A Statistical History
of Pro Football

A Statistical History of Pro Football

Players, Teams and Concepts

RUPERT PATRICK

McFarland & Company, Inc., Publishers
Jefferson, North Carolina

Michael "Rupert" Patrick O'Connor died on December 26, 2019, after completing the manuscript for this book.

Library of Congress Cataloguing-in-Publication Data

Names: Patrick, Rupert, 1964– author.
Title: A statistical history of pro football : players, teams and concepts / Rupert Patrick.
Description: Jefferson, North Carolina : McFarland & Company, Inc., Publishers, 2021. | Includes bibliographical references and index.
Identifiers: LCCN 2020057254 | ISBN 9781476682877 (paperback : acid free paper) ∞
ISBN 9781476640891 (ebook)
Subjects: LCSH: National Football League—Statistics. | National Football League—History. | Football—United States—Statistics. | Football—United States—History.
Classification: LCC GV955.5.N35 P383 2021 | DDC 796.332/640973—dc23
LC record available at https://lccn.loc.gov/2020057254

British Library cataloguing data are available

ISBN (print) 978-1-4766-8287-7
ISBN (ebook) 978-1-4766-4089-1

© 2021 The Estate of Michael "Rupert" Patrick O'Connor. All rights reserved

No part of this book may be reproduced or transmitted in any form or by any means, electronic or mechanical, including photocopying or recording, or by any information storage and retrieval system, without permission in writing from the publisher.

Front cover image by Franck Camhi (Shutterstock)

Printed in the United States of America

McFarland & Company, Inc., Publishers
Box 611, Jefferson, North Carolina 28640
www.mcfarlandpub.com

For Mary Ellen,
whose courage and strength seems unending
especially in the worst of times,
and whose heart and compassion has made me
a much better man than I thought I could possibly be.
This book would not have been possible
without your love and support,
and above all else, patience.

Table of Contents

Acknowledgments   ix
Preface   1
Team Names and Abbreviations   5

1. Home Field Advantage   9
2. Estimated Winning Percentage   25
3. Momentum   43
4. Cinderella and Surprise Teams, and One-Year Wonders   63
5. Rusher Ratings: YRAA   78
6. Passer Ratings: NPR   108
7. Kicker Ratings: PAL, PAL2, K%   142
8. Punter Ratings: 1961 and 2018   187
9. Coding   203
10. Dynasties   221

Glossary   259
Bibliography   265
Player Index   269

Acknowledgments

Rupert Patrick died December 26, 2019, having completed the writing of this book a short time before. Its posthumous publication was made possible with the help of his sister, Michelle Godfrey, and other family members, whose contributions are gratefully acknowledged by the publisher.

I would like to thank the rank and file of the PFRA (Pro Football Researchers Association). According to their site www/profootballresearchers.com, "PFRA is a nonprofit organization dedicated to the history of professional football. Founded in 1979, PFRA members include many of the game's foremost historians and writers." In particular, I would like to thank many PFRA members, including but not limited to: Ken Crippen, John Turney, Nick Webster, Mark Ford, Andy Piascik, John Maxymuk, Tod Maher, Gary Najarian, Roy Sye, Coach TJ Troup, Jeff Miller, George Bozeka, Denis Crawford, Joe Zagorski, Mark Durr, Chris Willis, and the late Bob Carroll. If I missed you, I apologize.

There are two PFRA members whose assistance I would like to call out for going above and beyond the call of duty. One is Ivan Urena, whose expertise in understanding the NFL tiebreakers is unparalleled and he was very helpful in my being able to retroactively apply NFL tiebreakers in the 1970s and '80s to symbolically award additional wild cards in Chapter 10.

The other is Ken Pullis, who provided me with an alternate field goal database from my own from which I was able to correct many of the errors in my database, and my database in turn helped correct errors in his database. His database also filled in hundreds of missed field goal distances, and he also had the distances of all the missed field goals for the entire history of the American Football League. This helped make possible Chapter 7, where I've developed a revolutionary method for evaluating kickers.

Pete Palmer was very helpful in providing weekly NFL stat sheets for the 1940s and 50s, which has made it much easier to locate the field goal misses in those decades. Pete also supplied me with most of the field goal miss distances for the 1946–49 AAFC.

Eric Goska assisted with Packer game books and play-by-play documents from the 30s through the 1970s. Also, thanks to Pro Football Reference.com and the Pro Football Archives, both invaluable websites for statistical information.

Thanks to the various PR and Media personnel with the Cardinals, Bills, Bears, Bengals, Lions, Packers, Colts, Chiefs, Chargers, Vikings, Patriots, Saints, Raiders, 49ers, Seahawks, Buccaneers, Titans and Redskins in assisting me with my game book requests.

Also, the Mid-Continent Public Library of Independence, MO, along with Newspapers.com, GeneologyBank.com and NewspaperArchive.com. The newspapers used in researching this book were mainly employed to chase down the distances of missed field goals and these papers are too many to name, and the great old sportswriters are too many to name also, they're all gone now, but you guys are not forgotten by me.

Also, a few people in general—Peter King, Bill James, John Madden, Chris Berman, the late Paul Zimmerman, and to Steve and Ed Sabol for creating NFL Films. I learned an awful lot from reading and or watching you gentlemen over the years. Thank you one and all.

And to Glenn and Stu, for encouraging me to risk big.

I would like to list those who I wished could have been here to have to see this come to fruition—Daniel Almasy, Terry (Beau) Connell Jr., Mary Jane Kennedy, John O'Connor II, Timothy O'Connor, and James and Mary Ellen Cooper. You are all missed.

Finally, I would like to thank my family—Mary Ellen, Kathy, Bobby, Baxson, Shireen, Danny and everybody else, too many to name. And the cats—Charly, Jo, Zoe and the late Miss Kitty, who put up with me for a remarkable 19 years. And to all my friends, again, too many to name.

Preface

Each of these chapters is devoted to a different subject in pro football history, and they detail my search for a mathematical explanation related to each topic, be it a kicker rating system, an historical analysis of home field advantage or a methodology for evaluating dynasties. It generally begins with a question, such as "How do we improve this?" or "How do we measure that?" follows with a search for an answer, and ends with a list of the best and worst.

Keeping this book within a manageable size, I wanted to cover as many different facets of pro football as I could, such as passing, rushing, and kicking, and attempt to come up with better ways to evaluate players than the current ways we do.

In addition, I also wanted to delve into a number of subjects that people have talked about with respect to football (and sports in general, I think), such as momentum, home field advantage, dynasties, Cinderella teams and one-year wonders, to name a few. I wanted to take these topics in a direction that nobody has really done before in that I made an effort to define and quantify these subjects to explain how they apply to football.

What am I saying here? Let's use Cinderella teams as an example—it's one of the chapters in the book. What is a Cinderella team? There is no clear-cut definition, but most would say something along the lines of, "It is a team who comes out of nowhere and has a big season, like the 1999 St. Louis Rams or the 1977 Denver Broncos." (However, I'm going to make a rather persuasive argument that the 1977 Broncos are not, in fact, a Cinderella team, but we'll get to that in time.)

The process I take is to develop a definition of what a Cinderella team actually is, and once we establish a set of rules or standards for doing so, we wind up with a list of Cinderella teams. By the end of the chapter, you, the reader, will realize this set of rules (with a little tweaking) can be applied to answer the question of identifying Cinderella teams in baseball, basketball, and hockey. I feel certain that a lot of the theories I put forward in this book can, and will, be applied to other sports.

I generally view the history of pro football as a tree, with each season being a ring on the tree, no ring more important than any other. The rings in the middle are small, and represent the early years of the NFL, and the rings get gradually larger in the subsequent years as the number of teams in the league increases. If you look casually, you may see something new or different on a particular ring, but you generally need to look carefully at all the rings to see patterns, or trends. Sometimes, if you really zoom in, you will see something nobody else will see.

This book is heavy in numbers, but I think if you've ever taken an algebra class, you'll get what I'm doing here; and even if you haven't taken an algebra class, you'll still get it, as I explain things in layman's terms. Please don't let the math frighten you.

Here we will cover the 1933 through 2018 seasons for the NFL, AFL and AAFC, The APFA and later the NFL were playing professional football from 1920 to 1932, but the statistics were sparse and often unreliable in those days, and so, my book begins with 1933. The player statistics from 1933 to 1940 are not 100 percent accurate and in many places my player rating systems do not fully cover these seasons, but the team and league stats are pretty accurate.

I know there are people who will ask "Why didn't I rate wide receivers?" The reason is that I have not yet found a way to rate receivers that is an improvement on something that hasn't already been done. I don't think a "Yards Receiving Above Average" statistic would really work as well as it does for running backs.

As for not rating offensive linemen, I think the only real way to evaluate them is by watching game film, and I've watched a lot of game film from the 1930s through '50s. It's frankly difficult to rate a lineman from back then if you only have one or two games from his entire career to go on as there is often not a lot of game film readily available. Some of my colleagues like Ken Crippen and Coach TJ Troup are adept at film study, but I just never had the eye for it. My mind tends to look at things mathematically, and offensive linemen have no statistics, so, unfortunately, I have never come up with a way of evaluating them.

As for not rating individual defensive players, again, the main reason is again a general lack of statistics. I'm trying to break down the game in a mathematical way and there's not much to go on other than the residual results; the number of sacks, number of interceptions, the yards allowed, the points allowed. I do have rating systems in this book for evaluating a teams' defenses against rushing and passing, and I also have a team total defensive statistic, (Points Allowed ^3 divided by Yards Allowed ^1.5 divided by Games Played ^1.5, I call it Defensive Rating and it is a good, quick way to rate defenses) but I have not broken apart each of the component parts of the defense. I do not rate middle linebackers or cornerbacks.

Nor do I try to rank the top 100 players of all time. I do not attempt to compare the career accomplishments of Jerry Rice against those of Tom Brady or Anthony Munoz or Lou Groza or anybody else and say, "This guy is better than that guy." I just don't want to go there. I do not try to compare a ribeye steak to a chicken parmesan or a sizzling platter of fajitas and say one is better than the other, because I love them all and all three taste totally different. I will compare quarterbacks against quarterbacks, running backs against running backs, and so on.

Like any math or science book, the early chapters lay out basic concepts, and as we get deeper into the book, we build and expand on those concepts. For the most part, each succeeding chapter is slightly more complex than the previous chapter. If you have just purchased this book, I would advise the reader not to pick a chapter from the middle of the book and start reading there. The reason is that I use a lot of new terms and methodology that I will explain in detail as I first introduce them, but if they return later, I might just quickly gloss over them as I presume you are already familiar with them, and you might find yourself lost if you don't start at the beginning. There is a glossary in the back of the book with all of the terminology and abbreviations I use, along with the chapters where they first appear. In some cases, I do not list a chapter because they are basic mathematical or statistical concepts like "percentage."

If there are two important things to take from this book, the first is, do not think of any of the numbers I come up with is a definitive conclusion. If I have Pete Stoyanovich rated two points higher in career PAL (Points Above League—a kicker rating statistic I have developed) than Shayne Graham, it doesn't mean that I believe beyond a shadow of a doubt that Stoyanovich was a better kicker than Graham. PAL is just a statistic, like field goals made, or points scored.

The second thing is that all statistics are a product of the era in which they occur, and for that reason, the standards change over time, are still changing, and will always be changing, and you have to adjust the best you can for the context in which they occur. I will occasionally provide graphs to show how the league averages of all the various statistics such as league passing completion percentage or field goal percentage by season change over time. We will have to adjust as best we can for the fact that the standards change over the years.

With that in mind, I hope you find this journey interesting, and it will cause you to think of the game of pro football in a different way. Enjoy.

Team Names and Abbreviations

Data through 2018

Current Franchises

Arizona/Chicago/Phoenix/St. Louis Cardinals and Card-Pitt:
    Chicago Cardinals (1933–43, 1945–59 NFL)—CHC
    Card-Pitt (1944 NFL)—CPT (merger of Steelers and Cardinals)
    St. Louis Cardinals (1960–87 NFL)—STL
    Phoenix Cardinals (1988–93 NFL)—PHX
    Arizona Cardinals (1994–2018 NFL)—ARZ
    Atlanta Falcons (1966–2018 NFL)—ATL
    Baltimore Ravens (1996–2018 NFL)—BAR
    Buffalo Bills (1960–69 AFL, 1970–2018 NFL)—BUF
    Carolina Panthers (1995–2018 NFL)—CAR
    Chicago Bears (1933–2018 NFL)—CHI
    Cincinnati Bengals (1968–2018 NFL)—CIN
    Cleveland Browns (1946–49 AAFC, 1950–95, 1999–2018 NFL)—CLE
    Dallas Cowboys (1960–2018 NFL)—DAL
Detroit Lions/Portsmouth Spartans:
    Portsmouth Spartans (1933 NFL)—PTS
    Detroit Lions (1934–2018 NFL)—DET
    Denver Broncos (1960–1969 AFL, 1970–2018 NFL)—DEN
    Green Bay Packers (1933–2018 NFL)—G B
    Houston Texans (2002–2018 NFL)—HOT
Indianapolis/Baltimore Colts:
    Baltimore Colts (1953–83 NFL)—BAL
    Indianapolis Colts (1984–2018 NFL)—IND
    Jacksonville Jaguars (1995–2018 NFL)—JAX
Kansas City Chiefs/Dallas Texans:
    Dallas Texans (AFL) (1960–62)—DTX
    Kansas City Chiefs (1963–69 AFL, 1970–2018 NFL)—K C
San Diego/Los Angeles Chargers:
    Los Angeles Chargers (1960 AFL, 2018 NFL)—LAC
    San Diego Chargers (1961–69 AFL, 1970–2016 NFL)—S D
Los Angeles/Cleveland/St. Louis Rams:
    Cleveland Rams (1937–45 NFL)—CLR

Los Angeles Rams (1946–94, 2016–2018 NFL)—L A
St. Louis Rams (1995–2015 NFL)—SLR
Miami Dolphins (1966–69 AFL, 1970–2018 NFL)—MIA
Minnesota Vikings (1961–2018 NFL)—MIN

New England/Boston Patriots:
Boston Patriots (1960–69 AFL, 1970 NFL)—BOP
New England Patriots (1971–2018 NFL)—N E
New Orleans Saints (1967–2018 NFL)—N O
New York Giants (1933–2018 NFL)—NYG

New York Jets/Titans:
New York Titans (1960–62 AFL)—NYT
New York Jets (1963–69 AFL, 1970–2018 NFL)—NYJ

Oakland/Los Angeles Raiders:
Oakland Raiders (1960–1969 AFL, 1970–81, 1995–2018 NFL)—OAK
Los Angeles Raiders (1982–1994 NFL)—LAR

Philadelphia Eagles and Phil-Pitt:
Philadelphia Eagles (1933–42, 1944–2018 NFL)—PHI
Phil-Pitt aka Steagles (1943 NFL)—PHP (merger of Steelers and Eagles)

Pittsburgh Steelers/Pirates, Phil-Pitt and Card-Pitt:
Pittsburgh Pirates (1933–39 NFL)—PIT
Pittsburgh Steelers (1940–42, 1945–2018 NFL)—PIT
Phil-Pitt aka Steagles (1943 NFL)—PHP (merger of Steelers and Eagles)
Card-Pitt (1944 NFL)—CPT (merger of Steelers and Cardinals)
San Francisco 49ers (1946–1949 AAFC, 1950–2018 NFL)—S F
Seattle Seahawks (1976–2018 NFL)—SEA
Tampa Bay Buccaneers (1976–2018 NFL)—T B

Tennessee Titans/Oilers and Houston Oilers:
Houston Oilers (1960–69 AFL, 1970–1996 NFL)—HOU
Tennessee Oilers (1997–98 NFL)—TEN
Tennessee Titans (1999–2018 NFL)—TEN

Washington/Boston Redskins:
Boston Redskins (1933–36 NFL)—BOR
Washington Redskins (1937–2018 NFL)—WAS

Defunct Franchises

Baltimore Colts (1947–49 AAFC, 1950 NFL)—BAA
Boston Yanks (1945–48 NFL)—BOS

Brooklyn Dodgers/Tigers (NFL):
Brooklyn Dodgers (1933–43 NFL)—BKN
Brooklyn Tigers (1944 NFL)–BKN
Brooklyn Dodgers (1946–48 AAFC)—BKA

Buffalo Bills/Bison (AAFC):
Buffalo Bison (1946 AAFC)—BFA
Buffalo Bills (1947–49 AAFC)—BFA

Chicago Rockets/Hornets (AAFC):

Chicago Rockets (1946–48 AAFC)—CHA
Chicago Hornets (1949 AAFC)—CHA
Cincinnati Reds/St. Louis Gunners (NFL): *
Cincinnati Reds (1933–34 NFL)—CST
St. Louis Gunners (1934 NFL)—CST
Dallas Texans (1952 NFL)—TEX
Los Angeles Dons (1946–49 AAFC)—LAA
Miami Seahawks (1946 AAFC)—MAA
New York Yankees (1946–49 AAFC)—NYA
New York Bulldogs/Yanks (NFL):
New York Bulldogs (1949 NFL)—NYB
New York Yanks (1950–51 NFL)—NYY

*In reality, the Cincinnati Reds and St. Louis Gunners were two completely separate franchises. The Reds folded late in the 1934 season and the NFL brought in the St. Louis Gunners, a semi-pro team in the way we would look at it today, to finish the final three games of Cincinnati's schedule. Some might consider it sacrilege to combine the 1934 team stats of the Reds and Gunners, but since the Gunners took over the remainder of the Reds schedule, it made sense when running EPCT or other team statistics, to merge the two teams into one. It's my book, we'll do it my way. The reader is free to write your own football history book and do it your way. I promise to purchase a copy.

Alphabetical List of Team Abbreviations

ARZ—Arizona Cardinals (1994–2018 NFL)
ATL—Atlanta Falcons (1966–2018 NFL)
BAA—Baltimore Colts (1947–49 AAFC, 1950 NFL)
BAL—Baltimore Colts (1953–83 NFL)
BAR—Baltimore Ravens (1996–2018 NFL)
BKA—Brooklyn Dodgers (1946–48 AAFC)
BKN—Brooklyn Dodgers (1933–43 NFL), Brooklyn Tigers (1944 NFL)
BOP—Boston Patriots (1960–69 AFL, 1970 NFL)
BOR—Boston Redskins (1933–36 NFL)
BOS—Boston Yanks (1944–48 NFL)
BFA—Buffalo Bison (1946 AAFC), Buffalo Bills (1947–49 AAFC)
BUF—Buffalo Bills (1960–69 AFL, 1970–2018 NFL)
CAR—Carolina Panthers (1995–2018 NFL)
CHA—Chicago Rockets (1946–48 AAFC), Chicago Hornets (1949 AAFC)
CHC—Chicago Cardinals (1933–43, 1945–59 NFL)
CHI—Chicago Bears (1933–2018 NFL)
CIN—Cincinnati Bengals (1968–2018 NFL)
CLE—Cleveland Browns (1946–49 AAFC, 1950–95, 1999–2018 NFL)
CLR—Cleveland Rams (1937–45 NFL)
CPT—Card-Pitt (1944 NFL)—CPT (merger of Steelers and Cardinals)
CST—Cincinnati Reds (1933–34 NFL), St. Louis Gunners (1934 NFL)
DAL—Dallas Cowboys (1960–2018 NFL)
DEN—Denver Broncos (1960–1969 AFL, 1970–2018 NFL)
DET—Detroit Lions (1934–2018 NFL)
DTX—Dallas Texans (AFL) (1960–62)

G B—Green Bay Packers (1933–2018 NFL)
HOU—Houston Oilers (1960–69 AFL, 1970–1996 NFL)
HOT—Houston Texans (2002–2018 NFL)
IND—Indianapolis Colts (1984–2018 NFL)
JAX—Jacksonville Jaguars (1995–2018 NFL)
K C—Kansas City Chiefs (1963–69 AFL, 1970–2018 NFL)
L A—Los Angeles Rams (1946–94, 2018 NFL)
LAA—Los Angeles Dons (1946–49 AAFC)
LAC—Los Angeles Chargers (1960 AFL, 2018 NFL)
LAR—Los Angeles Raiders (1982–1994 NFL)
MAA—Miami Seahawks (1946 AAFC)
MIA—Miami Dolphins (1966–69 AFL, 1970–2018 NFL)
MIN—Minnesota Vikings (1961–2018 NFL)
N E—New England Patriots (1971–2018 NFL)
N O—New Orleans Saints (1967–2018 NFL)
NYA—New York Yankees (1946–49 AAFC)
NYB—New York Bulldogs (1949 NFL)
NYG—New York Giants (1933–2018 NFL)
NYJ—New York Jets (1963–69 AFL, 1970–2018 NFL)
NYT—New York Titans (1960–62 AFL)
NYY—New York Yanks (1950–51 NFL)
OAK—Oakland Raiders (1960–1969 AFL, 1970–81, 1995–2018 NFL)
PIT—Pittsburgh Steelers (1940–42, 1945–2018 NFL), Pittsburgh Pirates (1933–39 NFL)
PHI—Philadelphia Eagles (1933–42, 1944–2018 NFL)
PHX—Phoenix Cardinals (1988–93 NFL)
PHP—Phil-Pitt aka Steagles (1943 NFL) (merger of Steelers and Eagles)
PTS—Portsmouth Spartans (1933 NFL)
S D—San Diego Chargers (1961–69 AFL, 1970–2018 NFL)
S F—San Francisco 49ers (1946–1949 AAFC, 1950–2018 NFL)
SEA—Seattle Seahawks (1976–2018 NFL)
STL—St. Louis Cardinals (1960–87 NFL)
SLR—St. Louis Rams (1995–2015 NFL)
T B—Tampa Bay Buccaneers (1976–2018 NFL)
TEX—Dallas Texans (1952 NFL)
TEN—Tennessee Titans (1999–2018 NFL), Tennessee Oilers (1997–98 NFL)
WAS—Washington Redskins (1937–2018 NFL)

1

Home Field Advantage

Home Field Advantage or HFA is a concept that exists in all sports. You hear announcers and fans and athletes talk about it all the time, but what is it really?

It's a lot of things. It could be not having to fly halfway across the country, or a familiarity with the stadium, or more accurately, having a team that is tailored to take advantage of the stadium (which is more of an issue with baseball, where the stadiums are all different and shape the way the games are played), or having the home crowd on your side, or a combination of the above. I'm not going to try to figure out exactly what it is, but I will try to figure out how much of a factor home field advantage is in pro football, and at particular stadiums.

There are two different paths to home field advantage, one is by looking at the differential in winning percentage between home and road games for teams, which we will refer to as HWA or Home Field Winning Advantage. The other way is to look at the point differential (or points for minus points against) between games played at home and games played on the road for teams which we will refer to as HPA for Home Field Point Advantage. We will also look at the HWA and HPA data for current stadiums to find teams who over-perform or under-perform at home.

In both cases, home field advantage (HFA) will be measured as:

HFA = (Home performance—Road performance) / 2

We'll begin with HWA, winning percentage differential between home and road games. The basic HWA formula for a given team-season is:

HWA = (Home Winning Percentage or HPCT—Road Winning Percentage or RPCT) / 2

HWA is half of the difference between home and road winning percentage, using end of regular season statistics. In other words, we are looking at how HPCT (Home Winning Percentage) differs from WPCT (Actual Winning Percentage). For purposes of calculating Home and Road Winning Percentage, a tie is considered a half a win and half a loss. (The value of a tie will change at different points in pro football history, which we will address.)

Let's apply this formula to a hypothetical team-season who has a 6–2–0 record in home games (HPCT = 0.7500) and a 1–7–0 record (RPCT = 0.1250) on the road. The HWA would be calculated as such:

HWA = (0.7500 - 0.1250) / 2 = 0.6250 / 2 = 0.3125

How do we measure HWA for a single game, where one team is at home (which we'll refer to as Asheville) and the other (which we'll refer to as Birmingham) is the road team?

What would be the HWA of the home team? First, we would have to figure out how often Asheville should win the game on a neutral field. We need to be able to answer this question before we can apply HWA. This can be easily estimated using Bayes Theorem, which is a basic principle of probability theory for measuring the success of two forces in competition against one another:

$$WPCT = (WA * LB) / ((WA * LB) + (WB * LA))$$
WA = Wins (or Winning Percentage) Asheville
LA = Losses (or 1—Winning Percentage) Asheville
WB = Wins (or Winning Percentage) Birmingham
LB = Losses (or 1—Winning Percentage) Birmingham

You wind up with the same result whether you use wins and losses or winning and losing percentage. For our hypothetical teams, Asheville had an overall record of 10 wins and 6 losses and Birmingham had a 7–9 record. We will use end of season statistics for HFA, and I always use the team with the better record (in this case Asheville) as Team A in the above equation.

Applying Bayes Theorem to this theoretical game:

$$\text{Win Probability (A versus B)} = (10 * 9) / ((10 * 9) + (6 * 7)) = 90 / (90+42) = 90 / 132 = 0.6818$$

Asheville should beat Birmingham 68.18 percent of the time on a neutral field, and Birmingham would therefore beat Asheville 31.82 percent (100 percent minus 68.18 percent) of the time playing on the same neutral field. The winning percentages of both teams must always equal one. When using Bayes Theorem, the concept of a tie game is disregarded.

Now that we know how often Asheville should win the game on a neutral field, we need to look at historical home/road records in order to determine what HWA has looked like throughout pro football history.

Below is Table 1.1, which contains all the team-seasons from 1933 to 2018, NFL, AFL and AAFC, grouped by common WPCT (winning percentage), with number of team-seasons (TS), aggregate home record (HW, HL, HT) and home winning percentage or HPCT; aggregate road record (RW, RL, RT) and road winning percentage or RPCT, followed by Home-Field Winning Advantage or HWA:

Table 1.1
HWA Calculated for All Team-Seasons, Grouped by WPCT

		HOME				ROAD				
WPCT	TS	HW	HL	HT	HPCT	RW	RL	RT	RPCT	HWA
1.0000	5	33	0	0	1.0000	35	0	0	1.0000	0.0000
0.9375	6	47	1	0	0.9792	43	5	0	0.8958	0.0417
0.9286	4	27	1	0	0.9643	25	3	0	0.8929	0.0357
0.9167	4	23	1	0	0.9583	21	3	0	0.8750	0.0417
0.9091	3	14	3	0	0.8235	16	0	0	1.0000	−0.0883
0.9000	1	4	0	0	1.0000	5	1	0	0.8333	0.0834
0.8929	2	13	1	0	0.9286	11	1	2	0.8571	0.0358

1. Home Field Advantage

WPCT	TS	HOME				ROAD				HWA
		HW	HL	HT	HPCT	RW	RL	RT	RPCT	
0.8889	2	7	1	0	0.8750	9	1	0	0.9000	−0.0125
0.8750	21	148	18	0	0.8916	142	23	1	0.8584	0.0166
0.8667	1	6	1	0	0.8571	7	1	0	0.8750	−0.0090
0.8636	2	10	1	0	0.9091	8	1	2	0.8182	0.0455
0.8571	24	149	17	3	0.8905	136	28	3	0.8234	0.0336
0.8500	2	10	1	0	0.9091	6	1	2	0.7778	0.0657
0.8333	7	35	6	1	0.8452	34	7	1	0.8214	0.0119
0.8214	6	33	4	5	0.8452	33	8	1	0.7976	0.0238
0.8182	2	11	1	0	0.9167	7	3	0	0.7000	0.1084
0.8125	47	333	43	0	0.8856	278	98	0	0.7394	0.0731
0.8077	1	6	0	0	1.0000	4	2	1	0.6429	0.1786
0.8000	4	20	2	2	0.8750	15	6	0	0.7143	0.0804
0.7917	6	33	2	1	0.9306	21	10	5	0.6528	0.1389
0.7857	23	138	23	0	0.8571	115	46	0	0.7143	0.0714
0.7778	2	8	0	0	1.0000	6	4	0	0.6000	0.2000
0.7727	4	19	3	2	0.8333	13	5	2	0.7000	0.0667
0.7692	1	6	2	0	0.7500	4	1	0	0.8000	−0.0250
0.7500	117	725	144	9	0.8309	585	285	14	0.6697	0.0806
0.7333	2	12	3	0	0.8000	10	5	0	0.6667	0.0667
0.7273	6	27	8	0	0.7714	21	10	0	0.6774	0.0470
0.7188	2	12	2	2	0.8125	10	6	0	0.6250	0.0938
0.7143	34	187	50	1	0.7878	152	85	1	0.6408	0.0735
0.7083	4	18	5	1	0.7708	14	7	3	0.6458	0.0625
0.7000	3	17	2	0	0.8947	7	8	1	0.4688	0.2130
0.6875	99	611	181	0	0.7715	478	314	0	0.6035	0.0840
0.6818	1	5	1	1	0.7857	2	2	0	0.5000	0.1429
0.6786	10	44	20	6	0.6714	46	20	4	0.6857	−0.0071
0.6667	23	100	34	1	0.7444	77	54	1	0.5871	0.0787
0.6563	6	35	11	2	0.7500	25	19	4	0.5625	0.0938
0.6500	5	20	8	1	0.7069	10	7	4	0.5714	0.0678
0.6429	30	145	62	3	0.6976	120	83	7	0.5881	0.0548
0.6364	7	26	13	2	0.6585	21	13	2	0.6111	0.0237
0.6250	134	751	307	2	0.7094	571	485	4	0.5406	0.0844
0.6154	1	5	1	0	0.8333	3	4	0	0.4286	0.2024
0.6111	1	3	1	0	0.7500	2	2	1	0.5000	0.1250
0.6071	16	68	36	9	0.6416	59	43	9	0.5721	0.0347
0.6000	4	19	9	0	0.6786	14	13	0	0.5185	0.0801

		HOME				ROAD				
WPCT	TS	HW	HL	HT	HPCT	RW	RL	RT	RPCT	HWA
0.5938	4	21	10	1	0.6719	15	14	3	0.5156	0.0782
0.5909	3	11	7	0	0.6111	7	5	3	0.5667	0.0222
0.5833	20	68	46	4	0.5932	69	51	2	0.5738	0.0097
0.5714	26	114	60	8	0.6484	86	88	8	0.4945	0.0770
0.5625	135	709	371	0	0.6565	506	574	0	0.4685	0.0940
0.5556	5	14	9	0	0.6087	11	11	0	0.5000	0.0544
0.5500	2	7	3	2	0.6667	3	5	0	0.3750	0.1459
0.5455	7	21	15	0	0.5833	21	20	0	0.5122	0.0356
0.5417	9	28	19	7	0.5833	26	26	2	0.5000	0.0417
0.5385	1	4	2	0	0.6667	3	4	0	0.4286	0.1191
0.5357	12	46	29	9	0.6012	38	43	3	0.4702	0.0655
0.5333	5	22	15	0	0.5946	18	20	0	0.4737	0.0605
0.5313	9	40	27	5	0.5903	32	36	4	0.4722	0.0591
0.5000	192	833	607	8	0.5780	605	831	11	0.4219	0.0781
0.4688	5	19	18	3	0.5125	16	22	2	0.4250	0.0438
0.4667	4	15	15	0	0.5000	13	17	0	0.4333	0.0334
0.4643	10	30	34	6	0.4714	27	33	10	0.4571	0.0071
0.4583	7	23	16	4	0.5814	12	26	3	0.3293	0.1261
0.4545	3	7	7	0	0.5000	8	11	0	0.4211	0.0395
0.4444	6	15	14	0	0.5172	9	16	0	0.3600	0.0786
0.4375	129	521	511	0	0.5048	380	652	0	0.3682	0.0683
0.4286	35	130	109	6	0.5429	73	164	8	0.3143	0.1143
0.4231	1	3	2	1	0.5833	2	5	0	0.2857	0.1488
0.4167	9	24	30	0	0.4444	21	33	0	0.3889	0.0278
0.4091	3	10	6	1	0.6176	2	12	2	0.1875	0.2151
0.4063	5	23	14	3	0.6125	7	31	2	0.2000	0.2063
0.4000	4	13	13	0	0.5000	9	20	0	0.3103	0.0949
0.3929	13	40	41	10	0.4945	25	63	3	0.2912	0.1017
0.3889	1	2	3	1	0.4167	1	2	0	0.3333	0.0417
0.3750	112	403	472	5	0.4608	253	624	3	0.2892	0.0858
0.3667	1	2	5	1	0.3125	3	4	0	0.4286	−0.0581
0.3636	5	10	17	0	0.3704	9	17	2	0.3571	0.0067
0.3571	35	94	144	7	0.3980	75	165	5	0.3163	0.0409
0.3500	4	8	10	3	0.4524	4	14	1	0.2368	0.1078
0.3438	4	13	17	2	0.4375	7	23	2	0.2500	0.0938
0.3333	21	46	76	0	0.3770	35	86	0	0.2893	0.0439
0.3214	19	40	82	11	0.3421	35	88	10	0.3008	0.0207

		HOME				ROAD				
WPCT	TS	HW	HL	HT	HPCT	RW	RL	RT	RPCT	HWA
0.3182	2	1	6	2	0.2222	5	8	0	0.3846	−0.0812
0.3125	90	287	433	0	0.3986	165	555	0	0.2292	0.0847
0.3000	1	2	3	0	0.4000	1	4	0	0.2000	0.1000
0.2917	5	10	17	3	0.3833	5	23	2	0.2000	0.0917
0.2857	29	79	123	0	0.3911	37	167	0	0.1814	0.1049
0.2813	4	12	18	2	0.4063	4	26	2	0.1563	0.1250
0.2727	4	6	10	3	0.3947	4	20	1	0.1800	0.1074
0.2667	4	7	22	0	0.2414	9	22	0	0.2903	−0.0245
0.2500	110	258	573	6	0.3118	155	677	5	0.1882	0.0618
0.2273	4	4	19	2	0.2000	4	13	2	0.2632	−0.0316
0.2222	2	2	8	0	0.2000	2	6	0	0.2500	−0.0250
0.2188	1	1	7	0	0.1250	2	5	1	0.3125	−0.0938
0.2143	23	42	118	1	0.2640	25	133	3	0.1646	0.0497
0.2083	3	4	13	1	0.2500	2	14	2	0.1667	0.0417
0.2000	4	6	16	0	0.2727	3	20	0	0.1304	0.0712
0.1875	38	76	228	0	0.2500	38	266	0	0.1250	0.0625
0.1818	5	2	23	0	0.0800	8	22	0	0.2667	−0.0934
0.1786	10	16	49	5	0.2643	4	61	5	0.0929	0.0857
0.1667	8	9	36	2	0.2128	5	42	2	0.1224	0.0452
0.1429	15	15	90	0	0.1429	15	90	0	0.1429	0.0000
0.1364	4	3	15	2	0.2000	1	21	2	0.0833	0.0584
0.1250	35	46	225	3	0.1734	21	253	0	0.0766	0.0484
0.1111	1	1	4	0	0.2000	0	4	0	0.0000	0.1000
0.1071	5	4	30	1	0.1286	1	30	4	0.0857	0.0215
0.1000	1	0	3	0	0.0000	1	6	0	0.1429	−0.0715
0.0909	5	3	22	0	0.1200	2	28	0	0.0667	0.0267
0.0833	4	3	21	0	0.1250	1	23	0	0.0417	0.0417
0.0714	8	7	49	0	0.1250	1	55	0	0.0179	0.0536
0.0625	10	3	77	0	0.0375	7	73	0	0.0875	−0.0250
0.0556	1	0	3	1	0.1250	0	5	0	0.0000	0.0625
0.0417	1	0	6	0	0.0000	0	5	1	0.0833	−0.0417
0.0000	7	0	42	0	0.0000	0	45	0	0.0000	0.0000
SUM	1995	8301	6215	196	0.5709	6215	8301	196	0.4291	0.0709

The TS column of Table 1.1 gives the number of team-seasons with that particular actual Winning Percentage or WPCT. A team-season is a given season for a given team, such as the 1981 St. Louis Cardinals, or the 1946 Washington Redskins, or the 2014 Washington Redskins. The bottom row is an aggregate summary, which is the sum of the above numbers. From the summary row we see there have been a total of 1,995 team-seasons between 1933 and 2018 between the NFL, AFL and AAFC.

Looking down the chart, you can see there have been a total of 21 teams who have finished their respective regular seasons with a 0.8750 winning percentage. These teams collectively had a home winning percentage (HPCT) of 0.8916, and a combined road winning percentage (RPCT) of 0.8584, and as a group, their HWA is 0.0166, or 0.8916 minus 0.8584 divided by two.

The rightmost column is for HWA, and we see on the summary row at the bottom that the average HWA for the entire group of all team-seasons is 0.0709. What that means is that on average, the home team wins 57.09 percent of the time throughout pro football history from 1933 to 2018. In fractional terms, the home team wins the game roughly four times in seven.

We'll go with seven percent for HWA, a good round number.

If we were dealing with real teams, we would use historical home and road won-loss data from the home stadium in question to determine what the HWA should be, but because we are dealing with theoretical teams, we'll just use the seven percent to show how it works. In that case, if the game is played at Asheville's home stadium, they would have a win probability of 0.7518, (or 0.6818 + 0.0700), and Birmingham would have a 0.2482 (or 1−0.7518) chance of winning the game. If the game were played at Birmingham, since we already know Birmingham would have a win probability of 0.3182 (or 1−0.6818) when playing at a neutral field, the HWA of 0.0700 would be added to 0.3182 to get a result of 0.3882, and Asheville's probability of winning at Birmingham is one minus 0.3882, or 0.6118.

This is how HWA works when applied to winning percentage. Now we have to establish a link between point differential and home field advantage.

Home Field Point Advantage (HPA)

Home Field Point Advantage (or HPA) is defined as one-half of the average point differential between home and road games, using end of regular season statistics. The basic formula looks like this:

$$HPA = (\text{Average Home Point Differential or APHD} - \text{Average Road Point Differential or ARPD})/2$$

Average Point Differential is simply total points for minus total points against divided by number of games played. The HPA formula is very similar to the HFA formula in its format of home performance minus road performance divided by two.

Once again, we'll use a hypothetical team to show its HPA. Here is the home and road point statistics for this sample team:

HPF (Home Points For) = 195   RPF (Road Points For) = 125
HPX (Home Points Against) = 155   RPA (Road Points Against) = 200
HG (Home Games) = 8   RG (Road Games) = 8
AHPD = (195 - 155)/8 = 40/8 = 5.000   ARPD = (125 - 200)/8 = -75/8 = -9.375
HPA = (5.000 - (-9.375)) / 2 = 14.375/2 = 7.1875

On average, this team has a five-point advantage at home, and a negative 9.375-point advantage on the road. Overall, this team improves by about 7.2 points when playing at home and is about 7.2 points worse on the road. If their HPA had been -7.2, it would mean they were 7.2 points worse at home and 7.2 points better away.

Let's return to our two hypothetical teams, Asheville and Birmingham, to explain the process. How should these two teams match up against each other playing on a neutral field, looking only at points? How many points should Asheville win by? The easiest way to do this is to look at the total points scored, and points allowed for both teams. Here are the point totals and games played for both teams for a hypothetical 16-game season:

Asheville: 395 points scored, 270 points allowed, 16 games played
Birmingham: 310 points scored, 370 points allowed, 16 games played

Knowing that the teams scored and allowed a total of 1345 points between them (adding the four above point totals together: 395 + 270 + 310 + 370 = 1345) and dividing by total games played by both teams (16 + 16 = 32), the total number of points scored by both teams should equal 1345 divided by 32, or 42.03.

A quick way to estimate points scored and points allowed by each team in a given game is by using the following formula:

PS = (PFA+ PAB) / (GA + GB)
PFA = Points for by team A   PAB = Points allowed by team B
GA = Games played by team A   GB = Games played by team B

When the above formula is applied to Asheville and Birmingham:

Points Asheville = (395 + 370) / (16 + 16) = 765 / 32 = 23.91
Points Birmingham = (310 + 270) / (16 + 16) = 580 / 16 = 18.12

Assuming a neutral field, we would expect Asheville to score 23.91 points and Birmingham 18.12 points, keeping in mind that 23.91 plus 18.12 equals 42.03. Since we know how the score should look when played at a neutral field, we will next come up with a standard figure for HPA, and then apply it to this hypothetical example to show what it should actually be.

Table 1.2 is a chart of the home and away point totals for all teams in NFL-AFL-AAFC history from 1933 through 2018, grouped by similar WPCT. Once again, these are the same 1,995 team-seasons, with aggregate home and road points scored and allowed, along with HPA for each group:

Table 1.2
HPA Calculated for All Team-Seasons, Grouped by Like WPCT

		HOME			ROAD			
WPCT	TS	GP	HPS	HPX	GP	RPS	RPA	HPA
1.0000	5	33	997	342	35	1028	463	1.85
0.9375	6	48	1512	711	48	1407	928	3.35
0.9286	4	30	846	315	30	789	447	3.38

WPCT	TS	HOME			ROAD			HPA
		GP	HPS	HPX	GP	RPS	RPA	
0.9167	4	24	817	333	24	621	341	4.25
0.9091	3	26	490	197	30	391	172	1.77
0.9000	1	4	78	14	6	166	122	4.33
0.8929	2	14	375	202	12	412	225	-0.50
0.8889	2	10	186	135	10	264	193	-0.36
0.8750	21	167	4583	2495	166	4442	2829	1.43
0.8667	1	8	247	105	11	212	148	6.14
0.8636	2	11	222	116	10	147	69	1.27
0.8571	24	166	4786	2276	164	4214	2205	1.41
0.8500	2	12	275	100	7	234	132	2.29
0.8333	7	47	1099	550	45	1069	687	1.99
0.8214	6	38	1149	648	42	1041	706	1.98
0.8182	2	14	266	158	14	212	137	0.75
0.8125	47	377	10740	6157	380	9456	6948	2.76
0.8077	1	9	67	46	13	66	36	-0.39
0.8000	4	24	666	362	23	470	314	2.62
0.7917	6	37	1067	472	35	881	670	5.33
0.7857	23	161	4316	2491	161	3886	2726	2.07
0.7778	2	8	198	106	11	232	202	4.25
0.7727	4	31	634	318	27	391	263	3.38
0.7692	1	8	163	36	5	75	23	2.74
0.7500	117	870	23723	13876	873	21129	16960	3.25
0.7333	2	15	375	273	18	360	294	1.20
0.7273	6	39	712	404	33	666	377	-0.26
0.7188	2	22	366	232	24	376	316	2.31
0.7143	34	237	5852	3668	237	5318	4186	2.21
0.7083	4	23	650	409	21	602	472	2.31
0.7000	3	21	493	252	15	353	363	6.65
0.6875	99	792	19753	13397	792	17676	15573	2.68
0.6818	1	13	174	100	6	62	62	5.29
0.6786	10	64	1568	1079	66	1616	1236	0.78
0.6667	23	143	3371	2199	134	2976	2609	2.95
0.6563	6	46	1219	885	44	926	895	3.16
0.6500	5	33	611	485	21	458	325	-0.99
0.6429	30	215	4895	3818	214	4462	4018	1.51
0.6364	7	42	638	408	36	482	436	2.17
0.6250	134	1058	26147	19049	1056	23317	22008	2.73

1. Home Field Advantage

WPCT	TS	HOME			ROAD			HPA
		GP	HPS	HPX	GP	RPS	RPA	
0.6154	1	12	77	20	17	70	87	5.96
0.6111	1	8	104	81	7	122	88	-0.53
0.6071	16	104	2576	2103	102	2589	2329	0.92
0.6000	4	28	685	538	27	589	536	1.64
0.5938	4	31	822	540	29	758	677	3.14
0.5909	3	24	346	285	20	300	260	0.36
0.5833	20	115	2556	2132	120	2447	2305	1.21
0.5714	26	174	4323	3075	174	3494	3670	3.91
0.5625	135	1081	25188	19825	1082	21555	23401	3.34
0.5556	5	26	456	476	24	350	426	1.29
0.5500	2	10	207	136	8	111	148	5.27
0.5455	7	46	591	513	44	691	622	0.24
0.5417	9	48	1220	941	52	1299	1222	1.87
0.5385	1	11	105	48	10	51	64	5.68
0.5357	12	76	2089	1632	81	1703	1788	3.23
0.5333	5	37	873	764	40	683	815	3.21
0.5313	9	74	1661	1460	73	1446	1624	2.63
0.5000	192	1443	32386	28753	1437	28420	32321	2.60
0.4688	5	39	788	812	40	907	944	0.16
0.4667	4	30	631	683	30	678	718	-0.20
0.4643	10	75	1506	1428	70	1391	1640	2.34
0.4583	7	41	799	753	38	538	878	4.68
0.4545	3	14	146	186	19	238	269	-0.61
0.4444	6	29	460	456	25	431	523	1.91
0.4375	129	1035	22393	22001	1034	19141	23739	2.42
0.4286	35	239	5145	4775	237	4152	5630	3.77
0.4231	1	7	120	40	9	50	67	7.88
0.4167	9	57	1095	1151	55	942	1254	2.37
0.4091	3	16	252	259	14	148	346	5.98
0.4063	5	43	845	782	43	777	970	3.20
0.4000	4	28	573	561	31	546	696	2.82
0.3929	13	81	2001	2012	88	1842	2357	2.77
0.3889	1	5	62	67	4	15	91	12.25
0.3750	112	876	18129	18837	880	15703	20841	2.52
0.3667	1	8	118	148	9	137	152	-0.80
0.3636	5	27	304	365	26	204	441	3.10
0.3571	35	238	4478	5192	240	4207	5847	1.89

		HOME			ROAD			
WPCT	TS	GP	HPS	HPX	GP	RPS	RPA	HPA
0.3500	4	18	302	289	18	216	448	6.41
0.3438	4	35	582	651	35	567	853	3.39
0.3333	21	124	2483	2791	123	2115	2798	1.56
0.3214	19	122	2655	3110	123	2218	3267	2.23
0.3182	2	9	76	134	15	133	237	0.78
0.3125	90	723	13783	15656	720	11754	17667	2.81
0.3000	1	5	112	123	5	80	112	2.10
0.2917	5	28	404	488	32	326	568	2.63
0.2857	29	202	3776	4490	204	3141	5202	3.28
0.2813	4	30	516	666	30	443	777	2.88
0.2727	4	16	156	251	24	241	526	3.20
0.2667	4	29	562	684	31	551	818	2.20
0.2500	110	831	15350	19942	832	13265	21850	2.39
0.2273	4	24	242	444	17	217	347	-0.62
0.2222	2	10	188	256	9	160	220	0.35
0.2188	1	8	135	175	7	132	172	0.00
0.2143	23	356	2624	3930	354	2451	4573	2.53
0.2083	3	17	359	451	16	337	549	3.33
0.2000	4	22	237	497	23	194	626	3.48
0.1875	38	304	5257	7499	304	4632	8313	2.37
0.1818	5	25	229	471	30	271	528	-0.56
0.1786	10	65	1058	1764	65	1094	2139	2.42
0.1667	8	45	739	1221	47	704	1398	1.95
0.1429	15	105	1570	2624	105	1382	2807	1.77
0.1364	4	18	160	339	22	214	454	0.53
0.1250	35	271	4485	6829	274	3913	7716	2.66
0.1111	1	5	81	137	4	55	108	1.03
0.1071	5	34	476	919	31	555	1097	1.41
0.1000	1	3	41	73	7	57	155	1.67
0.0909	5	25	182	567	30	267	719	-0.17
0.0833	4	24	286	625	24	332	811	2.92
0.0714	8	56	855	1458	56	798	1740	3.03
0.0625	10	80	1163	2187	80	1163	2149	-0.24
0.0556	1	3	57	98	5	56	138	3.08
0.0417	1	6	94	219	5	83	150	-4.83
0.0000	7	42	447	1110	45	490	1224	0.26
SUM	1995	14516	324158	286217	14516	286217	324158	2.58

The number in the lower right-hand corner of Table 1.2 is the average HPA, which is 2.58 points. The standard rule of thumb for HFA as everybody refers to it has always been three points, but it is actually a little under 2.6 points. The rule of thumb, perhaps, should be changed to 2.60 points.

As we found earlier, on a neutral field Asheville should be expected to score 23.91 points, and Birmingham should be expected to score 18.12 points. Again, because we are using fictitious teams, we'll use the average HPA results.

If the game were played at Asheville's stadium, 2.60 points would be added to Asheville's points and also subtracted from Birmingham's points, which would give us an estimated score of 26.51 (23.91 plus 2.60) for Asheville and 15.52 (18.12 minus 2.60) for Birmingham. If the game were played at Birmingham, 2.60 would have been added to Birmingham's points scored and also subtracted from Asheville's points scored to give an estimated score of 21.31 for Asheville and 20.72 for Birmingham.

Current Stadiums and HWA/HPA

How much of an HWA and HPA do the San Francisco 49ers have when playing in Levi's Stadium, and how does it differ from Candlestick Park? How does that compare to the HWA and HPA for other teams when playing in their home stadiums, past and present? What should we expect the HWA and HPA to be for 49ers games in their new stadium, and how does it differ from the actual results? How do the HWA and HPA results at their recent stadiums compare to Kezar Stadium, where the 49ers played from 1946 to 1970? We can answer these questions by looking at the data for all regular-season 49ers games played at Levi's and Candlestick and Kezar to find the actual HWA and HPA. Here is Table 1.3, with the HWA data, and Table 1.4, with the HPA data for all three of the 49ers home stadiums:

Table 1.3
San Francisco 49ers Historical HWA Data by Stadium

TM	YRS	VENUE	WPCT	HPCT	RPCT	HWA
S F	4670	Kezar Stadium	0.5353	0.6043	0.4663	0.0690
S F	7113	Candlestick Park	0.5683	0.6246	0.5120	0.0563
S F	1418	Levi's Stadium	0.3125	0.4000	0.2250	0.0153

Table 1.4
San Francisco 49ers Historical HPA Data by Stadium

TM	YRS	VENUE	PDHG	PDRG	HPA
S F	4670	Kezar Stadium	3.8160	-1.4724	2.64
S F	7113	Candlestick Park	5.7447	0.9249	2.41
S F	1418	Levi's Stadium	-3.4000	-9.0750	2.47

YRS (short for Years, but I guess you already figured that out) is a shorthand of sorts, in which the first two numbers are the last two digits of the season they first started playing there, and the final two numbers are the last two digits of the last season they played there. The San Francisco YRS notation 7113 for Candlestick Park means that the 49ers played their first game in Candlestick in 1971 and played there until 2013. It makes perfect sense.

From Table 1.3, we can see that the 49ers won 60.4 percent of the games at Kezar and won under 47 percent on the road, good for an HWA of 0.0690. At Candlestick, the Niners won 62 percent at home and over 51 percent on the road, and their HWA is 0.0563. After four seasons at Levi's Stadium, their HWA is 0.0153, but it generally takes a few years for the HWA and HPA to even out, due to the law of averages and getting a significant sample size of games.

Table 1.4 is the stadium history with respect to HPA. PDHG and PDRG are Point Differential in Home Games and Road Games, respectively.

How does that compare to other teams in other stadiums?

Table 1.5 is a list of the stadium history tables for all current stadiums with the name the stadium went by during the 2018 season. The teams are ranked by highest HWA:

Table 1.5
Current NFL Stadiums Ranked by Highest HWA Values, Through 2018

TM	YRS	VENUE	WPCT	HPCT	RPCT	HWA
BAR	9818	M&T Bank Stadium	0.5655	0.7083	0.4226	0.1429
SEA	0218	CenturyLink Field	0.5754	0.6971	0.4522	0.1225
G B	9518	Lambeau Field	0.6276	0.7448	0.5104	0.1172
MIN	1618	U.S. Bank Stadium	0.6146	0.7083	0.5208	0.0938
NYJ	1118	MetLife Stadium	0.3906	0.4844	0.2969	0.0938
JAX	9518	TIAA Bank Stadium	0.4427	0.5365	0.3490	0.0938
K C	7218	Arrowhead Stadium	0.5014	0.5932	0.4101	0.0916
BUF	7318	New Era Field	0.4786	0.5682	0.3886	0.0898
DET	0218	Ford Field	0.3676	0.4559	0.2794	0.0883
S F	1418	Levi's Stadium	0.3125	0.4000	0.2250	0.0875
HOT	0218	NRG Stadium	0.4449	0.5294	0.3603	0.0846
DEN	0118	Sport Authority Field	0.5694	0.6528	0.4861	0.0834
CIN	0018	Paul Brown Stadium	0.4753	0.5559	0.3947	0.0806
N E	0218	Gillette Stadium	0.7684	0.8456	0.6912	0.0772
IND	0818	Lucas Oil Stadium	0.5739	0.6477	0.5000	0.0739
MIA	8718	Hard Rock Stadium	0.5108	0.5843	0.4375	0.0734
T B	9818	Raymond James Stadium	0.4464	0.5179	0.3750	0.0715
PIT	0118	Heinz Field	0.6563	0.7257	0.5868	0.0695
CHI	0318	Soldier Field	0.4961	0.5625	0.4297	0.0664
WAS	9718	FedEx Field	0.4375	0.4972	0.3778	0.0597
ARZ	0618	State Farm Stadium	0.3125	0.3750	0.2500	0.0625
NYG	1118	MetLife Stadium	0.4375	0.4844	0.3906	0.0469
N O	0618	Mercedes Benz Superdome	0.6010	0.6538	0.5481	0.0529
L A	SUM	Los Angeles Coliseum	0.5875	0.6345	0.5403	0.0471
OAK	SUM	Oakland-Alameda Coliseum SUM	0.5195	0.5731	0.4659	0.0536

TM	YRS	VENUE	WPCT	HPCT	RPCT	HWA
TEN	9918	Nissan Stadium	0.5125	0.5688	0.4563	0.0563
CLE	9918	FirstEnergy Stadium	0.2984	0.3531	0.2438	0.0547
CAR	9618	Bank of America Stadium	0.4986	0.5489	0.4484	0.0503
OAK	9518	Oak-Alameda Coliseum	0.3984	0.4479	0.3490	0.0495
N O	SUM	Mercedes-Benz Superdome SUM	0.4378	0.4506	0.4249	0.0253
PHI	0318	Lincoln Financial Field	0.5762	0.5938	0.5586	0.0176
ATL	1718	Mercedes Benz Stadium	0.5313	0.5625	0.5000	0.0000
DAL	0918	AT&T Stadium	0.5563	0.5500	0.5625	-0.0062
LAC	1718	StubHub Center	0.6563	0.6250	0.6875	-0.0312
L A	1618	Los Angeles Coliseum	0.5833	0.5000	0.6667	-0.0833

Among the current stadiums, the Ravens, Seahawks and Packers stadiums top the list. If you pay close attention to the table, you'll notice that the dates listed for Lambeau Field are 1995 to 2018. Until 1994, the Packers split their home games between Milwaukee and Green Bay, and they've played their Green Bay games at Lambeau since 1957. When a team splits their games between two stadiums as the Packers did, those are handled as a separate entity from the games played strictly at Lambeau. In the long run, I don't think the Packers got some sort of special advantage from that annual game or two each season in Milwaukee.

After a decade at AT&T Stadium, the Cowboys have the lowest HFA in the entire NFL among active stadiums with the exception of the two new Los Angeles teams. The Cowboys play better on the road than they do at Jerryworld. Perhaps that giant TV screen they play underneath is too much of a distraction to the players.

For three of the teams, Oakland and New Orleans and the Rams, there are multiple entries; their entries are listed as SUM for their current tenure. What this means is the Raiders and Saints and Rams had breaks in the time they played in their respective stadium, as the Raiders moved to Los Angeles from 1982 to 1994 and then moved back to the Oakland Coliseum. The Raiders SUM record at the Oakland Coliseum covers from 1966 to 1981 and 1995 to present, but their 1966–81 and 1995–2018 records are also listed separately.

The Saints, on the other hand, found themselves a perpetual road team during the 2005 season due to Hurricane Katrina, and their HFA stats for 2005 are not included in their SUM totals, which cover 1975 to 2004 and 2006 to present. Because they played all their 2005 road games at different stadiums (San Antonio, Baton Rouge, The Meadowlands), I just lumped the Saints 2005 road games collectively.

The Rams record at the LA Coliseum runs from 1946 to 1979 (they moved to Anaheim Stadium from 1980 to 1994 before moving to St. Louis from 1995 to 2015) and their record picks up again at the LA Coliseum in 2016.

You will notice I have the Bears playing at Soldier Field 2, and I need to explain this. Soldier Field was renovated in 2002, and the Bears spent the entire season playing at the University of Illinois stadium at Champaign. In this case, the stadium was substantially redesigned to the point where the new Soldier Field is, from an architectural standpoint, a totally different stadium compared to the original Soldier Field. The before and after pics of the stadium do not look anything alike, other than the iconic colonnades. For this reason, I decided to split Soldier Field into two different stadiums.

Table 1.6
Current NFL Stadiums Ranked by Highest HPA Values, Through 2018

TM	YRS	VENUE	HG	HPDG	RG	RPDG	HPA
BAR	9818	M&T Bank Stadium	168	7.45	168	-1.14	4.29
SEA	0218	CenturyLink Field	137	7.04	136	-0.80	3.92
G B	9518	Lambeau Field	192	8.21	192	1.14	3.54
K C	7218	Arrowhead Stadium	365	3.95	367	-2.91	3.43
NYJ	1118	MetLife Stadium	64	-0.91	64	-7.66	3.38
BUF	7318	New Era Field	352	2.45	350	-4.26	3.36
ATL	1718	Mercedes Benz Stadium	16	4.19	16	-2.38	3.28
JAX	9518	TIAA Bank Stadium	192	1.80	192	-4.32	3.06
HOT	0218	NRG Stadium	136	1.13	136	-4.93	3.03
DET	0218	Ford Field	136	-0.95	136	-6.80	2.93
S F	1418	Levi's Stadium	40	-3.40	40	-9.08	2.84
L A	SUM	Los Angeles Coliseum SUM	249	6.83	248	1.25	2.79
PIT	0118	Heinz Field	144	7.72	144	2.16	2.78
IND	0818	Lucas Oil Stadium	88	3.08	88	-2.47	2.77
MIN	1618	U.S. Bank Stadium	24	6.25	24	0.79	2.73
CHI	0318	Soldier Field	128	2.41	128	-2.94	2.67
DEN	0118	Sport Authority Field	144	4.36	144	-0.94	2.65
TEN	9918	Nissan Stadium	160	1.34	160	-3.38	2.36
MIA	8718	Hard Rock Stadium	255	2.00	256	-2.50	2.25
ARZ	0618	State Farm Stadium	104	1.89	104	-4.54	2.19
OAK	9518	Oakland-Alameda Coliseum	192	-1.29	192	-5.63	2.17
OAK	SUM	Oak-Alameda Coliseum SUM	308	2.36	308	-1.96	2.16
T B	9818	Raymond James Stadium	168	0.85	168	-3.21	2.03
N E	0218	Gillette Stadium	136	11.28	136	7.44	1.92
PHI	0318	Lincoln Financial Field	128	4.73	128	0.92	1.91
N O	0618	Mercedes-Benz Superdome	104	6.29	104	2.56	1.87
CLE	9918	FirstEnergy Stadium	160	-4.36	160	-8.07	1.86
CAR	9618	Bank of America Stadium	184	1.91	184	-1.66	1.79
CIN	0018	Paul Brown Stadium	152	0.59	152	-2.82	1.70
LAC	1718	StubHub Center	16	7.19	16	4.19	1.50
N O	SUM	Mercedes Benz Superdome SUM	337	1.20	337	-1.56	1.38
NYG	1118	MetLife Stadium	64	-0.41	64	-2.89	1.24
WAS	9718	FedEx Field	176	-0.95	176	-3.42	1.23
DAL	0918	AT&T Stadium	80	2.65	80	0.38	1.14
L A	1618	Los Angeles Coliseum	24	1.92	24	3.17	-0.62

As you can see from Table 1.6, Baltimore, Seattle and Green Bay top the list again, with Dallas next to last, only ahead of the Los Angeles Rams.

Figuring the HWA and HPA of a Real Game

To show how to figure out HWA and HPA for a game if we have real home and road data, we'll use a real example. We'll figure the HWA and HPA of a game between the 2018 Los Angeles Rams and New England Patriots:

Table 1.7
2018 Patriots and Rams, HWA Values

TM	YRS	VENUE	WPCT	HPCT	RPCT	HWA
N E	0218	Gillette Stadium	0.7684	0.8456	0.6912	0.0772
L A	SUM	Los Angeles Coliseum	0.5875	0.6345	0.5403	0.0471

Using the data from Table 1.7, the HWA for the game is 0.0622, which is 0.0772 + 0.0471 or 0.1243 divided by 2. We could use win-loss records, but I would prefer we wait until we introduce EPCT in Chapter 2 before we can continue with this process for HWA, but we can complete the process for HPA right now.

Table 1.8
2018 Patriots and Rams, HPA Values

TM	YRS	VENUE	HOME		ROAD		HPA
			HG	HPDG	RG	RPDG	
N E	0218	Gillette Stadium	136	11.28	136	7.44	1.92
L A	SUM	Los Angeles Coliseum	249	6.83	248	1.25	2.79

From Table 1.8, the HPA for the game is 2.355, which is 1.92 + 2.79 or 4.71 divided by 2.

We know the 2018 Pats scored 436 points and allowed 325 points in regular season games, while the Rams scored 527 and allowed 384, for a total of 1,672 points. Dividing 1,672 by 32 (total number points scored and allowed by both teams divided by games played by both teams), we get 52.25. That predicted number of combined points scored by both teams is more than three times the combined number of points they scored in Super Bowl LIII, by the way.

Nobody, and I mean nobody, predicted the final score of Super Bowl LIII would be 13–3. Everybody figured it to be a high-scoring shootout, and it turned out to be the most unexpected, most bizarre world Super Bowl game since Super Bowl V between the Colts and Cowboys.

We'll use the formula from earlier for determining points scored by each team in the game:

PS = (PFA+ PAB) / (GA + GB)
PFA = Points for by team A PAB = Points allowed by team B
GA = Games played by team A GB = Games played by team B

For New England:

PS = (436+ 384) / (16 + 16) = 820/32 = 25.625

For Los Angeles:

$$PS = (527 + 325) / (16 + 16) = 852/32 = 26.625$$

If the game is played at New England, add 2.355 to New England and subtract 2.355 from Los Angeles, and if the game is played at Los Angeles, vice versa.

At New England:

$$\text{Patriots: } 25.625 + 2.355 = 27.98 \text{ or } 28$$
$$\text{Rams: } 26.625 - 2.355 = 23.27 \text{ or } 23$$

At Los Angeles:

$$\text{Rams: } 25.625 + 2.355 = 28.98 \text{ or } 29$$
$$\text{Patriots: } 25.625 - 2.355 = 23.27 \text{ or } 23$$

Now, we need to come up with a way to estimate WPCT in order to determine a little more accurately how teams might match up as opposed to using wins and losses to compare them.

2

Estimated Winning Percentage

It would be nice to have a formula for easily estimating a team's winning percentage based on points and possibly yards. This way, you could compare teams from different eras. I'm going to give it a shot here, to develop a Pythagorean formula for estimating a team's winning percentage from points scored and points allowed.

The Pythagorean formula was developed by Bill James of *Baseball Abstract* fame, and it looks like this:

$$\text{Winning Percentage} = (RS^2) / ((RS^2) + (RA^2))$$
$$RS, RA = \text{Runs Scored, Runs Allowed}$$

It has proven to be very accurate at predicting a team's winning percentage in baseball, and I think a similar formula will work for pro football.

What we are trying to come up with here is a formula for Estimated Winning Percentage, or EPCT, that looks like this:

$$EPCT = (PS^X) / ((PS^X) + (PA^X))$$

We have to solve for X, the power we are raising Points Scored (PS) and Points Allowed (PA) to.

The method I came up with for determining the X with the lowest average absolute error was to set up a spreadsheet with the WPCT (Actual Winning Percentage), Points Scored and Points Allowed data for every team-season from 1933 to 2018, and leave the X number open where I could pick a number for X and it would immediately apply to each team-season, and come up with an EPCT for every team-season, and thus calculate an average absolute error for the entire set of 1,995 team-seasons.

After a few minutes of trial and error plugging in numbers, I determined that the X value that gave the lowest absolute error or AERR was approximately 2.47…, which I rounded off to X = 2.50 with virtually the same AERR, which was 0.0666, or 1.06 games per 16-game season.

Absolute error is the absolute value of EPCT minus WPCT. Absolute value is a mathematical term to denote magnitude, regardless of whether it is positive or negative. The absolute value of six is six, and the absolute value of negative six is also six. By using absolute value for the error, the positive and negative errors don't cancel each other out, they all come back positive, and thus, we can get a real average of all the errors. The mathematical symbol for absolute value is a set of vertical lines | | around the items in question, and the absolute error formula is:

$$AERR = | EPCT - WPCT |$$

The EPCT formula is:

$$EPCT = (PS^{2.5}) / ((PS^{2.5}) + (PA^{2.5}))$$

Applying EPCT to Real Teams

Let's apply our EPCT formula to the two Super Bowl LIII opponents from the end of the Chapter 1, the 2018 Patriots and Rams, using their end of regular season points scored and points allowed numbers:

Patriots: 436 points scored; 325 points allowed
Rams: 527 points scored; 384 points allowed

Patriots EPCT = (436^2.5) / ((436^2.5) + (325^2.5)) = 0.6758
Rams EPCT = (527^2.5) / ((527^2.5) + (325^2.5)) = 0.6881

The Rams have the higher EPCT, so next, we'll run Bayes Theorem, using the Rams as Team A since they have the higher EPCT:

WPCT = (WA * LB) / ((WA * LB) + (WB * LA))
WPCT Rams = (0.6881 * 0 3242) / ((0.6881 * 0.3242) + (0.6758 * 0.3119)) = 0.5142

Since the Super Bowl was played at a neutral site (Atlanta), we would stop here if we were figuring projected winning percentages of their meeting in the Super Bowl, and the Rams would have a 51.42 percent probability of winning on a neutral field, but we want to see how it would look if they were to meet in Foxborough or Los Angeles.

Picking up where I left off last in Chapter 1, here is a repeat of the HWA table (previously Table 1.7, now Table 2.1) for both teams:

Table 2.1
2018 Patriots and Rams, HWA Values

TM	YRS	VENUE	WPCT	HPCT	RPCT	HWA
N E	0218	Gillette Stadium	0.7684	0.8456	0.6912	0.0772
L A	SUM	Los Angeles Coliseum	0.5875	0.6345	0.5403	0.0471

HWA = 0.0772 + 0.0471 or 0.1243; 0.1243 / 2 = 0.0622
N E at L A = 0.5142 + 0.0622 = 0.5762 Rams or 0.4238 Patriots
L A at N E = 0.4858 (or 1 - 0.5142) + 0.0622 = 0.5480 Patriots or 0.4520 Rams

Applying EPCT to an Entire League

The EPCT formula is applied to the 1966 AFL teams, with each teams' won-loss-tied record, WPCT, points scored (PS) and points allowed (PA) data as shown in Table 2.2:

Table 2.2
EPCT and AERR Applied to All 1966 AFL Teams

TM	W	L	T	WPCT	PS	PA	EPCT	AERR
BUF	9	4	1	0.6786	358	255	0.7002	0.0216

2. Estimated Winning Percentage

TM	W	L	T	WPCT	PS	PA	EPCT	AERR
BOP	8	4	2	0.6429	315	283	0.5666	0.0763
NYJ	6	6	2	0.5000	322	312	0.5197	0.0197
HOU	3	11	0	0.2143	335	396	0.3969	0.1827
MIA	3	11	0	0.2143	213	362	0.2098	0.0044
K C	11	2	1	0.8214	448	276	0.7705	0.0510
OAK	8	5	1	0.6071	315	288	0.5558	0.0514
S D	7	6	1	0.5357	335	284	0.6018	0.0661
DEN	4	10	0	0.2857	196	381	0.1595	0.1262
SUM	59	59	8		2837	2837		
AVG				0.5000				0.0666

From Table 2.2, the average absolute error between EPCT and WPCT for the 1966 AFL is at 0.0666. For the 1,995 team-seasons, the AERR is 0.0670.

Adjusting for Schedule

A team's statistics are biased by the schedules they play, and EPCT has to be adjusted for their schedule.

For the 1966 Buffalo Bills, Table 2.3 (shown below) lists their regular season schedule, the final score in PS and PA (Points Scored and Allowed) by Buffalo in each game, and the OPS (Opponents' Points Scored) and OPA (Opponents' Points Allowed) for their opponents for each week of the regular season:

Table 2.3
1966 Bills Opponents, PS, PA, OPS, OPA by Week

GM NO	OPP	GM SCORE		OPP POINTS	
		PS	PA	OPS	OPA
1	S D	7	27	335	284
2	K C	20	42	448	276
3	MIA	58	24	213	362
4	HOU	27	20	335	396
5	K C	29	14	448	276
6	BOP	10	20	315	283
7	S D	17	17	335	284
8	NYJ	33	23	322	312
9	MIA	29	0	213	362
10	NYJ	14	3	322	312
11	HOU	42	20	335	396
12	OAK	31	10	315	288
13	BOP	3	14	315	283

GM NO	OPP	GM SCORE		OPP POINTS	
		PS	PA	OPS	OPA
14	DEN	38	21	196	381
	SUM	358	255	4447	4495

In order to adjust the opposition, the results of their games against the Bills need to be removed from the opponents points for and against, so that we are looking at how the Bills opponents did in all games in which they did not play Buffalo.

Let's look at Buffalo's Week 1 opponent, the San Diego Chargers, who scored 335 points and allowed 284 points in the 1966 regular season. In the Week 1 meeting, the Bills lost the game, 27–7. The results of the Chargers game against the Bills will need to be removed from the Chargers points for and points against. Since the Bills allowed 27 points, it means the Chargers scored 27 points, which means we'll remove 27 points from San Diego's seasonal points scored total. The Bills scored seven points, which means the Chargers allowed seven points, which means seven points will need to be removed from the Chargers' seasonal points allowed total. In mathematical terms, 335 minus 27 equals 308, and 284 minus 7 equals 277. Simple enough.

Table 2.4 shows this "first stage" adjustment being made to each of the games on the Bills 1966 schedule, as shown, with OFF ADJ and DEF ADJ (offensive and defensive adjustment, respectively), taking care of the subtraction process, and ADJ OPP 1 being the adjusted offensive and defensive point totals:

Table 2.4
1966 Bills Weekly Schedule Adjustment, First Stage

GM NO	OPP	GM SCORE		OPP POINTS		OPP POINT ADJ 1		ADJ OPP 1	
		PS	PA	OPS	OPA	OFF ADJ	DEF ADJ	OPS	OPA
1	S D	7	27	335	284	335 minus 27	284 minus 7	308	277
2	K C	20	42	448	276	448 minus 42	276 minus 20	406	256
3	MIA	58	24	213	362	213 minus 24	362 minus 58	189	304
4	HOU	27	20	335	396	335 minus 20	396 minus 27	315	369
5	K C	29	14	448	276	448 minus 14	276 minus 29	434	247
6	BOP	10	20	315	283	315 minus 20	283 minus 10	295	273
7	S D	17	17	335	284	335 minus 17	284 minus 17	318	267
8	NYJ	33	23	322	312	322 minus 23	312 minus 33	299	279
9	MIA	29	0	213	362	213 minus 0	362 minus 29	213	333
10	NYJ	14	3	322	312	322 minus 3	312 minus 14	319	298
11	HOU	42	20	335	396	335 minus 20	396 minus 42	315	354
12	OAK	31	10	315	288	315 minus 10	288 minus 31	305	257
13	BOP	3	14	315	283	315 minus 14	283 minus 3	301	280w
14	DEN	38	21	196	381	196 minus 21	381 minus 38	175	343
	SUM	358	255	4447	4495			4192	4137

However, the Bills played the Chargers twice in 1966; they also played one another in Week 7 in addition to Week 1. This means we need to perform a second adjustment, because the Chargers Week 1 adjusted OPS and OPA still includes the results of the Week 7 game against the Bills and the Chargers Week 7 adjusted OPS and OPA still include the results of the Week 1 game against the Bills, which was a 17–17 tie by the way. In order for this adjustment to work for Buffalo with respect to San Diego, any games involving Buffalo have to be completely removed from San Diego's points for and points allowed results for 1966.

The Bills also played the Chiefs twice along with playing all of their Eastern Division foes (Boston, Jets, Miami and Houston) two times, so those will also require a second adjustment to all of these games. Buffalo faced both Oakland and Denver once, so no additional adjustment will be necessary for those two games.

Table 2.5
1966 Bills Weekly Schedule Adjustment, Second Stage

GM NO	OPP	ADJ OPP 1		GAME SCORE 2		ADJ OPP 2		FIN ADJ OPP	
		OPS	OPA	PS	PA	APS	APA	OPS	OPA
1	S D	308	277	17	17	308 minus 17	277 minus 17	291	260
2	K C	406	256	29	14	406 minus 14	256 minus 29	392	227
3	MIA	189	304	29	0	189 minus 0	304 minus 29	189	275
4	HOU	315	369	42	20	315 minus 20	369 minus 42	295	327
5	K C	434	247	20	42	434 minus 42	247 minus 20	392	227
6	BOP	295	273	3	14	295 minus 14	273 minus 3	281	270
7	S D	318	267	7	27	318 minus 27	267 minus 7	291	260
8	NYJ	299	279	14	3	299 minus 3	279 minus 14	296	265
9	MIA	213	333	58	24	213 minus 24	333 minus 58	189	275
10	NYJ	319	298	33	23	319 minus 23	298 minus 33	296	265
11	HOU	315	354	27	20	315 minus 20	354 minus 27	295	327
12	OAK	305	257	N/A	N/A	N/A	N/A	305	257
13	BOP	301	280	10	20	301 minus 20	280 minus 10	281	270
14	DEN	175	343	N/A	N/A	N/A	N/A	175	343
	SUM	4192	4137	289	224			3968	3848

As you can see in Table 2.5, the Chargers scored 291 points and allowed 261 points in the 12 games in which they did not play Buffalo, in the Final Adjustment Opposition columns for game numbers 1 and 7.

All told, the Bills' opponents in 1966 scored 3,968 points and allowed 3,848 points in games in which they did not face the Bills. Next, it is a matter of figuring the EPCT for a team who scores 3,968 points and allows 3,848 points. We will call this OSCH, short for Opponents' Schedule:

$$OSCH = (3968 \wedge 2.5) / ((3968 \wedge 2.5) + (3848 \wedge 2.5)) = 0.5192$$

If a team scores 3,968 points and allow 3,848 games in a season, regardless of the number of games they play, they would be expected to win 51.92 percent of the time.

Table 2.6 shows the above process performed on each of the teams in the AFL from 1966:

Table 2.6
OSCH Schedule Adjustment for All 1966 AFL Teams

TM	WPCT	PS	PA	EPCT	ADJ OPS	ADJ OPA	OSCH
BUF	0.6786	358	255	0.7002	3968	3848	0.5192
N E	0.6429	315	283	0.5666	3985	3872	0.5180
NYJ	0.5000	322	312	0.5197	3801	3789	0.5020
HOU	0.2143	335	396	0.3969	3505	3697	0.4667
MIA	0.2143	213	362	0.2098	3938	3981	0.4932
K C	0.8214	448	276	0.7705	3616	3598	0.5031
OAK	0.6071	315	288	0.5558	3850	3961	0.4822
S D	0.5357	335	284	0.6018	3920	3750	0.5277
DEN	0.2857	196	381	0.1595	3894	3981	0.4862
SUM		2837	2837		34477	34477	
AVG	0.5000			0.4979			0.4998

An Opponents' Schedule or OSCH above 0.5000 means the team faced a tougher than average schedule, and an OSCH under 0.5000 indicates the team faced an easier than average schedule.

Adjusting EPCT for OSCH

The next stage in the process is to put the EPCT and OSCH together to figure out what a team's Estimated Winning Percentage would be against average competition. If you are guessing that we will be using Bayes Theorem to do this, you would be correct, but we will first need to algebraically manipulate the Bayes Theorem formula to do this.

This is the basic Bayes Theorem formula that we have used:

$$W = (A - A * B) / (A + B - 2*A*B)$$

When we used this previously, we have known A and B, and were solving for W. This time, we know B, which is OSCH. We also know W, which is EPCT. Therefore, we have to solve for A.

Why is this? This is because EPCT, or W, has already been adjusted for schedule, or B, during the course of the season, because the Bills already played all of these teams and achieved this EPCT in spite of the competition they played. We are trying to remove the schedule bias and see how the team should be expected to perform against average, which we define as 0.5000, competition.

When you algebraically solve the equation for A (I'll save you a page of algebraic equations here; you're welcome to double-check the math to confirm my results if you wish):

$$A = (W * B) / (1 - B - W + 2 * W * B)$$

We will substitute AEWP (Adjusted Estimated Winning Percentage) for A, OSCH for B, and EPCT for W.

2. Estimated Winning Percentage

$$AEWP = (EPCT * OSCH) / (1 - EPCT - OSCH + 2 * EPCT * OSCH)$$

For the 1966 Bills:

$$AEWP = (0.7002 * 0.5192) / (1 - 0.7002 - 0.5192 + 2 * 0.7002 * 0.5192) = 0.7160$$

We know from Bayes Theorem that when a 0.7160 team plays a 0.5192 team, their probability of winning is 0.7002:

$$W = (A - A * B) / (A + B - 2*A*B)$$
$$W = (0.7160 - 0.7160 * 0.5192) / (0.7160 + 0.5192 - 2 * 0.7160 * 0.5192)$$
$$W = (0.7160 - 0.3717) / (0.7160 + 0.5192 - 0.7435) = (0.3443 / 0.4917) = 0.7002$$

Therefore, the 1966 Bills AEWP is 0.7160, because they played a 0.5192 schedule, and their Estimated Winning Percentage or EPCT is 0.7002. The AEWP is now adjusted for a 0.5000 schedule. This AEWP calculation is carried out for all 1966 AFL teams in Table 2.7:

Table 2.7
AEWP Adjustment for All 1966 AFL Teams

TM	WPCT	EPCT	OSCH	AEWP
BUF	0.6786	0.7002	0.5192	0.7160
N E	0.6429	0.5666	0.5180	0.5841
NYJ	0.5000	0.5197	0.5020	0.5217
HOU	0.2143	0.3969	0.4667	0.3655
MIA	0.2143	0.2098	0.4932	0.2054
K C	0.8214	0.7705	0.5031	0.7727
OAK	0.6071	0.5558	0.4822	0.5382
S D	0.5357	0.6018	0.5277	0.6280
DEN	0.2857	0.1595	0.4862	0.1523
AVG	0.5000	0.4979	0.4998	0.4982

Next, we will employ a basic statistical method in order to compare teams from different seasons against each other.

Rating by Standard Deviations

At this point, you'd think we were done, but rating teams from different seasons by AEWP just doesn't work. Here's why—presented for your approval is Table 2.8, which displays a ranking of the 21 team-seasons with an AEWP of 0.9000 or above.

Note—YL is a three-character abbreviation for Year League, where the first two characters are the last two digits of the year number and the last character is a letter signifying the league (N for NFL, F for AAFC or A for AFL)—.68A is short for 1968 AFL, 47F is short for 1947 AAFC and 00N is short for 2000 NFL. You'll get the hang of it pretty quickly.

Table 2.8
List of Team-Seasons with an AEWP of 0.9000 or Higher, 1933–2018

RK	TM	YL	W	L	T	WPCT	EPCT	OSCH	AEWP
1	DET	34N	10	3	0	0.7692	0.9703	0.5203	0.9726
2	CHI	42N	11	0	0	1.0000	0.9770	0.3911	0.9646
3	CHI	34N	13	0	0	1.0000	0.9528	0.5409	0.9596
4	CLE	46F	12	2	0	0.8571	0.9437	0.5000	0.9437
5	MIN	69N	12	2	0	0.8571	0.9320	0.5246	0.9380
6	NYG	33N	11	3	0	0.7857	0.9007	0.6220	0.9372
7	G B	62N	13	1	0	0.9286	0.9294	0.5062	0.9310
8	BAL	68N	13	1	0	0.9286	0.9287	0.5084	0.9309
9	PHI	49N	11	1	0	0.9167	0.9240	0.5255	0.9309
10	G B	36N	10	1	1	0.8750	0.8649	0.6669	0.9277
11	PIT	76N	10	4	0	0.7143	0.9063	0.5500	0.9220
12	CHI	48N	10	2	0	0.8333	0.9067	0.5466	0.9214
13	CHI	36N	9	3	0	0.7500	0.8955	0.5445	0.9111
14	MIA	73N	12	2	0	0.8571	0.8877	0.5607	0.9098
15	DET	36N	8	4	0	0.6667	0.8896	0.5529	0.9088
16	CHI	41N	10	1	0	0.9091	0.9225	0.4501	0.9070
17	PHI	48N	9	2	1	0.7917	0.9002	0.5166	0.9060
18	NYG	44N	8	1	1	0.8500	0.9259	0.4338	0.9055
19	CHI	33N	10	2	1	0.8077	0.7701	0.7405	0.9053
20	G B	35N	8	4	0	0.6667	0.8300	0.6562	0.9031
21	CLE	51N	11	1	0	0.9167	0.8750	0.5685	0.9022

Eight of the teams in Table 2.8 are from the 1930s, seven are from the 1940s, one is from the '50s, three are from the '60s, and two are from the 1970s. Any list of the greatest team-seasons of all time that does not include any team from the past 40 years (such as the 1978 Steelers, 1985 Bears, 1989 or 1994 49ers, early '90s Cowboys or any number of recent New England teams, for example) is what Jeff Spicoli would call bogus. However, it doesn't mean we're not close to the solution.

What I am saying is that the Buffalo Bills AEWP of 0.7061 in 1966 does not necessarily mean the same in 1936 or 1986 or 2018. The way to put all leagues on an equal level is by using standard deviations. For those of you who never took a Statistics class, I will have to give a quick explanation of the Bell-Shaped curve and Standard Deviations in layman's terms.

Standard Deviation is a basic statistical measure for determining the general variation of numbers from the center, an average distance from each data point to the center. This is the easiest way to explain Standard Deviations without using numbers:

Let's suppose two people are shooting at targets, and you are comparing their results. A pair of such targets are shown in Figure 2.1:

2. Estimated Winning Percentage

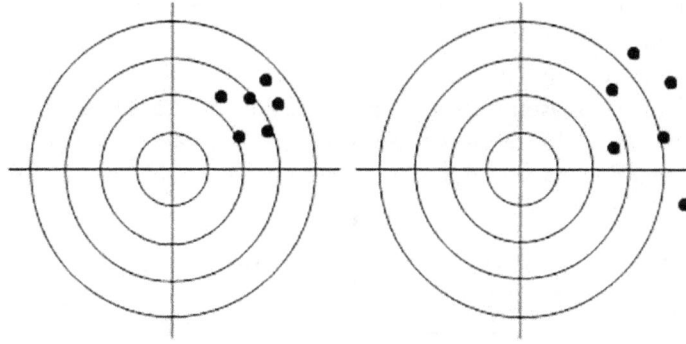

Figure 2.1. Two bullseye targets with bullet holes in them.

Looking at the target on the left in Figure 2.1, the bullet holes are more closely spaced together than those on the right, even though they are not centered near the target, but the holes on the target on the right are more closely centered around the target. This is another way of saying that the standard deviation of the distance between the shots on the target on the left is less than the standard deviation of the distance between the shots on the right, but the standard deviation of the shots on the right in relation to the center of the target is less than that of the standard deviation of the shots on the left in relation to the center of the target. Does it make sense?

Standard Deviation is a mathematical measure of how closely a group of numbers are grouped together. The lower the Standard Deviation, the closer the numbers are to the mean or center or average of all the numbers in the group.

This is the Bell-Shaped or Normal Distribution curve:

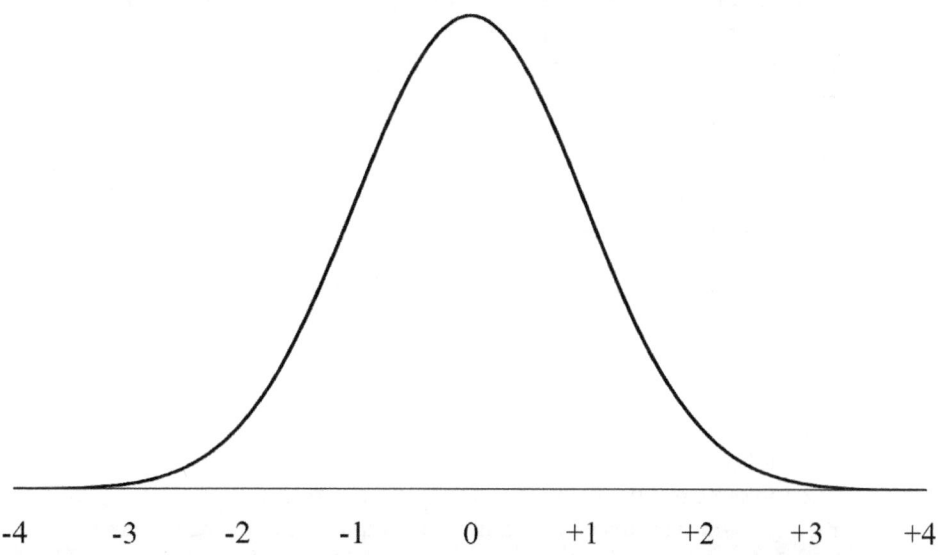

Figure 2.2. Bell-Shaped or normal curve, showing number of standard deviations.

The Bell-Shaped curve is applicable to any number of different applications in all walks of life. If you measured the height of every eight-year-old girl, or if you measured how far all

20-year-old men could throw a football, you would get the Bell-Shaped curve once you collected and plotted the distribution of the data.

In pro football, certain facets of the game follow the Bell-Shaped curve. If we look at the number of regular-season wins by teams since the NFL went to the 16-game schedule in 1978, removing the 1982 and 1987 seasons because they were shortened due to strikes, we would get the following data (FREQ = frequency), and Table 2.9 displays the results:

Table 2.9
Frequency of Team Wins in 16-Game Seasons 1978–2018

WINS	FREQ	WINS	FREQ	WINS	FREQ	WINS	FREQ
16	1	11.5	2	7	129	2.5	0
15.5	0	11	99	6.5	5	2	32
15	6	10.5	6	6	104	1.5	0
14.5	0	10	128	5.5	4	1	10
14	20	9.5	4	5	90	0.5	0
13.5	0	9	135	4.5	4	0	2
13	47	8.5	9	4	84	SUM	1177
12.5	0	8	131	3.5	1		
12	81	7.5	5	3	38		

Teams with ties in their final record are the 0.5's in the list above like 8.5, or an 8–7–1 record. Dropping out the 0.5 teams with ties from Table 2.9, the list becomes:

Table 2.10
Frequency of Team Wins in 16-Game Seasons, 1978–2018, Whole Numbers Only

WINS	FREQ	WINS	FREQ	WINS	FREQ	WINS	FREQ
16	1	11	97	7	129	3	38
15	6	10	128	6	104	2	32
14	20	9	135	5	90	1	10
13	47	8	131	4	84	0	2
12	81					SUM	1137

If we graph Wins (X-axis or horizontally) versus FREQ or frequency (Y-axis or vertically) from Table 2.10, we would get the following graph shown at top of next page. The thin trendline curve is a pretty close approximation of the Bell-Shaped Curve, and you can see the data follows it well.

If you did the same test using the 14-game schedule, or 12-game schedule, you would wind up with a very similar curve given a similar sample size of over 1,100 team-seasons.

The amount of variation (how far on average each item of data resides from the center or mean) is measured in Standard Deviations or SD's. In the original Bell-Shaped curve that I presented in Figure 2.2, at the bottom of the chart were notations for SD's. Figure 2.4 (shown below) explains the reason for the SD's on the Bell-Shaped curve, and they have to do with marking the percentages of data distribution within the curve.

2. Estimated Winning Percentage

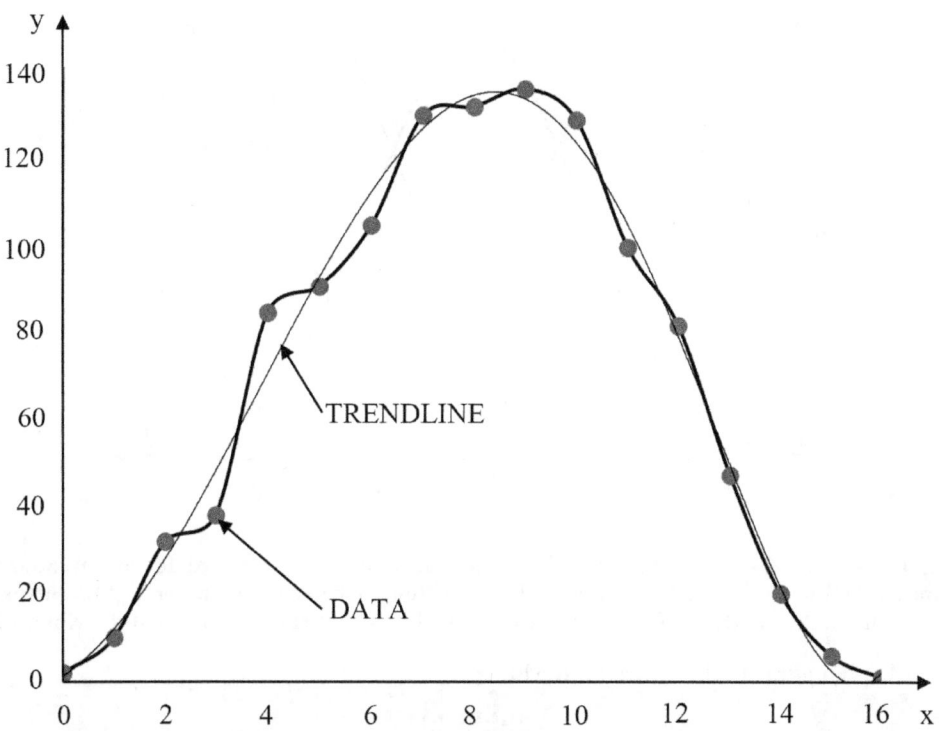

Figure 2.3. Graph of wins against frequency from Table 2.10 data, 16-game seasons, 1978–2018.

Approximately 34.1 percent of the total area under the curve should fall into the area between zero and positive one SD, which means we should expect 34.1 percent of the data that is collected to be between zero and positive one SD. Between positive one and positive two SD, approximately 13.6 percent of the data should fall, because that is the percentage of the area under the curve that lies between one and two SD. Between positive two and positive three SD, approximately 2.1 percent of the total area under the curve should fall into that region. Above positive three SD, about 0.1 percent of the data falls into that range.

The curve is symmetrical about zero SD, which means it is a mirror image on the negative side, meaning 34.1 percent of the data falls between zero and negative one SD, 13.6 falls between negative one and negative 2 SD, 2.1 percent falls between negative two and negative three, and 0.1 percent falls in the area above negative three SD.

This data percentage distribution that I've just explained is shown on the next page in Figure 2.4

The formula for determining a Standard Deviation (or SD) for a set of numbers is:

$$SD = [(\text{sum of (X-MEAN)}^2 \text{ for each of the numbers in the set}) / (\text{the total number of items in the set minus 1})]^{0.5}$$

Mean is a fancy statistical term for average, which would be the league average AEWP. The average AEWP for the 1966 AFL is 0.4982. For the 1966 Bills, it would look something like this:

$$(0.7160 - 0.4982)^2 = (0.2178)^2 = 0.0475$$

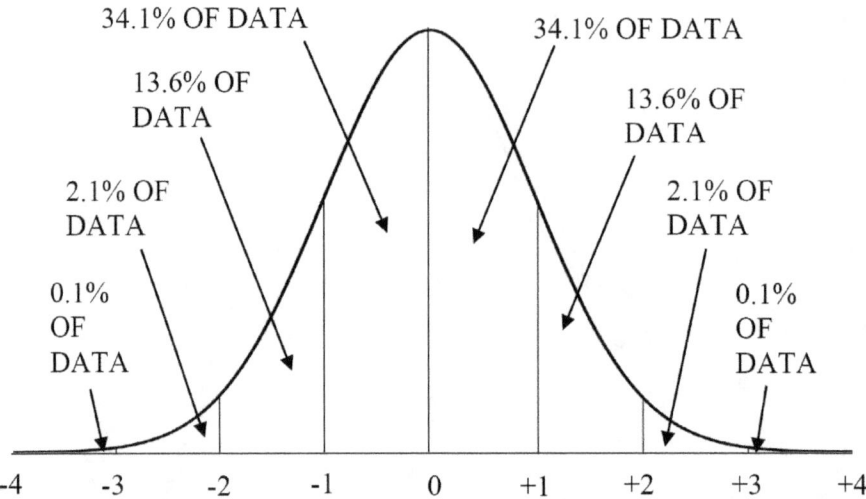

Figure 2.4. Data distribution for a Bell-Shaped Curve, showing standard deviations. Source: "Statistics How To," "What is a Normal Distribution," accessed September 4, 2019, https://www.statisticshowto.datasciencecentral.com/probability-and-statistics/normal-distributions/

Applying this to the entire 1966 AFL:

Table 2.11
Standard Deviation Calculation for 1966 AFL Teams

TM	WPCT	EPCT	OSCH	AEWP	MEAN	AEWP MINUS MEAN	(AEWP MINUS MEAN)^2
BUF	0.6786	0.7002	0.5192	0.7160	0.4982	0.2178	0.0475
BOP	0.6429	0.5666	0.5180	0.5841	0.4982	0.0859	0.0074
NYJ	0.5000	0.5197	0.5020	0.5217	0.4982	0.0235	0.0006
HOU	0.2143	0.3969	0.4667	0.3655	0.4982	-0.1327	0.0176
MIA	0.2143	0.2098	0.4932	0.2054	0.4982	-0.2928	0.0858
K C	0.8214	0.7705	0.5031	0.7727	0.4982	0.2745	0.0753
OAK	0.6071	0.5558	0.4822	0.5382	0.4982	0.0400	0.0016
S D	0.5357	0.6018	0.5277	0.6280	0.4982	0.1298	0.0169
DEN	0.2857	0.1595	0.4862	0.1523	0.4982	-0.3459	0.1197
SUM							0.3722
AVG	0.5000	0.4979	0.4998	0.4982			

SD = [0.3722/ (9 - 1)] ^ 0.5; SD = [0.3722 / 8] ^ 0.5; SD = [0.0465] ^ 0.5 = 0.2157

Now that we know the mean AEWP (0.4982) and SD (0.2157), Table 2.5 displays what the bell-shaped curve looks like in mathematical terms with respect to AEWP for the 1966 AFL.

One SD is equal to 0.2157, so at one SD away from the center, the AEWP value would

2. Estimated Winning Percentage

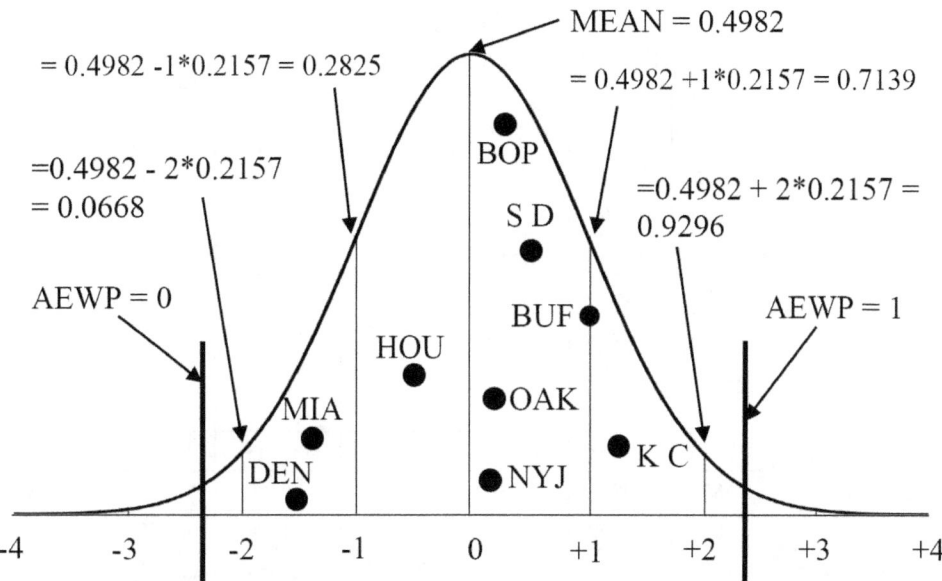

Figure 2.5 Bell-shaped curve for AEWP in the 1966 AFL. Source: "Statistics How To," "What is a Normal Distribution," accessed September 4, 2019, https://www.statisticshowto.datasciencecentral.com/probability-and-statistics/normal-distributions/

be equal to 0.4982 + 0.2157 or 0.7139, and three SD would be 0.4982 + 3*0.2157, or 1.1453. Of course, AEWP, like EPCT or OSCH, are akin to winning percentages in that they cannot be less than zero or greater than one. I added the two vertical lines to convey where the limits of AEWP actually are.

You will notice I added the data points for the nine 1966 AFL teams. As you can see, they are not equally distributed within the bell-shaped curve. Six of the teams are on the positive side, three are on the negative side, and there are four teams between zero and positive one SD compared to only one between zero and negative one SD. This is due to the small sample size. If you were to keep track of this over the course of all seasons and compile all the data, this would even out over time, and you would see that the data would follow the bell-shaped curve pretty well.

Once you have the SD for the league, you can determine the number of SD's a team is away from the center (known as Z or Z-score) using the following formula:

$$Z = (AEWP - MEAN) / SD$$

For the 1966 Bills, we know their AEWP is 0.7160, the mean is 0.4982, and the SD for the 1966 NFL is 0.2157. Plugging those numbers into the formula:

$$Z = (0.7160 - 0.4982) / 0.2157 = 0.2178 / 0.2157 = 1.0099$$

The 1966 Buffalo Bills have a Z-score of 1.0099, meaning they were 1.0099 SD's from the mean or center.

Running the same formula on the entire 1966 AFL:

Table 2.12
Z-Scores for All 1966 AFL Teams

TM	WPCT	EPCT	OSCH	AEWP	MEAN	AEWP MINUS MEAN	LG SD	Z-SCORE
BUF	0.6786	0.7002	0.5192	0.7160	0.4982	0.2178	0.2157	1.0099
BOP	0.6429	0.5666	0.5180	0.5841	0.4982	0.0859	0.2157	0.3983
NYJ	0.5000	0.5197	0.5020	0.5217	0.4982	0.0235	0.2157	0.1088
HOU	0.2143	0.3969	0.4667	0.3655	0.4982	-0.1327	0.2157	-0.6152
MIA	0.2143	0.2098	0.4932	0.2054	0.4982	-0.2928	0.2157	-1.3576
K C	0.8214	0.7705	0.5031	0.7727	0.4982	0.2745	0.2157	1.2725
OAK	0.6071	0.5558	0.4822	0.5382	0.4982	0.0400	0.2157	0.1853
S D	0.5357	0.6018	0.5277	0.6280	0.4982	0.1298	0.2157	0.6018
DEN	0.2857	0.1595	0.4862	0.1523	0.4982	-0.3459	0.2157	-1.6038
SUM								0.0000
AVG	0.5000	0.4979	0.4998	0.4982				

If you add the Z-scores for all the teams in the league, they will always equal zero. Z-scores are like a zero-sum game in that way, as the Z-score is the number of standard deviations a team is from the center, and for all the teams in a single league, the positives and negatives would cancel each other out and you would wind up at zero. If they don't wind up equaling zero at the end, you've done something wrong.

There have been seven team-seasons between 1933 and 2018 who finished the regular season with a Z-score between 1.00 and 1.01 in a season. They are listed in Table 2.13:

Table 2.13
All Team Seasons with a Z-Score Between 1.00 and 1.01

TM	YL	WPCT	EPCT	OSCH	AEWP	Z
BUF	66A	0.6786	0.7002	0.5192	0.7160	1.0099
DET	37N	0.6364	0.7937	0.5356	0.8161	1.0079
BAL	76N	0.7857	0.7891	0.4620	0.7626	1.0033
MIA	85N	0.7500	0.6741	0.5003	0.6744	1.0018
DAL	70N	0.7143	0.6804	0.5197	0.6973	1.0017
NYG	63N	0.7857	0.7640	0.4666	0.7391	1.0012
CHI	87N	0.7333	0.6417	0.5166	0.6568	1.0002

In that group, except for the 1937 7–4 Lions, every team went to the postseason. None went all the way, but there was a Super Bowl loser (1970 Cowboys), an NFL Championship game loser (1963 Giants), one team who lost an AFC Championship game (1985 Dolphins) and another who lost an AFL Title game (1966 Bills). All teams were deemed by the EPCT methodology to be virtually similar to one another. On the whole, I would generally agree.

2. Estimated Winning Percentage

And that, in a nutshell, is how standard deviation works. The higher the standard deviation, the further you are from the norm, the more you stand apart from your contemporaries, the more unique you are, the more impressive your performance is. But it works the other way also. Conversely, the lower the standard deviation, the further you are from the norm, the more you stand apart from your contemporaries, the more unique you are, and the less impressive your performance is. It works both ways.

If you calculate the SD of the EPCT results for all the teams in each league for each season, and graph the annual SD of EPCT (y) by season (x), it becomes clear that the NFL has become consistently a lot more competitive over the past 40 years, as shown in Figure 2.6:

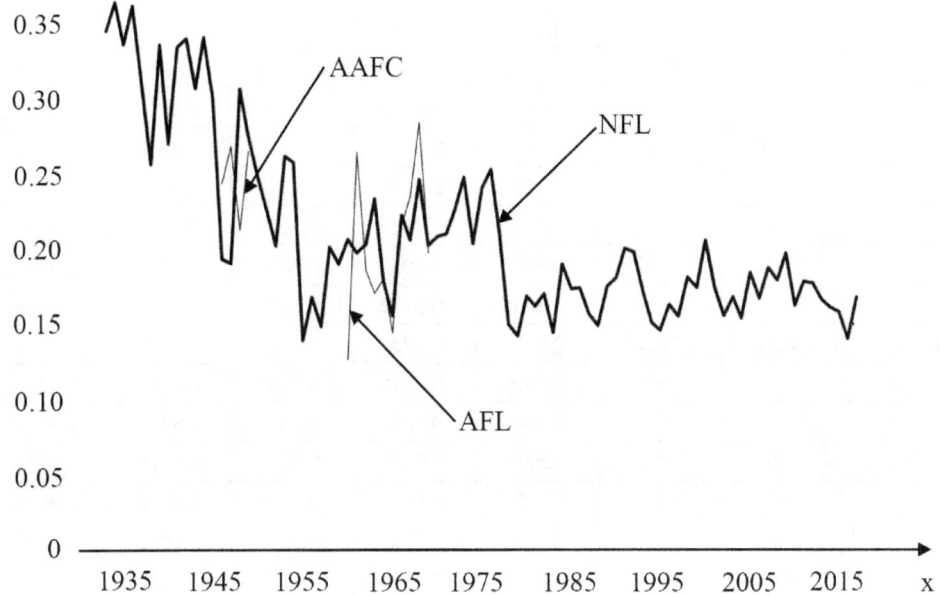

Figure 2.6. Graph of average EPCT by Season, 1933–2018 for NFL, AAFC and AFL.

What is most interesting about Figure 2.6 is that the SD for the NFL between 1978 and 2018 has fluctuated between 0.15 and 0.20 consistently. If you want to see what parity looks like, it is the right side of the graph. Somewhere, someplace, Pete Rozelle must be smiling right now.

I think there are a number of reasons for this—the balanced schedules, the competitive balance between teams in that the gap between the best and worst teams has narrowed, and the fact that the draft works in favor of the lesser teams in the league, propelling them upward. Also, it is clear that Free Agency also plays a big role, in that it keeps talent moving around freely, and in conjunction with the Salary Cap and the massive amounts of TV money that is shared equally amongst all teams, it ensures parity.

Best and Worst by Z-Score

What do the all-time best and worst lists look like? It is necessary to keep in mind that the more teams there are in a league, the easier it is to rack up a very high or very low

Z-score. This is because the more teams there are in a league, the more teams will disperse further from the center due to the law of averages; which means in larger leagues, you will see more very, very good teams and more very, very bad teams.

Table 2.14
List of Highest Single-Season Z-Scores, 1933–2018

RK	TM	YL	WPCT	EPCT	OSCH	AEWP	Z
1	G B	96N	0.8125	0.8741	0.5148	0.8775	2.3954
2	CHI	85N	0.9375	0.8898	0.5135	0.8952	2.2542
3	DAL	78N	0.7500	0.8228	0.5223	0.8353	2.1882
4	S F	95N	0.6875	0.8099	0.5269	0.8224	2.1357
5	G B	62N	0.9286	0.9298	0.5050	0.9317	2.0776
6	N E	07N	1.0000	0.8759	0.5396	0.8924	2.0765
7	MIN	69N	0.8571	0.9302	0.5232	0.9360	2.0609
8	S D	79N	0.7500	0.7841	0.5353	0.8073	2.0579
9	WAS	83N	0.8750	0.7769	0.5239	0.7933	2.0229
10	MIN	88N	0.6875	0.8035	0.5014	0.8045	2.0198
11	S F	87N	0.8667	0.8172	0.5007	0.8176	2.0013
12	MIN	70N	0.8571	0.8933	0.5121	0.8996	1.9951
13	PIT	79N	0.7500	0.7618	0.5508	0.7970	1.9891
14	T B	02N	0.7500	0.8063	0.5614	0.8419	1.9686
15	N E	04N	0.8750	0.7880	0.5531	0.8219	1.9598
16	BAL	64N	0.8571	0.8370	0.5338	0.8556	1.9575
17	DAL	94N	0.7500	0.7855	0.5309	0.8057	1.9560
18	SEA	13N	0.8125	0.8146	0.5143	0.8234	1.9457
19	SLR	01N	0.8750	0.8210	0.5065	0.8246	1.9457
20	N E	16N	0.8750	0.8058	0.4542	0.7750	1.9225
21	SLR	99N	0.8125	0.8746	0.3990	0.8209	1.9215
22	CLE	55N	0.7917	0.7676	0.5077	0.7735	1.9191
23	PIT	78N	0.8750	0.8187	0.4582	0.7923	1.9076
24	BAL	71N	0.7143	0.8802	0.4740	0.8680	1.9047
25	N E	10N	0.8750	0.7796	0.5415	0.8073	1.8761

There was a good spread of teams from different eras in Table 2.14, with one from the 1950s, three from the '60s, six from the '70s, four from the '80s, five from the '90s, four from the '00s, and three from this decade. All 25 made the postseason, with three teams appearing in pre–Super Bowl Championship games; two won and one lost. Fourteen of the teams went to the Super Bowl, nine won and five lost. Two teams lost in the Conference Championship game and the other six lost in the Divisional playoffs.

The 1996 Packers were a bit of a surprise at the top of the list, but in 1996, the league SD was low at 0.1604, and the Packers, like virtually all the teams on the list, benefited from an above average schedule difficulty or an OSCH above 0.5000.

Perhaps the other big surprise in the top 25 is the 2002 Tampa Bay Bucs. Although

2. Estimated Winning Percentage

they convincingly won Super Bowl XVII, they are kind of forgotten among the great team-seasons of the 21st century due to their win coming in the middle of the Patriots run of three titles in four years. Also, the fact the Bucs were unable to sustain their domination, as they remained a successful team for a few years afterward, but are seen by most, I would think, as a one-year wonder of sorts.

There were a couple repeat teams on the list—the 1969 and 70 Vikings, 1978 and 79 Steelers, and a near-miss, the 1999 and 2001 Rams.

One other interesting thing about the 11 teams that finished about 2.0000 in the Z-Score department, is that other than the top two, the 1996 Packers and 1985 Bears, the other eight teams from the Super Bowl era failed to win the Super Bowl, but several went into the Super Bowl as heavy favorites, such as the 2007 Patriots and 1969 Vikings. The 78 Cowboys were a slight underdog to the Steelers (3.5 or 4.5 points depending on when you bet, but you most likely won either way), and the 83 Redskins were about a three-point favorite over the Raiders. A couple others went into the postseason looking like the team to beat and were upset—the 1979 Chargers and 1987 49ers. The 1995 49ers were the defending Super Bowl Champs and were upset by the upstart Packers, and the 1988 Vikings were beaten by the 49er team whom they upset the previous postseason. The other non–Super Bowl teams on the list were of course the 1955 Browns, and the 1962 Packers, Vince Lombardi's greatest team in the opinion of most.

Table 2.15
List of Lowest Single-Season Z-Scores, 1933–2018

RK	TM	YL	WPCT	EPCT	OSCH	AEWP	Z
1	ATL	87N	0.2000	0.1326	0.5095	0.1370	-2.2879
2	BAL	81N	0.1250	0.1387	0.5121	0.1448	-2.2598
3	N E	90N	0.0625	0.0919	0.5458	0.1091	-2.2071
4	L A	16N	0.2500	0.1966	0.4882	0.1888	-2.1755
5	ARZ	18N	0.1875	0.1694	0.4994	0.1690	-2.1748
6	IND	91N	0.0625	0.0806	0.4464	0.0661	-2.1621
7	CAR	10N	0.1250	0.1384	0.5181	0.1476	-2.1516
8	SLR	09N	0.0625	0.0934	0.4715	0.0839	-2.1078
9	T B	86N	0.1250	0.1523	0.4459	0.1254	-2.1009
10	CLE	00N	0.1875	0.0824	0.5377	0.0945	-2.0977
11	PIT	65N	0.1429	0.1570	0.4514	0.1330	-2.0929
12	CLE	99N	0.1250	0.1482	0.5074	0.1507	-2.0918
13	ARZ	03N	0.2500	0.1507	0.5246	0.1642	-2.0908
14	NYJ	95N	0.1875	0.2263	0.4424	0.1847	-2.0890
15	PHI	98N	0.1875	0.1361	0.4719	0.1215	-2.0764
16	OAK	06N	0.1250	0.1581	0.5046	0.1604	-2.0425
17	IND	93N	0.2500	0.1512	0.4870	0.1444	-2.0322
18	N O	81N	0.2500	0.1784	0.5121	0.1859	-1.9985
19	S F	04N	0.1250	0.2014	0.4521	0.1727	-1.9929
20	ARZ	00N	0.1875	0.1317	0.4658	0.1169	-1.9822

RK	TM	YL	WPCT	EPCT	OSCH	AEWP	Z
21	DET	79N	0.1250	0.2192	0.4782	0.2048	-1.9771
22	SLR	08N	0.1250	0.1479	0.4864	0.1420	-1.9724
23	NE	70N	0.1429	0.0984	0.5165	0.1062	-1.9660
24	PHI	72N	0.1786	0.0953	0.4347	0.0742	-1.9474
25	SLR	11N	0.1250	0.1374	0.5572	0.1671	-1.9409

Once again, the worst teams list from Table 2.15 is dominated by teams from after the merger; the 1965 Steelers are the only pre–1970 team on the list.

The 1987 Falcons are an odd choice to top the list, and it has to be taken into consideration that the 1987 statistics are fluky due to the replacement players who played for three weeks due to the strike, and the Falcons did have one of the weakest replacement teams. I expected the 1976 Bucs to finish at the top, but the fact the league SD for the 1976 season was the highest the NFL has seen since 1954, the Bucs had to settle for 39th on the list with a Z-score of -1.8485. On the other hand, the Bucs AEWP of 0.0438 is the eighth worst of all time, and the lowest AEWP of any team since the end of World War II.

One odd fact about the 1987 Falcons is that one of their three wins during the 1987 season came at the expense of the team that would win the Super Bowl that year. They defeated the Washington Redskins 21–20 in Atlanta on 9/20/1987, a non-strike game, in fact.

Another odd fact is that neither the 2008 Lions or the 2017 Browns, both of which finished the regular season 0–16, finished in the bottom 25.

There aren't as many expansion teams on the list as one would expect; only the 1999 Browns (who also repeated in 2000) made the list. Among other repeat teams, the 2008 and 2009 Rams, who also appeared in 2011, along with near-misses the 1991 and 93 Colts and the 2000 and 03 Cardinals.

3

Momentum

Momentum is a factor that exists in pro football and all sports, and how much of a role it plays in predicting future success is debatable. It clearly exists within drives and within games, and it shifts back and forth from one team to another. Momentum in sports terms is a positive or negative carryover from one play to the next, one possession to the next, one game to the next, and maybe from one season to the next.

This chapter is about my search to find a way to quantify momentum (from one game to the next) within a particular season, and to see what effect, if any, it plays in predicting how a team performs the following season. Two types of momentum exist, positive momentum and negative momentum.

In order to explain the importance of momentum in sports, I must give a quick introduction to college level math and science.

Motion and Winning

At this point, I'm going to draw a short parallel between Calculus, Physics, and football, and I need to explain it as briefly as possible and attempt to put it into layman's terms. Here goes nothing:

As Algebra is, among other things, the study of the properties of a straight line, Calculus is, among other things, the study of the properties of a curved line. In any first semester Calculus course, you are going to learn the process of differentiation, which is a relatively simple (once you learn it) mathematical process by which you determine the slope of a curve, as the slope of the curve is constantly changing.

In Algebra, everything is based on the slope of a straight line, which is always constant, as shown in Figure 3.1. The slope of a straight line never changes:

In Calculus, the slope of a curve at a particular point is equal to the slope of a line which is tangent (meaning it is a straight line that only touches the curve at that point) to the curve at that particular point, as Figure 3.2 demonstrates.

As there are an infinite number of points on any curve, the slope of the curve is always changing. You can pick any point on the curve, measure the slope of the line tangent to it at that point, and you have the slope of the curve at that particular point. The curve in Figure 3.2 shows three different points, and the slope of the curve is different in all three places.

Differentiation is a process in Calculus that algebraically does this: it extracts from the original curve equation a new, totally different mathematical equation which will determine the slope of the curve at any point on the curve. This new equation is known as

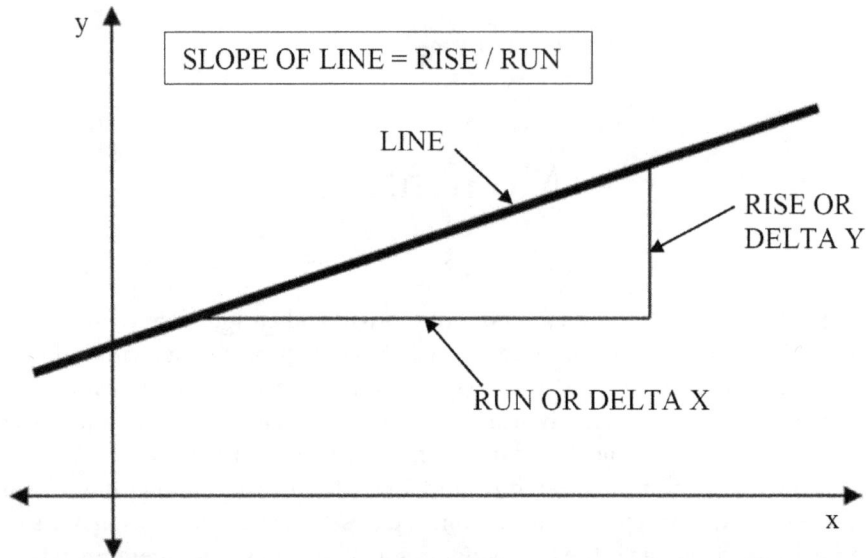

Figure 3.1. Graphical depiction of the slope of a straight line in Algebra.

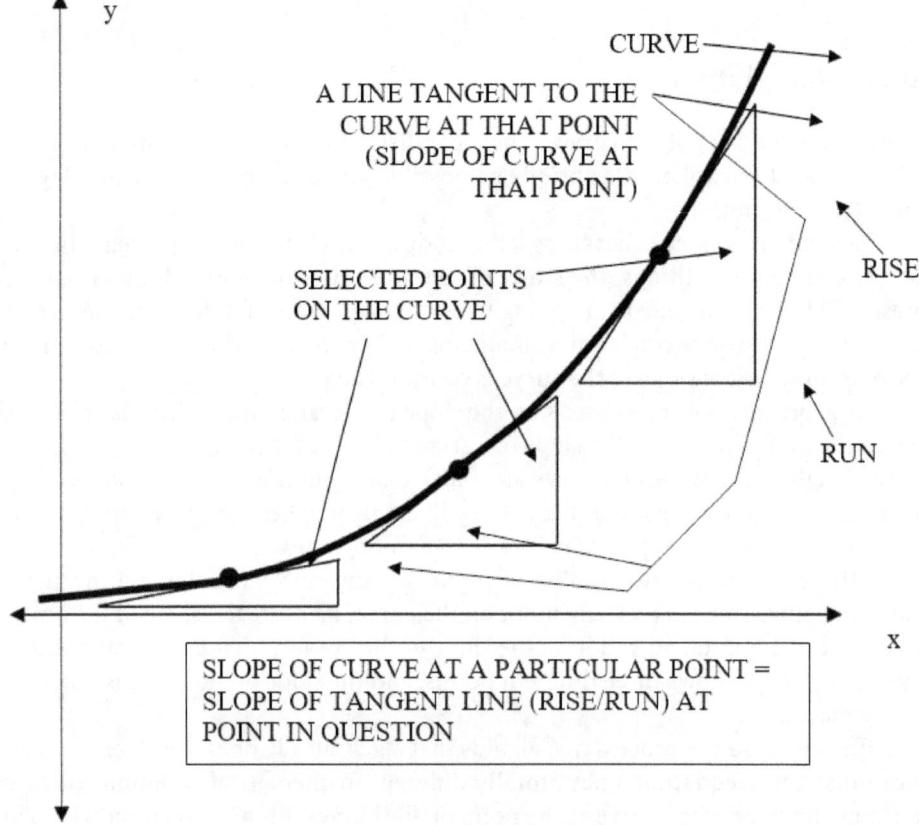

Figure 3.2. Graphical depiction of the slope of a curved line in Calculus.

the first derivative. This first derivative equation is very important to know when you get to Physics class, because when you are given an equation that defines the path or motion of a body, this first derivative equation will give you the speed or velocity of a body at any point on the curve when you plug the x-values into the equation. Velocity (also known as speed) is the rate of change, which is what the slope of the curve at that point measures. Velocity is the first derivative.

However, if you take the first derivative equation for the velocity that you got from the first differentiation process, and then you run the same differentiation process on it a second time, this will produce another totally different equation that is known as the second derivative equation. This second derivative, which is rate of rate of change, mathematically explains the acceleration of the body along a curve when you plug your x-values into the equation. Acceleration is the second derivative.

In a nutshell, that's basic Calculus, and how it relates to Physics. First derivative is velocity, rate of change or speed, which is determined from the original equation for a body's motion. Second derivative is acceleration, rate of rate of change, which is determined from the first derivative equation.

End of lesson, back to football.

Momentum and Winning

If you think of a team's football season as a series of victories and defeats, peaks and valleys, and graph it, you might get something that looks like Figure 3.3:

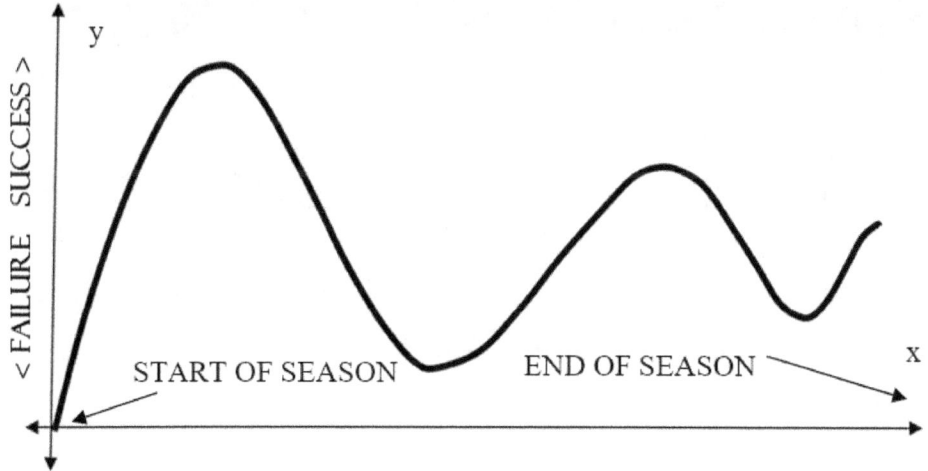

Figure 3.3. Graphical depiction of a fictional team's aggregate success during a season.

Let's take a team at random, the 1981 Detroit Lions. Table 3.1 is the Lions summary of week number (WK), opponent (OPP), RES or result of that game (win, loss, tie), aggregate record (REC) and aggregate WPCT (winning percentage) after each week of the 1981 season:

Table 3.1
1981 Detroit Lions Schedule and Aggregate Winning Percentage by Week

WK	OPP	RES	REC	WPCT	WK	OPP	RES	REC	WPCT
1	S F	W	1–0	1.0000	9	L A	L	4–5	0.4444
2	S D	L	1–1	0.5000	10	WAS	L	4–6	0.4000
3	MIN	L	1–2	0.3333	11	DAL	W	5–6	0.4545
4	OAK	W	2–2	0.5000	12	CHI	W	6–6	0.5000
5	T B	L	2–3	0.4000	13	K C	W	7–6	0.5385
6	DEN	L	2–4	0.3333	14	G B	L	7–7	0.5000
7	CHI	W	3–4	0.4286	15	MIN	W	8–7	0.5333
8	G B	W	4–4	0.5000	16	T B	L	8–8	0.5000

If you graph the Lions aggregate WPCT (y) by week (x), you would wind up with Figure 3.4:

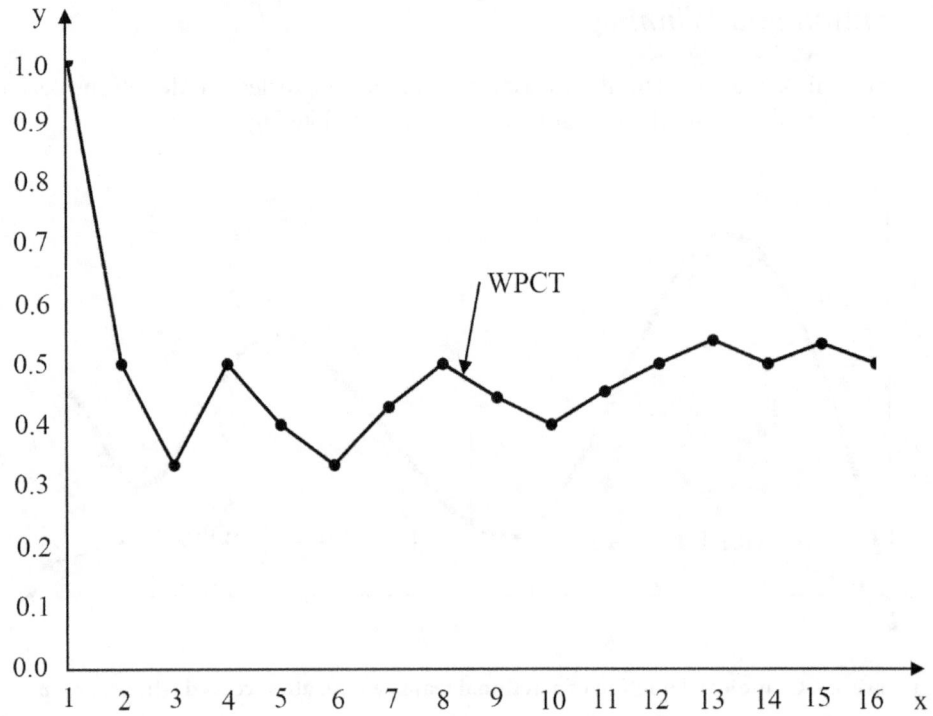

Figure 3.4. Graph of week number (WK) versus aggregate winning percentage (WPCT) for the 1981 Detroit Lions from data in Table 3.1

It is probably about what you would expect, a series of up and down lines. In pro football terms, or sports terms in general (as I think this probably applies to all team sports), a team's winning percentage or WPCT is similar to velocity, as WPCT is measuring the rate of winning, in the same way that velocity measures the rate of motion or rate of change.

Momentum is defined in physics as mass multiplied by acceleration, but in football terms (and in sports in general), when we talk about momentum, what we are really talking about is acceleration and deceleration. Momentum would therefore be akin to acceleration, the rate of rate of winning, as acceleration is the rate of rate of change. Positive momentum is acceleration, and negative momentum is deceleration.

When a car is accelerating, the speed (or velocity) is increasing, and when a car is decelerating, the speed is decreasing. Positive momentum means a team's rate of winning is increasing as the season progresses, while negative momentum means a team's rate of winning is decreasing as the season progresses. What I have developed is a weighted winning percentage, weighted by week, that when graphed, resembles acceleration and or deceleration and in my opinion satisfies our definition of Momentum. I call it Momentum Winning Percentage (MWP).

Winning Percentage (WPCT) is the first derivative of winning, while Momentum Winning Percentage is what I believe must be the second derivative of winning, at least for pro football. Momentum (MOM) is the difference between the two, or MWP minus WPCT.

Momentum Winning Percentage and Momentum

I've been playing around with the concept of momentum for many years, trying to figure out a mathematical formula that properly measures it. I've reached the conclusion that it comes down to properly weighing each week of the regular season, and then multiplying wins in weeks by said weights. After a number of tries, this is what I finally decided on, with MWT being our weight for each particular week, which I call Momentum Weight:

Table 3.2
Number of Momentum Weights (MWT) for Each Game Week (WK)

WK	MWT	WK	MWT	WK	MWT	WK	MWT
1	1.0	5	1.8	9	2.6	13	3.4
2	1.2	6	2.0	10	2.8	14	3.6
3	1.4	7	2.2	11	3.0	15	3.8
4	1.6	8	2.4	12	3.2	16	4.0

How does it work? Each week of the regular season is weighted by the number of MWT, and if the team wins in that week, you multiply the weekly MWT factor by one, and if the team ties (1972 to present), you multiply the above weekly MWT by 0.5. Losses are counted as zero, and we ignore the bye week; the week before and after a bye week are considered consecutive weeks. Pre-1972 ties are also skipped over like a bye week. As you can see in Table 3.2, the week 6 games are weighted twice as much as the week 1 games, the week 11 games are weighted three times as much as the week 1 games, and the week 16 games four times more than week 1 games.

Momentum Winning Percentage (MWP) is defined as the total MW (Momentum

Wins) a team has accumulated divided by the total MWT they could possibly accumulate had they won all their games, aggregate MWT to that week of the season.

Let's apply weekly MWP and MOM to the 1981 Detroit Lions:

Table 3.3
MWP and MOM by Week of Season for 1981 Lions

WK	RES	NRES	WPCT	MWT	MW	MWS	MWTS	MWP	MOM
1	W	1	1.0000	1.0	1.0	1.0	1.0	1.0000	0.0000
2	L	0	0.5000	1.2	0.0	1.0	2.2	0.4545	-0.0455
3	L	0	0.3333	1.4	0.0	1.0	3.6	0.2778	-0.0556
4	W	1	0.5000	1.6	1.6	2.6	5.2	0.5000	0.0000
5	L	0	0.4000	1.8	0.0	2.6	7.0	0.3714	-0.0286
6	L	0	0.3333	2.0	0.0	2.6	9.0	0.2889	-0.0444
7	W	1	0.4286	2.2	2.2	4.8	11.2	0.4286	0.0000
8	W	1	0.5000	2.4	2.4	7.2	13.6	0.5294	0.0294
9	L	0	0.4444	2.6	0.0	7.2	16.2	0.4444	0.0000
10	L	0	0.4000	2.8	0.0	7.2	19.0	0.3789	-0.0211
11	W	1	0.4545	3.0	3.0	10.2	22.0	0.4636	0.0091
12	W	1	0.5000	3.2	3.2	13.4	25.2	0.5317	0.0317
13	W	1	0.5385	3.4	3.4	16.8	28.6	0.5874	0.0490
14	L	0	0.5000	3.6	0.0	16.8	32.2	0.5217	0.0217
15	W	1	0.5333	3.8	3.8	20.6	36.0	0.5722	0.0389
16	L	0	0.5000	4.0	0.0	20.6	40.0	0.5150	0.0150

The left-most column in Table 3.3 is WK or week number, next is RES or the game result for that week (W, L, T for win, loss or tie), NRES or Numerical Result (1 for a win, 0 for a loss and 0.5 for a tie), aggregate WPCT up to that week, MWT is Momentum Weight or value for that particular week, then, the number of Momentum Wins (MW) the Lions got that particular week (MWT multiplied by NRES). MWS is the total MW the Lions have accumulated during the season to that point, and MWTS is the total MWT available for the season to that point. The rightmost columns are MWP or Momentum Winning Percentage (MWS divided by MWTS for the week in question) and finally, MOM, or Momentum, which is MWP minus WPCT for the row.

In short, the value of each game is weighted such that they are worth more each successive week as the season progresses. Weighted wins and weighted losses are used to find a weighted winning percentage, which is MWP.

If you were to graph WPCT (y) and MWP (y) by week (x) for the 1981 Lions season, you will see how MWP differs from WPCT (see top of next page). If the MWP is above the WPCT on Figure 3.5, you are looking at positive momentum, but if the MWP is below the WPCT, you are looking at negative momentum. One way to visualize momentum is to look at the area between the two lines. The actual winning percentage (WPCT) is the thicker line and the momentum winning percentage (MWP) is the thin line.

The 1981 Lions won their first game, then lost their next two. After three games, their MWP (the thin line) was below the WPCT (the thicker line); this indicates negative

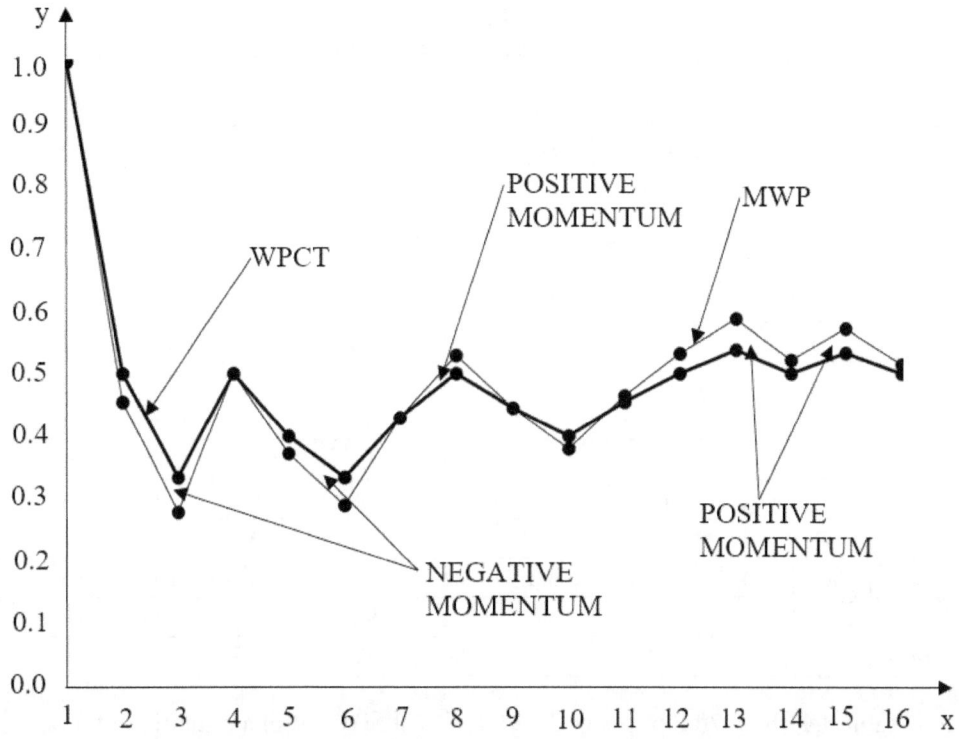

Figure 3.5. Graph of week number (WK) versus aggregate winning percentage (WPCT) and MWP for the 1981 Detroit Lions, from data in Table 3.3.

momentum as the MWP dropped below the WPCT. After losses in weeks six and seven, the Lions found themselves in negative momentum once again. Two wins in a row were followed by two losses in a row, and then they won three in a row in weeks 11 through 13, which built up a lot of positive momentum, so much that even though they lost two of their final three games, their momentum was on the positive side at the end of the season.

In the table, you can see the 1981 Lions final MOM score is 0.5150 minus 0.5000 or 0.0150.

I will give a couple more historical examples to demonstrate how momentum works:

1970 Bengals

The 1970 Cincinnati Bengals, who won their opening game, then went on a six-game losing streak, followed by a seven-game winning streak, to wind up the season 8–6 (0.5714 WPCT) which was enough to win the inaugural AFC Central Division. Their division title for an expansion team in their third season remained a record until the Carolina Panthers won the NFC West in 1996 in only their second season of existence.

Here is the weekly results and momentum table for the 1970 Bengals:

Table 3.4
1970 Cincinnati Bengals MWP and MOM by Week of Season

WK	RES	NRES	WPCT	MWT	MW	MWS	MWTS	MWP	MOM
1	W	1	1.0000	1.0	1.0	1.0	1.0	1.0000	0.0000
2	L	0	0.5000	1.2	0.0	1.0	2.2	0.4545	-0.0455
3	L	0	0.3333	1.4	0.0	1.0	3.6	0.2778	-0.0556
4	L	0	0.2500	1.6	0.0	1.0	5.2	0.1923	-0.0577
5	L	0	0.2000	1.8	0.0	1.0	7.0	0.1429	-0.0571
6	L	0	0.1667	2.0	0.0	1.0	9.0	0.1111	-0.0556
7	L	0	0.1429	2.2	0.0	1.0	11.2	0.0893	-0.0536
8	W	1	0.2500	2.4	2.4	3.4	13.6	0.2500	0.0000
9	W	1	0.3333	2.6	2.6	6.0	16.2	0.3704	0.0370
10	W	1	0.4000	2.8	2.8	8.8	19.0	0.4632	0.0632
11	W	1	0.4545	3.0	3.0	11.8	22.0	0.5364	0.0818
12	W	1	0.5000	3.2	3.2	15.0	25.2	0.5952	0.0952
13	W	1	0.5385	3.4	3.4	18.4	28.6	0.6434	0.1049
14	W	1	0.5714	3.6	3.6	22.0	32.2	0.6832	0.1118

From Table 3.4, the 1970 Bengals got a total of 22.0 MW out of a potential total of 32.2 MW (adding together the MW available for every week from one to fourteen), for an MWP of 0.6832, and incidentally, one of the ten highest MOM totals of all time.

Figure 3.6 displays the weekly WPCT and MWP graph for the 1970 Bengals:

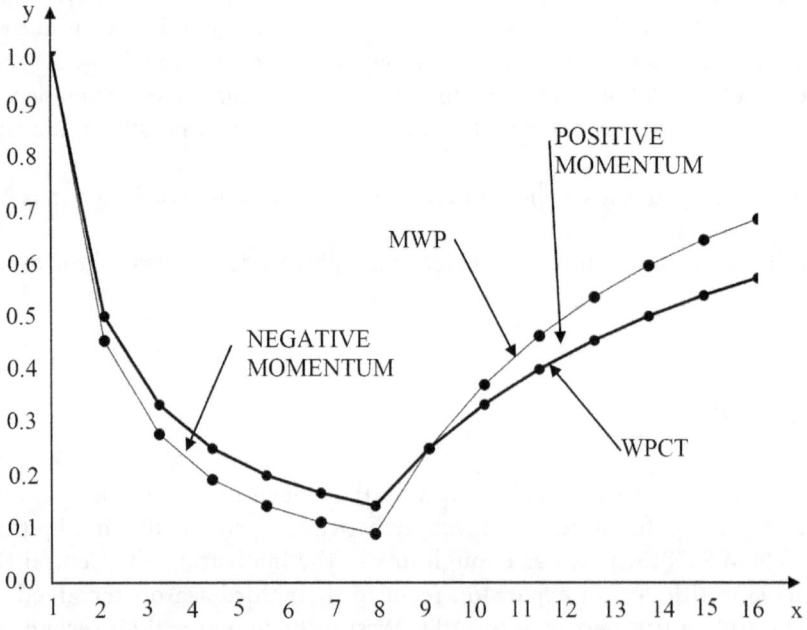

Figure 3.6. Graph of week number (WK) versus aggregate winning percentage (WPCT) and MWP for the 1970 Cincinnati Bengals, from data in Table 3.4

The WPCT rises constantly over the second half of the season because the Bengals kept winning every week, raising the WPCT slightly each week they won. However, the MWP was rising even faster in the second half of the season; this is acceleration versus speed. When you are speeding up in your car, your acceleration will exceed your velocity.

1970 Chargers

The 1970 San Diego Chargers finished 5-6-3, winning in weeks 5, 7, 8, 9 and 14 and tying in weeks 2, 6 and 13.

It is important to keep in mind that before 1972, a tie was not included in winning percentage as the NFL calculated it. In the standings, it was as though the game did not happen, and WPCT was calculated as (Wins) / (Wins + Losses). If it is pre-1972, for the MOM methodology, the tie is treated as though the game didn't happen, which means the Chargers played 11 games, not 14. This is how the revised results will look:

Table 3.5
1970 San Diego Chargers MWP and MOM by Week of Season

WK	RES	NRES	WPCT	MWT	MW	MWS	MWTS	MWP	MOM
1	L	0	0.0000	1.0	0.0	0.0	1.0	0.0000	0.0000
TIE GAME, DISREGARDED									
2	L	0	0.0000	1.2	0.0	0.0	2.2	0.0000	0.0000
3	L	0	0.0000	1.4	0.0	0.0	3.6	0.0000	0.0000
4	W	1	0.2500	1.6	1.6	1.6	5.2	0.3077	0.0577
TIE GAME, DISREGARDED									
5	W	1	0.4000	1.8	1.8	3.4	7.0	0.4857	0.0857
6	W	1	0.5000	2.0	2.0	5.4	9.0	0.6000	0.1000
7	W	1	0.5714	2.2	2.2	7.6	11.2	0.6786	0.1071
8	L	0	0.5000	2.4	0.0	7.6	13.6	0.5588	0.0588
9	L	0	0.4444	2.6	0.0	7.6	16.2	0.4691	0.0247
10	L	0	0.4000	2.8	0.0	7.6	19.0	0.4000	0.0000
TIE GAME, DISREGARDED									
11	W	1	0.4545	3.0	3.0	10.6	22.0	0.4818	0.0273

From Table 3.5, the Chargers have accumulated 10.6 MW, out of a potential 22.0 MW, giving them an MWP of 0.4818 and their MOM is 0.0273. Their graph is shown in Figure 3.7.

One final example, which will cover ties in the post-1971 era:

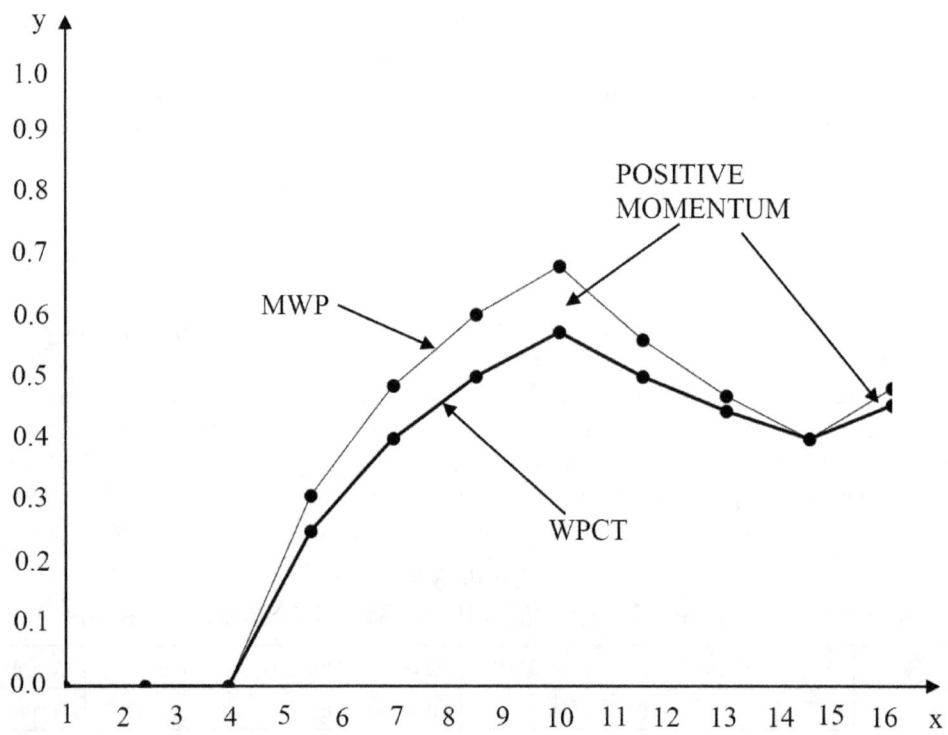

Figure 3.7. Graph of week number (WK) versus aggregate winning percentage (WPCT) and MWP for the 1970 San Diego Chargers, from data in Table 3.5.

1973 Broncos

Denver won games 1, 5, 7, 9 through 11 and 13, and tied games 6 and 8 and had a record of 7-5-2 (WPCT 0.5714). Ties in the post-1971 era are treated as a half-win, so the MW is multiplied by 0.5 for that particular week:

Table 3.6
1973 Denver Broncos MWP and MOM by Week of Season

WK	RES	NRES	WPCT	MWT	MW	MWS	MWTS	MWP	MOM
1	W	1	1.0000	1.0	1.0	1.0	1.0	1.0000	0.0000
2	L	0	0.5000	1.2	0.0	1.0	2.2	0.4545	-0.0455
3	L	0	0.3333	1.4	0.0	1.0	3.6	0.2778	-0.0556
4	L	0	0.2500	1.6	0.0	1.0	5.2	0.1923	-0.0577
5	W	1	0.4000	1.8	1.8	2.8	7.0	0.4000	0.0000
6	T	0.5	0.4167	2.0	1.0	3.8	9.0	0.4222	0.0056
7	W	1	0.5000	2.2	2.2	6.0	11.2	0.5357	0.0357
8	T	0.5	0.5000	2.4	1.2	7.2	13.6	0.5294	0.0294
9	W	1	0.5556	2.6	2.6	9.8	16.2	0.6049	0.0494
10	W	1	0.6000	2.8	2.8	12.6	19.0	0.6632	0.0632
11	W	1	0.6364	3.0	3.0	15.6	22.0	0.7091	0.0727

WK	RES	NRES	WPCT	MWT	MW	MWS	MWTS	MWP	MOM
12	L	0	0.5833	3.2	0.0	15.6	25.2	0.6190	0.0357
13	W	1	0.6154	3.4	3.4	19.0	28.6	0.6643	0.0490
14	L	0	0.5714	3.6	0.0	19.0	32.2	0.5901	0.0186

Denver had a total of 19.0 MW out of a possible 32.2 for an MWP of 0.5901. The MOM was 0.5901 minus 0.5714 or 0.0186. I won't do a graph for Denver; Table 3.6 was added just to demonstrate how the ties are handled.

Sudden Improvements/Declines

This subject is marginally related to momentum, a team who suddenly improves or declines from one season to the next. A good number of these may be related to momentum, but in many cases, there are certainly other factors at work.

In order to study this issue, we will be looking at the differential between the winning percentage of season two and season one, using the following formula:

$$NSDIF = NSWP - WPCT$$

NSDIF = Winning percentage differential between season two and season one
NSWP = Next Season's Winning Percentage
WPCT = Winning Percentage for the season in question, the target season

For the 2009–10 Minnesota Vikings, who finished 10–6 (0.6250) in 2009 and 6–10 (0.3750) in 2010, their NSDIF would be:

$$NSDIF = 0.3750 - 0.6250 = -0.2500$$

A negative score in NSDIF is a team who declines in season two relative to season one, and a positive score in NSDIF is a team who improves in season two compared to season one.

Best and Worst

Table 3.7
25 Highest Single-Season WP, 1933–2018

RK	TM	YL	WPCT	MWP	MOM
T1	CHI	34N	1.0000	1.0000	0.0000
T1	CHI	42N	1.0000	1.0000	0.0000
T1	CLE	48F	1.0000	1.0000	0.0000
T1	MIA	72N	1.0000	1.0000	0.0000
T1	N E	07N	1.0000	1.0000	0.0000
6	PIT	04N	0.9375	0.9700	0.0325
7	CLE	51N	0.9167	0.9603	0.0437

RK	TM	YL	WPCT	MWP	MOM
8	CHC	48N	0.9167	0.9524	0.0357
T9	OAK	67A	0.9286	0.9503	0.0217
T9	OAK	76N	0.9286	0.9503	0.0217
T11	G B	36N	0.9091	0.9455	0.0364
T11	WAS	42N	0.9091	0.9455	0.0364
13	S F	84N	0.9375	0.9450	0.0075
14	MIN	98N	0.9375	0.9400	0.0025
15	BAL	68N	0.9286	0.9379	0.0093
T16	L A	67N	0.9167	0.9365	0.0198
T16	PHI	49N	0.9167	0.9365	0.0198
18	G B	41N	0.9091	0.9364	0.0273
19	N E	03N	0.8750	0.9350	0.0600
20	CLE	47F	0.9231	0.9301	0.0070
21	OAK	69A	0.9231	0.9231	0.0000
22	CHI	63N	0.9167	0.9206	0.0040
T23	NYG	86N	0.8750	0.9200	0.0450
T23	WAS	83N	0.8750	0.9200	0.0450
T25	S D	06N	0.8750	0.9150	0.0400
T25	CHI	85N	0.9375	0.9150	-0.0225

Many football fans don't realize that the 1972 Dolphins were not the first team to finish the regular season undefeated. Like the 2007 Patriots, the 1934 and 1942 Bears were undefeated during the regular season but lost the championship game, and the 1948 Browns did win the AAFC title game after finishing the regular season 14–0. However, the AAFC statistics and records were not recognized by the NFL when the Browns, 49ers and original Baltimore Colts (AAFC) (not to be confused with the current Baltimore/Indianapolis Colts franchise) joined the NFL when the AAFC dissolved after the 1949 season. However, I'm not the NFL, and I recognize AAFC statistics in this book. This book isn't titled *The Statistical History of the NFL*, is it?

Only eleven of the 26 teams in Table 3.7 won their league championship, and ten of them lost in the final postseason game of the season, be it a league championship or Super Bowl.

Table 3.8
25 Lowest Single-Season MWP, 1933–2018

RK	TM	YL	WPCT	MWP	MOM
T1	BKN	44N	0.0000	0.0000	0.0000
T1	CHC	43N	0.0000	0.0000	0.0000
T1	CLE	17N	0.0000	0.0000	0.0000
T1	CPT	44N	0.0000	0.0000	0.0000
T1	DAL	60N	0.0000	0.0000	0.0000

RK	TM	YL	WPCT	MWP	MOM
T1	DET	42N	0.0000	0.0000	0.0000
T1	DET	08N	0.0000	0.0000	0.0000
T1	T B	76N	0.0000	0.0000	0.0000
9	CAR	01N	0.0625	0.0250	-0.0375
10	N E	90N	0.0625	0.0300	-0.0325
11	PIT	69N	0.0714	0.0311	-0.0404
12	PHI	36N	0.0833	0.0397	-0.0437
T13	CHA	48F	0.0714	0.0435	-0.0280
T13	HOU	72N	0.0714	0.0435	-0.0280
15	CLR	37N	0.0909	0.0545	-0.0364
16	HOT	13N	0.1250	0.0550	-0.0700
17	BUF	68A	0.0769	0.0559	-0.0210
18	SLR	09N	0.0625	0.0600	-0.0025
19	NYG	66N	0.0769	0.0629	-0.0140
20	WAS	60N	0.1000	0.0632	-0.0368
21	CHC	39N	0.0909	0.0636	-0.0273
T22	DAL	89N	0.0625	0.0650	0.0025
T22	NYJ	96N	0.0625	0.0650	0.0025
24	BAL	82N	0.0556	0.0679	0.0123
25	ATL	67N	0.0769	0.0699	-0.0070

The battle for the worst team-season of all time, in my opinion, is between the 1976 expansion Bucs and the 1944 Card-Pitt team, a team so dreadful they were dubbed the Carpets. During World War II, the NFL was reeling from losing most of their stars to the military, and a number of teams were in danger of going under, which could have pulled the entire NFL under. To keep the league afloat, it was necessary to merge teams in 1943 (the Steelers and Eagles, known as the Steagles) and 1944 (the Steelers and Cardinals, dubbed as Card-Pitt). Given the best players from both franchises, the Cardinals and Steelers amalgamation failed to mesh, and did not win in ten tries, and the only time they came within two touchdowns in a game was on opening day when they lost to the Cleveland Rams 30–28.

The Cards failed to win a game in 1943 in addition to 1944 when they merged with the Steelers, but by 1947 the Chi Cards turned things around and beat the Eagles for their only NFL title.

Table 3.9
Single-Season MOM, 1933–2018

RK	TM	YL	WPCT	MWP	MOM
1	S F	17N	0.3750	0.5200	0.1450
2	DET	89N	0.4375	0.5700	0.1325

RK	TM	YL	WPCT	MWP	MOM
3	OAK	64A	0.4167	0.5397	0.1230
4	CIN	84N	0.5000	0.6200	0.1200
5	S D	92N	0.6875	0.8050	0.1175
6	DET	95N	0.6250	0.7400	0.1150
7	NYJ	74N	0.5000	0.6149	0.1149
8	K C	15N	0.6875	0.8000	0.1125
T9	BUF	62A	0.5385	0.6503	0.1119
T9	PHI	71N	0.4615	0.5734	0.1119
11	CIN	70N	0.5714	0.6832	0.1118
12	N E	65A	0.3333	0.4444	0.1111
T13	PIT	58N	0.6364	0.7455	0.1091
T13	NYG	55N	0.5455	0.6545	0.1091
15	DET	15N	0.4375	0.5450	0.1075
16	DET	60N	0.5833	0.6905	0.1071
17	PIT	76N	0.7143	0.8199	0.1056
T18	STL	78N	0.3750	0.4800	0.1050
T18	WAS	98N	0.3750	0.4800	0.1050
T18	NYJ	99N	0.5000	0.6050	0.1050
T18	WAS	81N	0.5000	0.6050	0.1050
T18	HOU	93N	0.7500	0.8550	0.1050
23	CIN	08N	0.2813	0.3850	0.1038
25	CHI	59N	0.6667	0.7698	0.1032
T25	CLE	09N	0.3125	0.4150	0.1025
T25	N E	93N	0.3125	0.4150	0.1025
T25	ATL	97N	0.4375	0.5400	0.1025

None of these teams won a Super Bowl or league championship.

The most famous of these teams was the 1976 Steelers, who lost four of their first five games, which included losses to both eventual Super Bowl teams, the Vikings and Raiders, along with New England and Cleveland. The Steelers proceeded to run the table for the rest of the regular season, winning nine games in a row by a truly astounding combined score of 234–28, which included five shutouts, three of them in a row.

The 1995 Lions started out 3–6 and then went on a seven-game winning streak to snag a wild card. In this particular case, much of this was related to the schedule, as the early part of the season saw the Lions took on the Steelers and 49ers, and two games with Green Bay and another with Atlanta. The final seven games included weaker competition, two games each against the Bears and Bucs, in addition to Jacksonville and Houston, and a 44–38 Thanksgiving shootout against the Vikings.

The 1992 Chargers dropped their first four games, and then went 11–1 the rest of the regular season on the way to their first division title since 1981.

The first year of the Joe Gibbs regime in Washington was 1981, and they dropped their first five games but rebounded to finish 8–8. There was a strong carryover to 1982 as they became Super Bowl Champs.

Table 3.10
25 Lowest Single-Season MOM, 1933–2018

RK	TM	YL	WPCT	MWP	MOM
1	WAS	78N	0.5000	0.3650	-0.1350
2	WAS	62N	0.4167	0.2937	-0.1230
3	SEA	06N	0.5625	0.4400	-0.1225
4	N E	74N	0.5000	0.3789	-0.1211
5	DEN	09N	0.5000	0.3800	-0.1200
6	S D	67A	0.6154	0.4965	-0.1189
7	DET	39N	0.5455	0.4273	-0.1182
8	S D	01N	0.3125	0.1950	-0.1175
T9	CHI	89N	0.3750	0.2600	-0.1150
T9	OAK	95N	0.5000	0.3850	-0.1150
T9	S D	02N	0.5000	0.3850	-0.1150
12	DEN	62A	0.5000	0.3851	-0.1149
13	STL	66N	0.6154	0.5035	-0.1119
T14	S D	87N	0.5333	0.4222	-0.1111
T14	WAS	43N	0.6667	0.5556	-0.1111
T16	PHI	94N	0.4375	0.3300	-0.1075
T16	K C	13N	0.6875	0.5800	-0.1075
18	NYJ	86N	0.6250	0.5200	-0.1050
T19	DET	34N	0.7692	0.6643	-0.1049
T19	DEN	60A	0.3077	0.2028	-0.1049
21	PIT	55N	0.3333	0.2302	-0.1032
T22	DAL	86N	0.4375	0.3350	-0.1025
T22	SLR	95N	0.4375	0.3350	-0.1025
T22	MIA	93N	0.5625	0.4600	-0.1025
T22	NYG	68N	0.5000	0.3975	-0.1025
T22	L A	69N	0.7857	0.6832	-0.1025

Many of these are among the great late-season collapses in pro football history.

The 1978 Redskins top this list, as they started the season 6–0, which included upsets of the Patriots and Cowboys, but they cooled off and finished 8–8, and out of the playoffs.

In 1974, the Patriots looked like the surprise team the first half of the season, starting 6–1 which included wins over the Dolphins, Rams and Vikings, with their only defeat a two-point loss to the Bills. They were playing over their heads, but they were still in control of the AFC East as December began. At that point, New England lost their final three games to the Raiders, Steelers and Dolphins to finish 7–7 and out of the playoffs.

The 2009 Broncos began the season 6–0, but a pair of four-game losing streaks left them with an 8–8 record.

The Jets of 1986 were probably the most notorious team on this list, as they began the season 10–1 before Paul Maguire correctly predicted on the NBC NFL pre-game show that they would lose their final five games.

Going back to 1934, the Bears and Lions both went into late November undefeated at 10–0. But the Lions lost to Green Bay 3–0, and the Bears and Lions met the final two weeks of the season, with Chicago winning each game by a field goal. Detroit finished 10–3, while the Bears went undefeated only to lose to the Giants in the Sneakers game.

Table 3.11
Single-Season NSDIF, 1933–2018

RK	TM	YRS	WPCT	MWP	MOM	NSWP	NSDIF
1	OAK	6263	0.0714	0.1113	0.0399	0.7143	0.6429
T2	IND	9899	0.1875	0.2053	0.0178	0.8125	0.6250
T2	MIA	0708	0.0625	0.0902	0.0277	0.6875	0.6250
T4	BAL	7475	0.1429	0.1491	0.0062	0.7143	0.5714
T4	N E	7576	0.2143	0.1925	-0.0217	0.7857	0.5714
T6	DAL	1516	0.2500	0.2056	-0.0444	0.8125	0.5625
T6	IND	1112	0.1250	0.1844	0.0594	0.6875	0.5625
T6	K C	1213	0.1250	0.1152	-0.0098	0.6875	0.5625
T6	PIT	0304	0.3750	0.3807	0.0057	0.9375	0.5625
T9	SLR	9899	0.2500	0.2353	-0.0147	0.8125	0.5625
T11	CHI	0001	0.3125	0.3763	0.0638	0.8125	0.5000
T11	CLR	4445	0.4000	0.3027	-0.0973	0.9000	0.5000
T11	DET	5556	0.2500	0.2913	0.0413	0.7500	0.5000
T11	IND	9192	0.0625	0.0701	0.0076	0.5625	0.5000
T11	NYJ	9697	0.0625	0.0649	0.0024	0.5625	0.5000
T11	PIT	4142	0.1000	0.1371	0.0371	0.6364	0.5000
T11	S D	0304	0.2500	0.3006	0.0506	0.7500	0.5000
T11	S D	6263	0.2857	0.2351	-0.0506	0.7857	0.5000
19	CIN	8788	0.2667	0.2333	-0.0333	0.7500	0.4833
20	CHI	4546	0.3000	0.3995	0.0995	0.8000	0.4727
21	CAR	1415	0.4688	0.4957	0.0269	0.9375	0.4688
T22	MIA	6970	0.2308	0.2680	0.0372	0.7143	0.4643
T22	HOU	6667	0.2143	0.1259	-0.0884	0.6923	0.4643
T24	BOS	4950	0.0909	0.0904	-0.0005	0.5833	0.4583
T24	G B	5859	0.0909	0.0751	-0.0158	0.5833	0.4583

I used the same four-digit code for years (YRS) as I used in the HFA section, with the last two digits of the first and second season; thus 8485 stands for 1984–1985, and 4849 stands for 1948–49.

NSP is Next Season's WPCT, and NSDIF is short for Next Season Differential, or

3. Momentum

NSP minus WPCT, which is the WPCT for the first season, so this is a list of the biggest single-season turnarounds. Most of these teams fall into one class or another:

Four of these teams would win a league championship or Super Bowl in the second year, the 1945 and 1999 Rams, along with the 1946 Bears and 1963 Chargers. The 1988 Bengals and 2015 Panthers lost the Super Bowl.

A number of these teams were successful teams rebounding from off seasons, such as the 2004 Steelers, 2013 Chiefs and 1956 Lions along with the aforementioned 1946 Bears.

Others were surprise teams who were starting very successful runs such as the 1970 Dolphins, 1959 Packers, 1998 Colts, and 1976 Patriots, who except for the Victor Kiam era, have been pretty successful over the past 40 years.

On the other hand, other teams were starting runs that would be successful for a few years, such as the 1997 Jets (until Bill Parcells left), and the 1975 Colts, who had a good three-year run (1975–77) until Bert Jones got injured.

The others were one-year wonders, or were they? Don't worry, we'll discuss one-year wonders in the next chapter.

Table 3.12
25 Lowest Single-Season NSDIF, 1933–2018

RK	TM	YRS	WPCT	MWP	MOM	NSWP	NSDIF
T1	HOT	1213	0.7500	0.6705	-0.0795	0.1250	-0.6250
T1	HOU	9394	0.7500	0.8552	0.1052	0.1250	-0.6250
3	DET	4546	0.7000	0.6828	-0.0172	0.0909	-0.6091
T4	NYG	6364	0.7857	0.8098	0.0240	0.1667	-0.5714
T4	S D	6162	0.8571	0.7853	-0.0718	0.2857	-0.5714
T6	ATL	1213	0.8125	0.7504	-0.0621	0.2500	-0.5625
T6	ATL	9899	0.8750	0.9101	0.0351	0.3125	-0.5625
T6	CAR	1516	0.9375	0.9053	-0.0322	0.3750	-0.5625
T6	CHI	0102	0.8125	0.8352	0.0227	0.2500	-0.5625
10	DET	5455	0.8182	0.7995	-0.0187	0.2500	-0.5417
T11	BAR	0607	0.8125	0.8272	0.0147	0.3125	-0.5000
T11	CHI	6364	0.9167	0.9187	0.0021	0.3571	-0.5000
T11	DAL	1415	0.7500	0.7705	0.0205	0.2500	-0.5000
T11	DEN	9899	0.8750	0.8152	-0.0598	0.3750	-0.5000
T11	IND	1011	0.6250	0.6493	0.0243	0.1250	-0.5000
T11	L A	5859	0.6667	0.7290	0.0624	0.1667	-0.5000
T11	N E	8081	0.6250	0.5900	-0.0350	0.1250	-0.5000
T11	NYG	1617	0.6875	0.7054	0.0179	0.1875	-0.5000
T11	NYG	4445	0.8889	0.8956	0.0067	0.3333	-0.5000
T11	S F	4950	0.7500	0.7335	-0.0165	0.2500	-0.5000
T11	S F	9899	0.7500	0.7353	-0.0147	0.2500	-0.5000
22	S F	8182	0.8125	0.8650	0.0525	0.3333	-0.4792
23	NYG	8687	0.8750	0.9200	0.0450	0.4000	-0.4750

RK	TM	YRS	WPCT	MWP	MOM	NSWP	NSDIF
24	PHI	6162	0.7143	0.6839	-0.0304	0.2308	-0.4643
T25	9192 DET, 0001 DET, 0708 DET, 0708 GB, 9900 JAX, 7980 N O, 0203 OAK, 0405 PHI, 9900 S D, 0102 SLR, 0506 T B, 0304 TEN AND 1213 WAS ALL TIED AT -0.4375						

Table 3.12 displays the shocking collapses from one season to the next.

The 1994 Houston Oilers were coming off a 12–4 record and thought they could trade Warren Moon to Minnesota and adequately replace him with Billy Joe Tolliver, Bucky Richardson and/or Cody Carlson. Did their plan work out? Not so much. The Oilers fell to 2–14, which ended the Jack Pardee era and ushered in the Jeff Fisher era.

In 2012, the Texans were coming off an AFC South division title, where they lost to New England in the divisional playoffs. The 2013 seemed to start out fine, as Houston started out 2–0, but late in the second quarter of Week Three against the Ravens, Matt Schaub gave up a pick six to Daryl Smith. On the ensuing drive, Schaub was sacked, which led to a punt that was returned for a TD, and from that point, the Texans season mysteriously fell apart. They lost to Baltimore and then proceeded to lose the other 13 games in the 2013 season. I've always found this to be one of the most mysterious single-season collapses in pro football history. If anybody knows what happened to the 2013 Texans, I'm all ears.

The 1961–63 Giants lost three straight NFL championship games, two to the Packers and one to the Bears. Sam Huff, the heart and soul of the Giants defense, was traded to Washington, and YA Tittle made the mistake later repeated by Johnny Unitas and Brett Favre of playing one season too many. The Giants offense and defense were led by a bunch of older guys and they all gave out at the same time. The team fell apart, and they tumbled to 2–10–2 in 1964. It wouldn't be until they drafted Lawrence Taylor in 1981 that their fortunes would turn around and the Gothams would again return to the postseason.

A few of these collapses are championship teams or Super Bowl winners who tailed off the next season, such as the 1963 Bears, 1981 49ers, 1986 Giants and 1998 Broncos.

Four of these teams appear on the highest and lowest DIF lists in consecutive seasons—Carolina 2014–15, Chicago 2000–01, Detroit 1954–55 and Dallas 2014–15. In the first two cases, the team had a historic improvement followed by a historic collapse the following season, and the last two teams had a massive collapse followed by a massive improvement the next season. In the case of the Lions, they won an NFL championship in 1957.

Using Momentum as a Predictive Tool

Do positive and negative momentums carry over to the next season?

I don't believe that it plays much of a role, as teams by and large turn over their personnel (players and coaches) quite a bit from one season to the next, and that momentum gets lost after an eight-month hiatus between the end of one season and the beginning of the next. But there are cases where you can look back in retrospect and declare that a team has turned a corner, as the Jets did several weeks into the 1981 season, and the 1981 Redskins who started 0–5, but rallied to finish 8–8 on the season and would win the next two NFC titles, including a Super Bowl. There are cases that go the other way, such as the 1986 Jets who went from 10–1 to 10–6 and dropped to 6–9 in 1987.

To begin, we would need to rank teams by MOM, and track how each of them did the next year, and then compare the WPCT in the season in question with the WPCT the following season, which is NSDIF. However, some of the 1,995 teams will need to be removed from the study, and those are teams who were playing their final season, who went defunct and did not play the following season such as the AAFC teams who didn't come over to the NFL, and including the 2018 teams, since they have no "next season." This leaves us with a total of 1,947 teams for the differential study.

Figure 3.8 is a scatter plot of all the 1,947 data points of Momentum or MOM of season one (x) against WPCT Differential between season one and season two (y), and I generated a linear least squares curve (degree one) from it. This is what the graph looks like:

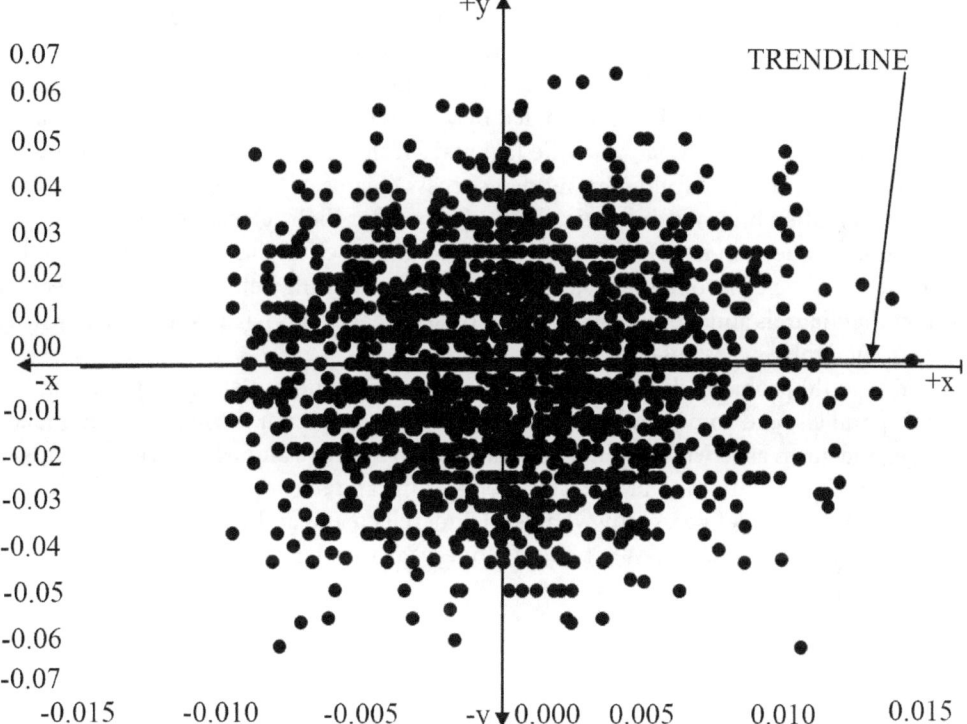

Figure 3.8. A scatter plot of MOM versus NSDIF for 1,947 two-year team-season eras.

OK, I admit, Figure 3.8 does looks like somebody sneezed ink all over the place, but the payoff is the least squares line running through it. The line is very nearly horizontal and has a very slight positive slope; the equation for the line is: Y = 0.0746X + 0.0013. We will drop the Y-intercept of +0.0013 and go with Y = 0.0746X, or IMP = 0.0746*MOM.

What does this improvement really look like? Let's pick a team at random, say, the 2006 Houston Texans, who started the season with three straight losses and were 3–8 in late November before winning three of their final five games to finish 6–10. Their strong finish gave them a MOM of 0.0539. How much improvement should we have expected in 2007?

$$IMP = 0.0746 * 0.0539 = 0.0040$$

Sixteen times 0.0040 equals 0.0643, or one-sixteenth of a game improvement, which is positive but is not the kind of improvement we were looking for in a formula. By the way, the Texans did improve in 2007; they improved to 8–8.

I think we can conclude that there is a very slight mathematical relationship between Momentum and WPCT differential, but I don't think a blanket formula like this will work for all teams. I think we need to look at the extreme cases, cases where a team has a positive or negative momentum in excess of the factor of 1.5 divided by the number of games played. For a 16-game schedule, this would be 1.5 divided by 16 or plus or minus 0.0938; meaning in the modern era, if a team has a positive momentum over 0.0938 or a negative momentum less than -0.0938, they should definitely be looked at for other factors to see if there should be carryover to the following season.

The most obvious question to ask is, "Is this team a true surprise team? Are they a Cinderella team?" such as the 1981 49ers or 1999 Rams? Did this team come out of nowhere? If the answer is yes, expect them to decline the following season.

The next question is, "Is this team led by younger players that are successful for the first time, such as the 2017 Jacksonville Jaguars?" If the answer is yes, these teams often face crises of confidence following sudden success. Teams of this kind are vulnerable to relapses, but often improve dramatically the season after their relapse season.

Another question is, "How did the team conduct itself in the off-season?" Did they keep their noses clean, so to speak, and stay focused on getting better, or did they seem to rest on their laurels and let their success get to their heads? It is hard to stay hungry when you are suddenly successful.

You could probably draw up a list of a questions, some statistical, some using historical parallels, and some questions like those above, and from those you could make a pretty good guess as to which teams will continue to improve and which will not.

We really need to look at the Cinderella teams and surprise teams. But before we do that, we need to define exactly what is a Cinderella team, and what is a surprise team. Are they one and the same? What about a one-year wonder team? Are the three terms synonymous?

We shall see.

4

Cinderella and Surprise Teams, and One-Year Wonders

Since I brought up the topic of Cinderella teams and surprise teams, I thought I would try to develop a method to spot them throughout the history of pro football. Instead of some statistical study as I usually do, I instead came up with four simple questions:

    1. Did the team in question have a below 0.5000 record in each of the previous two seasons?
    2. In the third-most previous season, did they fail to play in a post-season game? For pre–Super Bowl seasons, I am counting division tiebreaker games as postseason games.
    3. Did the team in question reach the postseason but come up short of a league (pre–Super Bowl) or conference championship game in the season in question, the target season?
    4. Did the team in question reach at least a league (pre–Super Bowl) or conference championship game in the target season?
    5. If you answer "yes" to questions (1), (2) and (3), you are a surprise team. If you answer "yes" to questions (1), (2) and (4), you are a Cinderella team.

After thinking it over, I realized that there were actually two slightly different animals here, the surprise teams and the Cinderella teams. There are a lot of surprise teams, but relatively few Cinderella teams. The only difference between them is how deep they advance into the postseason. For example, the 1975 Colts were a surprise team. They did not appear in a postseason game in 1972, and finished below 0.5000 in 1973 and 1974, and they surprised everybody by winning the AFC East, and then lost to the Steelers in the first round of the playoffs. If they had upset the Steelers and advanced to the AFC Championship game against the Raiders, they would have captured the attention of the football world and the national public and become a Cinderella team. But they lost to Pittsburgh, which made them a surprise team.

Applying the above four questions to all team-seasons from 1933 to 2018, I found a total of 57 team-seasons who made the postseason after not having a 0.5000 or better season in any of the previous two seasons, and did not win a playoff season in that third most-previous season, which makes them either surprise teams or Cinderella teams. To this list, I have added three team-seasons and a fourth that comes with an asterisk:

    1. The 1970 Bengals, who won the AFC Central in their third season of existence; but they were below 0.5000 in each of their first two seasons.

2. The 1996 Panthers and Jaguars, who made the playoffs in their second season after finishing below 0.5000 in their inaugural season.

3. (With an asterisk) The 1945 Cleveland Rams, who suspended operations for the 1943 season (due to World War II), and (I skipped over the 1943 season) they were below 0.5000 in 1941, 1942 and 1944.

I think we can bend the rules for the three expansion teams who got to the postseason in less than three seasons in the league while being below 0.5000 in their previous seasons, along with the 1945 Rams, who had disbanded in 1943 and two years later won an NFL title and were under 0.5000 the three previous seasons they were playing. Nobody predicted the Panthers to win the NFC Western Division before the 1996 season; their getting to the 1996 conference championship game (as did the Jaguars), shocked the football world.

Of these 61 team-seasons, 19 of them lost the wild-card game: the 1978 Eagles, 1982 Cards, 1987 Saints, 1991 Jets, 1994 Patriots, 1995 Falcons, 1997 Giants, 2002 Browns, 2003 Cowboys, 2008 Dolphins and Falcons, 2009 Bengals, 2010 Chiefs, 2011 Lions, 2012 Redskins, the 2016 Raiders and Giants, the 2017 Rams and the 2018 Bears. These 19 teams are all surprise teams.

Of the remaining 42 team-seasons, 27 of them would lose in the divisional playoff game. These teams would include the 1968 Vikings, 1970 Bengals and Dolphins, 1972 Packers, 1974 Cardinals, 1975 Colts, 1980 Bills, 1981 Giants, 1987 Colts and Oilers, 1988 Eagles, 1991 Falcons and Cowboys, 1992 Chargers, 1994 Browns (where Bill Belichick got his first postseason victory leading the Browns to a victory against New England in an AFC Wild Card game, which is a great trivia question by the way), 1997 Bucs, 1998 Cards, 2000 Saints and Eagles, 2001 Bears, 2002 Falcons, 2005 Bears and Redskins, 2012 Seahawks, 2013 Panthers and 2017 Saints. The 1957 49ers lost the Western Conference tiebreaker game to the Lions, and (we'll get into this in more detail in Chapter 10) I consider this to be roughly equivalent to a divisional playoff game. I'm adding the 1957 Lions to this group. These 27 team-seasons are also surprise teams.

The 15 team-seasons that remain are the Cinderella teams, according to my definition. Of them, nine of them lost the league or conference championship game, they include the 1967 Oilers, 1972 Steelers, 1979 Bucs, 1983 Seahawks, 1988 Bills, 1991 Lions, the 1996 Jaguars and Panthers, and the 2017 Jaguars.

Six more Cinderella teams are left, and two of them lost the Super Bowl—the 1981 Bengals and 2003 Panthers. The four teams left standing are the Cinderella teams who won a league Championship or the Super Bowl: they are the 1945 Cleveland Rams, 1981 San Francisco 49ers, 1999 St. Louis Rams and the 2017 Philadelphia Eagles.

Table 4.1 details the 15 Cinderella teams:

Table 4.1
Cinderella Teams from Pro Football History, 1933–2018

TM	YR	WPCT	RES	STRAW	3S%	3+A	COMMENTS
CLR	1945	0.9000	CGW	Bob Waterfield	0.3810	0.5429	No postseason appearances in 1946–48

4. Cinderella and Surprise Teams, and One-Year Wonders 65

TM	YR	WPCT	RES	STRAW	3S%	3+A	COMMENTS
HOU	1967	0.6786	CCL	Miller Farr, Ken Houston	0.3125	0.5366	Lost 1969 AFL Divisional
PIT	1972	0.7857	CCL	Franco Harris	0.3733	0.6250	Lost 1973 AFC Divisional, Won Super Bowl IX
T B	1979	0.6250	CCL	Defense jelled, weak division	0.3333	0.7292	Lost 1981 NFC Divisional, Lost 1982 NFC Wild Card
S F	1981	0.8125	SBW	Ronnie Lott, Jack Reynolds	0.2500	0.4167	Lost 1983 NFC Champ, Won Super Bowl XIX
CIN	1981	0.7500	SBL	Ken Anderson comeback, collapse of Browns	0.2111	0.4756	Lost 1982 AFC Wild Card
SEA	1983	0.5625	CCL	Curt Warner, Dave Krieg	0.3750	0.5000	Lost 1984 AFC Divisional
BUF	1988	0.7500	CCL	Thurman Thomas	0.2500	0.7500	Lost 1989 AFC Divisional, Lost Super Bowl XXV, XXVI
DET	1991	0.7500	CCL	Mike Utley injury	0.4375	0.3958	Lost 1993 NFC Wild Card, Lost 1994 NFC Wild Card
JAX	1996	0.5625	CCL	Mark Brunell	0.2500	0.6458	Lost 1997 AFC Wild Card, Lost 1998 AFC Divisional, Lost 1999 AFC Champ.
CAR	1996	0.7500	CCL	Kerry Collins, Wesley Walls	0.2500	0.6829	No postseason appearances in 1997–99.
SLR	1999	0.8125	SBW	Kurt Warner, Marshall Faulk	0.3452	0.7738	Lost 2000 NFC Wild Card, Lost Super Bowl XXXVI,
CAR	2003	0.6875	CCL	Jake Delhomme, Stephen Davis	0.4375	0.5417	Lost 2005 NFC Champ
JAX	2017	0.6250	CCL	Leonard Fournette, Calais Campbell	0.2292	N/A	No playoffs in 2018
PHI	2017	0.8125	SBW	Blount/Ajayi, Nick Foles	0.4688	N/A	Lost 2018 NFC Divisional

The first five columns of Table 4.1 apply to the team-season in question, with column four the result (RES) of the season, how far they went into the postseason. It's a pretty simple three-letter code where the first two letters are either (CG) an abbreviation for Championship Game from the pre–Super Bowl era, (DT) for Division Tiebreaker game from the pre–Super Bowl era, (SB) for Super Bowl game, (CC) for Conference Championship game, (DP) for Divisional Playoff game, and (WC) for Wild Card or First Round game. The third letter is either (W) for win or (L) for loss, and the third letter will always be a loss except for SBW or CGW. If a RES for a team is a CCW, it means they lost the

Conference Championship game during the target season, and if a team's RES is SBW, it means they won the Super Bowl that year.

STRAW is a nod to the famous Reggie Jackson comment about how when he got to the New York Yankees he announced he was the straw that stirred the drink and everything came together with his showing up there. The Straw column is for the catalyst, the player or players (often new or young players who developed quickly, or a missing piece that arrived on the scene) who were perhaps most responsible, or an incident or other reason for the turnaround.

3S% is a weighted winning percentage to predict their winning percentage for the team-season in question. It is just an estimate of what we perhaps should have expected this team to do in the target season based on how they did over the past three years. The formula is:

$$3S\% = [(WPCT\ T\text{-}3) + 2*(WPCT\ T\text{-}2) + 3*(WPCT\ T\text{-}1) + 3*.5000] / 9$$

In the formula, WPCT T-3 is the team's winning percentage three seasons before the target season, WPCT T-2 is the team's WPCT two seasons before, and WPCT T-1 is the team's WPCT last year. The 0.5000 is in there because good teams usually decline and bad teams usually improve. Previous performance carries two-thirds of the weight and 0.5000 carries a third of the weight.

For the 1981 San Francisco 49ers, as an example, the 1978 season would be T-3 (their WPCT was 0.1250), 1979 would be T-2 (their WPCT was 0.1250 once again) and 1980 would be T-1 (their WPCT was 0.3750), and plugging those numbers into the formula:

$$3S\% = [.1250 + 2 * 0.1250 + 3 * 0.3750 + 3 * 0.5000] / 9 =$$
$$[.1250 + .2500 + 1.1250 + 1.5000] / 9 = 3 / 9 = 0.3333$$

A rough estimate is that the 1981 49ers should have been expected to finish about 5–11 or 6–10, which seems a fair guess.

The next column 3+A is the aggregate winning percentage over the following three seasons (1982–1984) after the Cinderella season, the target season, and the final column is comments, which is a summary of postseason appearances over those three seasons following the target season, 1982 through 1984.

A few comments about the list:

Two of the greatest dynasties ever (1970s Steelers, 1980s 49ers) started as Cinderella teams. Another notable dynasty, the Kelly-Thomas-Levy Bills, came together as a Cinderella team. It is interesting that only two of them were one-and-done, the 1945 Rams and 1996 Panthers, in that neither made the postseason in the subsequent three seasons.

The 2017 Eagles are by definition the weakest possible example of a Cinderella team. In 2015 and 2016, they went 7–9 each season, and in 2014, they went 10–6 and were the top seeded NFC team that did not make the postseason.

None of the Cinderella teams appeared in a league or conference championship game the following season. They all took at least a slight step back. Eight of the 15 teams did not make the playoffs the following season.

Out of a total of 1,995 team-seasons that we are covering in this book, to find only 15 true Cinderella teams indicates the odds of a Cinderella team are 15 in 1,995 or about 133 to one. In the modern NFL of 32 teams, we should expect to see one of these teams about once every four seasons. The odds of a surprise team were 1,995 to 46, or about 43 to one. A surprise team should occur about three times every four seasons these days.

The 1977 Denver Broncos

When I showed this Cinderella team/surprise team thought process to some of my colleagues in the football historian community, a number of them immediately stated that the 1977 Denver Broncos were a Cinderella team, because it's been drilled into everybody's heads for the past 40 years that they were a Cinderella team. The 1977 Broncos were not a Cinderella team. Here's why:

The Broncos were 9–5 in 1976, finishing seventh in the NFL in points scored and sixth in the NFL in points allowed, and this is with the venerable Steve Ramsey at quarterback. The Broncos finished 6–8 in 1975 and 7–6–1 in 1974. They already had a lot of good players, the only real positional weakness they had was at quarterback, and they made a brilliant off-season move in bringing in Craig Morton. There was a lot of discontent among the Broncos players with coach John Ralston, leading to a players' revolt of sorts with Ralston being replaced with Red Miller after the 1976 season.

The team immediately responded to Miller, and with Morton at quarterback, it all came together. However, at the end of the day, the 1977 Broncos improved by three games over the previous season, beating a weak Steelers team at home in the Divisional round, and beating the Raiders at home in the AFC Championship game, albeit aided by a controversial touchdown play. I'm not taking anything away from the Broncos, they were the big story of the 1977 NFL season and how could you not root for them, but on closer inspection, they were not a Cinderella team. The Broncos were already a very good team that addressed the two biggest problems with the team (replacing their quarterback and head coach) and both moves turned out perfectly, with the team taking a step forward to become a great team, if only for a brief time.

Table 4.2 demonstrates another way to look at the whole "Cinderella Broncos" argument, by examining the Broncos three-game improvement in 1977 against other Super Bowl losers.

Table 4.2
18 Highest IMP Values of Super Bowl Losing Teams

RK	TM	YL	WPCT	PRVW	IMP
1	CIN	88N	0.7500	0.2667	0.4833
2	CAR	15N	0.9375	0.4688	0.4688
3	ATL	98N	0.8750	0.4375	0.4375
4	CIN	81N	0.7500	0.3750	0.3750
5	MIN	73N	0.8571	0.5000	0.3571
6	OAK	67A	0.9286	0.6154	0.3132
T7	N E	96N	0.6875	0.3750	0.3125
T7	NYG	00N	0.7500	0.4375	0.3125
T7	TEN	99N	0.8125	0.5000	0.3125
10	MIN	69N	0.8571	0.5714	0.2857
12	K C	66A	0.8462	0.5833	0.2628
T13	BUF	90N	0.8125	0.5625	0.2500

RK	TM	YL	WPCT	PRVW	IMP
T13	CAR	03N	0.6875	0.4375	0.2500
T13	N E	07N	1.0000	0.7500	0.2500
T13	SEA	05N	0.8125	0.5625	0.2500
T13	SLR	01N	0.8750	0.6250	0.2500
18	DEN	77N	0.8571	0.6429	0.2143

WPCT is for the year they lost the Super Bowl, PRVW is the WPCT for the previous year, and IMP is improvement between the Super Bowl losing season and the previous season. (IMP is basically the opposite of NSDIF from Chapter 3, except it's the WPCT for the season in question minus the WPCT for the previous season. NSDIF was the other way around.) Two of the teams in Table 8.2 were Cinderella teams, the 1981 Bengals and 2003 Panthers, and there were a number of these teams I was more surprised to see in the Super Bowl than the 1977 Broncos.

The first that comes to mind were the 1999 Titans, who pulled major road upsets over the Colts and Jaguars and of course won the Music City Miracle game. The Titans came within one yard of taking the Greatest Show on Turf to OT in the Super Bowl, but you never heard them referred to as a Cinderella team during the 1999 playoffs.

Surprise Teams

I mentioned the surprise teams along the way as I got to the Cinderella teams, but Table 4.3 details each of the surprise teams:

Table 4.3
List of Surprise Teams in Pro Football History, 1933–2018

TM	YRS	WPCT	RES	STRAW	3S%	3+A	COMMENTS
S F	1957	0.6667	DTL	Won five games by four points or less	0.4444	0.5556	No postseason appearances
MIN	1968	0.5714	DPL	Good rookie crop; collapse of Packers	0.3512	0.8333	Lost Super Bowl IV, Lost 1970 and 1971 NFC Divisionals
CIN	1970	0.5714	DPL	Rookies Mike Reid and Lamar Parrish, seven-game winning streak	N/A	0.5238	Lost 1973 AFC Divisional
MIA	1970	0.7143	DPL	Collapse of Jets, Don Shula	0.3036	0.8690	Lost Super Bowl VI, Won Super Bowls VII and VIII
G B	1972	0.7143	DPL	Vikings off-season, rookies Willie Buchanon and Chester Marcol	0.4167	0.3810	No postseason appearances

4. Cinderella and Surprise Teams, and One-Year Wonders

TM	YRS	WPCT	RES	STRAW	3S%	3+A	COMMENTS
STL	1974	0.7143	DPL	Terry Metcalf	0.3214	0.6667	Lost 1975 NFC Divisional
BAL	1975	0.7143	DPL	HC Ted Marchibroda	0.2262	0.5909	Lost 1976 and 1977 AFC Divisionals
PHI	1978	0.5625	DPL	Wilbert Montgomery	0.3214	0.6875	Lost 1979 NFC Divisional, Lost Super Bowl XV, Lost 1981 NFC Wild Card
BUF	1980	0.6875	DPL	Rookie Joe Cribbs	0.3617	0.5366	Lost 1981 AFC Divisional
NYG	1981	0.5625	DPL	Rookie Lawrence Taylor	0.3125	0.4024	Lost 1984 NFC Divisional
STL	1982	0.5556	WCL	Won four games by three points	0.3750	0.4688	No postseason appearances
HOU	1987	0.6000	DPL	Warren Moon, Mike Rozier	0.2917	0.5833	Lost 1988 AFC Divisional, Lost 1989 and 1990 AFC Wild Cards
IND	1987	0.6000	DPL	Best defense in NFL, Eric Dickerson trade	0.2396	0.5000	No postseason appearances
N O	1987	0.8000	WCL	Bobby Hebert	0.3958	0.5625	Lost 1990 NFC Wild Card
PHI	1988	0.6250	DPL	Rookies Keith Jackson and Eric Allen	0.4194	0.6458	Lost 1989 and 1990 NFC Wild Cards
ATL	1991	0.6250	DPL	MC Hammer	0.2708	0.3958	No postseason appearances
DAL	1991	0.6875	DPL	Norv Turner helps the Triplets mature	0.2708	0.7708	Won Super Bowl XXVII and XXVIII, Lost 1994 NFC Championship
NYJ	1991	0.5000	WCL	Offensive and defensive improvement	0.3594	0.3750	No postseason appearances
S D	1992	0.6875	DPL	Bobby Ross, 11-1 after 0-4 start	0.3125	0.5833	Lost Super Bowl XIX, Lost 1995 AFC Wild Card
CLE	1994	0.6875	DPL	Bill Belichick and DC Nick Saban	0.4271	0.2083	No postseason appearance in 1995, not in NFL in 1996–1997
N E	1994	0.6250	WCL	Drew Bledsoe improvement, won final four to end 1993 season, won final seven to end 1994 season	0.2604	0.5625	Lost Super Bowl XXXI, Lost 1997 AFC Divisional

TM	YRS	WPCT	RES	STRAW	3S%	3+A	COMMENTS
ATL	1995	0.5625	WCL	Free agents Eric Metcalf, Chris Doleman and Morten Andersen	0.4063	0.5000	Lost Super Bowl XXXIII
NYG	1997	0.6563	WCL	DC John Fox	0.3854	0.5625	Lost Super Bowl XXXV
T B	1997	0.6250	DPL	Rookie Warrick Dunn, new uniforms	0.3958	0.6042	Lost 1999 NFC Championship, lost 2000 NFC Wild Card
ARZ	1998	0.5625	DPL	Won seven games by three points or less	0.3125	0.3333	No postseason appearances
N O	2000	0.6250	DPL	OC Mike McCarthy, offensive and defensive improvement	0.2813	0.5000	No postseason appearances
PHI	2000	0.6875	DPL	Donovan McNabb; Andy Reid and coaching staff	0.2865	0.7292	Lost 2001, 2002 and 2003 NFC Championship games
CHI	2001	0.8125	DPL	Collapse of Vikings and Lions, Mike Brown, rookie Anthony Thomas	0.3229	0.3333	No postseason appearances
ATL	2002	0.5938	DPL	Healthy Michael Vick, Warrick Dunn, DC Wade Phillips	0.3542	0.5000	Lost 2004 NFC Championship
CLE	2002	0.5625	WCL	Offensive and defensive improvement	0.3021	0.3125	No postseason appearances
DAL	2003	0.6250	WCL	Bill Parcells	0.3125	0.5000	Lost 2006 NFC Wild Card
CHI	2005	0.6875	DPL	DC Ron Rivera, healthy Brian Urlacher	0.3438	0.6042	Lost Super Bowl XLI
WAS	2005	0.6250	DPL	Mark Brunell, Santana Moss, defensive improvement	0.3646	0.4583	Lost 2007 NFC Wild Card
ATL	2008	0.6875	WCL	Michael Turner	0.3542	0.6667	Lost 2010 NFC Divisional, Lost 2011 NFC Wild Card
MIA	2008	0.6875	WCL	Bill Parcells, Chad Pennington	0.2500	0.4167	No postseason appearances
CIN	2009	0.6250	WCL	Healthy Carson Palmer, Cedric Benson career season	0.3698	0.4792	Lost 2011 and 2012 AFC Wild Cards

TM	YRS	WPCT	RES	STRAW	3S%	3+A	COMMENTS
K C	2010	0.6250	WCL	OC Charlie Weis and DC Romeo Crennel	0.2083	0.4167	Lost 2013 AFC Wild Card
DET	2011	0.6250	WCL	Matthew Stafford career season	0.2292	0.4583	Lost 2014 NFC Wild Card
SEA	2012	0.6875	DPL	Rookie Russell Wilson, Legion of Boom	0.4167	0.7292	Won Super Bowl XLVIII, Lost Super Bowl XLIX, Lost 2015 NFC Divisional
WAS	2012	0.6250	WCL	Rookies Alfred Morris and Robert Griffin III	0.3229	0.3333	Lost 2015 NFC Wild Card
CAR	2013	0.7500	DPL	Defensive improvement	0.3646	0.5938	Lost 2014 NFC Divisional, Lost Super Bowl 50
NYG	2016	0.6875	WCL	Dramatic defensive improvement	0.3854	N/A	No postseason appearances
OAK	2016	0.7500	WCL	Won five games by three points or less	0.3229	N/A	No postseason appearances
N O	2017	0.6875	DPL	Rookie Alvin Kamara, overhauled defense	0.4375	N/A	Lost 2018 NFC Championship
L A	2017	0.6875	WCL	Sean McVay, Jared Goff, Todd Gurley et al	0.3333	N/A	Lost Super Bowl LIII
CHI	2018	0.7500	WCL	Mitchell Trubinsky, defensive improvement, new coaching staff	0.2813	N/A	N/A

One-Year Wonders

What then, is a one-year wonder? A one-year wonder team, or OYW for short, I shall define, is when a team has a markedly improved season in the midst of a number of much lesser seasons. We're going to look at it by examining winning percentage patterns over a consecutive number of seasons in chronological order for a specific team.

I created a couple sets of vertical bars, and let's suppose each of those bars or rectangles represents amounts of winning percentage for a single season, with the smaller rectangles or bars representing lower winning percentages and the larger rectangles representing larger winning percentages, and the bars are arranged in chronological order (season one, season two, etc.) for a fictional team.

In the pair of bar sets shown in Figure 4.1, the five-season bar sets that represent winning percentages over five consecutive seasons, and the season number in the lower part of the bar (S1 = season one, S2 = season two, and so on). In which set does the third season or S3 clearly represent an OYW?

Figure 4.1. A pair of vertical bar sets, each representing five-year spans.

It is the one on the right, of course.

Which one of the two seven-season bar sets in Figure 4.2 clearly has an OYW season (the target season) at season four (S4)?

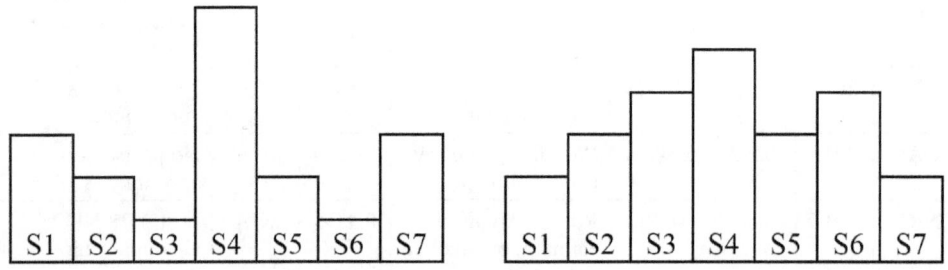

Figure 4.2. A pair of vertical bar sets, each representing seven-year spans.

It is, of course, the bar chart on the left side.

That is what a one-year wonder season is; it is a year that doesn't look like any of the other seasons around it. We have to come up with a way to explain this mathematically so we can find team-seasons like this.

Five, Seven, Nine and Eleven

I think that looking at team-seasons in the middle of chronological strings, as we did with the bar charts above, is the correct approach. In the example we used five and seven-year strings, but I don't really know what the correct length is, or if there is a correct length. For that reason, we're going to look at strings of five, seven, nine and eleven consecutive seasons, examining the middle season in the string (the target season), and comparing that season to the rest of the string.

I came up with a simple algebraic process for doing it, using a weighted winning percentage of the string except for the target season. The WPCT T-2, T-1, etc., are the same as in the 3S% formula from earlier in the chapter, they are for winning percentage in seasons relative to the target season. Here's how it works for five-year strings:

$$W5 = [(WPCT\ T-2) + 2 * (WPCT\ T-1) + 2 * (WPCT\ T+1) + (WPCT\ T+2)] / 6$$

Quite simply, it's the WPCT from two seasons before the target season, plus two times the WPCT from the season before the target season, plus two times the WPCT from the season after the target season, plus the WPCT from two seasons after the target season, with the sum divided by six.

After that, it's a matter of subtracting W5 from WPCT TAR or the winning percentage of the target season, which we abbreviate W - W5, to get the differential between the target and the rest of the string.

Here are the weighted winning percentage formulas for seven, nine and eleven-year strings:

$$W7 = [(WPCT\ T-3) + 2 * (WPCT\ T-2) + 3 * (WPCT\ T-1) + 3 * (WPCT\ T+1) + 2 * (WPCT\ T+2) + (WPCT\ T+3)] / 12$$

$$W9 = [(WPCT\ T-4) + 2 * (WPCT\ T-3) + 3 * (WPCT\ T-2) + 4 * (WPCT\ T-1) + 4 * (WPCT\ T+1) + 3 * (WPCT\ T+2) + 2 * (WPCT\ T+3) + (WPCT\ T+4)] / 20$$

$$W11 = [(WPCT\ T-5) + 2 * (WPCT\ T-4) + 3 * (WPCT\ T-3) + 4 * (WPCT\ T-2) + 5 * (WPCT\ T-1) + 5 * (WPCT\ T+1) + 4 * (WPCT\ T+2) + 3 * (WPCT\ T+3) + 2 * (WPCT\ T+4) + (WPCT\ T+5)] / 30$$

And, naturally, you would subtract each of these from the target to get W-W7, W-W9 and W-W11.

We'll use the history of the Carolina Panthers as an example to demonstrate the process. This table gives the target season (YL), winning percentage (WPCT) with weighted winning percentage (W5, W7, W9 and W11) and WPCT minus Wx columns below for all Panthers seasons:

Table 4.4
Carolina Panthers Franchise Analysis for OYW's

TM	YL	WPCT	W5	W-W5	W7	W-W7	W9	W-W9	W11	W-W11
CAR	95N	0.4375								
CAR	96N	0.7500								
CAR	97N	0.4375	0.4896	-0.0521						
CAR	98N	0.2500	0.5104	-0.2604	0.4740	-0.2240				
CAR	99N	0.5000	0.3125	0.1875	0.3542	0.1458	0.3875	0.1125		
CAR	00N	0.4375	0.3021	0.1354	0.3490	0.0885	0.3875	0.0500	0.4146	0.0229
CAR	01N	0.0625	0.4896	-0.4271	0.4740	-0.4115	0.4781	-0.4156	0.4896	-0.4271
CAR	02N	0.4375	0.3958	0.0417	0.4323	0.0052	0.4375	0.0000	0.4396	-0.0021
CAR	03N	0.6875	0.4167	0.2708	0.4219	0.2656	0.4281	0.2594	0.4354	0.2521
CAR	04N	0.4375	0.6146	-0.1771	0.5417	-0.1042	0.5250	-0.0875	0.5167	-0.0792
CAR	05N	0.6875	0.5000	0.1875	0.5208	0.1667	0.5031	0.1844	0.4813	0.2063
CAR	06N	0.5000	0.5729	-0.0729	0.5781	-0.0781	0.5500	-0.0500	0.5167	-0.0167
CAR	07N	0.4375	0.6146	-0.1771	0.5573	-0.1198	0.5375	-0.1000	0.5229	-0.0854
CAR	08N	0.7500	0.4167	0.3333	0.4271	0.3229	0.4313	0.3188	0.4521	0.2979
CAR	09N	0.5000	0.4271	0.0729	0.4323	0.0677	0.4625	0.0375	0.4740	0.0260
CAR	10N	0.1250	0.4896	-0.3646	0.5156	-0.3906	0.5203	-0.3953	0.5417	-0.4167
CAR	11N	0.3750	0.3958	-0.0208	0.4505	-0.0755	0.4906	-0.1156	0.5031	-0.1281

TM	YL	WPCT	W5	W-W5	W7	W-W7	W9	W-W9	W11	W-W11
CAR	12N	0.4375	0.4740	-0.0365	0.5000	-0.0625	0.5141	-0.0766	0.5229	-0.0854
CAR	13N	0.7500	0.5208	0.2292	0.4870	0.2630	0.4875	0.2625	0.4948	0.2552
CAR	14N	0.4688	0.6979	-0.2292	0.6458	-0.1771	0.5938	-0.1250		
CAR	15N	0.9375	0.5208	0.4167	0.5234	0.4141				
CAR	16N	0.3750	0.6927	-0.3177						
CAR	17N	0.6875								
CAR	18N	0.4375								

The process displayed in Table 4.3 was run on every other franchise in pro football history, although we had to skip a few teams, namely, most of the AAFC teams, because you need at least five consecutive seasons in order to generate a single target season. I actually set the minimum number of seasons for a franchise at eleven, which wiped out all the defunct franchises except for the Brooklyn Dodgers. It was also necessary to remove any strings that contained the 1943 Rams and the 1996–1998 Browns because the teams were not in the league those particular years, along with the 1943–44 Steelers, the 1943 Eagles, and 1944 Cardinals, due to the Steagles and Card-Pitt amalgamations.

Where to Draw the Line

After reviewing the distributions of W-W5, W-W7, et al, I chose to look at team-seasons which finished with a W-Wx of 0.3 or higher as being exceptional and thus indicative of being a one-year wonder. As there were between 1632 and 1830 team-seasons in each of the four Wx groups, there were between 44 and 54 team-seasons with a W-Wx figure of 0.3 or higher, which is in the top three percent.

Between the four Wx groups, there were a total of 191 team-seasons, of which 89 were unique, as most of the team-seasons appeared in several of the W-Wx groups. Twenty-one team-seasons appeared in all four W-Wx groups. When you were done, you were left with a total of 84 unique team-seasons.

However, there was a problem with these 84 team-seasons—some of them didn't belong among the list of one-year wonders, like the 1984 San Francisco 49ers. While the 49ers did go 14-2 and win the Super Bowl, they won the Super Bowl three years earlier, and they did narrowly lose the NFC Championship game the year before, and would go to the postseason in 13 of the next 14 seasons. How could you be an OYW if you lost the NFC Championship game by three points the previous season?

The 1949 NFL Champion Philadelphia Eagles qualified as an OYW; except they also won the NFL Championship in 1948. The 1948 Chicago Cardinals qualified as an OYW also, except they won the NFL title the previous season. The 1999 Rams qualified as an OYW also, except they went to the playoffs in 2000, and in 2001, lost the Super Bowl by three points. The 2004 Steelers are another OYW, but won the Super Bowl the next season. The 2007 Patriots qualified as an OYW in the W-W5 group, but narrowly lost the AFC Championship to the Colts in 2006. The 2011 Packers qualified as an OYW one year after winning the Super Bowl.

It's clear a couple rules need to be put in place to fix these kinds of problems.

4. Cinderella and Surprise Teams, and One-Year Wonders   75

Narrowing Down the List

Logic dictates that we should apply a couple of rules to fine-tune this list of one-year wonders, and I will suggest four:

1. All OYW teams must have an above-0.5000 record in their target (OYW) season. That makes sense, I think, that in order to be a one-year wonder, you actually have to finish better than 0.5000. Two team-seasons finished below 0.5000 (1938 Eagles, 2007 Lions), so they were removed.

2. All OYW teams cannot have a season within their five or seven-year span with a better WPCT than they did during the target season. This did happen with some of them—1966 Eagles, 1967 Oilers, 1981 49ers and 2010 Chiefs, but they qualified in others, so they will stay.

3. For seasons during the Super Bowl era, an OYW team cannot have made the postseason in the year before, or the year after, their target season; it violates the entire principal of a one-year wonder if you think about it. (This includes tiebreaker games from the pre–Super Bowl era.) This rule removed 27 team-seasons from the list, the 1972 Dolphins, 1976 Colts, 1977 Broncos, 1982 Bengals, 1984 49ers, 1985 Bears, 1986 Giants, 1991 Redskins, 1993 Oilers, 1998 Vikings, 1999 Colts, Jaguars and Rams, 2001 Rams and 49ers, 2003 Titans, 2004 Steelers 2005 Seahawks, 2006 Bears, 2007 Patriots, 2008 Titans, 2009 Vikings, 2011 Packers and 49ers, 2012 Falcons and Texans and 2015 Panthers. Bringing it back to the 1977 Broncos once again, how can they be a one-year wonder team if they won the AFC West in 1978 also?

4. For seasons before the Super Bowl existed, any OYW team cannot have made the postseason the year before, or the year after, their target season, nor could they have had a WPCT at or above 0.5500 in the before or after the target season. This is of course because only the division champions made it to the postseason, and as such, there were still a number of strong teams in the league who finished above 0.5000. I consider division tiebreaker games from before the Super Bowl era to be postseason games because they occur outside the realm of the regular schedule. Nine team-seasons were dropped from the list due to this rule, including the 1944 Giants and Lions, 1945 Lions, 1948 Cards, 1949 Eagles, 1950 Giants, 1960 Eagles, 1963 Giants and 1964 Bills.

We are left with 41 team-seasons, meaning just over half the list was cut. Table 4.5 (below) details the team-seasons that remain, with the YL or target, WPCT for the target season, RES (with a NO if they did not make the postseason), and the STRAW column for the catalyst, or missing piece, or main reason for the improvement. Next is a C/S column indicating if they were a Cinderella (C) or surprise (S) team (there are three Cinderella teams and nine surprise teams on the list) a WPCT minus Weighted WPCT for the four groups (W-W5, W-W7, W-W9, and W-W11), and to make them less complex, I made them N/A if the results in the block were less than 0.3000.

Table 4.5
One-Year Wonder Teams from Pro Football History, 1933–2018

TM	TAR	WPCT	RES	C/S	STRAW	W-W5	W-W7	W-W9	W-W11
BKN	1940	0.7273	NO		Defensive improvement	N/A	N/A	0.3359	N/A

TM	TAR	WPCT	RES	C/S	STRAW	W-W5	W-W7	W-W9	W-W11
CHC	1956	0.5833	NO		Defensive improvement, Browns off-season.	0.3125	0.3403	0.3292	0.3167
L A	1958	0.6667	NO		Bill Wade and Del Shofner	0.3264	N/A	N/A	N/A
DET	1962	0.7857	NO		Defensive improvement	N/A	N/A	0.3021	0.3065
DAT	1962	0.7857	CGW		Len Dawson	0.3214	N/A	N/A	N/A
OAK	1963	0.7143	NO		Tom Flores, Art Powell, Head Coach Al Davis,	0.4226	0.3780	N/A	N/A
PHI	1966	0.6429	NO		I couldn't find a straw for this team; they could be a fluke	N/A	N/A	0.3143	N/A
HOU	1967	0.6786	CHL	C	Miller Farr, Ken Houston	0.3095	0.3244	0.3268	N/A
L A	1967	0.8571	NO		Roman Gabriel becomes a star	N/A	N/A	N/A	0.3000
G B	1972	0.7143	DPL	S	Vikings off-season, Willie Buchanon, Chester Marcol	0.3095	0.3036	0.3018	N/A
BUF	1973	0.6429	NO		OJ Simpson and the Electric Company	N/A	N/A	N/A	0.3098
HOU	1975	0.7143	NO		Bum Phillips, Robert Brazile, Don Hardeman	0.3214	0.3348	0.3263	0.3176
N E	1976	0.7857	DPL		DROY Mike Haynes, return to early 1974 level	0.3021	N/A	0.3022	0.3182
ATL	1980	0.7500	DPL		Steve Bartkowski, revamped defense	N/A	N/A	N/A	0.3182
S F	1981	0.8125	SBW	C	Ronnie Lott, Jack Reynolds	0.4514	N/A	N/A	N/A
N O	1987	0.8000	WCL	S	Bobby Hebert	0.3000	0.3104	0.3031	N/A
CIN	1988	0.7500	SBL		Boomer Esiason, Ickey Woods	N/A	0.3083	0.3154	0.3264
G B	1989	0.6250	NO		Don Majkowski	0.3139	N/A	N/A	N/A
ATL	1991	0.6250	DPL	S	MC Hammer	0.3021	N/A	N/A	N/A
DET	1991	0.7500	CGL	C	Mike Utley injury	0.3438	0.3333	0.3273	0.3322
IND	1992	0.5625	NO		Ted Marchibroda	0.3021	N/A	N/A	N/A
ATL	1998	0.8750	SBL		Top to bottom improvement	0.5521	0.5313	0.5078	0.5000
NYJ	1998	0.7500	CGL		Vinny Testaverde, Curtis Martin	N/A	0.3125	0.3156	0.3167

TM	TAR	WPCT	RES	C/S	STRAW	W-W5	W-W7	W-W9	W-W11
CHI	2001	0.8125	DPL	S	Collapse of Vikings and Lions, Anthony Thomas, Mike Brown	0.4896	0.4896	0.4750	0.4500
K C	2003	0.8125	DPL		Dante Hall	0.3333	0.3281	0.3344	0.3500
T B	2005	0.6875	WCL		Cadillac Williams, Joey Galloway comeback	0.3333	N/A	N/A	N/A
BAR	2006	0.8125	DPL		Steve McNair, Ray Lewis comeback	0.3750	0.3333	0.3094	N/A
CLE	2007	0.6250	NO		Derek Anderson, Jamal Lewis	0.3438	0.3385	0.3375	0.3271
G B	2007	0.8125	CGL		New OC and DC, Favre turnaround	0.3646	0.3333	N/A	N/A
CAR	2008	0.7500	DPL		DeAngelo Williams, a healthy Jake Delhomme	0.3333	0.3229	0.3188	N/A
MIA	2008	0.6875	WCL	S	Bill Parcells, Chad Pennington	0.3854	0.3490	0.3375	0.3188
MIN	2009	0.7500	CGL		Brett Favre	0.3021	N/A	N/A	N/A
K C	2010	0.6250	WCL	S	OC Charlie Weis and DC Romeo Crennel	0.3542	N/A	N/A	N/A
T B	2010	0.6250	NO		Josh Freeman improvement, LeGarrette Blount	0.3125	N/A	N/A	N/A
DET	2011	0.6250	WCL	S	Matthew Stafford career season	0.3229	N/A	N/A	N/A
MIN	2012	0.6250	WCL		Adrian L Peterson, defensive improvement	0.3125	N/A	N/A	N/A
WAS	2012	0.6250	WCL		Robert Griffin III, Alfred Morris	0.3542	0.3281	N/A	N/A
NYJ	2015	0.6250	NO		Todd Bowles, Ryan Fitzpatrick, Brandon Marshall	0.3021	N/A	N/A	N/A
DAL	2016	0.8125	WCL		Ezekiel Elliott, Dak Prescott	0.3125	N/A	N/A	N/A
NYG	2016	0.6875	WCL	S	Dramatic defensive improvement	0.3854	N/A	N/A	N/A
OAK	2016	0.7500	DPL	S	Won five games by three points or less	0.4063	N/A	N/A	N/A

Of the 41 one-year wonders in Table 4.5, 14 did not make the playoffs during their target season, nine lost in the wild card/first round, nine lost in the divisional round, four lost conference championship games, two lost Super Bowls (1988 Bengals and 1998 Falcons), one was victorious in the Super Bowl (the 1981 49ers), and there was a team who won and lost AFL Title games.

5

Rusher Ratings: YRAA

To date, seven players have rushed for more than 2,000 yards in a season. The record for most yards rushing in a season is Eric Dickerson with 2,105 yards rushing in 1984, a record which surprisingly has never been broken, but I believe it will be broken in the next ten years. But was it the best of the 2,000-yard seasons? Which of those seven seasons was the most impressive?

The knee-jerk answer is, of course, Dickerson, because he had the most rushing yards, or RY. Here's how they rank by RY:

Eric Dickerson, 1984, 2,105 RY
Adrian L Peterson, 2012, 2,097 RY
Jamal Lewis, 2003, 2,066 RY
Barry Sanders, 1997, 2,053 RY
Terrell Davis, 1998, 2,008 RY
Chris Johnson, 2009, 2,006 RY
OJ Simpson, 1973, 2,003 RY

But Simpson accomplished his in 1973 when there were only 14 games. The others on the list played in a 16-game season. If you adjust the yards for games played, or yards rushing per game (RY/G), Simpson jumps to the top of the list:

OJ Simpson, 2,003/14 = 143.1 RY/G
Eric Dickerson, 2,105/16 = 131.6 RY/G
Adrian L Peterson, 2,097/14 = 131.1 RY/G
Jamal Lewis, 2,066/16 = 129.1 RY/G
Barry Sanders, 2,053/16 = 128.3 RY/G
Terrell Davis, 2,008/16 = 125.5 RY/G
Chris Johnson, 2,006/16 = 125.4 RY/G

How do we properly compare these seven seasons to the context in which they occurred? One way to examine the issue is to look at how many yards an average rusher in the league that particular season would have rushed for given the same number of attempts, and then compare that to the rusher in question. The attempts and yards of the rusher in question would first have to be removed from the league statistics so that a rusher is not being compared against his own performance.

In 1984, the NFL, as a whole, rushed 13,432 times (league attempts or LA) for a total of 53,398 yards (league yards or LY), and subtracting Dickerson's numbers (379 rushing attempts or RA and 2105 rushing yards or RY), from the NFL totals:

5. Rusher Ratings

Adjusted League Attempts (ALA) = LA - RA = 13,811 - 379 = 13,432
Adjusted League Rushing Yards (ALY) = LY - RY = 55,503 - 2105 = 53,398
Adjusted Rushing Yards per Attempt (ALYA) = ALY / ALA = 53,398 / 13,432 = 3.975
ALYA multiplied by Dickerson's RA = 3.975 * 379 = 1,506.689

An average rusher in the NFL in 1984 (anybody besides Eric Dickerson), given 379 rushing attempts, would have been expected to rush for approximately 1,507 yards. It is important to keep in mind that the 1,507 yards that an average rusher would have gained in 1984 if he had simply carried the ball 379 times in a season, is a lot of yards. In some seasons, as we will find out, such a player could actually lead the league in rushing, simply for being an average or even below-average running back who ran the ball a lot more than everybody else.

In the NFL in 1984, 1,507 yards would have been enough to finish fourth in the entire NFL in rushing, behind Dickerson (of course), along with Walter Payton of Chicago and James Wilder of Tampa Bay, all NFC teams. It would have been more than enough to lead the AFC in rushing in 1984 as Earnest Jackson of San Diego led the AFC in rushing with only 1,179 yards.

Dickerson exceeded this "average" mark by 598.311 yards, which is 2,105 (his actual total) minus 1,506.689. The 598.311 is Yards Rushing Above Average or YRAA. This is the value added, the portion of the iceberg that sits above the water, the part of Dickerson's performance that is above the league average.

Table 5.1 displays the YRAA values for the seven members of the 2K club, evaluating them against the leagues they played in, ranked from highest YRAA to lowest:

Table 5.1
List of 2,000-Yard Rushers Ranked by Highest YRAA

RUSHER	YL	TM	G	RA	RY	AVY	YRAA
Barry Sanders	97N	DET	16	335	2053	1362.7	690.3
OJ Simpson	73N	BUF	14	332	2003	1331.6	671.4
Adrian L Peterson	12N	MIN	16	348	2097	1482.8	614.2
Eric Dickerson	84N	SLR	16	379	2105	1506.7	598.3
Chris Johnson	09N	TEN	16	358	2006	1505.3	500.7
Jamal Lewis	03N	BAR	16	387	2066	1597.1	468.9
Terrell Davis	98N	DEN	16	392	2008	1549.6	458.4

RA, RY = Rusher Attempts, Rusher Yards

AVY = Average Rusher Yards, which is how many yards an average rusher that season would have accumulated given the same number of attempts as the rusher in question during the season in question.

YRAA = Yards Rushing Above Average, which equals RY - AVY.

In Table 5.1, Barry Sanders moves to the top of the YRAA list, with Simpson close behind, but once again Simpson played in 14 games and Sanders played in 16. YRAA can and should be adjusted for games played, or YRAA/G, which is YRAA divided by games, which we'll do in Table 5.2:

Table 5.2
List of 2,000-Yard Rushers Ranked by Highest YRAA/G

RUSHER	YL	TM	G	RA	RY	AVY	YRAA	YRAA/G
OJ Simpson	73N	BUF	14	332	2003	1331.6	671.4	47.960
Barry Sanders	97N	DET	16	335	2053	1362.7	690.3	43.142
Adrian L Peterson	12N	MIN	16	348	2097	1482.8	614.2	38.385
Eric Dickerson	84N	SLR	16	379	2105	1506.7	598.3	37.394
Chris Johnson	09N	TEN	16	358	2006	1505.3	500.7	31.291
Jamal Lewis	03N	BAR	16	387	2066	1597.1	468.9	29.307
Terrell Davis	98N	DEN	16	392	2008	1549.6	458.4	28.651

In 1973, Simpson rushed for almost 48 more yards per game (671.4 divided by 14) than an average rusher that season would have rushed for given the same number of attempts. You would probably think that is the highest single season YRAA/G figure of all time, being that he was one of the seven guys who had rushed for more than 2000 yards in a single season, but you would be wrong. There is one figure that is higher, and I doubt one football fan in a hundred can name the guy who I'm talking about or has ever even heard of him. A hint—he is the first running back to rush for more than 1,000 yards in a season and he did it during that season. Another hint—he did it during the 1934 season. Still don't know? I'll make you think about it a bit.

Throughout the 2018 season, there have been, according to my count, a total of 630 separate 1,000-yard rushing seasons between the NFL, AFL and AAFC. (A quick aside—I also found the average 1,000-yard rusher rushed for an average of 1,253 yards during the season in question.) I calculated the YRAA for each of those player-seasons, a player-season being a particular season for a particular player, such as Franco Harris, 1975, or John Riggins, 1983, or Melvin Gordon, 2017. Table 5.3 is a list of what the top twenty-five 1,000-yard player-seasons looks like, ranked by YRAA/G:

Table 5.3
List of 25 Highest Single-Season Rusher YRAA/G Values

RK	RUSHER	YL	TM	G	ATT	YDS	Y/A	YRAA	YRAA/G
1	Beattie Feathers	34N	CHI	11	119	1004	8.437	564.482	51.317
2	Jim Brown	63N	CLE	14	291	1863	6.402	717.747	51.268
3	OJ Simpson	73N	BUF	14	332	2003	6.033	671.444	47.960
4	Barry Sanders	97N	DET	16	335	2053	6.128	690.265	43.142
5	Jim Brown	58N	CLE	12	257	1527	5.942	482.396	40.200
6	Walter Payton	77N	CHI	14	339	1852	5.463	559.863	39.990
7	Barry Sanders	94N	DET	16	331	1883	5.689	638.119	39.882
8	Adrian L Peterson	12N	MIN	16	348	2097	6.026	614.162	38.385
9	Eric Dickerson	84N	LA	16	379	2105	5.554	598.311	37.394
10	OJ Simpson	75N	BUF	14	329	1817	5.523	509.615	36.401
11	Michael Vick	06N	ATL	16	123	1039	8.447	532.179	33.261

5. Rusher Ratings

RK	RUSHER	YL	TM	G	ATT	YDS	Y/A	YRAA	YRAA/G
12	Jim Brown	60N	CLE	12	215	1257	5.847	396.735	33.061
13	Spec Sanders	47F	NYA	14	231	1432	6.199	459.090	32.792
14	Jamaal Charles	10N	K C	16	230	1467	6.378	507.015	31.688
15	Chris Johnson	09N	TEN	16	358	2006	5.603	500.653	31.291
16	Joe Perry	64N	S F	12	173	1049	6.064	374.856	31.238
17	Earl Campbell	80N	HOU	15	373	1934	5.185	464.442	30.963
18	Jim Brown	65N	CLE	14	289	1544	5.343	431.184	30.799
19	Clinton Portis	03N	DEN	13	290	1591	5.486	392.695	30.207
20	Jamal Lewis	03N	BAR	16	387	2066	5.339	468.916	29.307
21	Terrell Davis	98N	DEN	16	392	2008	5.122	458.416	28.651
22	Otis Armstrong	74N	DEN	14	263	1407	5.350	395.017	28.216
23	Emmitt Smith	93N	DAL	14	283	1486	5.251	394.963	28.212
24	John David Crow	60N	STL	12	183	1071	5.852	336.614	28.051
25	Tiki Barber	05N	NYG	16	357	1860	5.210	440.888	27.556

All seven of the 2,000-yard club members appear in Table 5.3, but it is a nice mix of rushers from different eras. Beattie Feathers, who was the first rusher to crack the 1,000-yard mark, tops the list. He was a halfback with the 1934 Bears team that went 13–0 during the regular season, only to lose the NFL Championship game to the Giants that is better known as the Sneakers game.

That being said, I do not consider Feathers' 1934 season to be the greatest rushing season of all-time, or even in the discussion for being the greatest of all-time. Individual statistics from the 1930s can be prone to errors, as we will find when we get to kickers, and the teams of 1934 did not play balanced schedules or even the same number of games. There is also the wide gap between the best and worst players and teams, also known as lack of parity; in 1934, an NFL team was disbanded mid-season and replaced by a minor league team who played out the three remaining games on the disbanded team's schedule. Feathers had a great season for a running back, maybe one of the 25 best ever, maybe not, but I can't see it as the greatest of all time.

Perhaps the next biggest surprise on the list was Michael Vick at number eleven; he was the only NFL quarterback to rush for 1,000 yards in a season. Jim Brown appears four times on the list, OJ and Barry Sanders show up twice, and nobody else appears more than once.

The other two who need to be discussed are the two quarterbacks who also ran a lot—Spec Sanders and Michael Vick. Sanders played for the 1947 New York Yankees of the AAFC and is the first 1000–1000 passer-rusher in pro football history, with Vick being the first in NFL history to rush for 1000 yards and pass for 1000 yards in the same season. Do they derive an advantage because a lot of the times they are caught behind the line of scrimmage, those lost rushing yards are written off as a sack? I've never studied it but would like to see the data if anybody has.

Other than that, I think if you remove Feathers, Spec Sanders and Vick, the list was pretty good.

To calculate games played, I do not use total team games played, but rather the games the player was active on the roster, as determined by profootballreference.com. This way, if the rusher is injured and not activated for the game, it does not affect his totals as he does not get credited for a game. However, if he is eligible to play and sits on the bench the whole game, he will be credited for a game played. I know it hurts certain rushers (Marcus Allen comes to mind) but on the whole, it seems the fairest way to do it.

The bottom twenty-five 1,000-yard seasons looks like this:

Table 5.4
List of 25 Lowest Single-Season Rusher YRAA/G Values

RK	RUSHER	YL	TM	G	ATT	YDS	Y/A	YRAA	YRAA/G
1	Eddie George	02N	TEN	16	343	1165	3.397	-288.219	-18.014
2	Eddie George	03N	TEN	16	312	1031	3.304	-272.516	-17.032
3	Ottis Anderson	89N	NYG	16	325	1023	3.148	-268.099	-16.756
4	Ricky Williams	03N	MIA	16	392	1372	3.500	-265.564	-16.598
5	Edgerrin James	06N	ARZ	16	337	1159	3.439	-247.802	-15.488
6	Cedric Benson	10N	CIN	16	321	1111	3.461	-246.174	-15.386
7	James Stewart	00N	DET	16	339	1184	3.493	-204.863	-12.804
8	James Wilder	85N	T B	16	365	1300	3.562	-203.593	-12.725
9	Curtis Martin	98N	NYJ	15	369	1287	3.488	-189.280	-12.619
10	Rodney Hampton	94N	NYG	14	327	1075	3.287	-176.585	-12.613
11	Jamal Anderson	97N	ATL	16	290	1002	3.455	-197.225	-12.327
12	Jerome Bettis	94N	L A	16	319	1025	3.213	-196.483	-12.280
13	John Riggins	83N	WAS	15	375	1347	3.592	-168.779	-11.252
14	Edgar Bennett	95N	G B	16	316	1067	3.377	-179.511	-11.219
15	Jamal Lewis	06N	BAR	16	314	1132	3.605	-177.255	-11.078
16	Jamal Lewis	08N	CLE	16	279	1002	3.591	-174.638	-10.915
17	Adrian Murrell	97N	NYJ	16	300	1086	3.620	-153.583	-9.599
18	Steven Jackson	10N	SLR	16	330	1241	3.761	-151.993	-9.500
19	Joe Morris	88N	NYG	16	307	1083	3.528	-149.996	-9.375
20	Franco Harris	78N	PIT	16	310	1082	3.490	-146.162	-9.135
21	Walter Payton	81N	CHI	16	339	1222	3.605	-143.714	-8.982
22	Thomas Jones	07N	NYJ	16	310	1119	3.610	-142.919	-8.932
23	LaDainian Tomlinson	01N	S D	16	339	1236	3.646	-142.792	-8.924
24	Eddie George	00N	TEN	16	403	1509	3.744	-140.161	-8.760
25	Lamar Smith	00N	MIA	15	309	1139	3.686	-125.154	-8.344

It was a surprise to see Eddie George occupy the top, or actually, bottom two spots on Table 5.4, but Jamal Lewis also appeared twice in the bottom twenty-five. It is noteworthy that several of the bottom guys on this list are already in the Hall of Fame, and a couple others on the list will probably join them in time. We'll discuss a couple of those HOFers later.

To calculate Career YRAA, it is simply the sum of YRAA of each season of the player's career, and to calculate career YRAA/G, divide Career YRAA by total games the player was active on the roster for. Table 5.5 is the top 25 career chart of those among the top 250 in career rushing yards, ranked by Career YRAA/G:

Table 5.5
List of 25 Highest Career Rusher YRAA/G Values

RK	RUSHER	G	ATT	YDS	Y/A	YRAA	YRAA/G
1	Jim Brown	118	2359	12312	5.219	2831.464	23.995
2	Barry Sanders	153	3062	15269	4.987	3224.858	21.078
3	Michael Vick	143	873	6109	6.998	2483.398	17.366
4	Gale Sayers	68	991	4956	5.001	1074.147	15.796
5	Terrell Davis	78	1655	7607	4.596	1036.142	13.284
6	Jamaal Charles	127	1401	7556	5.393	1685.367	13.271
7	Marion Motley	106	828	4720	5.700	1321.402	12.466
8	Robert Smith	98	1411	6818	4.832	1217.910	12.428
9	OJ Simpson	135	2404	11236	4.674	1644.251	12.180
10	Randall Cunningham	158	775	4928	6.359	1847.997	11.696
11	Adrian L Peterson	133	2574	12276	4.769	1512.830	11.375
12	Joe Perry	181	1929	9723	5.040	1904.546	10.522
13	Steve Van Buren	83	1320	5860	4.439	863.771	10.407
14	Billy Sims	60	1131	5106	4.515	616.477	10.275
15	Napoleon Kaufman	91	978	4792	4.900	897.839	9.866
16	Paul Lowe	100	1026	4995	4.868	957.051	9.571
17	Wendell Tyler	108	1344	6378	4.746	1020.152	9.446
18	Mercury Morris	99	804	4133	5.141	898.172	9.072
19	Eric Dickerson	146	2996	13259	4.426	1310.068	8.973
20	Tiki Barber	154	2217	10449	4.713	1366.225	8.872
21	William Andrews	87	1315	5986	4.552	760.779	8.745
22	Fred Taylor	153	2534	11695	4.615	1320.373	8.630
23	Steve Young	169	722	4239	5.871	1388.002	8.213
24	Priest Holmes	113	1780	8172	4.591	902.821	7.990
25	Cam Newton	109	828	4320	5.217	858.945	7.880

Most of the guys listed in Table 5.5 had shorter careers. On average, the top 25 careers in YRAA/G played an average of about 119 career games (seven and a half 16-game seasons) while the 1–250 list had an average career of about 117 games played. Even Barry Sanders, who retired while still in his prime and is thought of as having had a short career, played the fifth-most career games of anybody in the top 25. His total of 153 career games tied with Fred Taylor only ranks behind Joe Perry, Tiki Barber (another guy who it was felt retired early), and quarterbacks Randall Cunningham and Steve Young.

Table 5.6 lists the bottom 25 careers as rated by YRAA/G, among those who are in the top 250 all-time in career rushing yardage:

Table 5.6
List of 25 Lowest Career Rusher YRAA/G Values

RK	RUSHER	G	ATT	YDS	Y/A	YRAA	YRAA/G
1	Eddie George	141	2865	10441	3.644	-1194.113	-8.469
2	Cedric Benson	96	1600	6017	3.761	-718.083	-7.480
3	Leonard Russell	85	1164	3973	3.413	-568.821	-6.692
4	Ron A Johnson	81	1204	4308	3.578	-519.862	-6.418
5	Reggie Cobb	92	1065	3743	3.515	-476.293	-5.177
6	Errict Rhett	86	1174	4143	3.529	-442.755	-5.148
7	Anthony Thomas	87	1044	3891	3.727	-425.303	-4.889
8	Rashard Mendenhall	72	1081	4236	3.919	-341.982	-4.750
9	Lamar Smith	115	1322	4853	3.671	-513.747	-4.467
10	Bill Mathis	137	1044	3589	3.438	-607.799	-4.436
11	Sammy Winder	127	1495	5427	3.630	-554.768	-4.368
12	Dick Hoak	135	1132	3965	3.503	-587.459	-4.352
13	BenJarvus Green-Ellis	85	1008	3914	3.883	-367.718	-4.326
14	Cadillac Williams	81	1055	4038	3.827	-341.762	-4.219
15	Bill Brown	194	1649	5838	3.540	-736.931	-3.799
16	Natrone Means	88	1409	5215	3.701	-321.496	-3.653
17	Altie Taylor	102	1170	4308	3.682	-365.591	-3.584
18	Edgar Bennett	112	1115	3992	3.580	-366.303	-3.271
19	Ron Dayne	96	983	3722	3.786	-313.387	-3.264
20	James R Jones	135	1010	3626	3.590	-428.136	-3.171
21	Jim Kiick	115	1029	3759	3.653	-353.448	-3.073
22	Antowain Smith	131	1784	6881	3.857	-391.160	-2.986
23	Thomas Jones	180	2678	10591	3.955	-530.535	-2.947
24	Dalton Hilliard	108	1126	4164	3.698	-315.182	-2.918
25	Rudi Johnson	91	1517	5979	3.941	-261.265	-2.871

Eddie George had the best career of any player on Table 5.6, and his career certainly falls short of enshrinement in Canton, and my research will probably not help his Canton case.

Attempts and Yards Per 16 Games

Another way of examining the rushing data outside the realm of YRAA is by pro-rating each rusher's career rushing statistics to Rushing Attempts per 16 Games (A16G) and Rushing Yards per 16 Games (Y16G). This type of analytical measure standardizes each

5. Rusher Ratings

rusher's performance and puts those who play in a differing number of games on equal footing. It's nothing more than dividing career attempts and career yards by career games played and multiplying by 16 and rounding off to the nearest whole number.

For Jim Brown, his A16G would be his career attempts (2359) divided by his career games played (118), multiplied by 16, and rounded off to the nearest whole number, which would be 320. Over his career, during a 16-game season, Number 32 would have rushed 320 times. This way, he can be directly compared to modern rushers, and using modern single-season numbers, it is easier to put into perspective.

Of the top 250 all-time in career rushing yards, Table 5.7 lists the top 25 in highest Y16G, with A16G and Y16G:

Table 5.7
List of 25 Rushers Ranked by Highest Y16G

RK	RUSHER	G	ATT	YDS	Y/A	A16G	Y16G
1	Jim Brown	118	2359	12312	5.219	320	1669
2	Barry Sanders	153	3062	15269	4.987	320	1597
3	Terrell Davis	78	1655	7607	4.596	339	1560
4	Adrian L Peterson	133	2574	12276	4.769	310	1477
5	Eric Dickerson	146	2996	13259	4.426	328	1453
6	Walter Payton	190	3838	16726	4.358	323	1409
7	Clinton Portis	113	2230	9923	4.450	316	1405
8	Le'Veon Bell	62	1229	5336	4.342	317	1377
9	Billy Sims	60	1131	5106	4.515	302	1362
10	Curtis Martin	168	3518	14101	4.008	335	1343
11	OJ Simpson	135	2404	11236	4.674	285	1332
12	Edgerrin James	148	3028	12246	4.044	327	1324
13	Earl Campbell	115	2187	9407	4.301	304	1309
14	Arian Foster	80	1476	6527	4.422	295	1305
15	Emmitt Smith	226	4409	18355	4.163	312	1299
16	Jamal Lewis	131	2542	10607	4.173	310	1296
17	LaDainian Tomlinson	170	3174	13684	4.311	299	1288
18	George Rogers	92	1692	7176	4.241	294	1248
19	Shaun Alexander	123	2187	9453	4.322	284	1230
20	Fred Taylor	153	2534	11695	4.615	265	1223
21	LeSean McCoy	133	2185	10092	4.619	263	1214
22	Corey Dillon	150	2618	11241	4.294	279	1199
23	Chris Johnson	130	2163	9651	4.462	266	1188
24	Eddie George	141	2865	10441	3.644	325	1185
25	Ricky Watters	144	2622	10643	4.059	291	1183

Once again Brown and Sanders rate 1 and 2, this time in Y16G, but it should be kept in mind that Brown and Sanders retired before they passed their prime, and their numbers probably would have dropped somewhat if they had hung around a few more years than they did. Terrell Davis and Billy Sims were both in the top ten, but their careers were derailed by injuries. Le'Veon Bell has averaged 1,377 per 16 games, although after five seasons in the NFL (not including the 2018 season when he held out for the entire season), he has never actually rushed for that many yards in a season; his career high in RY is 1,361.

Table 5.7 could be viewed as a "Peak Value" list, as it includes players from different eras rated by Yards per 16 Games. It is difficult, I believe, to draw up a list of greatest running backs that does not have Brown, Sanders and Walter Payton in the top three, whether you rate them by Peak Value or Career Value. Even for Emmitt Smith, the career Rushing Yards leader with three Super Bowl rings, I think it would be a challenge to make a "best running back ever" argument on his behalf. Emmitt was a great running back, maybe number four or five all time, but not the greatest.

Yards to Points

Converting Yards Rushing Above Average, or YRAA, to Points Above Average is a simple matter. In their classic 1988 book *The Hidden Game of Football*, Pete Palmer, John Thorn and (the late) Bob Carroll set the ratio of yards to points at 14 to one, so that one point is equal to 14 yards. I believe that 14 is probably pretty close to the correct number, as historically from 1933 to 2018 the aggregate ratio of yards to points is 15.30 (approximately 9,156,793 yards and 598,423 points in regular season games). Also, it is interesting to note that the playing field is one hundred yards long, and you get seven points for scoring a TD (with extra point), and one hundred divided by seven equals approximately 14.286. Fourteen yards per point works for me.

Over his career, Jim Brown averaged 24 yards above average per game according to YRAA, which works out to about 1.7 points per game, or about 20.6 points per 12-game season or 24.0 points per 14-game season. Working it out over his career, Brown was 202 points above average. As a comparison, over the course of his career, the Browns as a team were a little over 700 points above average, as they had more points scored than allowed every season from 1957 to 1965; a total of 2,934 points scored and 2,227 points allowed over his career. It could therefore be argued that almost 30 percent (28.6 percent actually; 202 divided by 707) of the amount that the Browns were above average during his career was entirely due to the rushing of Jim Brown.

Top 25 Career Rushers

Table 5.8 contains the top 25 career rushers based of rushing yards as of the end of the 2018 season.

Table 5.8
List of 25 Highest Career Rushing Yards
Through 2018, YRAA, A16G, Y16G

RK	RUSHER	G	ATT	YDS	Y/A	YRAA/G	A16G	Y16G
1	Emmitt Smith	226	4409	18355	4.163	3.426	312	1299

RK	RUSHER	G	ATT	YDS	Y/A	YRAA/G	A16G	Y16G
2	Walter Payton	190	3838	16726	4.358	7.651	323	1409
3	Barry Sanders	153	3062	15269	4.987	21.078	320	1597
4	Curtis Martin	168	3518	14101	4.008	-0.563	335	1343
5	Frank Gore	196	3226	14026	4.348	2.885	263	1145
6	LaDainian Tomlinson	170	3174	13684	4.311	3.233	299	1288
7	Jerome Bettis	192	3479	13662	3.927	-1.403	290	1139
8	Eric Dickerson	146	2996	13259	4.426	8.973	328	1453
9	Tony Dorsett	173	2936	12739	4.339	6.158	272	1178
10	Jim Brown	118	2359	12312	5.219	23.995	320	1669
11	Marshall Faulk	176	2836	12279	4.330	5.217	258	1116
12	Adrian L Peterson	133	2574	12276	4.769	11.375	310	1477
13	Edgerrin James	148	3028	12246	4.044	-0.927	327	1324
14	Marcus Allen	221	3022	12243	4.051	1.071	219	886
15	Franco Harris	173	2949	12120	4.110	2.120	273	1121
16	Thurman Thomas	182	2877	12074	4.197	3.949	253	1061
17	Fred Taylor	153	2534	11695	4.615	8.630	265	1223
18	Steven Jackson	160	2764	11438	4.138	-0.767	276	1144
19	John Riggins	174	2916	11352	3.893	-1.968	268	1044
20	Corey Dillon	150	2618	11241	4.294	3.790	279	1199
21	OJ Simpson	135	2404	11236	4.674	12.18	285	1332
22	Warrick Dunn	181	2669	10967	4.109	0.304	236	969
23	Ricky Watters	144	2622	10643	4.059	1.904	291	1183
24	Jamal Lewis	131	2542	10607	4.173	0.754	310	1296
25	Thomas Jones	180	2678	10591	3.955	-2.947	238	941

A similar list of the top 250 rushers can be found at the end of the chapter, Table 5.22.

A few things to note:

Six members on the list have negative YRAA, and three of them are currently in the Pro Football Hall of Fame. There is a good reason for this, and this is the major problem with YRAA.

John Riggins is one of these players. If you look at Riggo's career in YRAA/G, his big years in Washington (1982–84), his YRAA/G were -15.8, -11.3 and -5.5 respectively. In all of those seasons, the Redskins ran a high-powered pass offense and in many of those games, Washington was well ahead by halftime. In the second half, on most downs Theismann was handing off to Riggins who was burning up the clock and icing the victory.

When Riggins wasn't killing the clock, he was taking the pressure off Theismann's passing game; he forced the opposing defenses to key on him, which opened up Theismann. Even if you keyed on Riggins, as the Dolphins learned the hard way on a fourth-and-one early in the fourth quarter of Super Bowl XVII, Riggins (who twice won the Kansas high school 100-yard dash championship) would leave you in his dust.

In that era, Riggins was not a below-average player but actually one of the half-dozen most valuable men in pro football. However, the magnitude of the negative YRAA values of those big-yardage seasons weighed down his career. John Riggins is a deserving Hall of Famer and if I were a coach, I would be happy to have him in my backfield.

Jerome Bettis suffers from much of the same dilemma. Bettis was big and slow coming out of the gate, but like Riggins, he was punishing, and once he got it up to full speed, he was damn near impossible to bring down. In Pittsburgh he played for a lot of successful teams under Bill Cowher, and he ate up a lot of the clock late in the game in Pittsburgh victories. In his 13-year career, he only had a positive YRAA in four seasons. He was a great running back and the team leader during his tenure in Pittsburgh and after Franco Harris, the second greatest running back in Steelers history. Like Riggins, I would have Bettis on my team any time. He is considered a controversial Hall of Fame decision but I think he definitely belongs in Canton.

Curtis Martin cost his team about half a yard a game during his career, which isn't very bad as that works out to half a point a season and less than seven points or one touchdown over the course of his career. However, Martin was one of the most dependable running backs in pro football history, and was rarely injured.

On a personal note, Curtis Martin was always a favorite of mine because as a high school freshman, I attended the same high school that he would attend about ten years later, Taylor Allderdice High School in Pittsburgh.

Of the other three, Edgerrin James probably has the best chance of making the Hall of Fame. Edge, in my opinion, more of what the folks at the PFRA refer to as a HOVG (Hall of the Very Good) type, but he could very well get into Canton.

But I don't feel any of the three guys are really below average, nor do I feel Eddie George (career YRAA/G of -8.47) was necessarily a below average or terrible running back. Even in 2002 and 2003 when George was -18 and -17 in YRAA/G, the Titans finished 11–5 and 12–4 respectively. However, when you run the ball over 300 times in a season for an average of 3.3 or 3.4 yards, your YRAA isn't going to be good. The Titans were willing to live with his low rushing average, but when he went to Dallas in 2004 and brought his 3.3 YPC rushing average with him, he only lasted for one season before calling it a career.

Annual Rushing Leaders—Lowest YRAA/G

I mentioned earlier in this chapter that you could lead the league in rushing just by being average, or in some cases, even below average, if you carried the ball enough times. I've checked, and there have been two occasions where the league leading rusher since 1933 had a negative YRAA. The first time was in 1951 when Eddie Price of the Giants won the rushing title with 971 yards, beating Washington's Rob Goode by 20 yards. However, it took Price 271 attempts to get those 971 yards. Price's yards per attempt was 3.583, and because his Y/A was below the league average of 4.051 yards per rush in 1951, Price's YRAA was -133.49, which worked out to minus 11.124 YRAA/G, the worst in the league.

The second time it occurred was in 1971 when Floyd Little led the NFL with 1,133 yards, and his 3.989 yards per rush was just a shade under the league average of 4.022.

Little wound up with a YRAA of -9.570, or -0.684 YRAA/G. Table 5.9 contains the ten worst league rushing champions according to YRAA/G:

Table 5.9
List of 10 Lowest YRAA/G Values for League-Leading Rushers

RK	RUSHER	YL	TM	G	ATT	YDS	Y/A	YRAA/G	LG Y/A
1	Eddie Price	51N	NYG	12	271	971	3.583	-11.124	4.051
2	Floyd Little	71N	DEN	14	284	1133	3.989	-0.684	4.022
3	Christian Okoye	89N	K C	15	370	1480	4.000	1.216	3.952
4	OJ Simpson	72N	BUF	14	292	1251	4.284	3.110	4.139
5	Whizzer White	40N	DET	11	146	514	3.521	4.660	3.182
6	Cookie Gilchrist	64A	BUF	14	230	981	4.265	5.326	3.965
7	Paul Robinson	68A	CIN	14	238	1023	4.298	5.983	3.965
8	Whizzer White	38N	PIT	11	152	567	3.730	6.047	3.309
9	Charles White	87N	L A	15	324	1374	4.241	6.526	3.946
10	Gale Sayers	69N	CHI	14	236	1032	4.373	6.529	3.999

Some interesting names on the list, including three future Hall of Famers, two Heisman Trophy winners, and the only person to appear twice was future U.S. Supreme Court Justice Byron "Whizzer" White.

Rushing Average Per Attempt—1994–2012 and 2018

I will offer one final observation after compiling this rushing data, and it seems that the League Average Yards per Rushing Attempt, which has hovered between 3.8 and 4.1 from the end of World War II through the next 50 years, suddenly began to move upward. The league rushing average went as high as 4.305 in 2012, the highest annual average the NFL has ever seen. The average has begun to drop over the past five seasons, but in 2018, shot up a third of a yard, to 4.416 yards per attempt, as you can see in Figure 5.1, which pits season (x) against league Y/A (y).

I think the reason for this movement upward is obvious, and that is the number of running quarterbacks who have entered the league over the past 15 years. A good scrambling quarterback will almost always have a Y/A much higher than the league rushing average because a number of their losses will be written off as sacks, and as there are now more quarterbacks that can also run well in the league than at any point in pro football history, it seems logical that the rushing quarterbacks are probably responsible for the upswing in Rushing Average.

I'm open to theories about the 2018 rise in rushing average. Will it go up or down in 2019?

Here are the best and worst team YRAA tables, and the top 250 rusher YRAA tables:

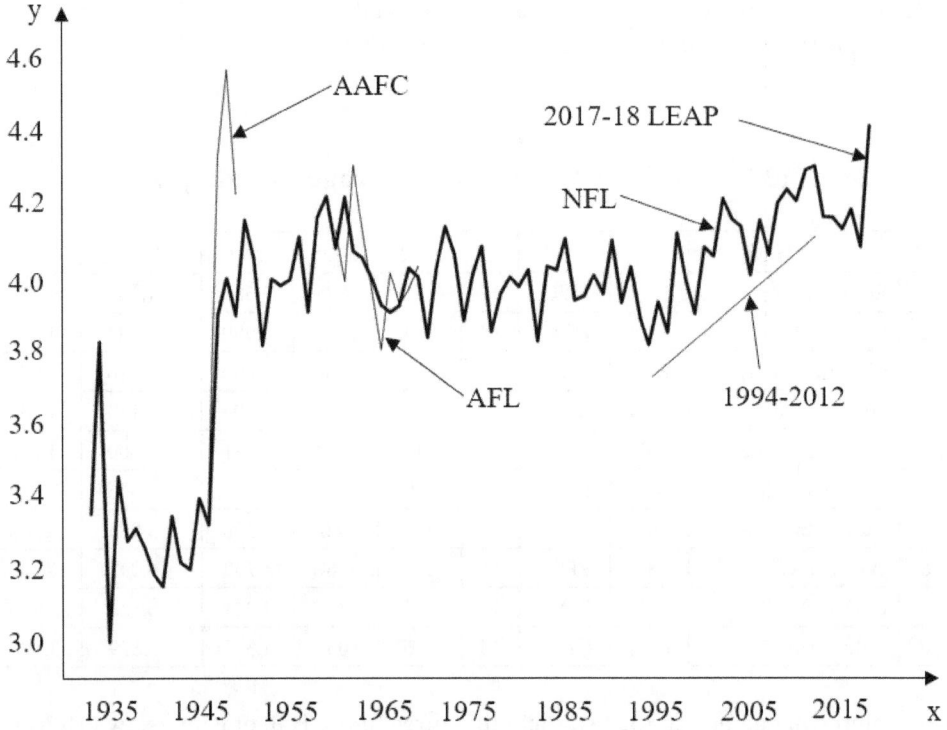

Figure 5.1. Graph of league rushing average by season, 1933–2018 for NFL, AAFC and AFL.

Table 5.10
25 Highest and Lowest Single Season Offensive Team YR/A Values, 1933–1969

RK	TM	YL	G	ATT	YDS	Y/A	RK	TM	YL	G	ATT	YDS	Y/A
1	S F	48F	14	603	3663	6.075	1	PHI	40N	11	317	298	0.940
2	CLE	63N	14	460	2639	5.737	2	BOS	44N	10	324	471	1.454
3	S F	54N	12	442	2498	5.652	3	PIT	35N	12	327	508	1.554
4	S D	63A	14	395	2201	5.572	4	DET	46N	11	274	472	1.723
5	S F	49F	12	506	2798	5.530	5	BKN	43N	10	333	610	1.832
6	NYA	47F	14	534	2930	5.487	6	PHI	39N	11	329	631	1.918
7	CLE	47F	14	479	2557	5.338	7	MAA	46F	14	408	848	2.078
8	CLE	58N	12	475	2526	5.318	8	CHC	43N	10	334	709	2.123
9	CLE	66N	14	415	2166	5.219	9	PIT	36N	12	472	1100	2.331
10	L A	51N	12	426	2210	5.188	10	PHI	41N	11	360	849	2.358
11	K C	66A	14	439	2274	5.180	11	CLR	38N	11	336	798	2.375
12	L A	56N	12	384	1978	5.151	12	NYG	45N	10	317	769	2.426
13	BAL	56N	12	432	2202	5.097	13	BOS	45N	10	345	846	2.452
14	BFA	48F	14	539	2738	5.080	14	CST	33N	10	320	795	2.484

RK	TM	YL	G	ATT	YDS	Y/A		RK	TM	YL	G	ATT	YDS	Y/A
15	L A	53N	12	426	2148	5.042		15	CLR	37N	11	370	930	2.514
16	CLE	60N	12	383	1930	5.039		16	PHI	35N	11	411	1054	2.564
17	S F	53N	12	443	2230	5.034		17	G B	34N	13	456	1183	2.594
18	L A	58N	12	345	1734	5.026		18	CHC	39N	11	321	835	2.601
19	K C	62A	14	479	2407	5.025		19	BKN	44N	10	367	960	2.616
20	CHI	34N	13	567	2847	5.021		20	NYG	53N	12	398	1049	2.636
21	K C	61A	14	439	2183	4.973		21	WAS	44N	10	342	904	2.643
22	CLE	64N	14	435	2163	4.972		22	PIT	39N	11	428	1138	2.659
23	G B	61N	14	474	2350	4.958		23	PHI	42N	11	407	1089	2.676
24	L A	54N	12	432	2140	4.954		24	PIT	45N	10	358	961	2.684
25	BUF	62A	14	501	2480	4.950		25	CHC	36N	12	559	1509	2.699

Table 5.11
25 Highest and Lowest Single-Season Offensive
Team YR/A Values, 1970–2018

RK	TM	YL	G	ATT	YDS	Y/A		RK	TM	YL	G	ATT	YDS	Y/A
1	DET	97N	16	447	2464	5.512		1	N E	94N	16	478	1332	2.787
2	ATL	06N	16	537	2939	5.473		2	IND	92N	16	379	1102	2.908
3	PHI	10N	16	428	2324	5.430		3	N E	86N	16	469	1373	2.928
4	MIN	12N	16	486	2634	5.420		4	S D	00N	16	351	1062	3.026
5	CAR	11N	16	445	2408	5.411		5	S D	99N	16	410	1246	3.039
6	BUF	16N	16	492	2630	5.346		6	MIN	78N	16	505	1536	3.042
7	MIN	07N	16	494	2634	5.332		7	ARZ	99N	16	396	1207	3.048
8	MIN	02N	16	473	2507	5.300		8	T B	77N	14	465	1424	3.062
9	L A	84N	16	541	2864	5.294		9	HOU	71N	14	361	1106	3.064
10	DET	90N	16	366	1927	5.265		10	PHI	71N	14	407	1248	3.066
11	SEA	14N	16	525	2762	5.261		11	WAS	74N	14	470	1443	3.070
12	WAS	12N	16	519	2709	5.220		12	CHI	70N	14	353	1092	3.093
13	TEN	09N	16	499	2592	5.194		13	BOP	70N	14	334	1040	3.114
14	S F	98N	16	491	2544	5.181		14	ATL	78N	16	533	1660	3.114
15	MIN	11N	16	448	2318	5.174		15	G B	77N	14	469	1464	3.122
16	K C	02N	16	462	2378	5.147		16	MIA	97N	16	430	1343	3.123
17	S D	03N	16	417	2146	5.146		17	PHI	91N	16	446	1396	3.130
18	PHI	13N	16	500	2566	5.132		18	WAS	73N	14	459	1439	3.135
19	DET	94N	16	406	2080	5.123		19	BAR	13N	16	423	1328	3.139
20	BUF	73N	14	605	3088	5.104		20	CHI	07N	16	423	1330	3.144

RK	TM	YL	G	ATT	YDS	Y/A
21	ATL	04N	16	524	2672	5.099
22	PIT	72N	14	497	2520	5.070
23	S F	12N	16	492	2491	5.063
T24	BUF	75N	14	588	2974	5.058
T24	PHI	11N	16	450	2276	5.058

RK	TM	YL	G	ATT	YDS	Y/A
T21	T B	83N	16	428	1353	3.161
T21	ARZ	05N	16	360	1138	3.161
23	MIN	16N	16	380	1205	3.171
T24	ARZ	97N	16	395	1255	3.177
T24	HOT	02N	16	424	1347	3.177

Table 5.12
25 Highest and Lowest Single-Season Defensive Team YR/A Values, 1933–1969

RK	TM	YL	G	ATT	YDS	Y/A
1	PHI	44N	10	321	558	1.738
2	CHI	42N	11	294	519	1.765
3	S F	46F	14	425	873	2.054
4	CHI	37N	11	412	933	2.265
5	CHI	39N	11	353	812	2.300
6	WAS	42N	11	367	848	2.311
7	NYG	51N	12	392	913	2.329
8	DET	35N	12	443	1039	2.345
9	NYA	46F	14	449	1055	2.350
10	NYG	40N	11	413	977	2.366
11	WAS	39N	11	412	999	2.425
12	BOR	35N	11	404	998	2.470
13	NYG	35N	12	436	1089	2.498
14	PHP	43N	10	312	793	2.542
15	DET	45N	10	356	912	2.562
16	PHI	45N	10	318	817	2.569
17	BOR	36N	12	434	1148	2.645
18	CHC	34N	11	360	954	2.650
19	NYG	44N	10	374	1000	2.674
20	G B	40N	11	387	1040	2.687
21	PHI	46N	11	418	1123	2.687
22	CHI	40N	11	372	1003	2.696
23	WAS	41N	11	410	1110	2.707
24	WAS	46N	11	407	1103	2.710
25	G B	35N	12	448	1219	2.721

RK	TM	YL	G	ATT	YDS	Y/A
1	NYY	50N	12	434	2445	5.634
2	BAA	50N	12	514	2857	5.558
3	TEX	52N	12	421	2334	5.544
4	WAS	59N	12	404	2214	5.480
5	MIN	61N	14	493	2667	5.410
6	BKA	48F	14	585	3146	5.378
7	S F	58N	12	380	2038	5.363
8	CST	34N	11	391	2082	5.325
9	HOU	65A	14	507	2683	5.292
10	CHI	55N	12	398	2100	5.276
11	CHI	51N	12	372	1958	5.263
12	BAL	53N	12	445	2315	5.202
13	NYY	51N	12	464	2397	5.166
14	G B	56N	12	512	2619	5.115
15	OAK	62A	14	478	2440	5.105
16	CIN	69A	14	523	2651	5.069
17	DAL	60N	12	447	2242	5.016
18	BAA	48F	14	504	2522	5.004
19	PIT	34N	12	517	2569	4.969
20	CHA	49F	12	467	2309	4.944
21	PHI	60N	12	449	2200	4.900
22	BKA	47F	14	514	2516	4.895
23	MIA	68A	14	445	2172	4.881
24	CHA	47F	14	564	2752	4.879
25	NYT	60A	14	393	1914	4.870

Table 5.13
25 Highest and Lowest Single-Season Defensive Team YR/A Values, 1970–2018

RK	TM	YL	G	ATT	YDS	RY/A	RK	TM	YL	G	ATT	YDS	RY/A
1	BAR	00N	16	361	970	2.687	1	CHI	13N	16	483	2583	5.348
2	S D	98N	16	422	1140	2.701	2	IND	06N	16	519	2768	5.333
3	MIN	06N	16	348	985	2.830	3	K C	03N	16	453	2344	5.174
4	BAR	07N	16	446	1268	2.843	4	DAL	90N	16	382	1976	5.173
5	PHI	91N	16	383	1136	2.966	5	N O	12N	16	457	2361	5.166
6	PIT	10N	16	333	1004	3.015	6	K C	76N	14	555	2861	5.155
7	S D	00N	16	470	1422	3.026	7	IND	12N	16	428	2200	5.140
8	S F	95N	16	348	1061	3.049	8	DET	08N	16	536	2754	5.138
9	S D	99N	16	432	1321	3.058	9	N E	73N	14	560	2850	5.089
10	MIN	94N	16	355	1090	3.070	10	OAK	11N	16	430	2178	5.065
11	WAS	04N	16	419	1304	3.112	11	T B	11N	16	498	2497	5.014
12	MIN	07N	16	379	1185	3.127	12	DET	11N	16	410	2050	5.000
13	BAR	99N	16	392	1231	3.140	13	K C	08N	16	509	2543	4.996
14	NYJ	70N	14	408	1283	3.145	14	DEN	08N	16	469	2337	4.983
15	DET	82N	9	271	854	3.151	15	BUF	12N	16	470	2333	4.964
16	BAL	71N	14	352	1113	3.162	16	N E	72N	14	548	2717	4.958
17	DET	14N	16	350	1109	3.169	17	N O	11N	16	351	1738	4.952
18	S D	93N	16	414	1314	3.174	18	ATL	92N	16	464	2294	4.944
19	JAX	03N	16	442	1406	3.181	19	SLR	08N	16	501	2475	4.940
20	DET	70N	14	362	1152	3.182	20	NYG	14N	16	438	2162	4.936
21	DEN	82N	9	293	935	3.191	21	N O	06N	16	418	2063	4.935
22	CHI	70N	14	459	1471	3.205	22	N O	15N	16	421	2076	4.931
23	N O	86N	16	486	1559	3.208	23	N O	80N	16	630	3106	4.930
24	NYG	00N	16	359	1156	3.220	24	ATL	08N	16	415	2040	4.916
25	DAL	74N	14	417	1344	3.223	25	DAL	00N	16	538	2636	4.900

Table 5.14
25 Highest and Lowest Single-Season Offensive Team YR/G Values, 1933–1969

RK	TM	YL	G	ATT	YDS	YR/G	RK	TM	YL	G	ATT	YDS	YR/G
1	S F	48F	14	603	3663	261.643	1	PHI	40N	11	317	298	27.091
2	DET	36N	12	591	2885	240.417	2	PIT	35N	12	327	508	42.333
3	S F	49F	12	506	2798	233.167	3	DET	46N	11	274	472	42.909
4	CHI	34N	13	567	2847	219.000	4	BOS	44N	10	324	471	47.100

RK	TM	YL	G	ATT	YDS	YR/G		RK	TM	YL	G	ATT	YDS	YR/G
5	PHI	49N	12	632	2607	217.250		5	PHI	39N	11	329	631	57.364
6	CHC	48N	12	531	2560	213.333		6	MAA	46F	14	408	848	60.571
7	DET	34N	13	632	2740	210.769		7	BKN	43N	10	333	610	61.000
8	CLE	58N	12	475	2526	210.500		8	NYJ	63A	14	306	978	69.857
9	NYA	47F	14	534	2930	209.286		9	CHC	43N	10	334	709	70.900
10	S F	54N	12	442	2498	208.167		10	CLR	38N	11	336	798	72.545
11	CHI	56N	12	536	2468	205.667		11	BKA	46F	14	374	1017	72.643
12	CHI	48N	12	557	2452	204.333		12	WAS	65N	14	354	1037	74.071
13	CHI	51N	12	539	2408	200.667		13	CHC	39N	11	321	835	75.909
14	CHI	55N	12	487	2388	199.000		14	WAS	61N	14	361	1072	76.571
15	PHI	48N	12	528	2378	198.167		15	NYG	45N	10	317	769	76.900
16	S F	47F	14	587	2767	197.643		16	PHI	41N	11	360	849	77.182
17	S F	51N	12	523	2366	197.167		17	WAS	62N	14	371	1088	77.714
18	STL	60N	12	484	2356	196.333		18	DEN	61A	14	333	1091	77.929
19	CHI	41N	11	495	2156	196.000		19	PIT	66N	14	375	1092	78.000
20	BFA	48F	14	539	2738	195.571		20	CIN	33N	10	320	795	79.500
21	NYG	50N	12	515	2336	194.667		21	CLR	42N	11	310	875	79.545
22	PHI	50N	12	581	2328	194.000		22	BOP	65A	14	373	1117	79.786
23	CHI	50N	12	574	2308	192.333		23	PHI	37N	11	285	884	80.364
24	DET	37N	11	484	2074	188.545		24	BOS	47N	12	343	973	81.083
25	CLE	63N	14	460	2639	188.500		25	DET	43N	10	294	817	81.700

Table 5.15
25 Highest and Lowest Single-Season Offensive
Team YR/G Values, 1970–2018

RK	TM	YL	G	ATT	YDS	YR/G		RK	TM	YL	G	ATT	YDS	YR/G
1	BUF	73N	14	605	3088	220.571		1	S D	00N	16	351	1062	66.375
2	BUF	75N	14	588	2974	212.429		2	CLE	00N	16	336	1085	67.813
3	PIT	76N	14	653	2971	212.214		3	IND	92N	16	379	1102	68.875
4	MIA	72N	14	613	2960	211.429		4	DET	06N	16	304	1129	70.563
5	N E	76N	14	591	2948	210.571		5	ARZ	05N	16	360	1138	71.125
6	L A	73N	14	659	2925	208.929		6	CLE	99N	16	313	1150	71.875
7	CHI	77N	14	599	2811	200.786		7	ATL	89N	16	318	1155	72.188
8	N E	78N	16	671	3165	197.813		8	IND	91N	16	354	1169	73.063
9	PIT	75N	14	581	2633	188.071		9	ARZ	08N	16	340	1178	73.625
10	OAK	77N	14	681	2627	187.643		10	CAR	00N	16	363	1186	74.125

RK	TM	YL	G	ATT	YDS	YR/G	RK	TM	YL	G	ATT	YDS	YR/G
11	K C	78N	16	663	2986	186.625	11	N E	70N	14	334	1040	74.286
12	CHI	84N	16	674	2974	185.875	12	ATL	99N	16	373	1196	74.750
13	L A	77N	14	621	2575	183.929	13	ARZ	12N	16	352	1204	75.250
14	OAK	75N	14	643	2573	183.786	T14	MIN	16N	16	380	1205	75.313
15	ATL	06N	16	537	2939	183.688	T14	MIA	88N	16	335	1205	75.313
16	BUF	76N	14	548	2566	183.286	16	ARZ	99N	16	396	1207	75.438
17	L A	76N	14	613	2528	180.571	17	ATL	00N	16	350	1214	75.875
18	MIA	73N	14	507	2521	180.071	18	CLE	90N	16	345	1220	76.250
19	PIT	72N	14	497	2520	180.000	19	DET	17N	16	363	1221	76.313
20	OAK	73N	14	547	2510	179.286	20	OAK	14N	16	337	1240	77.500
21	L A	84N	16	541	2864	179.000	21	DET	88N	16	391	1243	77.688
22	MIA	75N	14	594	2500	178.571	22	DET	99N	16	356	1245	77.813
23	DAL	74N	14	542	2454	175.286	23	S D	99N	16	410	1246	77.875
24	L A	80N	16	615	2799	174.938	24	ATL	13N	16	321	1247	77.938
25	S F	76N	14	576	2447	174.786	T25	CHI	70N	14	353	1092	78.000
							T25	K C	07N	16	383	1248	78.000

Table 5.16
25 Highest and Lowest Single-Season Defensive
Team YR/G Values, 1933–1969

RK	TM	YL	G	ATT	YDS	YR/G	RK	TM	YL	G	ATT	YDS	YR/G
1	CHI	42N	11	294	519	47.182	1	BAA	50N	12	514	2857	238.083
2	PHI	44N	10	321	558	55.800	2	BKA	48F	14	585	3146	224.714
3	S F	46F	14	425	873	62.357	3	G B	56N	12	512	2619	218.250
4	BUF	64A	14	300	913	65.214	4	PIT	34N	12	517	2569	214.083
5	CHI	39N	11	353	812	73.818	5	NYA	50N	12	434	2445	203.750
6	BOP	61A	14	350	1041	74.357	6	NYY	51N	12	464	2397	199.750
7	DAL	69N	14	313	1050	75.000	7	BAA	49F	12	511	2396	199.667
8	BUF	66A	14	344	1051	75.071	8	DET	48N	12	495	2382	198.500
9	NYA	46F	14	449	1055	75.357	9	NYB	49N	12	535	2360	196.667
10	NYG	51N	12	392	913	76.083	10	CHA	47F	14	564	2752	196.571
11	WAS	42N	11	367	848	77.091	11	BKN	34N	11	496	2153	195.727
12	DAL	67N	14	339	1081	77.214	12	TEX	52N	12	421	2334	194.500
13	MIN	69N	14	337	1089	77.786	13	BOS	48N	12	511	2320	193.333
14	K C	69A	14	314	1091	77.929	14	WAS	49N	12	487	2316	193.000
15	S D	65A	14	306	1094	78.143	15	BAL	53N	12	445	2315	192.917

RK	TM	YL	G	ATT	YDS	YR/G
16	BOP	63A	14	312	1108	79.143
17	PHP	43N	10	312	793	79.300
18	BUF	65A	14	360	1114	79.571
19	L A	67N	14	361	1119	79.929
20	OAK	67A	14	352	1129	80.643
21	BOP	66A	14	369	1135	81.071
22	BOP	64A	14	356	1143	81.643
23	PHI	45N	10	318	817	81.700
24	DAL	66N	14	356	1176	84.000
25	CHI	37N	11	412	933	84.818

RK	TM	YL	G	ATT	YDS	YR/G
16	CHA	49F	12	467	2309	192.417
17	HOU	65A	14	507	2683	191.643
18	MIN	61N	14	493	2667	190.500
19	BAA	47F	14	571	2665	190.357
20	CIN	69A	14	523	2651	189.357
21	CST	34N	11	391	2082	189.273
22	DAL	60N	12	447	2242	186.833
23	CHA	48F	14	538	2614	186.714
24	WAS	59N	12	404	2214	184.500
25	L A	51N	12	478	2206	183.833

Table 5.17
25 Highest and Lowest Single-Season Defensive Team YR/G Values, 1970–2018

RK	TM	YL	G	ATT	YDS	YR/G
1	BAR	00N	16	361	970	60.625
2	MIN	06N	16	348	985	61.563
3	PIT	10N	16	333	1004	62.750
4	S F	95N	16	348	1061	66.313
5	MIN	94N	16	355	1090	68.125
6	DET	14N	16	350	1109	69.313
7	PHI	91N	16	383	1136	71.000
8	S D	98N	16	422	1140	71.250
9	NYG	00N	16	359	1156	72.250
10	PHI	90N	16	337	1169	73.063
11	MIN	07N	16	379	1185	74.063
12	SLR	99N	16	338	1189	74.313
13	PIT	01N	16	339	1195	74.688
14	ATL	98N	16	361	1203	75.188
15	N O	91N	16	334	1213	75.813
16	BAR	06N	16	367	1214	75.875
17	MIN	08N	16	371	1230	76.875
18	BAR	99N	16	392	1231	76.938
19	S F	11N	16	353	1236	77.250
20	DAL	92N	16	345	1244	77.750
21	S F	90N	16	353	1258	78.625

RK	TM	YL	G	ATT	YDS	YR/G
1	K C	77N	14	634	2971	212.214
2	SEA	76N	14	614	2876	205.429
3	K C	76N	14	555	2861	204.357
4	N E	73N	14	560	2850	203.571
5	BUF	78N	16	677	3228	201.750
6	NYJ	75N	14	574	2737	195.500
7	N O	77N	14	623	2729	194.929
8	K C	75N	14	562	2724	194.571
9	N O	80N	16	630	3106	194.125
10	N E	72N	14	548	2717	194.071
11	BAL	78N	16	662	3010	188.125
12	NYJ	76N	14	582	2592	185.143
13	HOU	72N	14	546	2591	185.071
14	N E	81N	16	644	2950	184.375
15	ATL	76N	14	574	2577	184.071
16	ATL	74N	14	627	2564	183.143
17	T B	76N	14	588	2560	182.857
18	ATL	87N	15	600	2734	182.267
19	G B	79N	16	639	2885	180.313
20	CHI	73N	14	563	2509	179.214
21	BUF	71N	14	562	2496	178.286

RK	TM	YL	G	ATT	YDS	YR/G
22	PHI	17N	16	337	1267	79.188
23	BAR	07N	16	446	1268	79.250
24	BAL	71N	14	352	1113	79.500
25	HOU	93N	16	369	1273	79.563

RK	TM	YL	G	ATT	YDS	YR/G
22	SEA	77N	14	596	2485	177.500
23	BUF	76N	14	533	2465	176.071
24	HOU	85N	16	588	2814	175.875
25	SEA	81N	16	588	2806	175.375

Table 5.18
25 Highest and Lowest Single-Season Offensive Team YRAA/G Values, 1933–1969

RK	TM	YL	G	YRAA	YRAA/G
1	DET	36N	12	974.426	79.766
2	S F	48F	14	1070.386	73.915
3	S F	54N	12	816.503	67.376
4	BOR	33N	12	784.940	63.556
5	S F	49F	12	790.342	62.386
6	CHI	39N	11	687.606	61.704
7	CHI	41N	11	679.156	60.048
8	CLE	63N	14	837.659	59.734
9	CHI	34N	13	780.392	58.084
10	NYA	47F	14	716.171	49.984
11	CLR	45N	10	504.026	49.643
12	DET	37N	11	551.411	49.084
13	CLE	58N	12	572.028	47.196
14	S D	63A	14	653.830	46.154
15	CHI	35N	12	552.384	44.536
16	L A	51N	12	525.776	43.815
17	S F	53N	12	506.716	41.841
18	CLE	66N	14	583.702	41.606
19	WAS	45N	10	416.990	41.071
20	K C	66A	14	583.255	41.051
21	CHI	55N	12	488.821	40.444
22	L A	53N	12	489.307	40.404
23	CHC	48N	12	495.999	39.980
24	BAL	56N	12	463.073	38.589
25	CLE	47F	14	550.863	38.446

RK	TM	YL	G	YRAA	YRAA/G
1	PHI	40N	11	-769.623	-69.966
2	BOS	44N	10	-618.021	-61.802
3	BKN	43N	10	-518.783	-51.878
4	BAA	47F	14	-721.673	-51.548
5	PIT	36N	12	-591.897	-49.325
6	NYG	53N	12	-589.834	-49.153
7	G B	34N	13	-623.149	-47.935
8	PHI	51N	12	-551.916	-45.980
9	PHI	39N	11	-478.958	-43.542
10	MAA	46F	14	-599.374	-42.812
11	PIT	35N	12	-513.131	-42.761
12	DET	46N	11	-468.628	-42.603
13	PIT	61N	14	-582.109	-41.579
14	CHC	43N	10	-410.943	-41.094
15	CHC	36N	12	-480.805	-40.067
16	CHA	48F	14	-560.555	-40.040
17	PHI	54N	12	-434.587	-36.216
18	BOS	45N	10	-358.390	-35.839
19	PIT	55N	12	-426.350	-35.529
20	WAS	60N	12	-413.563	-34.464
21	CHA	49F	12	-411.996	-34.333
22	WAS	61N	14	-479.703	-34.264
23	NYG	45N	10	-335.650	-33.565
24	BOS	47N	12	-394.906	-32.909
25	WAS	62N	14	-449.568	-32.112

Table 5.19
25 Highest and Lowest Single-Season Offensive Team YRAA/G Values, 1970–2018

RK	TM	YL	G	YRAA	YRAA/G	RK	TM	YL	G	YRAA	YRAA/G
1	BUF	73N	14	661.033	46.951	1	WAS	73N	14	-441.403	-31.529
2	ATL	06N	16	733.787	45.693	2	N E	86N	16	-490.016	-30.626
3	BUF	75N	14	643.355	45.637	3	MIN	78N	16	-475.048	-29.690
4	L A	84N	16	717.979	44.727	4	N E	94N	16	-464.776	-29.008
5	DET	97N	16	708.935	44.201	5	ATL	78N	16	-462.123	-28.883
6	MIN	07N	16	651.117	40.554	6	PHI	71N	14	-403.019	-28.787
7	N E	76N	14	556.900	39.582	7	HOT	02N	16	-454.396	-28.400
8	S F	98N	16	608.498	37.887	8	WAS	74N	14	-395.181	-28.227
9	CHI	77N	14	526.479	37.533	9	BAR	13N	16	-448.235	-28.015
10	SEA	14N	16	598.663	37.278	10	NYG	73N	14	-388.238	-27.731
11	BUF	16N	16	592.317	36.930	11	IND	92N	16	-438.149	-27.384
12	DET	94N	16	587.923	36.745	12	T B	77N	14	-378.174	-27.012
13	MIN	12N	16	582.992	36.246	13	ATL	77N	14	-365.105	-26.079
14	MIA	71N	14	494.556	35.192	14	ARZ	06N	16	-415.988	-25.999
15	PIT	72N	14	482.634	34.237	15	TEN	03N	16	-412.155	-25.760
16	MIA	73N	14	480.069	34.098	16	T B	83N	16	-409.833	-25.615
17	PHI	10N	16	538.562	33.560	17	HOU	71N	14	-357.007	-25.500
18	N E	78N	16	535.058	33.328	18	G B	77N	14	-352.867	-25.205
19	MIN	02N	16	530.458	33.043	19	S D	09N	16	-399.775	-24.986
20	ATL	04N	16	522.447	32.592	20	CHI	07N	16	-399.675	-24.980
21	WAS	12N	16	516.239	32.096	21	BAL	79N	16	-399.588	-24.974
22	CAR	11N	16	513.970	32.065	22	MIN	16N	16	-397.043	-24.815
23	MIA	72N	14	445.242	31.585	23	S D	00N	16	-380.535	-23.783
24	CIN	86N	16	501.670	31.236	24	MIA	97N	16	-379.637	-23.727
25	PHI	13N	16	500.635	31.185	25	PIT	03N	16	-378.622	-23.664

Table 5.20
25 Highest and Lowest Single-Season Defensive Team YRAA/G Values, 1933–1969

RK	TM	YL	G	YRAA	YRAA/G	RK	TM	YL	G	YRAA	YRAA/G
1	NYG	51N	12	-727.766	-60.647	1	TEX	52N	12	795.466	65.990
2	NYG	50N	12	-630.185	-52.515	2	BAA	50N	12	791.069	65.609
3	PHI	44N	10	-512.094	-51.209	3	HOU	65A	14	898.345	61.307

RK	TM	YL	G	YRAA	YRAA/G		RK	TM	YL	G	YRAA	YRAA/G
4	S F	46F	14	-638.943	-45.639		4	CST	34N	11	644.954	58.377
5	CHI	42N	11	-499.673	-45.425		5	NYA	50N	12	693.289	57.500
6	CHI	49N	12	-518.438	-43.203		6	PIT	34N	12	672.016	55.758
7	CHI	37N	11	-460.951	-41.905		7	BAL	53N	12	591.796	48.686
8	CHC	34N	11	-458.566	-41.688		8	NYY	51N	12	565.995	46.989
9	CLE	54N	12	-465.036	-38.753		9	G B	56N	12	567.891	46.919
10	CLE	48F	14	-531.272	-37.948		10	WAS	59N	12	554.249	46.187
11	NYA	46F	14	-529.917	-37.851		11	CHI	55N	12	552.691	45.907
12	WAS	42N	11	-416.034	-37.821		12	MIN	61N	14	638.173	45.139
13	DET	34N	13	-486.441	-37.419		13	CIN	69A	14	619.697	42.819
14	NYA	49F	12	-439.810	-36.651		14	BKA	46F	14	591.766	41.344
15	G B	34N	13	-465.396	-35.800		15	CHI	51N	12	484.421	40.217
16	WAS	39N	11	-381.082	-34.644		16	S F	58N	12	466.475	38.727
17	NYG	40N	11	-374.485	-34.044		17	BKA	48F	14	554.916	38.515
18	CHI	39N	11	-369.440	-33.585		18	WAS	49N	12	468.823	38.504
19	DET	45N	10	-327.779	-32.778		19	DAL	60N	12	458.909	37.812
20	BOR	36N	12	-387.792	-32.316		20	DET	48N	12	453.283	36.903
21	S F	49F	12	-381.351	-31.779		21	PHI	35N	11	413.349	36.895
22	NYG	60N	12	-377.728	-31.477		22	MAA	46F	14	525.435	36.710
23	PHI	54N	12	-371.817	-30.985		23	BOS	46N	11	394.065	35.527
24	NYG	59N	12	-367.309	-30.575		24	OAK	61A	14	487.427	34.070
25	PIT	53N	12	-364.984	-30.415		25	NYG	45N	10	340.346	33.719

Table 5.21
25 Highest and Lowest Single-Season Defensive
Team YRAA/G Values, 1970–2018

RK	TM	YL	G	YRAA	YRAA/G		RK	TM	YL	G	YRAA	YRAA/G
1	BAR	07N	16	-560.864	-35.054		1	K C	76N	14	617.892	43.925
2	S D	98N	16	-559.845	-34.990		2	N E	73N	14	600.950	42.676
3	BAR	00N	16	-517.241	-32.328		3	K C	77N	14	554.192	39.438
4	S D	00N	16	-514.192	-32.137		4	IND	06N	16	633.087	39.398
5	MIN	06N	16	-473.149	-29.572		5	N O	80N	16	631.209	39.274
6	PIT	76N	14	-401.688	-28.692		6	CHI	13N	16	591.004	36.882
7	JAX	03N	16	-445.932	-27.871		7	BUF	78N	16	576.277	35.881
8	WAS	04N	16	-442.855	-27.678		8	K C	75N	14	489.875	34.894
9	WAS	73N	14	-360.430	-25.745		9	N E	72N	14	470.003	33.446

RK	TM	YL	G	YRAA	YRAA/G	RK	TM	YL	G	YRAA	YRAA/G
10	PIT	10N	16	-407.776	-25.486	10	NYJ	75N	14	453.594	32.309
11	MIA	03N	16	-394.168	-24.635	11	DET	08N	16	519.871	32.301
12	PIT	73N	14	-343.515	-24.537	12	NYJ	71N	14	420.305	29.877
13	PHI	91N	16	-380.449	-23.778	13	K C	03N	16	474.726	29.614
14	HOU	75N	14	-330.664	-23.619	14	T B	86N	16	471.149	29.329
15	T B	88N	16	-376.759	-23.547	15	SEA	81N	16	461.688	28.755
16	G B	72N	14	-328.315	-23.451	16	DAL	00N	16	457.917	28.521
17	S D	99N	16	-375.183	-23.449	17	HOU	83N	16	449.416	27.961
18	DEN	76N	14	-328.098	-23.436	18	ATL	92N	16	441.649	27.571
19	SEA	16N	16	-371.363	-23.210	19	SEA	76N	14	384.527	27.335
20	N O	86N	16	-367.124	-22.945	20	N O	12N	16	427.267	26.650
21	PIT	08N	16	-366.050	-22.878	21	DAL	90N	16	422.787	26.297
22	BAR	09N	16	-363.815	-22.738	22	HOU	85N	16	418.603	25.999
23	MIN	07N	16	-363.783	-22.736	23	IND	98N	16	417.934	25.970
24	DEN	15N	16	-359.122	-22.445	24	K C	08N	16	417.729	25.954
25	DET	14N	16	-357.678	-22.355	25	SEA	00N	16	416.075	25.915

Table 5.22
List of 250 Highest Career Rushing Yards 1933–2018,
YRAA, A16G, Y16G

RK	RUSHER	G	ATT	YDS	Y/A	YRAA/G	A16G	Y16G
1	Emmitt Smith	226	4409	18355	4.163	3.426	312	1299
2	Walter Payton	190	3838	16726	4.358	7.651	323	1409
3	Barry Sanders	153	3062	15269	4.987	21.078	320	1597
4	Curtis Martin	168	3518	14101	4.008	-0.563	335	1343
5	Frank Gore	196	3226	14026	4.348	2.885	263	1145
6	LaDainian Tomlinson	170	3174	13684	4.311	3.233	299	1288
7	Jerome Bettis	192	3479	13662	3.927	-1.403	290	1139
8	Eric Dickerson	146	2996	13259	4.426	8.973	328	1453
9	Tony Dorsett	173	2936	12739	4.339	6.158	272	1178
10	Jim Brown	118	2359	12312	5.219	23.995	320	1669
11	Marshall Faulk	176	2836	12279	4.330	5.217	258	1116
12	Adrian L Peterson	133	2574	12276	4.769	11.375	310	1477
13	Edgerrin James	148	3028	12246	4.044	-0.927	327	1324
14	Marcus Allen	221	3022	12243	4.051	1.071	219	886
15	Franco Harris	173	2949	12120	4.110	2.120	273	1121

5. Rusher Ratings

RK	RUSHER	G	ATT	YDS	Y/A	YRAA/G	A16G	Y16G
16	Thurman Thomas	182	2877	12074	4.197	3.949	253	1061
17	Fred Taylor	153	2534	11695	4.615	8.630	265	1223
18	Steven Jackson	160	2764	11438	4.138	-0.767	276	1144
19	John Riggins	174	2916	11352	3.893	-1.968	268	1044
20	Corey Dillon	150	2618	11241	4.294	3.790	279	1199
21	OJ Simpson	135	2404	11236	4.674	12.180	285	1332
22	Warrick Dunn	181	2669	10967	4.109	0.304	236	969
23	Ricky Watters	144	2622	10643	4.059	1.904	291	1183
24	Jamal Lewis	131	2542	10607	4.173	0.754	310	1296
25	Thomas Jones	180	2678	10591	3.955	-2.947	238	941
26	Tiki Barber	154	2217	10449	4.713	8.872	230	1086
27	Eddie George	141	2865	10441	3.644	-8.469	325	1185
28	Ottis Anderson	182	2562	10273	4.010	0.169	225	903
29	LeSean McCoy	133	2185	10092	4.619	7.144	263	1214
30	Ricky Williams	147	2431	10009	4.117	-0.210	265	1089
31	Marshawn Lynch	142	2351	10003	4.255	1.106	265	1127
32	Clinton Portis	113	2230	9923	4.450	6.300	316	1405
33	Matt Forte	146	2356	9796	4.158	-0.764	258	1074
34	Joe Perry	181	1929	9723	5.040	10.522	171	859
35	Chris Johnson	130	2163	9651	4.462	4.173	266	1188
36	Shaun Alexander	123	2187	9453	4.322	3.862	284	1230
37	Earl Campbell	115	2187	9407	4.301	6.032	304	1309
38	Ahman Green	148	2056	9205	4.477	4.975	222	995
39	Terry Allen	130	2152	8614	4.003	0.937	265	1060
40	Jim Taylor	132	1941	8597	4.429	5.898	235	1042
41	Willis McGahee	142	2095	8474	4.045	-1.676	236	955
42	Earnest Byner	211	2095	8261	3.943	-0.519	159	626
43	Herschel Walker	187	1954	8225	4.209	2.556	167	704
44	Roger Craig	165	1991	8189	4.113	1.429	193	794
45	Gerald Riggs	129	1989	8188	4.117	1.825	247	1016
46	Priest Holmes	113	1780	8172	4.591	7.990	252	1157
47	Maurice Jones-Drew	125	1797	8167	4.545	4.905	230	1045
48	DeAngelo Williams	142	1730	8096	4.680	5.985	195	912
49	Larry Csonka	146	1891	8081	4.273	3.757	207	886
50	Freeman McNeil	144	1798	8074	4.491	6.214	200	897
51	Stephen Davis	143	1945	8052	4.140	0.974	218	901

RK	RUSHER	G	ATT	YDS	Y/A	YRAA/G	A16G	Y16G
52	Garrison Hearst	126	1831	7966	4.351	4.822	233	1012
53	James Brooks	162	1685	7962	4.725	7.701	166	786
54	Chris Warren	162	1791	7696	4.297	4.118	177	760
55	Terrell Davis	78	1655	7607	4.596	13.284	339	1560
56	Jamaal Charles	127	1401	7556	5.393	13.271	177	952
57	Mike Pruitt	152	1844	7378	4.001	0.177	194	777
58	Michael Turner	134	1639	7338	4.477	3.134	196	876
59	Jonathan Stewart	131	1699	7318	4.307	1.533	208	894
60	Leroy Kelly	136	1727	7274	4.212	3.051	203	856
61	George Rogers	92	1692	7176	4.241	4.599	294	1248
62	DeMarco Murray	99	1609	7174	4.459	4.585	260	1159
63	Charlie Garner	147	1537	7097	4.617	6.223	167	772
64	Rodney Hampton	104	1824	6897	3.781	-2.437	281	1061
65	Antowain Smith	131	1784	6881	3.857	-2.986	218	840
66	Curt Warner	100	1698	6844	4.031	0.509	272	1095
67	Robert Smith	98	1411	6818	4.832	12.428	230	1113
68	John Henry Johnson	143	1571	6803	4.330	3.006	176	761
69	Wilbert Montgomery	107	1540	6789	4.408	6.247	230	1015
70	Chuck Muncie	110	1561	6702	4.293	4.621	227	975
71	Mark van Eeghen	136	1652	6651	4.026	0.770	194	782
72	Lawrence McCutcheon	109	1521	6578	4.325	4.979	223	966
73	Lydell Mitchell	111	1675	6534	3.901	-1.230	241	942
74	Arian Foster	80	1476	6527	4.422	3.558	295	1305
75	Wendell Tyler	108	1344	6378	4.746	9.446	199	945
76	Brian Westbrook	121	1385	6335	4.574	5.099	183	838
77	Floyd Little	117	1641	6323	3.853	-2.035	224	865
78	Larry Johnson	85	1428	6223	4.358	6.374	269	1171
79	Don Perkins	107	1500	6217	4.145	1.863	224	930
80	Ray Rice	92	1430	6180	4.322	1.258	249	1075
81	Neal Anderson	116	1515	6166	4.070	1.186	209	850
82	Michael Vick	143	873	6109	6.998	17.366	98	684
83	Ken Willard	132	1622	6105	3.764	-2.483	197	740
84	Deuce McAllister	96	1429	6096	4.266	1.644	238	1016
85	Travis Henry	89	1488	6086	4.090	-0.752	268	1094
86	Calvin Hill	156	1452	6083	4.189	1.820	149	624
87	Cedric Benson	96	1600	6017	3.761	-7.480	267	1003

5. Rusher Ratings

RK	RUSHER	G	ATT	YDS	Y/A	YRAA/G	A16G	Y16G
88	James Wilder	129	1586	6008	3.788	-2.816	197	745
89	William Andrews	87	1315	5986	4.552	8.745	242	1101
90	Rudi Johnson	91	1517	5979	3.941	-2.871	267	1051
91	Chuck Foreman	109	1556	5950	3.824	-2.183	228	873
92	LeGarrette Blount	116	1341	5888	4.391	2.416	185	812
93	Larry Brown	102	1530	5875	3.840	-2.478	240	922
94	Steve Van Buren	83	1320	5860	4.439	10.407	254	1130
95	James Stewart	101	1478	5841	3.952	-1.120	234	925
96	Bill Brown	194	1649	5838	3.540	-3.799	136	481
97	Rick Casares	130	1431	5797	4.051	-0.401	176	713
98	Duce Staley	114	1430	5785	4.045	-0.147	201	812
99	Fred Jackson	122	1305	5746	4.403	2.045	171	754
100	Greg Pruitt	158	1196	5672	4.742	5.920	121	574
101	Michael Pittman	151	1392	5627	4.042	-0.655	147	596
102	Pete Johnson	110	1489	5626	3.778	-2.564	217	818
103	Delvin Williams	100	1312	5598	4.267	3.951	210	896
104	Joe Morris	110	1411	5585	3.958	-0.471	205	812
105	Alfred Morris	91	1262	5503	4.361	2.413	222	968
106	Reggie Bush	134	1286	5490	4.269	0.618	154	656
107	Mike Garrett	104	1308	5481	4.190	2.368	201	843
108	Sam Cunningham	107	1385	5453	3.937	-0.403	207	815
109	Sammy Winder	127	1495	5427	3.630	-4.368	188	684
110	Darren McFadden	104	1302	5421	4.164	-0.586	200	834
111	Dick Bass	112	1218	5417	4.447	4.994	174	774
112	Jim Nance	101	1341	5401	4.028	1.212	212	856
113	Ronnie Brown	133	1281	5391	4.208	0.476	154	649
114	Willie Parker	79	1253	5378	4.292	3.191	254	1089
115	Mark Ingram	94	1183	5362	4.533	4.509	201	913
116	Joe Cribbs	102	1309	5356	4.092	1.404	205	840
T117	Jamal Anderson	88	1329	5336	4.015	0.078	242	970
T117	Le'Veon Bell	62	1229	5336	4.342	3.959	317	1377
119	Hugh McElhenny	143	1124	5281	4.698	5.244	126	591
120	Ryan Mathews	80	1184	5261	4.443	3.399	237	1052
121	Natrone Means	88	1409	5215	3.701	-3.653	256	948
122	Adrian Murrell	122	1375	5199	3.781	-2.095	180	682
T123	John Brockington	95	1347	5185	3.849	-2.469	227	873

RK	RUSHER	G	ATT	YDS	Y/A	YRAA/G	A16G	Y16G
T123	Marion Butts	104	1345	5185	3.855	-1.306	207	798
125	Lenny Moore	143	1069	5174	4.840	6.027	120	579
126	Ollie Matson	171	1170	5173	4.421	2.675	109	484
127	Clem Daniels	110	1146	5138	4.483	5.157	167	747
128	Emerson Boozer	118	1291	5135	3.978	-0.098	175	696
129	Kevin Mack	99	1291	5123	3.968	-0.470	209	828
130	Billy Sims	60	1131	5106	4.515	10.275	302	1362
131	Dexter Bussey	150	1203	5105	4.244	2.074	128	545
132	Brandon Jacobs	109	1141	5094	4.465	2.953	167	748
133	Mike Alstott	158	1359	5088	3.744	-2.563	138	515
134	Julius Jones	94	1280	5068	3.959	-2.374	218	863
135	John L Williams	149	1245	5006	4.021	0.418	134	538
136	Paul Lowe	100	1026	4995	4.868	9.571	164	799
137	John David Crow	125	1157	4963	4.290	2.394	148	635
138	Tyrone Wheatley	124	1270	4962	3.907	-1.403	164	640
139	Greg Bell	80	1204	4959	4.119	1.644	241	992
T140	Gale Sayers	68	991	4956	5.001	15.796	233	1166
T140	Dorsey Levens	144	1243	4955	3.986	-0.369	138	551
T142	Randall Cunningham	158	775	4928	6.359	11.696	78	499
T142	Ahmad Bradshaw	103	1083	4928	4.550	3.338	168	766
144	Christian Okoye	79	1246	4897	3.930	-0.952	252	992
145	Lamar Miller	91	1144	4891	4.275	1.545	201	860
146	Lamar Smith	115	1322	4853	3.671	-4.467	184	675
147	Chris Ivory	95	1112	4852	4.363	2.273	187	817
148	Joe Washington	119	1195	4839	4.049	0.651	161	651
149	Napoleon Kaufman	91	978	4792	4.900	9.866	172	843
150	Robert Newhouse	168	1160	4784	4.124	1.062	110	456
151	Marion Barber	99	1156	4780	4.135	-0.362	187	773
152	Chester Taylor	151	1160	4740	4.086	-0.463	123	502
153	Marion Motley	106	828	4720	5.700	12.466	125	712
154	Donny Anderson	126	1197	4696	3.923	-0.584	152	596
155	JD Smith	131	1100	4672	4.247	1.191	134	571
156	MacArthur Lane	133	1206	4656	3.861	-1.243	145	560
157	Stump Mitchell	116	986	4649	4.715	6.197	136	641
158	Tony Collins	106	1191	4647	3.902	-0.948	180	701
159	Tom Matte	142	1200	4646	3.872	-1.110	135	523

5. Rusher Ratings

RK	RUSHER	G	ATT	YDS	Y/A	YRAA/G	A16G	Y16G
160	Alex Webster	109	1196	4638	3.878	-2.312	176	681
161	Doug Martin	68	1150	4633	4.029	-2.676	271	1090
162	Abner Haynes	112	1036	4630	4.469	3.828	148	661
163	Bob Hoernschemeyer	113	1059	4548	4.295	2.157	150	644
164	Ted Brown	103	1117	4546	4.070	0.874	174	706
165	Marv Hubbard	103	951	4544	4.778	7.177	148	706
166	Dave Hampton	93	1148	4536	3.951	-1.004	198	780
167	Mike Rozier	92	1159	4462	3.850	-1.857	202	776
T168	Joseph Addai	78	1095	4453	4.067	-1.572	225	913
T168	Otis Armstrong	96	1023	4453	4.353	4.228	171	742
170	Ed Podolak	104	1157	4451	3.847	-1.625	178	685
171	Darrin Nelson	152	1020	4442	4.355	2.430	107	468
172	Harold Green	124	1151	4365	3.792	-1.441	149	563
173	Rob Carpenter	118	1172	4363	3.723	-2.623	159	592
174	Jim Otis	116	1160	4350	3.750	-2.320	160	600
175	Dave Osborn	143	1179	4336	3.678	-2.268	132	485
176	Cam Newton	109	828	4320	5.217	7.880	122	634
T177	Ron A Johnson	81	1204	4308	3.578	-6.418	238	851
T177	Altie Taylor	102	1170	4308	3.682	-3.584	184	676
179	Craig Heyward	149	1031	4301	4.172	1.599	111	462
180	Gary Brown	99	1032	4300	4.167	2.153	167	695
181	Cookie Gilchrist	65	1010	4293	4.250	3.597	249	1057
182	Matt Snell	87	1057	4285	4.054	1.381	194	788
183	Johnny Hector	126	1052	4280	4.068	0.580	134	543
184	Lorenzo White	107	1062	4242	3.994	0.377	159	634
185	Steve Young	169	722	4239	5.871	8.213	68	401
186	Rashard Mendenhall	72	1081	4236	3.919	-4.750	240	941
187	Tommy Mason	124	1040	4203	4.041	0.323	134	542
T188	Tony Canadeo	116	1025	4197	4.095	3.639	141	579
T188	Carl Garrett	110	1031	4197	4.071	0.623	150	610
190	Mike Thomas	77	1087	4196	3.860	-1.722	226	872
191	Earnest Jackson	81	1059	4167	3.935	-1.028	209	823
192	Dalton Hilliard	108	1126	4164	3.698	-2.918	167	617
193	Ryan Grant	67	956	4148	4.339	1.960	228	991
194	Errict Rhett	86	1174	4143	3.529	-5.148	218	771
195	Mercury Morris	99	804	4133	5.141	9.072	130	668

RK	RUSHER	G	ATT	YDS	Y/A	YRAA/G	A16G	Y16G
196	Shonn Greene	85	993	4110	4.139	-1.369	187	774
197	Johnny Johnson	72	1046	4078	3.899	-0.749	232	906
198	Tony Galbreath	170	1031	4072	3.950	-0.164	97	383
199	Mike Anderson	98	919	4067	4.425	3.324	150	664
200	Alan Ameche	70	964	4045	4.196	1.675	220	925
201	Cadillac Williams	81	1055	4038	3.827	-4.219	208	798
202	Nick Pietrosante	116	955	4026	4.216	1.130	132	555
203	Curtis Dickey	85	937	4019	4.289	3.364	176	757
204	Edgar Bennett	112	1115	3992	3.580	-3.271	159	570
205	Frank Pollard	111	953	3989	4.186	1.474	137	575
206	Kevan Barlow	84	1022	3984	3.898	-2.772	195	759
207	Leonard Russell	85	1164	3973	3.413	-6.692	219	748
208	Dick Hoak	135	1132	3965	3.503	-4.352	134	470
209	Leroy Hoard	253	1008	3964	3.933	0.033	64	251
210	Harvey Williams	110	1021	3952	3.871	-0.314	149	575
211	Barry Foster	62	915	3943	4.309	5.509	236	1018
212	BenJarvus Green-Ellis	85	1008	3914	3.883	-4.326	190	737
213	Anthony Thomas	87	1044	3891	3.727	-4.889	192	716
214	Justin Forsett	122	820	3890	4.744	3.737	108	510
215	Walt Garrison	119	899	3886	4.323	2.514	121	522
216	Randy McMillan	88	990	3876	3.915	-0.989	180	705
217	Rocky Bleier	140	928	3865	4.165	1.250	106	442
218	Timmy Brown	108	889	3862	4.344	2.899	132	572
219	Clarke Hinkle	100	1076	3529	3.280	-0.592	172	565
220	Wilbur Jackson	94	971	3852	3.967	0.036	165	656
221	Jon Arnett	123	964	3833	3.976	-0.735	125	499
222	Gerry Ellis	103	836	3826	4.577	4.711	130	594
T223	Bam Morris	74	974	3809	3.911	-0.325	211	824
T223	Pierre Thomas	110	833	3809	4.573	2.718	121	554
T225	Pete Banaszak	173	964	3772	3.913	-0.427	89	349
T225	Rashad Jennings	93	930	3772	4.056	-1.306	160	649
227	Jim Kiick	115	1029	3759	3.653	-3.073	143	523
228	Wendell Hayes	133	988	3758	3.804	-1.240	119	452
229	Johnny Roland	103	1015	3750	3.695	-2.764	158	583
230	Reggie Cobb	92	1065	3743	3.515	-5.177	185	651
231	LeMont Jordan	114	897	3734	4.163	0.471	126	524

RK	RUSHER	G	ATT	YDS	Y/A	YRAA/G	A16G	Y16G
232	Ron Dayne	96	983	3722	3.786	-3.264	164	620
233	Paul Hornung	104	893	3711	4.156	0.697	137	571
234	Michael Bennett	107	842	3703	4.398	2.174	126	554
235	Fran Tarkenton	246	675	3674	5.443	3.990	44	239
236	Rickey Young	131	1011	3666	3.626	-2.758	123	448
237	Clarence Peaks	105	951	3660	3.849	-2.190	145	558
238	Hoyle Granger	83	805	3653	4.538	5.742	155	704
239	Maurice Morris	145	867	3648	4.208	0.253	96	403
T240	Tank Younger	112	770	3640	4.727	5.094	110	520
T240	Clarence Davis	88	804	3640	4.527	5.045	146	662
242	James R Jones	135	1010	3626	3.590	-3.171	120	430
243	Knowshon Moreno	63	877	3616	4.123	-1.427	223	918
244	Eddie Lacy	60	857	3614	4.217	0.939	229	964
T245	Preston Pearson	176	941	3609	3.835	-0.756	86	328
T245	Frank Gifford	136	840	3609	4.296	1.558	99	425
247	Kevin Faulk	161	864	3607	4.175	0.293	86	358
248	Reuben Droughns	114	929	3602	3.877	-1.739	130	506
249	Steve McNair	161	669	3590	5.366	5.441	66	357
250	Bill Mathis	137	1044	3589	3.438	-4.436	122	419

6

Passer Ratings: NPR

Who is the greatest quarterback of all time? Is it Joe Montana, or John Elway, or Otto Graham? Brady or Peyton? Unfortunately, we will not answer that question here, but we will address the problems inherent in the NFL Passer Rating System (which we will abbreviate as PRS), and then use the design of the PRS to build a better, more sensible measurement.

The main problem with the PRS, as I see it, is that it favors contemporary quarterbacks because it rates them against fixed standards, and some of those standards have been constantly changing. The average completion percentage continues to creep upward, and the interception percentage continues to decline. As a result, most of the career highest rated passers according to PRS are mostly contemporary quarterbacks, and if you looked at a list of the career highest rated passers from, say, 1988, or 2000, most of them would have been active at that time. It always made more sense to me to rate players against their contemporaries instead of fixed standards, and from that I have developed a Normalized Passer Rating (NPR).

Before we start redesigning the PRS, we have to take a look at how the PRS works and show where the problems lie.

Passer Rating System (PRS) Explanation

The NFL PRS was first used in 1973, and it relies on four different factors to evaluate passers: Completion Percentage or completions divided by attempts (C/A), Yards per Attempt (Y/A), Touchdown Percentage (TD/A) and Interception Percentage (I/A). The four factors are weighed equally; each of the four is responsible for 25 percent of the rating. Points are awarded for each of the four categories, and a passer can receive between zero and 2.375 points for each category.

To demonstrate how the PRS works, we'll apply it to Terry Bradshaw's 1978 season. Here are Bradshaw's regular season statistics for 1978:

Attempts or A = 368
Completions or C = 207
Yards or Y = 2915
Touchdown Passes or TD = 28
Interceptions or I = 20

The completions, yards, touchdowns, and interceptions have to be divided by attempts in order to be used in the formulas:

6. Passer Ratings

Completion Percentage (C/A) = 207 / 368 = 0.5625
Yards per Attempts (Y/A) = 2915/368 = 7.9212
Touchdown Percentage (TD/A) = 28 / 368 = 0.0761
Interception Percentage (I/A) = 20 / 368 = 0.0543

There are four formulas for determining points awarded for each category:

For Completion Percentage, the formula is: 5 * (C/A - 0.3)
C/A Points or P = 5 * (0.5625-0.3) = 5 * 0.2625 = 1.3125

For Yards per Attempt, the formula is: ((Y/A) - 3) / 4
Y/A P = (7.9212 - 3) / 4 = 4.9212 / 4 = 1.2303

The Touchdown Percentage formula is 20 * (TD/A).
TD/A P = 20 * 0.0761 = 1.5217

The Interception Percentage formula is ((0.095 - (I/A)) / 0.04)
I/A P = ((0.095 - 0.0543) / 0.04) = ((0.0407) / 0.04) = 1.0163

Finally, the four scores have to be added together and the sum is multiplied by fifty and divided by three:

Passer Rating or PR = (50 / 3) * (C/A P + Y/A+ TD/A P + I/A P)
PR = (50 / 3) * (1.3125 + 1.2303 + 1.5217 + 1.0163) = (50/3) * (5.0808) = 84.681

This was a good figure, enough for Bradshaw to lead the AFC and finish second in the NFL, just behind Roger Staubach of Dallas, who had a PR of 84.91.

Bradshaw's 1978 rating of 84.681 would have been good enough to finish ninth in the AFC in 2005. When it gets to the point where a league leading performance in 1978 is middle of the pack in 2005, there is clearly something wrong with the system. As a comparison here are the statistics for the 2005 AFC PR leader, Peyton Manning of Indianapolis:

Attempts = 453
Completions = 305; Completion Percentage (C/A) = 305 / 453 = 0.6733
Yards = 3747; Yards per Attempts (Y/A) = 3747 / 453 = 8.2715
Touchdowns = 28; Touchdown Percentage (TD/A) = 28 / 453 = 0.0618
Interceptions = 10; Interception Percentage (I/A) = 10 / 453 = 0.0221

C/A P = (0.6733 - 0.3) / 2 = 0.3733 / 0.2 = 1.8664
Y/A P = (8.2715 - 3) / 4 = 4.9212 / 4 = 1.3179
TD/A P = (0.0618 / 0.05) = 1.2360
I/A P = (0.095 - 0.0221) / 04 = ((0.0729) / 0.04) = 1.8225
PR = (50 / 3) * (1.8664 + 1.3179 + 1.2360 + 1.8225) = (50 / 3) * (6.2428) = 104.061

The PRS was designed that an average passer would score a 66.67, which is the average, if they got a point in every category.

PR = (50 / 3) * (1+1+1+1) = (50 / 3) * (4) = 200 / 3 = 66.667

The object of the NPR is to create a system where the weighted league average in each season comes in close to 66.667.

To determine the average PR in 1978 and 2005 plug the league statistics into the PRS formulas.

1978	2005
Attempts = 11829	Attempts = 16464
Completions = 6278; C/A P = 1.154	Completions = 9790; C/A P = 1.473
Yards = 79557; Y/A P = 0.931	Yards = 111721; Y/A P = 0.947
Touchdowns = 468; TD/A P = 0.791	Touchdowns = 644; TD/A P = 0.782
Interceptions = 639; I/A P 1.025	Interceptions = 506; I/A P = 1.601
PR = 65.014	PR = 80.143

As shown below, the average PR has increased quite a bit between 1978 and 2005, and the increase has been due to a higher C/A and lower I/A. The other two factors (Y/A and TD/A) have remained relatively stable since the merger, with the league Y/A staying pretty much between 6.5 and 7.2 yards per attempt and TD/A staying between 3.9 and 4.5 percent. Passer Rating has been steadily increasing upward throughout pro football history due to the rising completion percentage and dropping interception percentage.

Figure 6.1 displays a graph of the average league Passer Rating, or PR (y) per season (x):

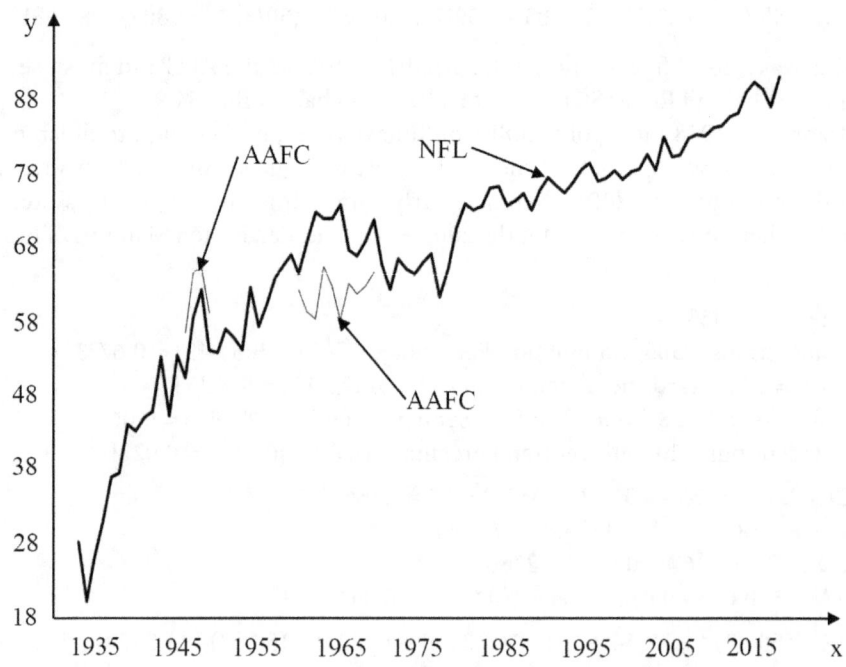

Figure 6.1. Graph of league Passer Rating by season, 1933–2018 for NFL, AAFC and AFL.

Figure 6.1 illustrates the problem with rating passers with this statistic, the league average for PR is increasing nearly every season.

By the way, did you happen to notice where the average league PR jumped between 1977 and 1980? It went from 60.5 in 1977 to 64.6 in 1978 to 70.3 in 1979 to 73.7 in 1980. That leap is in response to the rule changes in 1978 that opened up the passing game and increased offense.

If you plot the league average of Completion Percentage, or C/A (y) by season (x), you would have Figure 6.2:

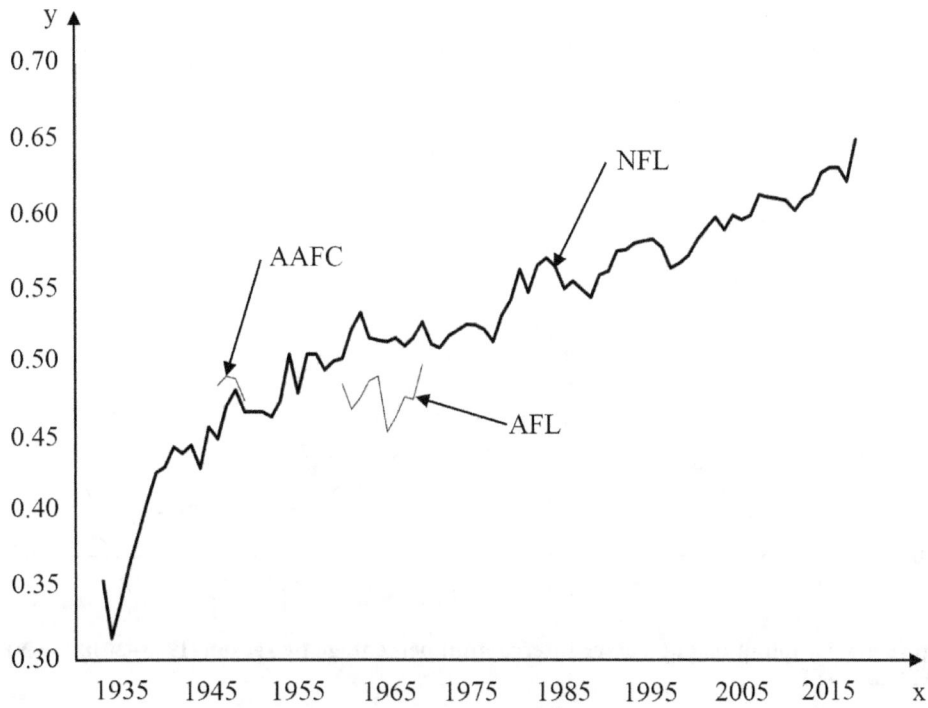

Figure 6.2. Graph of league passer completion percentage by season, 1933–2018 for NFL, AAFC and AFL.

As you can see, completion percentage has been steadily increasing, and shot up from 62.1 percent to 64.9 percent between 2017 and 2018. The reasons for this would include a continued reliance on the short to medium passing games (i.e., the West Coast offense) along with the catching gloves that have come into vogue in the past five years or so.

As a purist of sorts, I don't like the Stickum gloves at all. I think they artificially inflate the passing and receiving statistics in a manner not unlike the steroid epidemic in baseball inflated home runs and made a mockery of the game, and if I were Commissioner of the NFL, I would ban them.

Figure 6.3 is the graph for Interception Percentage (I/A) (y) by season (x). As you can see, Figure 6.3 is inverted compared to the two earlier graphs, and it makes sense, because it is better to have a lower I/A on offense as opposed to the other categories.

Now it's time to build the new measurement. Be forewarned, we're going to get into some algebraic equations, but stick with me, it makes sense.

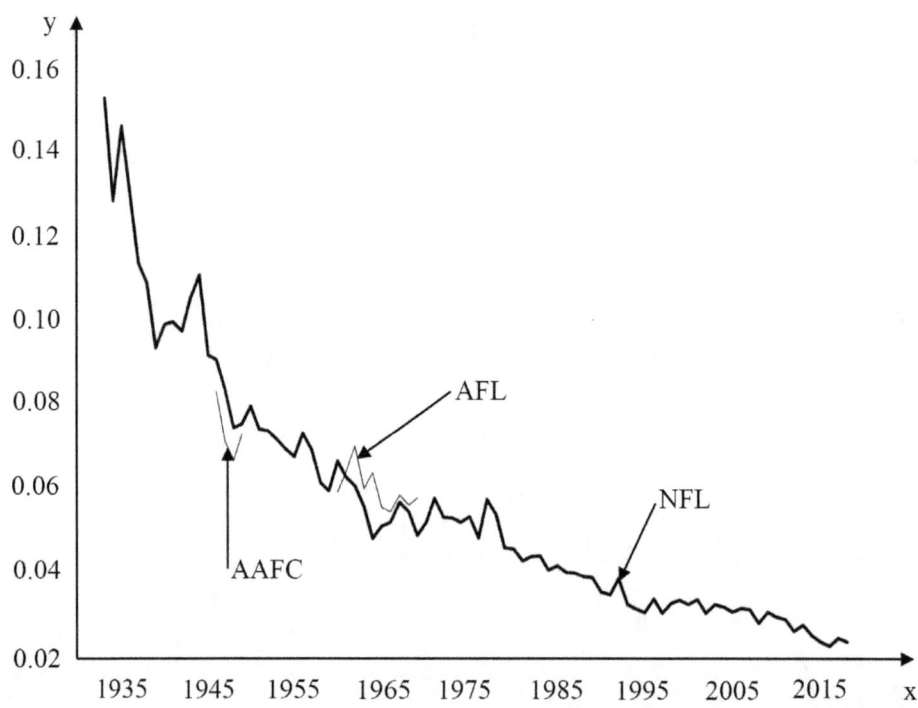

Figure 6.3. Graph of league passer interception percentage by season, 1933–2018 for NFL, AAFC and AFL.

NPR—Using League Averages Instead of Standards

To fix the PR system, we must first understand how the system was put together and we'll start with Completion Percentage, or C/A. When the PRS was developed, passing statistics were analyzed between 1950 and 1970 and an average performance in C/A was determined to be 50 percent, an outstanding performance was determined to be 70 percent, and a poor performance was determined to be 30 percent. Translating the above figures to points awarded by the system, and a ratio of the C/A divided by the average performance, as shown in Table 6.1:

Table 6.1
Completion % to Ratio Comparison for PRS

C/A	POINTS	RATIO
.70	2	.70/.50 = 1.40 * average performance
.50	1	.50/.50 = 1.00 or average performance
.30	0	.30/.50 = 0.60 * average performance

There are two small rules to keep in mind with respect to the points a passer can accumulate in a particular category, the maximum number is 2.375 and the minimum is zero. In all PR categories, two points is considered outstanding, one point is average and zero points is poor.

If we substitute the league average performance for a particular season in place of the standardized "average" performance as determined by the PRS in Table 6.1, we are left with:

Table 6.2
Points to League Completion % for NPR

POINTS	RATIO
2	1.4 * League Average C/A
1	1 * League Average C/A
0	0.6 * League Average C/A

When we rate a passer against the league average in a particular season, it is actually the league average with the particular passer's statistics removed, so in effect he is being rated against the average performance of the rest of the league that season similar to what we did with YRAA. What that means is that we'll substitute the term "League Average C/A" from Table 6.2 with player and league passing statistical variables, as shown in Table 6.3:

Table 6.3
Algebraic Substitution of Values from Table 6.2

POINTS	RATIO
2	1.4 * (LC-PC) / (LAT-PAT)
1	(LC-PC) / (LAT-PAT)
0	0.6 * (LC-PC) / (LAT-PAT)

LC, PC = League Completions, Passer Completions
LAT, PAT = League Attempts, Passer Attempts

The basic form for converting performance to points or P is:

$$P = (\text{Player Performance} - \text{Zero Point Value}) / (\text{One Point Value} - \text{Zero Point Value})$$

The One and Zero-Point Values are the places where one and zero points are awarded on the above table, and in the case of completion percentage it is 100 percent and 60 percent of the league average with the player's statistics removed, respectively. The difference between the one-point value and the zero-point value, is the league average minus 60 percent of the league average, or 40 percent of the league average.

Converting this into an algebraic formula and solving for Points (P):

$$N\ C/A\ P = ((PC/PAT) - (0.6 * ((LC - PC)/(LAT - PAT)) / (0.4 * ((LC - PC)/(LAT - PAT))))$$

Simplifying it to make it easier to work with:

$$N\ C/A\ P = ((5*(PC/PAT))/(2*(LC - PC)/(LAT - PAT))) - 1.5$$

For converting Yards per Attempt (or Y/A), Table 6.4 shows the Y/A and Points:

Table 6.4
Yards/Attempt to Ratio Comparison for PRS

Y/A	POINTS	RATIO
11	2	11/7 = 1.571 * average performance
7	1	7/7 = 1.000 or average performance
3	0	3/7 = 0.429 * average performance

Substituting the league average for the one-point performance from Table 6.4, we now have Table 6.5:

Table 6.5
Points to League Yards/Attempt Ratio for NPR

POINTS	RATIO
2	1.571 (OR 11/7) * League Average Y/A
1	1*League Average Y/A
0	0.429 (OR 3/7) * League Average Y/A

The League Average will be defined as (LY-PY)/(LAT - PAT).

LY, PY = League Passing Yards, Passer Yards
LAT, PAT = League Attempts, Passer Attempts

Table 6.6
Algebraic Substitution of Values from Table 6.5

POINTS	RATIO
2	1.571 * (LY - PY) / (LAT - PAT)
1	(LY - PY) / (LAT - PAT)
0	0.429 * (LY - PY) / (LAT - PAT)

The formula, using the above format for converting performance to P:

$$N\ Y/A\ P = ((PY/PAT) - ((3/7) * (LY - PY)/(LAT - PAT))/ ((LY - PY)/(LAT - PAT) - (3/7) * (LY - PY)/(LAT - PAT))$$

Simplifying the equation:

$$N\ Y/A\ P = [(PY/PAT) / ((4/7) * (LY - PY)/(LAT - PAT))] - 3/4$$

For Touchdown Percentage (TD/A):

Table 6.7
Touchdown % to Ratio Comparison for PRS

TD/A	POINTS	RATIO
.10	2	.10/.05 = 2.00 * average performance
.05	1	.05/.05 = 1.00 or average performance
0	0	.00/.05 = 0 * average performance or 0

Table 6.8
Points to League Touchdown % for NPR

POINTS	RATIO
2	2 * League Average TD/A
1	1 * League Average TD/A
0	0 * League Average TD/A or 0

Since the Zero Value is zero for Touchdowns, the formula will instead be:

Points = Player Performance / League Average

N TD/A P = (PTD/PAT) / ((LTD - PTD)/(LAT - PAT))

PTD, LTD = Passer Touchdowns, League Touchdowns

PAT, LAT = Passer Attempts, League Attempts

No algebraic simplification is necessary.

Interceptions are handled a little differently. If you remember the graph of interception average per season, it was reversed, which meant a lower I/A was better than a higher one. This means the formula for converting performance to P will also have to be reversed:

I/A P = (Zero Value—Player Performance) / (Zero Value—One Value)

Table 6.9
Interception % to Ratio Comparison for PRS

I/A	POINTS	RATIO
.015	2	0.015/0.055 = 0.273 * average performance
.055	1	0.055/0.055 = 1.00 or average performance
.095	0	0.095/0.055 = 1.727 * average performance

Table 6.10
Points to League Interception % for NPR

POINTS	RATIO
2	0.273 (OR 3/11) * League Average I/A
1	1 * League Average I/A
0	1.727 (OR 19/11) * League Average I/A

PI, LI = Passer Interceptions, League Interceptions

PAT, LAT = Passer Attempts, League Attempts

Table 6.11
Algebraic Substitution of Values from Table 6.10

POINTS	RATIO
2	0.273 * (LI - PI) / (LAT - PAT)
1	(LI - PI) / (LAT - PAT)
0	1.727 * (LI - PI) / (LAT - PAT)

$$N\ I/A\ P = (((19/11) * ((LI - PI)/(LAT - PAT)) - (PI/PAT)) / ((19/11) * ((LI - PI)/(LAT - PAT)) - (LI - PI)/(LAT - PAT)))$$

Simplifying the equation:

$$N\ I/A\ P = (19/8\ or\ 2.375) - [(PI/PAT)/ ((8/11) * ((LI - PI)/(LAT - PAT)))]$$

Putting the four formulas we just created back into the main formula to create a Normalized Passer Rating, or NPR:

$$N\ C/A\ P = ((5*(PC/PAT))/(2*(LC-PC)/(LAT - PAT))) - 1.5$$
$$N\ Y/A\ P = [(PY/PAT) / ((4/7) * (LY - PY)/(LAT - PAT))] - 0.75$$
$$N\ TD/A\ P = (PTD/PAT) / ((LTD - PTD)/(LAT - PAT))$$
$$N\ I/A\ P = 2.375 - [(PI/PAT)/ ((8/11) * ((LI - PI)/(LAT - PAT)))]$$
$$NPR = (50/3) * (N\ C/A\ P + N\ Y/A\ P + N\ TD/A\ P + N\ I/A\ P)$$

Keep in mind that the two rules that the maximum P score is 2.375 and the minimum P score is zero for any of the four categories.

We'll use the aforementioned league passing statistics and player statistics to determine the NPR for Bradshaw and Manning.

Bradshaw's 1978 NPR:
$$N\ C/A\ P = ((5*(207/368)) / (2*(6278 - 207) / (11829 - 368))) - 1.5 = 1.155$$
$$N\ Y/A\ P = (2915/368) / ((4/7) * (79557 - 2915)/ (11829 - 368)) - 3/4 = 1.323$$
$$N\ TD/A\ P = (28/368) / ((468 - 28) / (11829 - 368)) = 1.982$$
$$N\ I/A\ P = (19/8) - ((20/368) / ((8/11) * ((639 - 20) / (11829 - 368)))) = 0.991$$
$$NPR = (50/3) * (1.155 + 1.323 + 1.982 + 0.991) = 90.849$$

Manning's 2005 NPR:
$$N\ C/A\ P = ((5*(305/453)) / (2*(9790 - 305) / (16464 - 453))) - 1.5 = 1.341$$
$$N\ Y/A\ P = ((3747/453) / ((4/7) * (111721 - 3747) / (16464 - 453)) - 0.75 = 1.396$$
$$N\ TD/A\ P = (28/453) / ((644 - 28) / (16464 - 453)) = 1.607$$
$$N\ I/A\ P = (2.375) - ((10/453) / ((8/11) * ((506 - 10) / (16464 - 453)))) = 1.395$$
$$NPR = (50/3) * (1.341 + 1.396 + 1.607 + 1.395) = 95.659$$

When you compare them relative to the season in which they played, Manning still comes out ahead of Bradshaw, but they are much closer. Peyton 2005 dropped from 105.06 to 95.659 between PR and NPR, while Bradshaw 1978 improved from 84.681 to 90.849.

Final Adjustment

As I mentioned earlier, the average NPR for the entire league for each season has to come out at 66.667 (or something close to it) in order to directly compare passers from different seasons. We're close, very close right now; we can tell by looking at the weighted average of NPR for 2005. But we're not close. This needs to be very, very close.

The weighted average for each passer was found by multiplying the passer's NPR by the number of passes he attempted; in other words, Peyton's NPR multiplied by the number of passes he attempted. After doing that for every quarterback in the league in 2005, and adding all of those products together, then dividing that sum by the total number of

6. Passer Ratings

pass attempts in the league in 2005. When you do that, the weighted average of NPR for the 2005 NFL dropped to 66.984.

By comparison, the weighted average of PR (using PR instead of NPR) for the 2005 NFL was 80.072, which shows how far we have come. This is documented in Table 6.12, with passers ranked by attempts. An aggregate sum (SUM) row was added underneath, along with an average (AVG), which is aggregate NPR*ATT divided by aggregate ATT:

Table 6.12
Abbreviated List of 2005 NFL Passers, PR*Attempts and NPR*Attempts

PASSER	TM	YR	ATT	PR	PR*ATT	NPR	NPR*ATT
Brett Favre	G B	05N	607	70.871	43018.697	50.056	30384.07
Kerry Collins	OAK	05N	565	77.297	43672.805	67.347	38051.06
Eli Manning	NYG	05N	557	75.857	42252.349	63.622	35437.49
Tom Brady	N E	05N	530	92.256	48895.680	81.296	43086.77
Carson Palmer	CIN	05N	509	101.101	51460.409	92.165	46912.05
(90 percent of the list edited for brevity)							
Tony Fisher	G B	05N	1	118.750	118.750	118.750	118.750
DeShaun Foster	CAR	05N	1	39.583	39.583	39.58	39.583
Samkon Gado	G B	05N	1	39.583	39.583	39.58	39.583
Keyshawn Johnson	DAL	05N	1	39.583	39.583	39.58	39.583
BJ Sandler	G B	05N	1	83.833	83.833	83.833	83.833
SUM			16464		1318304.313		1102824.24
AVG				80.072		66.984	

Note that most of the passers are missing from Table 6.12 so the list doesn't run a couple pages longer, but the sum is for all NFL passers not just those listed. We're close, very close. Here's how we get very, very close.

A small adjustment needs to be made to the NPR to ensure the average NPR for the league comes in at 66.667. The method I chose was to take the P or point scores for each passer (C/A P, Y/A P, TD/A P and I/A P) and individually adjust each of those four factors so the weighted average of each of the factors came out an average of 1.000 for the entire league,

We'll return to our partial list of 2005 NFL passers ranked by attempts from Table 6.12, but instead, we'll display attempts (ATT), C/A P, and attempts multiplied by C/A P (ATT*P), with the aggregate or total sum row, and an average (AVG) row, which is aggregate ATT*P divided by aggregate ATT, at the bottom:

Table 6.13
Abbreviated List of 2005 NFL Passers, ATT*P

PASSER	TM	YL	ATT	C/A P	ATT*P
Brett Favre	G B	05N	607	1.080	655.332
Kerry Collins	OAK	05N	565	0.739	417.650
Eli Manning	NYG	05N	557	0.710	395.718

PASSER	TM	YL	ATT	C/A P	ATT*P
Tom Brady	N E	05N	530	1.155	612.032
Carson Palmer	CIN	05N	509	1.362	693.481
(90 percent of the list edited for brevity)					
Tony Fisher	G B	05N	1	2.704	2.375
DeShaun Foster	CAR	05N	1	-1.500	0.000
Samkon Gado	G B	05N	1	-1.500	0.000
Keyshawn Johnson	DAL	05N	1	-1.500	0.000
BJ Sandler	G B	05N	1	2.704	2.375
SUM			16464		16498.327
AVG				0.998	

For Brett Favre, his attempts (607) was multiplied by his Completion Percentage P score (1.080), which equals 655.332. In order to figure out the adjustment, look at the SUM row in Table 6.13, and the adjustment is made by dividing total attempts by total weighted P score (A*P), or 16464 divided by 16498.327, which equals 0.998. (Note that on the lowest passers on the list, their C/A P score was either below zero or above 2.375, and was corrected accordingly before the P score was multiplied by attempts.) The C/A P score for each passer is multiplied by the adjustment or ADJ as follows, in Table 6.14:

Table 6.14
Abbreviated List of 2005 NFL Passers, ATT*P*ADJ

PASSER	TM	YL	ATT	P	ATT * P	ADJ	ATT*P*ADJ
B Favre	G B	05N	607	1.080	655.332	0.998	653.969
K Collins	OAK	05N	565	0.739	417.650	0.998	416.781
E Manning	NYG	05N	557	0.710	395.718	0.998	394.895
T Brady	N E	05N	530	1.155	612.032	0.998	610.758
C Palmer	CIN	05N	509	1.362	693.481	0.998	692.038
(90 percent of the list edited for brevity)							
T Fisher	G B	05N	1	2.704	2.375	0.998	2.370
D Foster	CAR	05N	1	-1.500	0.000	0.998	0.000
S Gado	G B	05N	1	-1.500	0.000	0.998	0.000
K. Johnson	DAL	05N	1	-1.500	0.000	0.998	0.000
BJ Sandler	G B	05N	1	2.704	2.375	0.998	2.370
SUM			16464		16498.327		16464.000

When the attempts are multiplied by the adjusted or final C/A P, the sum of that product for all the passers (16464.000) in the SUM row for Table 6.14 equals the number of attempts, this is a confirmation that the adjustment is correct. This ADJ for C/A (0.998) will be abbreviated AC/A.

The same procedure will be performed in Table 6.15, with Y/A P (which we'll abbreviate as Y) multiplying the Y score by attempts for every passer, with SUM and AVG rows:

Table 6.15
Abbreviated List of 2005 NFL Passers, ATT*Y

PASSER	TM	YL	ATT	Y	ATT*Y
Brett Favre	G B	05N	607	0.895	543.422
Kerry Collins	OAK	05N	565	0.965	544.995
Eli Manning	NYG	05N	557	0.992	552.282
Tom Brady	N E	05N	530	1.259	667.496
Carson Palmer	CIN	05N	509	1.200	611.029
(90 percent of the list edited for brevity)					
Tony Fisher	G B	05N	1	2.375	2.375
DeShaun Foster	CAR	05N	1	0.000	0.000
Samkon Gado	G B	05N	1	0.000	0.000
Keyshawn Johnson	DAL	05N	1	0.000	0.000
BJ Sandler	G B	05N	1	0.282	0.282
SUM			16464		16489.476
AVG				0.998	

The adjustment from the SUM and AVG rows of Table 6.15 will be 16464/16489.476 or 0.998, each passer's ATT*Y will be multiplied by 0.998, and the process of multiplying the final adjusted value by attempts is repeated in Table 6.16:

Table 6.16
Abbreviated List of 2005 NFL Passers, ATT*Y*ADJ

PASSER	TM	YL	ATT	Y	ATT * Y	ADJ	ATT*Y*ADJ
B Favre	G B	05N	607	0.895	543.422	0.998	542.582
K Collins	OAK	05N	565	0.965	544.995	0.998	544.153
E Manning	NYG	05N	557	0.992	552.282	0.998	551.429
T Brady	N E	05N	530	1.259	667.496	0.998	666.465
C Palmer	CIN	05N	509	1.200	611.029	0.998	610.085
(90 percent of the list edited for brevity)							
T Fisher	G B	05N	1	2.375	2.375	0.998	2.371
D Foster	CAR	05N	1	0.000	0.000	0.998	0.000
S Gado	G B	05N	1	0.000	0.000	0.998	0.000
K Johnson	DAL	05N	1	0.000	0.000	0.998	0.000
BJ Sandler	G B	05N	1	0.282	0.282	0.998	0.281
SUM			16464		16489.476		16464.000

Again, the adjustment is correct, and the adjustment for Y/A (0.998) will be abbreviated AY/A. The same process will be repeated for TD/A P and I/A P, which I will not go through.

The adjustment will be different for every season and for every one of the four P factors, and will always be very small, almost always between 0.95 and 1.05. Each of those adjustments has to be multiplied by the corresponding P value for each player.

The NPR formula with final adjustment becomes:

$$NPR = (50/3) * [(AC/A * N C/A P) + (AY/A * N Y/A P) + (ATD/A * N TD/A P) + (AI/A * N I/A P)]$$

We'll calculate Peyton Manning's adjusted NPR for 2005, since we already have his point values in the four categories. Manning's 2005 NPR points and 2005 NFL adjustments for the corresponding categories:

N C/A P = 1.341	AC/A = 0.998
N Y/A P = 1.396	AY/A = 0.998
N TD/A P = 1.607	ATD/A = 1.005
N I/A P = 1.395	AI/A = 0.980

NPR = (50/3) * [(0.998 * 1.341) + (0.998 * 1.396) + (1.005 * 1.607) + (0.980 * 1.395)] = (50/3) * [1.339 + 1.394 + 1.615 + 1.367] = (50/3) * (5.715) = 95.246

Table 6.17 demonstrates how the raw, unadjusted NPR (what we started with) compares to the final, adjusted NPR for the 2005 passers:

Table 6.17
Abbreviated List of 2005 NFL Passers, NPR*ATT

PASSER	TM	YL	ATT	CMP	YDS	TD	INT	RAW NPR	NPR	NPR * ATT
Brett Favre	G B	05N	607	372	3881	20	29	50.056	50.001	30350.607
K Collins	OAK	05N	565	302	3759	20	12	67.347	66.894	37795.110
E Manning	NYG	05N	557	294	3762	24	17	63.622	63.328	35273.696
Tom Brady	N E	05N	530	334	4110	26	14	81.296	80.930	42892.900
C Palmer	CIN	05N	509	345	3836	32	12	92.165	91.781	46716.529
(90 percent of the list edited for brevity)										
T Fisher	G B	05N	1	1	14	0	0	118.750	117.82	117.817
D Foster	CAR	05N	1	0	0	0	0	39.583	38.79	38.794
S Gado	G B	05N	1	0	0	0	0	39.583	38.79	38.794
K Johnson	DAL	05N	1	0	0	0	0	39.583	38.79	38.794
BJ Sandler	G B	05N	1	1	4	0	0	83.833	82.98	82.980
SUM			16464							1097599.46
AVG										66.666634

The average NPR for all the passers in the entire league, weighted by attempts, comes in at 66.666634, as shown in the AVG row in Table 6.17. I intentionally ran it out to six decimal places just to demonstrate how mathematically close this is to 66.6667. This is what I call very, very close.

6. Passer Ratings

As far as the two player-seasons we covered earlier in the chapter, Terry Bradshaw and, the final adjustment changed Bradshaw's 1978 NPR from 90.849 to 90.214 and Peyton Manning's 2005 NPR from 95.659 to 95.246.

This is how the NPR system works for rating passers.

Lists Disclaimer

Now come a couple lists; we'll start with a pair of lists of the top 25 passers ranked by attempts and then the top and bottom 25 in NPR with more than 1500 career attempts. I also listed career PR and NPR; the career ratings are figured by multiplying the PR or NPR in each season by the number of pass attempts in that season, and those seasonal products are added up and the career total is divided by career attempts.

In the career section, since the AAFC statistics are not officially recognized by the NFL as the AFL statistics are, I have decided in the case of Frankie Albert and Otto Graham to create two separate listings for them, one with their complete career statistics (AAFC and NFL) and the other NFL statistics only, when determining career passer ratings. The NFL stats only versions of Albert and Graham have NFL after their name (such as O GRAHAM NFL), if there is no NFL after their name on the list (such as O GRAHAM), then it is the combined AAFC and NFL stats. In cases where both versions of the same person appeared on the career list, I added an extra player to the top 25 to make up for the extra position being taken up by the duplicate, to ensure 25 unique individuals appeared in the top 25 career lists.

Table 6.18
25 Highest Career PR and NPR Values, Minimum 1500 Attempts

RK	PASSER	PR	RK	PASSER	NPR
1	Aaron Rodgers	102.860	1	Otto Graham	96.094
2	Russell Wilson	99.892	2	Sid Luckman	94.372
3	Drew Brees	97.630	3	Sammy Baugh	92.051
4	Tom Brady	97.510	4	Steve Young	90.342
5	Tony Romo	97.105		Otto Graham NFL	90.133
6	Steve Young	96.664	5	Aaron Rodgers	89.309
7	Peyton Manning	96.460	6	Len Dawson	88.849
8	Phillip Rivers	95.493	7	Roger Staubach	86.518
9	Matt Ryan	94.652	8	Joe Montana	86.435
10	Kirk Cousins	94.610	9	Tom Brady	84.756
11	Ben Roethlisberger	94.152	10	Peyton Manning	83.338
12	Kurt Warner	93.713	11	Norm Van Brocklin	82.473
13	Joe Montana	92.258	12	Frankie Albert	82.389
14	Chad Pennington	90.081	13	Russell Wilson	81.616
15	Andrew Luck	89.364	14	Sonny Jurgensen	81.423

RK	PASSER	PR	RK	PASSER	NPR
16	Matt Schaub	89.192	15	Drew Brees	81.271
17	Colin Kaepernick	88.892	16	Tony Romo	80.788
18	Marcus Mariota	88.742	17	Ken Anderson	80.725
19	Andy Dalton	88.629	18	Kurt Warner	80.634
20	Nick Foles	88.363	19	Fran Tarkenton	80.604
21	Derek Carr	88.363	20	Bob Griese	80.345
22	Matthew Stafford	88.247	21	Dan Marino	79.170
23	Carson Palmer	87.892	22	Bart Starr	78.957
24	Daunte Culpepper	87.778	23	Daryle Lamonica	78.457
25	Jeff Garcia	87.544	24	Bert Jones	78.036
			25	YA Tittle	77.706

Eight of the top 12 in career PR, and 16 of the top 25, were active in 2018. By comparison, only four of the top 25 in career NPR (Rodgers, Brady, Wilson and Brees) played in 2018. It is perhaps the most damning indictment of the Passer Rating system that nearly half of the NFL's current starting quarterbacks (except for Matt Schaub, who threw seven passes as Matt Ryan's backup in Atlanta) comprise the list of highest career passer ratings of all time.

Perhaps the biggest surprise on the NPR list is Frankie Albert at number 12, and his score was inflated by his AAFC stats, or his peak coincided with the AAFC seasons. His AAFC (1946–49) PR/NPR totals of 83.37/90.06 are much higher than his NFL (1950–52) totals of 57.73/70.10. There was also a drop in Otto Graham's PR and NPR between the AAFC and his NFL years (1950–55), from 99.10/104.89 for AAFC to 78.17/90.13 for NFL. His AAFC stats were extraordinary, and surely inflated due to the inferior competition (Luckman effect), but his standalone NFL stats were outstanding on their own accord.

Only nine passers appear on both lists; three are already in the Hall of Fame (Montana, Young and Warner), and four of the other six are locks or near-locks to make the HOF. Tony Romo had a good career but came up short of Canton, and it's too early in Russell Wilson's career to judge, but he's well on his way.

Of the nine retired passers on the PR list, three are in the HOF and Peyton Manning is a lock. On the other hand, 15 of the 21 retired passers from the NPR list are already in Canton, and Peyton is a lock and I think Ken Anderson will eventually get in also.

Table 6.19
25 Lowest Career Passer PR and NPR Values Minimum 1500 Attempts

RK	PASSER	PR	RK	PASSER	NPR
1	Frank Tripucka	53.125	1	Rick Mirer	49.742
2	Mike Phipps	53.199	2	Mark Sanchez	51.647
3	Cotton Davidson	55.110	3	Mike Phipps	52.193
4	Jeff Kemp	57.447	4	Mark Malone	52.758
5	Frankie Albert NFL	57.734	5	Rex Grossman	53.320

RK	PASSER	PR	RK	PASSER	NPR
6	Tobin Rote	57.735	6	Derek Anderson	53.482
7	Dan Pastorini	59.121	7	Jack Trudeau	53.494
8	Babe Parilli	60.602	8	Joey Harrington	54.055
9	George Blanda	61.369	9	Kyle Boller	54.147
10	Mark Malone	61.893	10	Dave Brown	54.673
11	Bob Waterfield	62.378	11	Mike Pagel	55.086
12	Eddie LeBaron	63.087	12	Chad Henne	55.424
13	Mike Pagel	63.291	13	Blake Bortles	55.482
14	Ed Brown	63.402	14	Trent Dilfer	55.818
15	Mike Livingston	63.415	15	Billy Joe Tolliver	57.013
16	Rick Mirer	63.531	16	Kordell Stewart	57.679
17	Bobby Layne	63.584	17	Marc Wilson	58.292
18	Jack Trudeau	63.770	18	Ryan Fitzpatrick	58.581
19	Joe Namath	65.505	19	Josh Freeman	59.101
20	Norm Snead	65.543	20	Mike Tomczak	59.276
21	Jim Hart	66.561	21	Dan Pastorini	59.406
22	Archie Manning	67.101	22	Matt Cassel	59.519
23	Jim Zorn	67.333	23	David Carr	59.686
24	Jim Plunkett	67.451	24	Rodney Peete	59.850
25	John Hadl	67.473	25	Cotton Davidson	60.142

Four of the 25 worst in career PR are in the HOF (Blanda, Waterfield, Layne and Namath), and none of the 25 were active in 2018.

None of the 25 worst in career NPR are in the HOF, and six played in the 2018 season.

Peyton Manning appears in the top 25 career PR and NPR list, while his father Archie finished in the bottom 25 in career PR.

The only reason Ryan Leaf did not top the worst career lists is that he didn't last long enough to get 1500 career attempts. Based on his 665 career pass attempts, his PR was 49.96 and his NPR was 32.46.

Derek Carr is in the top 25 in PR, while his brother David is in the bottom 25 in NPR.

The Luckman Effect

Before I present the best and worst individual single season NPR lists, I wanted to bring attention to a problem with NPR, or any type of system where you rate people against their peers, such as PAL, which we'll get to shortly. I call it the Luckman Effect which is when in a small league of ten teams or less, if one passer has a great season and the rest of the passers in the league are rather mediocre or worse, it makes the

Sid Luckman or Sammy Baugh or Lou Groza (in PAL and PAL2 ratings, which we'll get to in Chapter 7) look much better by comparison as he is rated by the average performance of the rest of the league once his own stats are removed from the league stats.

In some cases, due to the law of averages, in a small league, the average performance level of the rest of the league except for the guy in question will be well below average, which will artificially make him look much better. It is a sample size issue. The more teams there are in the league, the less likely it is for this to occur. In a 32-team league, there is no chance you could have one really good quarterback and 31 quarterbacks who are all average or below average; the odds against that are astronomical. In an 8 or 10-team league, it is very possible that this can occur.

In late '30s and early–mid '40s NFL, you had two outstanding quarterbacks, Luckman and Baugh, and you had Arnie Herber of Green Bay who was also pretty good. For the most part, the rest were fair to poor, and a number played at or near the replacement level. And when World War II came along and a lot of the NFL players went to war and they were replaced with lesser players, the gap in talent between the guys like Baugh and Luckman (who both played in the NFL during the war years) and the rest of the league widened considerably.

It's difficult to put into words, but it's like you have a big fish in a pond full of a few small fish, it makes the big fish look larger when you compare him relatively to the size of the other fish. This so-called Luckman effect may have also occurred in the 1960s AFL when Len Dawson led the league in NPR a record six times (tied with Peyton Manning), three of which appear on the best list. There were some good QBs in the AFL in the 1960s, but none who were on a statistical level near Dawson, and many of them (Joe Namath, George Blanda, and John Hadl come to mind) threw a lot of interceptions, while Dawson was very good at avoiding them.

As a result, here is a list of highest single season NPR values:

Table 6.20
25 Highest Qualifying Single Season Passer NPR Values

RK	PASSER	TM	YL	A	C	Y	TD	I	PR	NPR
1	Sid Luckman	CHI	43N	202	110	2194	28	12	107.550	134.176
2	Sid Luckman	CHI	41N	119	68	1181	9	6	95.256	124.403
3	Sammy Baugh	WAS	45N	182	128	1669	11	4	109.890	121.839
4	Otto Graham	CLE	46F	174	95	1834	17	5	112.093	119.620
5	Sammy Baugh	WAS	40N	177	111	1367	12	10	85.581	117.122
6	Cecil Isbell	G B	42N	268	146	2021	24	14	86.987	116.850
7	Otto Graham	CLE	53N	258	167	2722	11	9	99.661	114.793
8	Aaron Rodgers	GB	11N	502	343	4643	45	6	122.460	114.262
9	Otto Graham	CLE	47F	269	163	2753	25	11	109.162	112.560
10	Frank Filchock	WAS	44N	147	84	1139	13	9	85.955	112.386

6. Passer Ratings

RK	PASSER	TM	YL	A	C	Y	TD	I	PR	NPR
11	Len Dawson	KC	62A	310	189	2759	29	17	98.306	112.151
12	Roger Staubach	DAL	71N	211	126	1882	15	4	104.808	111.939
13	Peyton Manning	IND	04N	497	336	4557	49	10	121.106	111.625
14	Milt Plum	CLE	60N	250	151	2297	21	5	110.367	111.095
15	Nick Foles	PHI	13N	317	203	2891	27	2	119.210	110.641
16	Len Dawson	KC	66A	284	159	2527	26	10	101.658	110.551
17	Tom Brady	NE	07N	578	398	4806	50	8	117.178	110.341
18	Arnie Herber	GB	36N	173	77	1239	11	13	58.899	109.876
19	Cecil Isbell	GB	41N	206	117	1479	15	11	81.351	109.667
20	Joe Montana	SF	89N	386	271	3521	26	8	112.414	108.553
21	Steve Young	SF	94N	461	324	3969	35	10	112.794	108.368
22	Sammy Baugh	WAS	42N	225	132	1524	16	11	82.528	108.279
23	Otto Graham	CLE	49F	285	161	2785	19	10	97.478	108.181
24	Ken Stabler	OAK	76N	291	194	2737	27	17	103.415	107.950
25	Bert Jones	BAL	76N	343	207	3104	24	9	102.472	107.028

The problem with Table 6.20 should already be clear, but this is how the list looks broken down by decades:

1933–39: 1	1960–69: 4	1990–99: 2
1940–49: 9	1970–79: 2	2000–09: 2
1950–59: 2	1980–89: 1	2010–18: 2

The 1940s are clearly over-represented, as there are nine on the list. This is due to the small leagues, and the war. Four of them occurred between 1942 and 1945, during World War II, when many of the best players were not in the league. It would be suspect to rate any player-season from the war years, when the competition was weakened due to the players who left football to join the war.

Another reason you can tell the 1940s NPR data doesn't seem right is by looking at Sammy Baugh's 1940 season (NPR 115.033) and comparing it to the 2011 season for Aaron Rodgers, where his NPR was 112.897. I cannot defend the fact that the system rates the season with Baugh's TD-INT ratio of 12–10 higher than the season with the 45–6 ratio of Rodgers. Slingin' Sammy had a very good season, leading the Redskins to the Eastern Division title until they lost to the Bears 73-zip in the NFL Championship game.

I don't think that Baugh's 1940 season was of historic magnitude, but it was one of the three or four best seasons of his career. But the fact that the passers in the 1940 season had much worse seasons made Baugh's performance look much better than it really was. This is the Luckman Effect in a nutshell, and why I will segregate the team and passer data between pre- (1933–1969) and post- (1970–2018) merger.

Table 6.21
25 Highest Qualifying Single Season Passer PR Values, 1933–69 and 1970–2018

RK	PASSER	TM	YL	PR	RK	PASSER	TM	YL	PR
1	Otto Graham	CLE	46F	112.093	1	A Rodgers	GB	11N	122.460
2	Milt Plum	CLE	60N	110.367	2	P Manning	IND	04N	121.106
3	S Baugh	WAS	45N	109.890	3	Nick Foles	PHI	13N	119.210
4	Otto Graham	CLE	47F	109.162	4	Tom Brady	NE	07N	117.178
5	Sid Luckman	CHI	43N	107.550	5	Matt Ryan	ATL	16N	117.127
6	Bart Starr	GB	66N	104.955	6	P Manning	DEN	13N	115.114
7	YA Tittle	NYG	63N	104.774	7	Drew Brees	NO	18N	114.651
8	Bart Starr	GB	68N	104.349	8	Tony Romo	DAL	14N	113.242
9	F Albert	SF	48F	102.936	9	Steve Young	SF	94N	112.794
10	C Conerly	NYG	59N	102.728	10	P Mahomes	KC	18N	112.615
11	Len Dawson	KC	66A	101.658	11	Joe Montana	SF	89N	112.414
12	Otto Graham	CLE	53N	99.661	12	A Rodgers	GB	14N	112.188
13	Len Dawson	KC	68A	98.605	13	Tom Brady	NE	16N	112.172
14	T Thompson	PHI	48N	98.374	14	Tom Brady	NE	10N	110.993
15	Len Dawson	DTX	62A	98.306	15	D Culpepper	MIN	04N	110.941
16	Otto Graham	CLE	49F	97.478	16	Drew Brees	NO	11N	110.632
17	John Unitas	BAL	65N	97.385	17	R Wilson	SEA	15N	110.123
18	Bart Starr	GB	64N	97.120	18	Drew Brees	NO	09N	109.638
19	John Unitas	BAL	64N	96.400	19	Kurt Warner	SLR	99N	109.239
20	E LeBaron	DAL	62N	95.356	20	J McCown	CHI	13N	109.022
21	John Brodie	SF	65N	95.348	21	Dan Marino	MIA	84N	108.939
22	Sid Luckman	CHI	41N	95.256	22	A Rodgers	GB	12N	108.024
23	Otto Graham	CLE	55N	93.998	23	R Wilson	SEA	18N	107.401
24	Bill Wade	CHI	61N	93.717	24	Brett Favre	MIN	09N	107.247
25	Rudy Bukich	CHI	65N	93.710	25	Steve Young	SF	92N	107.027

Table 6.22
25 Lowest Qualifying Single Season Passer PR Values, 1933–69 and 1970–2018

RK	PASSER	TM	YL	PR	RK	PASSER	TM	YL	PR
1	B Patterson	PIT	40N	14.886	1	T Bradshaw	PIT	70N	30.352
2	H McCullough	CHC	40N	23.886	2	G Marangi	BUF	76N	30.783
3	C Ortmann	PIT	51N	23.996	3	Joe Kapp	BOP	70N	32.601
4	D Panciera	NYA	49F	24.194	4	B Douglass	CHI	71N	36.972

RK	PASSER	TM	YL	PR	RK	PASSER	TM	YL	PR
5	D Smuckler	PHI	37N	24.364	5	Ryan Leaf	S D	98N	38.971
6	B Schwenk	CHC	42N	25.530	6	J Namath	NYJ	76N	39.946
7	A Herber	G B	33N	26.210	7	S DeBerg	S F	78N	40.025
8	Tobin Rote	G B	50N	26.693	8	J Pisarcik	NYG	77N	42.298
9	Tobin Rote	DET	59N	26.826	9	D Pastorini	HOU	71N	43.781
10	M Taliaferro	BOP	68A	26.918	10	A Manning	N O	75N	44.280
11	Ja Jacobs	G B	48N	27.899	11	B Hoying	PHI	98N	45.629
12	F Tripucka	DCC	52N	28.271	12	J Plunkett	N E	72N	45.698
13	E LeBaron	WAS	53N	28.328	13	N Snead	NYG	73N	45.754
14	Babe Parilli	G B	53N	28.514	14	D Shaw	BUF	71N	46.084
14	G Herring	DEN	61A	30.036	15	M Malone	PIT	87N	46.677
16	G Taliaferro	LAA	49F	30.040	16	M Phipps	CLE	74N	46.745
17	Dick Wood	MIA	66A	30.580	17	M Phipps	CLE	75N	47.464
18	J McCormick	DEN	66A	30.861	18	C Whelihan	S D	98N	47.956
19	H Gilmer	WAS	49N	30.966	19	Testaverde	T B	88N	48.757
20	P Hall	CLR	41N	30.987	20	R Hilger	DET	88N	48.897
21	J Grigas	CPT	44N	31.520	21	D Pastorini	HOU	73N	48.951
22	Jug Girard	G B	49N	31.631	22	B Avellini	CHI	76N	49.439
23	S Romanik	CHC	53N	31.750	23	M Phipps	CLE	73N	49.450
24	R Norton	MIA	69A	32.179	24	Jim Zorn	SEA	76N	49.454
25	Tobin Rote	G B	53N	32.376	25	B Douglass	CHI	72N	49.769

Table 6.23
25 Highest Qualifying Single Season Passer NPR Values, 1933–69 and 1970–2018

RK	PASSER	TM	YL	NPR	RK	PASSER	TM	YL	NPR
1	S Luckman	CHI	43N	134.176	1	A Rodgers	GB	11N	114.262
2	S Luckman	CHI	41N	124.403	2	R Staubach	DAL	71N	111.939
3	S Baugh	WAS	45N	121.839	3	P Manning	IND	04N	111.625
4	O Graham	CLE	46F	119.620	4	Nick Foles	PHI	13N	110.641
5	S Baugh	WAS	40N	117.122	5	Tom Brady	N E	07N	110.341
6	C Isbell	G B	42N	116.850	6	J Montana	S F	89N	108.553
7	O Graham	CLE	53N	114.793	7	S Young	S F	94N	108.368
8	O Graham	CLE	47F	112.560	8	K Stabler	OAK	76N	107.950
9	F Filchock	WAS	44N	112.386	9	Bert Jones	BAL	76N	107.028
10	L Dawson	K C	62A	112.151	10	K Warner	SLR	99N	105.825
11	Milt Plum	CLE	60N	111.095	11	S Young	S F	92N	104.907

RK	PASSER	TM	YL	NPR	RK	PASSER	TM	YL	NPR
12	L Dawson	K C	66A	110.551	12	D Marino	MIA	84N	104.693
13	A Herber	G B	36N	109.876	13	K Stabler	OAK	74N	104.116
14	C Isbell	G B	41N	109.667	14	P Manning	DEN	13N	103.118
15	S Baugh	WAS	42N	108.279	15	T Brady	NE	10N	102.951
16	O Graham	CLE	49F	108.181	16	M Ryan	ATL	16N	101.605
17	L Dawson	K C	68A	106.648	17	K Anderson	CIN	74N	101.429
18	B Starr	G B	66N	106.569	18	Tom Brady	NE	16N	101.244
19	G Blanda	HOU	61A	105.772	19	R Staubach	DAL	73N	100.372
20	O Graham	CLE	55N	105.650	20	Randall Cunningham	MIN	98N	100.358
21	F Albert	S F	48F	105.539	21	S Young	S F	97N	100.108
22	B Starr	G B	68N	103.224	22	D Culpepper	MIN	04N	99.327
23	T Thompson	PHI	48N	103.080	23	Br Griese	DEN	00N	99.159
24	C Conerly	NYG	59N	102.314	24	J McCown	CHI	13N	99.151
25	A Parker	BKN	40N	101.857	25	A Rodgers	GB	14N	98.917

Table 6.24
25 Lowest Qualifying Single Season Passer NPR Values, 1933–69 and 1970–2018

RK	PASSER	TM	YL	NPR	RK	PASSER	TM	YL	NPR
1	Tobin Rote	DET	59N	24.682	1	Ryan Leaf	S D	98N	21.232
2	D Panciera	NYA	49F	28.104	2	G Marangi	BUF	76N	27.809
3	M Taliaferro	BOS	68A	28.588	3	J Russell	OAK	09N	28.500
4	B Patterson	PIT	40N	30.271	4	B Hoying	PHI	98N	29.556
5	Jack Jacobs	G B	48N	30.824	5	C Whelihan	S D	98N	30.281
6	J McCormick	DEN	66A	31.958	6	Joe Kapp	BOP	70N	30.781
7	Dick Wood	MIA	66A	32.029	7	T Bradshaw	PIT	70N	31.804
8	H McCullough	CHC	40N	32.447	8	D Kizer	CLE	17N	32.480
9	G Taliaferro	LAA	49F	32.530	9	J Rosen	ARZ	18N	33.088
10	R Norton	MIA	69A	33.310	10	M Malone	PIT	87N	34.522
11	G Herring	DEN	61A	33.562	11	J Plummer	ARZ	99N	34.586
12	B Parilli	G B	53N	34.804	12	J Allen	BUF	18N	34.590
13	E LeBaron	WAS	53N	34.863	13	A Walter	OAK	06N	35.182
14	D Darragh	BUF	68A	35.057	14	J Namath	NYJ	76N	35.910
15	C Ortmann	PIT	51N	35.997	15	J Delhomme	CAR	09N	36.440
16	T Rote	G B	50N	36.912	16	M Stafford	DET	09N	37.656
17	R Cahill	CHC	43N	37.029	17	K Collins	CAR	97N	37.713

6. Passer Ratings

RK	PASSER	TM	YL	NPR
18	L McHan	CHC	54N	37.602
19	Z Bratkowski	CHI	60N	38.280
20	H Gilmer	WAS	49N	38.717
21	T Nofsinger	STL	66N	39.179
22	B Thomason	PHI	56N	39.840
23	R Johnson	ATL	68N	40.460
24	F Tripucka	DCC	52N	41.071
25	F Sinkwich	DET	43N	41.346

RK	PASSER	TM	YL	NPR
18	Ryan Leaf	S D	00N	38.037
19	G Smith	NYJ	13N	38.583
20	R Fitzpatrick	NYJ	16N	38.686
21	M Cassel	KC	12N	38.787
22	P Manning	DEN	15N	39.100
23	J McCown	TB	14N	39.564
24	B Douglass	CHI	71N	39.699
25	V Ferragamo	BUF	85N	39.729

Best and Worst Teams

What follows is a list of best and worst teams in PR and NPR, separated into two lists, 1933–1969 on the left and 1970–2018 on the right. On the defensive lists, remember that defensive stats are opposite of offensive stats, therefore, the lower ratings are better than higher ones.

Table 6.25
25 Highest Single Season Offensive Team PR Values

RK	TM	YL	PR	RK	TM	YL	PR
1	CLE	60N	109.454	1	G B	11N	122.562
2	CLE	47F	105.546	2	IND	04N	119.667
3	CLE	46F	103.806	3	ATL	16N	116.764
4	G B	66N	102.070	4	N E	07N	115.984
5	CLE	53N	101.905	5	S F	89N	114.782
6	CLE	55N	98.326	6	DEN	13N	114.380
7	DTX	62A	97.114	7	K C	18N	112.539
8	CLE	49F	96.805	8	S F	94N	111.363
9	K C	68A	96.404	9	N O	18N	111.284
10	CHI	43N	95.342	10	DAL	14N	110.872
11	CHI	41N	95.238	11	N O	11N	110.498
12	NYG	63N	94.396	12	G B	14N	109.880
13	S F	48F	93.866	13	MIN	04N	109.828
14	BAL	59N	92.061	14	SEA	15N	109.795
15	S F	65N	91.777	15	N E	10N	109.759
16	BAL	64N	91.757	16	N E	16N	109.477
17	K C	66A	91.418	17	MIA	84N	108.479
18	BAL	65N	91.369	18	G B	12N	108.281

RK	TM	YL	PR	RK	TM	YL	PR
19	G B	64N	91.310	19	SEA	18N	107.401
20	HOU	61A	90.671	20	MIN	09N	107.290
21	CLE	66N	90.413	21	SLR	99N	106.643
22	CHI	65N	89.803	22	S F	87N	106.167
23	MIN	64N	89.430	23	ATL	18N	106.034
24	NYG	67N	88.721	24	N O	09N	106.020
25	DAL	62N	88.651	25	N E	11N	105.685

Table 6.26
25 Highest Single Season Defensive Team PR Values

RK	TM	YL	PR	RK	TM	YL	PR
1	PHI	34N	7.099	1	PIT	73N	33.101
2	CHI	34N	7.227	2	OAK	75N	37.238
3	DET	34N	9.958	3	ATL	77N	37.435
4	G B	34N	12.064	4	MIA	73N	39.920
5	CHI	33N	13.102	5	MIN	70N	40.435
6	NYG	34N	13.406	6	MIN	88N	41.172
7	BOR	34N	13.758	7	WAS	76N	42.585
8	NYG	33N	14.666	8	PIT	75N	42.845
9	NYG	38N	15.118	9	DET	76N	43.670
10	BKN	33N	16.149	10	PIT	77N	43.797
11	NYG	35N	17.012	11	BAL	71N	44.177
12	G B	33N	17.086	12	PIT	74N	44.266
13	G B	35N	18.136	13	ATL	73N	44.766
14	CHI	35N	19.759	14	MIA	82N	44.875
15	CHI	36N	20.026	15	WAS	71N	45.149
16	BOR	36N	20.455	16	PIT	76N	45.191
17	DET	37N	20.682	17	BAL	77N	45.375
18	WAS	39N	20.730	18	L A	76N	45.608
19	CHI	42N	21.414	19	MIN	71N	45.725
20	CHI	43N	22.024	20	K C	70N	45.792
21	G B	36N	23.990	21	MIN	75N	46.227
22	NYG	44N	24.031	22	CIN	75N	46.867
23	CHC	35N	24.401	23	PIT	72N	47.025
24	NYG	39N	24.493	24	MIA	72N	47.450
25	CLE	46F	24.610	25	MIN	72N	47.539

Table 6.27
25 Lowest Single Season Offensive Team PR Values

RK	TM	YL	PR	RK	TM	YL	PR
1	CST	33N	2.083	1	T B	77N	22.514
2	CHC	34N	2.525	2	ATL	74N	27.844
3	DET	42N	8.014	3	S F	78N	32.984
4	PHI	36N	8.162	4	PIT	70N	35.417
5	CST	34N	8.390	5	BOP	70N	36.682
6	CHC	33N	8.783	6	S D	73N	37.311
7	PIT	45N	9.773	7	NYJ	76N	37.590
8	BKN	36N	10.993	8	NYG	77N	38.552
9	BOR	34N	11.021	9	HOU	71N	39.347
10	G B	49N	11.427	10	CHI	71N	41.342
11	BOR	35N	11.476	11	ATL	76N	41.502
12	BOR	33N	11.792	12	BUF	73N	42.694
13	PIT	35N	12.358	13	N O	75N	42.698
14	BKN	34N	12.785	14	DEN	70N	44.453
15	PIT	41N	13.641	15	NYJ	75N	44.705
16	BKN	35N	13.670	16	S D	98N	44.891
17	PIT	40N	14.418	17	DEN	71N	44.949
18	PHI	33N	14.821	18	BAL	73N	45.222
19	G B	46N	14.958	19	BUF	71N	45.828
20	PIT	33N	14.987	20	CHI	78N	45.893
21	DET	41N	16.288	21	CHI	74N	46.475
22	BKN	44N	16.412	22	G B	73N	46.904
23	PHI	34N	16.539	23	ATL	75N	47.197
24	BKN	42N	16.850	24	G B	74N	47.560
25	PIT	34N	16.980	25	N E	72N	47.987

Table 6.28
25 Lowest Single Season Defensive Team PR Values

RK	TM	YL	PR	RK	TM	YL	PR
1	ATL	68N	101.334	1	N O	15N	116.169
2	MIN	63N	99.051	2	DET	08N	110.878
3	DEN	63A	97.529	3	T B	18N	109.067
4	N O	69N	97.437	4	WAS	14N	108.305
5	NYG	66N	97.158	5	MIN	11N	107.574

RK	TM	YL	PR	RK	TM	YL	PR
6	STL	69N	96.098	6	HOU	82N	107.321
7	WAS	59N	94.638	7	DET	09N	106.969
8	L A	65N	93.344	8	DET	16N	106.485
9	ATL	67N	92.424	9	OAK	13N	105.089
10	PHI	63N	91.706	10	MIN	84N	104.413
11	WAS	62N	91.080	11	IND	11N	103.875
12	CHI	64N	91.075	12	S F	18N	103.652
13	WAS	54N	90.800	13	T B	15N	102.485
14	DAL	62N	89.841	14	ATL	13N	102.439
15	WAS	61N	89.828	15	CLE	17N	102.250
16	BAL	56N	89.387	16	G B	17N	101.994
17	L A	59N	89.119	17	OAK	17N	101.816
18	WAS	63N	88.254	18	CLE	15N	101.798
19	S F	63N	87.463	19	CLE	16N	101.784
20	WAS	60N	87.338	20	CHI	14N	101.673
21	ATL	66N	87.269	21	NYJ	14N	101.495
22	PHI	61N	86.972	22	TEN	15N	101.262
23	PIT	68N	86.627	23	DET	15N	100.923
24	CHC	59N	86.341	24	TEN	05N	100.683
25	NYG	64N	86.328	25	ATL	96N	100.649

Table 6.29
25 Highest Single Season Offensive Team NPR Values

RK	TM	YL	NPR	RK	TM	YL	NPR
1	CHI	41N	129.085	1	G B	11N	113.929
2	CHI	43N	120.420	2	S F	89N	111.553
3	WAS	39N	119.780	3	IND	04N	110.551
4	NYG	33N	118.606	4	N E	07N	108.578
5	CLE	53N	117.221	5	OAK	76N	107.486
6	CLE	55N	112.162	6	S F	94N	106.675
7	G B	42N	111.717	7	MIA	84N	104.116
8	CLE	46F	111.644	8	BAL	76N	103.665
9	K C	62A	110.553	9	S F	92N	102.597
10	CLE	60N	110.163	10	DEN	13N	102.400
11	WAS	40N	109.638	11	SLR	99N	102.335
12	CLE	47F	109.124	12	S F	87N	102.238

RK	TM	YL	NPR	RK	TM	YL	NPR
13	CLE	49F	108.765	13	ATL	16N	101.287
14	HOU	61A	107.491	14	N E	10N	101.199
15	G B	36N	106.527	15	N E	16N	98.833
16	NYG	35N	104.928	16	S F	70N	98.757
17	K C	68A	104.735	17	MIN	09N	98.092
18	WAS	45N	104.560	18	DAL	73N	97.860
19	G B	66N	103.963	19	MIN	04N	97.713
20	G B	34N	103.366	20	N O	11N	97.029
21	CHI	42N	103.210	21	S F	84N	96.936
22	G B	38N	102.796	22	G B	12N	96.650
23	CHI	44N	102.474	23	WAS	91N	95.945
24	G B	41N	101.949	24	DAL	71N	95.804
25	CHI	37N	101.881	25	G B	14N	95.795

Table 6.30
25 Highest Single Season Defensive Team NPR Values

RK	TM	YL	NPR	RK	TM	YL	NPR
1	CLE	46F	23.017	1	T B	02N	29.402
2	CHI	63N	30.087	2	MIN	88N	31.942
3	NYG	38N	30.417	3	PIT	73N	34.335
4	CLE	47F	31.934	4	OAK	75N	35.913
5	NYG	39N	32.625	5	BAR	08N	36.441
6	CHC	56N	33.289	6	BUF	09N	37.124
7	MIN	69N	34.196	7	MIA	82N	37.469
8	CLE	49F	34.529	8	PHI	91N	37.524
9	CHI	43N	34.674	9	CHI	86N	37.546
10	BAL	58N	34.955	10	S F	13N	37.674
11	S D	61A	37.906	11	N O	91N	37.960
12	PHI	50N	38.021	12	PIT	90N	37.971
13	CHI	42N	38.240	13	N E	03N	37.984
14	G B	62N	38.717	14	CHI	18N	38.155
15	CHI	48N	38.839	15	MIA	00N	38.218
16	DET	34N	38.948	16	MIN	70N	38.372
17	CLE	50N	39.242	17	JAX	17N	38.905
18	WAS	64N	39.301	18	MIA	73N	38.987
19	NYG	51N	40.074	19	MIA	98N	39.229

RK	TM	YL	NPR	RK	TM	YL	NPR
20	NYG	33N	40.233	20	WAS	76N	39.393
21	G B	67N	40.437	21	G B	96N	39.533
22	G B	65N	40.548	22	CHI	85N	39.903
23	G B	40N	40.998	23	DET	76N	40.467
24	CHI	67N	41.680	24	WAS	80N	40.610
25	BAL	60N	41.934	25	NYJ	09N	40.651

Table 6.31
25 Lowest Single Season Offensive Team NPR Values

RK	TM	YL	NPR	RK	TM	YL	NPR
1	PHI	36N	12.866	1	T B	77N	24.536
2	DET	42N	15.325	2	ATL	74N	25.147
3	PIT	41N	16.470	3	S D	98N	26.947
4	PIT	45N	18.772	4	BUF	18N	29.701
5	NYA	49F	21.525	5	S F	78N	31.673
6	G B	49N	21.714	6	S F	05N	31.904
7	BKN	42N	25.477	7	CLE	08N	32.481
8	CHC	33N	25.712	8	NYJ	76N	33.108
9	PIT	40N	25.788	9	CAR	10N	33.704
10	CST	33N	26.311	10	PIT	70N	33.817
11	CHC	43N	27.699	11	ARZ	99N	33.831
12	PIT	39N	28.107	12	OAK	06N	34.432
13	CHC	39N	28.684	13	CLE	17N	34.492
14	BOS	48N	29.735	14	ARZ	18N	34.761
15	CPT	44N	30.306	15	DET	09N	34.773
16	G B	46N	30.348	16	BOP	70N	34.835
17	G B	48N	30.551	17	K C	12N	35.925
18	WAS	33N	31.054	18	CLE	09N	36.207
19	CHC	40N	31.336	19	T B	91N	36.228
20	PHI	33N	31.756	20	S D	73N	36.325
21	BUF	68A	31.939	21	SEA	92N	36.605
22	BKN	44N	32.849	22	L A	16N	37.162
23	WAS	35N	33.240	23	T B	09N	37.320
24	BKA	47F	33.403	24	NYJ	16N	37.914
25	PIT	48N	33.995	25	PIT	87N	38.077

Table 6.32
25 Lowest Single Season Defensive Team NPR Values

RK	TM	YL	NPR	RK	TM	YL	NPR
1	CST	34N	131.788	1	HOU	82N	106.474
2	CPT	44N	107.683	2	DET	08N	103.240
3	DET	42N	104.245	3	NYJ	75N	99.715
4	DEN	63A	102.411	4	MIN	84N	99.571
5	NYG	66N	101.930	5	BAL	81N	98.853
6	ATL	68N	101.528	6	ATL	96N	97.930
7	CHC	43N	100.368	7	N O	15N	97.758
8	WAS	33N	100.026	8	BAL	78N	97.670
9	PIT	45N	99.734	9	CLE	75N	97.388
10	DET	46N	97.544	10	STL	73N	97.326
11	CHC	39N	97.248	11	DET	09N	96.793
12	WAS	54N	97.219	12	BAL	82N	96.718
13	BAL	56N	96.305	13	MIN	11N	96.002
14	WAS	59N	96.113	14	N E	72N	95.272
15	N O	69N	95.372	15	S F	99N	95.243
16	MIN	63N	94.595	16	SEA	76N	95.046
17	ATL	67N	94.230	17	TEN	05N	94.541
18	PHI	36N	94.096	18	NYJ	77N	94.255
19	STL	69N	94.083	19	HOT	05N	92.991
20	PIT	33N	93.509	20	WAS	06N	92.739
21	NYB	49N	92.288	21	WAS	14N	92.651
22	PHI	40N	91.344	22	NYJ	96N	92.295
23	CHC	45N	91.098	23	CIN	02N	92.258
24	HOU	66A	90.942	24	MIA	76N	92.025
25	CIN	68A	90.782	25	L A	91N	91.664

Table 6.33
List of Passers with at Least 1,500 Attempts, Ranked by Most Attempts, with Career Stats, Career PR, Rank, Career NPR, Rank

RK	PASSER	ATT	COMP	YARDS	TD	INT	PR	RK	NPR	RK
1	Brett Favre	10170	6300	71838	508	336	86.103	32	73.709	51
2	Drew Brees	9783	6586	74316	520	233	97.630	3	81.271	15
3	Peyton Manning	9380	6125	71940	539	251	96.460	7	83.338	10
4	Tom Brady	9375	6004	70367	517	171	97.510	4	84.756	9

RK	PASSER	ATT	COMP	YARDS	TD	INT	PR	RK	NPR	RK
5	Dan Marino	8358	4967	61361	420	252	86.384	30	79.170	21
6	Eli Manning	7972	4804	55623	360	239	83.934	44	64.515	136
7	John Elway	7250	4123	51475	300	226	79.862	75	72.026	63
8	Ben Roethlisberger	7168	4616	56028	363	190	94.152	11	75.580	36
9	Phillip Rivers	7000	4518	54452	374	178	95.493	8	76.919	28
10	Warren Moon	6823	3988	49325	291	233	80.901	65	71.811	67
11	Drew Bledsoe	6717	3839	44611	251	206	77.062	99	65.325	128
12	Vinny Testaverde	6701	3787	46233	275	267	74.971	114	63.226	150
13	Fran Tarkenton	6467	3686	47003	342	266	80.355	71	80.604	19
14	Carson Palmer	6307	3941	46247	294	187	87.892	23	69.481	89
15	Kerry Collins	6261	3487	40922	208	196	73.758	125	60.573	162
16	Matt Ryan	6201	4052	46424	295	133	94.652	9	76.614	30
17	Joe Flacco	5670	3499	38166	212	136	84.025	41	64.716	134
18	Dan Fouts	5604	3297	43040	254	242	80.227	74	76.016	33
19	Aaron Rodgers	5492	3560	42591	338	80	102.860	1	89.309	5
20	Matthew Stafford	5405	3372	38271	237	129	88.247	22	68.949	96
21	Joe Montana	5391	3409	40551	273	139	92.258	13	86.435	8
22	Donovan McNabb	5374	3170	37276	234	117	85.584	35	74.583	42
23	Matt Hasselbeck	5330	3222	36638	212	153	82.398	52	67.374	107
24	Dave Krieg	5311	3105	5311	261	199	81.517	59	72.783	57
25	Boomer Esiason	5205	2969	37920	247	184	81.062	63	72.633	58
26	John Unitas	5186	2830	40239	290	253	78.278	87	77.515	26
27	Jim Hart	5076	2593	34665	209	247	66.561	170	66.122	118
28	Steve DeBerg	5024	2874	34241	196	204	74.477	120	67.510	104
29	Alex Smith	4941	3082	33947	193	101	87.193	27	71.133	79
30	Jim Everett	4923	2841	34837	203	175	78.592	82	68.989	94
31	Jay Cutler	4920	3048	35133	227	160	85.292	36	64.412	138
32	Jim Kelly	4779	2874	35467	237	175	84.394	40	75.598	35
33	Troy Aikman	4715	2898	32942	165	141	81.619	58	71.736	69
34	John Hadl	4687	2363	33503	244	268	67.473	166	71.915	65
35	Phil Simms	4647	2576	4647	199	157	78.479	86	72.107	62
36	Mark Brunell	4640	2761	32072	184	108	83.958	42	74.747	41
37	Steve McNair	4544	2733	31304	174	119	82.761	48	71.875	66
38	Joe Ferguson	4519	2369	29817	196	209	68.573	160	65.080	131
39	Roman Gabriel	4498	2366	29444	201	149	74.286	123	74.054	46
40	John Brodie	4491	2458	31388	214	224	72.447	138	71.190	78

RK	PASSER	ATT	COMP	YARDS	TD	INT	PR	RK	NPR	RK
41	Ken Anderson	4475	2654	32838	197	160	81.858	53	80.725	17
42	Jon Kitna	4442	2677	29745	169	165	77.509	94	62.411	152
43	YA Tittle	4395	2427	33070	242	248	74.366	122	77.706	25
44	Norm Snead	4353	2276	30797	196	257	65.543	171	63.433	145
45	Jake Plummer	4350	2484	29253	161	161	74.605	119	60.573	163
46	Tony Romo	4335	2829	34183	248	117	97.105	5	80.788	16
47	Brad Johnson	4326	2668	29054	166	122	82.502	51	71.488	71
48	R Cunningham	4289	2429	29979	207	134	81.505	60	73.887	48
49	Ryan Fitzpatrick	4285	2575	29281	190	148	81.022	64	58.581	172
50	Sonny Jurgensen	4262	2433	32224	255	189	82.725	49	81.423	14
51	Rich Gannon	4206	2533	28743	180	104	84.749	37	76.349	32
52	Steve Young	4149	2667	33124	232	107	96.664	6	90.342	4
53	Ron Jaworski	4117	2187	28190	179	164	72.782	137	68.736	97
54	Kurt Warner	4070	2666	32344	208	128	93.713	12	80.634	18
55	George Blanda	4007	1911	26920	236	277	61.369	182	67.794	102
56	Chris Chandler	4005	2328	28484	170	146	79.336	79	69.197	92
57	Jeff George	3967	2298	27602	154	113	80.419	69	71.268	77
59	Andy Dalton	3921	2443	27943	188	104	88.629	19	67.481	105
58	Jim Harbaugh	3918	2305	26288	129	117	77.598	93	67.660	103
60	Terry Bradshaw	3901	2025	27989	212	210	71.183	146	71.581	70
61	Cam Newton	3891	2321	28256	182	107	86.183	31	64.386	139
62	Ken Stabler	3793	2270	27938	194	222	75.347	110	73.795	49
63	Craig Morton	3786	2053	27908	183	187	73.661	126	72.838	56
64	Joe Namath	3762	4182	58959	173	220	65.505	172	69.313	90
65	Len Dawson	3741	2136	28711	239	183	82.919	46	88.849	6
66	Trent Green	3740	2266	28475	162	114	86.045	33	74.081	45
67	Jim Plunkett	3701	1943	25882	164	198	67.451	167	65.054	132
68	Bobby Layne	3700	1814	26768	196	243	63.584	174	69.870	88
69	Jeff Garcia	3676	2264	25537	161	83	87.544	25	77.483	27
70	Tommy Kramer	3651	2012	24777	159	158	72.858	136	66.620	112
71	Archie Manning	3642	2011	23911	125	173	67.101	169	65.176	129
T72	Ken O'Brien	3602	2110	25094	128	98	80.436	68	73.521	52
T72	Joe Theismann	3602	2044	25206	160	138	77.458	95	73.083	54
74	Steve Grogan	3593	1879	26886	182	208	69.606	153	66.114	119
75	Steve Bartkowski	3456	1932	24124	156	144	75.449	108	71.437	73
76	Brian Sipe	3439	1944	23713	154	149	74.795	118	71.376	75

RK	PASSER	ATT	COMP	YARDS	TD	INT	PR	RK	NPR	RK
77	Bob Griese	3429	1926	25092	192	172	77.144	98	80.345	20
78	Charley Johnson	3392	1737	24410	170	181	69.339	156	67.282	108
79	Bernie Kosar	3365	1994	23301	124	87	81.827	54	74.847	39
80	Babe Parilli	3330	1552	22681	178	220	60.602	183	65.649	124
81	Steve Beuerlein	3328	1894	24046	147	112	80.316	73	70.550	81
82	Andrew Luck	3290	2000	23537	171	83	89.364	15	67.821	101
83	Matt Schaub	3281	2098	24887	133	90	89.192	16	72.339	60
84	Russell Wilson	3261	2095	25269	196	63	99.892	2	81.616	13
85	Jeff Blake	3241	1827	21711	134	99	78.029	90	67.404	106
86	Neil O'Donnell	3229	1865	21690	120	68	81.816	55	74.381	43
87	Michael Vick	3217	1807	22464	133	88	80.370	70	65.736	123
88	Daunte Culpepper	3199	2016	24153	149	106	87.778	24	74.169	44
89	Trent Dilfer	3172	1759	20518	113	129	70.203	151	55.818	176
90	Mark Bulger	3171	1969	22814	122	93	84.410	39	70.025	86
91	Neil Lomax	3153	1817	22771	136	90	82.682	50	76.782	29
T92	Bart Starr	3149	1808	24718	152	138	80.465	67	78.957	22
T92	Jim Zorn	3149	1669	21115	111	141	67.333	168	64.061	142
94	Lynn Dickey	3125	1747	23322	141	179	71.500	144	65.511	125
95	Bobby Hebert	3121	1839	21683	135	124	78.064	89	69.103	93
96	Gus Frerotte	3106	1699	21291	114	106	74.255	124	61.805	155
97	Jeff Kemp	3073	1436	21218	114	183	57.447	186	61.913	154
98	Dan Pastorini	3055	1556	18515	103	161	59.121	184	59.406	169
99	Sammy Baugh	2995	1693	21886	187	203	72.868	134	92.051	3
100	Bill Kilmer	2984	1585	20495	152	146	71.872	141	72.973	55
T101	Sam Bradford	2967	1855	19416	103	61	84.456	38	66.504	113
T101	Richard Todd	2967	1610	20610	124	161	67.702	165	61.962	153
103	Aaron Brooks	2963	1673	20261	123	92	78.527	83	66.010	121
104	Roger Staubach	2958	1685	22700	153	109	83.460	45	86.518	7
105	Danny White	2950	1761	21959	155	132	81.736	56	74.751	40
106	Jake Delhomme	2932	1741	20975	126	101	81.338	61	66.167	117
107	Ryan Tannehill	2911	1829	20155	123	75	86.640	28	64.328	140
108	Tobin Rote	2907	1329	18850	148	191	57.735	185	63.324	146
109	Norm Van Brocklin	2895	1553	23611	173	178	75.102	113	82.473	11
110	Chris Miller	2892	1580	19320	123	102	74.965	115	66.051	120
111	Charlie Conerly	2833	1418	19488	173	167	68.845	159	75.159	38
112	Jay Schroeder	2808	1426	20063	114	108	71.680	143	63.271	148

6. Passer Ratings

RK	PASSER	ATT	COMP	YARDS	TD	INT	PR	RK	NPR	RK
113	Derek Carr	2800	1759	18440	122	54	88.363	21	68.367	99
114	Brian Griese	2796	1752	19440	119	99	82.821	47	68.413	98
115	Kyle Orton	2712	1613	18037	101	69	81.133	62	64.805	133
116	Kirk Cousins	2702	1797	20242	129	65	94.610	10	72.331	61
117	Earl Morrall	2689	1379	20809	161	148	74.444	121	73.379	53
118	Matt Cassel	2683	1578	17495	104	82	78.511	84	59.519	168
119	Blake Bortles	2632	1561	17473	103	75	80.340	72	55.482	177
120	Josh McCown	2628	1581	17672	98	82	79.761	76	60.157	164
121	Otto Graham	2626	1464	23584	174	135	86.629	29	96.094	1
122	Mark Rypien	2613	1466	18473	115	88	78.932	80	70.524	82
123	Daryle Lamonica	2601	1288	19154	164	138	73.448	129	78.457	23
124	Jim McMahon	2573	1492	18148	100	90	78.167	88	70.144	85
125	Bert Jones	2551	1430	18190	124	101	78.498	85	78.036	24
126	Joey Harrington	2538	1424	14693	79	85	69.382	155	54.055	182
127	Bill Wade	2523	1370	18530	124	134	72.188	140	70.982	80
128	Jason Campbell	2518	1519	16771	87	60	81.695	57	66.362	115
129	Stan Humphries	2516	1431	17191	89	84	75.838	104	65.348	127
130	Doug Williams	2507	1240	16998	100	93	69.407	154	64.572	135
131	Chad Pennington	2471	1632	17823	102	64	90.081	14	76.428	31
132	Elvis Grbac	2445	1446	16774	99	81	79.646	78	68.958	95
133	Bill Kenney	2430	1330	17277	105	86	76.975	100	69.992	87
134	Wade Wilson	2428	1391	17283	99	102	75.703	105	66.433	114
135	Milt Plum	2419	1306	17536	122	127	73.023	132	70.426	83
136	Kordell Stewart	2358	1316	14746	77	84	70.666	147	57.679	174
137	Tony Banks	2356	1278	15315	77	73	72.356	139	61.734	156
T138	Scott Mitchell	2346	1301	15692	95	81	75.666	106	65.157	130
T138	Rodney Peete	2346	1344	16338	76	92	73.312	130	59.850	166
140	Jeff Hostetler	2338	1357	16430	94	71	80.480	66	71.347	76
141	Mike Tomczak	2337	1248	16079	88	106	68.905	158	59.276	170
142	Mark Sanchez	2320	1314	15315	86	89	73.227	131	51.647	188
143	Don Meredith	2308	1170	17199	135	111	74.836	116	72.022	64
144	Greg Landry	2300	1276	16052	98	103	73.580	127	74.033	47
145	Erik Kramer	2299	1317	15337	92	79	76.639	101	66.693	110
146	David Garrard	2281	1406	16003	89	54	85.824	34	71.394	74
147	David Carr	2267	1353	14452	65	71	74.804	117	59.686	167
148	Bubby Brister	2212	1207	14445	81	78	72.866	135	63.912	143

RK	PASSER	ATT	COMP	YARDS	TD	INT	PR	RK	NPR	RK
149	Doug Flutie	2151	1177	14715	86	68	76.355	103	66.686	111
150	Frank Ryan	2133	1090	16042	149	111	77.965	91	75.491	37
151	Marc Wilson	2081	1085	14391	86	102	67.703	164	58.292	173
152	Josh Freeman	2048	1179	13873	81	68	77.631	92	59.101	171
153	Rick Mirer	2043	1088	11969	50	76	63.531	175	49.742	189
154	Ed Brown	1987	949	15600	102	138	63.402	177	63.250	149
155	Bill Munson	1982	1070	12896	84	80	71.712	142	70.387	84
156	Chad Henne	1959	1161	12960	58	63	75.544	107	55.424	178
157	Gary Danielson	1932	1105	13764	81	78	76.569	102	71.458	72
158	Jameis Winston	1922	1183	14471	88	58	87.435	26	61.231	158
T159	Bill Nelsen	1905	963	14165	98	101	70.300	150	69.267	91
T159	Don Majkowski	1905	1056	12700	66	67	72.950	133	63.439	144
161	Case Keenum	1844	1144	12426	64	42	83.939	43	61.492	157
162	Mike Phipps	1799	886	10506	55	108	53.199	188	52.193	187
163	Eddie LeBaron	1796	898	13399	104	141	63.087	179	65.418	126
164	Cotton Davidson	1752	770	11760	73	108	55.110	187	60.142	165
165	Mike Livingston	1751	912	11295	56	83	63.415	176	64.441	137
166	Frank Tripucka	1745	879	10282	69	124	53.125	189	61.217	159
167	Sid Luckman	1744	904	14685	137	131	75.282	111	94.372	2
168	Jay Fiedler	1717	1008	11844	69	66	77.208	97	63.293	147
169	Tom Flores	1715	838	11959	93	92	67.943	161	73.739	50
170	Tim Couch	1714	1025	11131	64	67	75.136	112	60.690	161
171	Billy Joe Tolliver	1707	891	10760	59	64	67.744	163	57.013	175
172	Steve Bono	1701	934	10439	62	42	75.384	109	66.786	109
173	Colin Kaepernick	1692	1011	12271	72	30	88.892	17	71.742	68
174	Derek Anderson	1674	909	10845	60	64	70.318	149	53.482	184
175	Mark Malone	1648	839	10175	60	81	61.893	181	52.758	186
176	Jack Trudeau	1644	873	10243	42	69	63.770	173	53.494	183
177	Dave Brown	1634	892	10248	44	58	67.893	162	54.673	180
178	Bob Waterfield	1617	814	11849	98	128	62.378	180	75.924	34
179	Vince Ferragamo	1615	902	11336	76	91	70.508	148	63.060	151
T180	Byron Leftwich	1605	930	10532	58	42	78.854	81	66.323	116
T180	Marcus Mariota	1605	1015	11761	69	42	88.742	18	64.208	141
182	Charlie Batch	1604	908	11085	61	52	77.221	96	65.863	122
183	Nick Foles	1581	974	11118	68	33	88.363	20	68.217	100
T184	Frankie Albert	1564	831	10795	115	98	73.522	128	82.389	12

6. Passer Ratings

RK	PASSER	ATT	COMP	YARDS	TD	INT	PR	RK	NPR	RK
T184	Tony Eason	1564	911	11142	61	51	79.721	77	72.565	59
186	Rex Grossman	1562	863	10232	56	60	71.403	145	53.320	185
187	Eric Hipple	1546	830	10711	55	70	69.030	157	61.196	160
188	Kyle Boller	1519	861	8931	48	54	69.800	152	54.147	181
189	Mike Pagel	1509	756	9414	49	63	63.291	178	55.086	179

7

Kicker Ratings: PAL, PAL2, K%

The all-time single season leader in points by a kicker was established in 1983, when Mark Moseley of the Washington Redskins scored a total of 161 points solely on field goals and extra points, a record that was broken by Gary Anderson of the Minnesota Vikings 15 years later. (Anderson's record lasted until David Akers of the 49ers scored 166 points in 2011.) Moseley did this by converting 62 of 63 extra points and 33 of 47 field goals. It also helped that he had one of the greatest offensive units of all time giving him all those extra point opportunities and setting up good field position for all those field goal attempts. The question is—was it among the greatest seasons ever by a kicker?

I don't believe it was. I'll make the argument that Mark Moseley's 1983 season, while prolific in the number of points scored, was, in reality, slightly below average, and I think he cost his team a few points over the course of the season.

I arrived at that conclusion after creating three mathematical systems for rating kickers. The first is called Kicking Percentage (or K% for short), which is a simple way of putting the number of points a kicker scores into a ratio of how many points he would have scored had he not missed any field goals or extra points. It is a simple way of measuring kicking accuracy with respect to points.

The second system is PAL (short for Points Above League), which gives a rough estimate of how many points a kicker was above or below the number of points an average kicker in the league that season would have scored given the same number of field goal and extra point attempts.

Finally, the PAL2 system (Points Above League 2) which is a more complex (and more accurate) version of PAL, but it doesn't work for everybody. This is because it requires data on missed field goal attempt distances, and that information wasn't officially kept until the early 1980s. But I've been working to rebuild this missing part of statistical information; more on that later.

After I explain how these systems work, I will supply a series of lists of the best and worst from all the rating systems, followed by a look at the parallel careers of Gary Anderson and Morten Anderson, and concluding with an explanation of the field goal success curve.

Kicking Percentage

We'll start with Kicking Percentage, or K%. The formula for computing K% is:

$$K\% = 100*(XPM + 3*FGM) / (XPA + 3*FGA)$$

XPM, XPA = Extra Points Made, Attempted
FGM, FGA = Field Goals Made, Attempted

In short, it is a ratio of how many points a kicker scored on his kicks compared to how many points he would have scored if he had been successful on all his kicks. For the 1983 season, Moseley's K% would be:

$$K\% = 100*(62 + 3*33) / (63+3*47) = 100*(161/204) = 78.9$$

Had Moseley been successful on all of his field goal and extra point attempts in 1983, he would have scored 204 points, but in reality, he only scored 161, and 161 divided by 204 is 78.9 percent. Moseley converted nearly 79 percent of all potential points, but if he had been successful on all his field goals and extra points, his K% would be the maximum 100.0, one hundred percent.

Is that an impressive performance? If there is one thing you've learned from reading this much of the book, it is that you have to look at statistics within the context in which they occur. In 1983 NFL kickers were successful on 1104 of 1160 extra point attempts and 551 of 771 field goal tries. The K% for the NFL as a whole in 1983 was:

$$K\% = 100*(1104 + 3*551)/ (1160 + 3*771) = 100*(2757)/ (3473) = 79.4$$

Kicking Percentage is rounded off to one decimal point.

According to Kicking Percentage, Mark Moseley was slightly below the league average during his record-setting 1983 season. The highest K% in 1983 was by Gary Anderson, then of Pittsburgh, who hit 38 of 39 extra point and 27 of 31 field goals for a K% of 90.2 and Matt Bahr of Cleveland, who was 38 of 40 in extra point and 21 of 24 in field goals and also scored a 90.2. Among those eligible, Gary Anderson in 1998, Jeff Wilkins in 2000, Mike Vanderjagt in 2003 and Garrett Hartley in 2008 share the single season record for K% in a season when they did not miss a single field goal or extra point in the regular season, thus scoring a perfect 100 on K% because they converted every potential point that was put in front of them.

The major disadvantage to using K% is that average kicking skill has steadily improved throughout virtually all of pro football history. The success rates for field goals and extra points have always been constantly increasing except for when the goal posts were moved to the back of the end zone, and when the extra point distance was increased from 20 yards to 33 yards and because of expansion, but in the years following these changes, they started increasing once again. For this reason, the all-time best rankings for a statistic like K% at any point in pro football history will always be comprised of contemporary kickers. What I am saying is, if you created a list of the best single season and career K% scores in, say, 1980, the lists would be comprised of kickers who were active at that time and most of the best seasons would be in the couple years immediately before 1980. It would be the same if you chose any other particular season in the past.

In order to demonstrate this, we need to look at how extra point and field goal percentages have been pretty much steadily increasing throughout the history of pro football. These, of course, drive K%. We'll look at field goals first; Figure 7.1 is a graph of seasons since 1938 (x) plotted against field goal success percentage (y). The field goal success percentage hit a new high in 2013, to 86.47 percent, and has stayed steady between 84 and 85 percent since then. Field goal success rates were fairly immune to the moving of the goal posts in 1974 (compared to extra points) as the coaches quickly adapted their

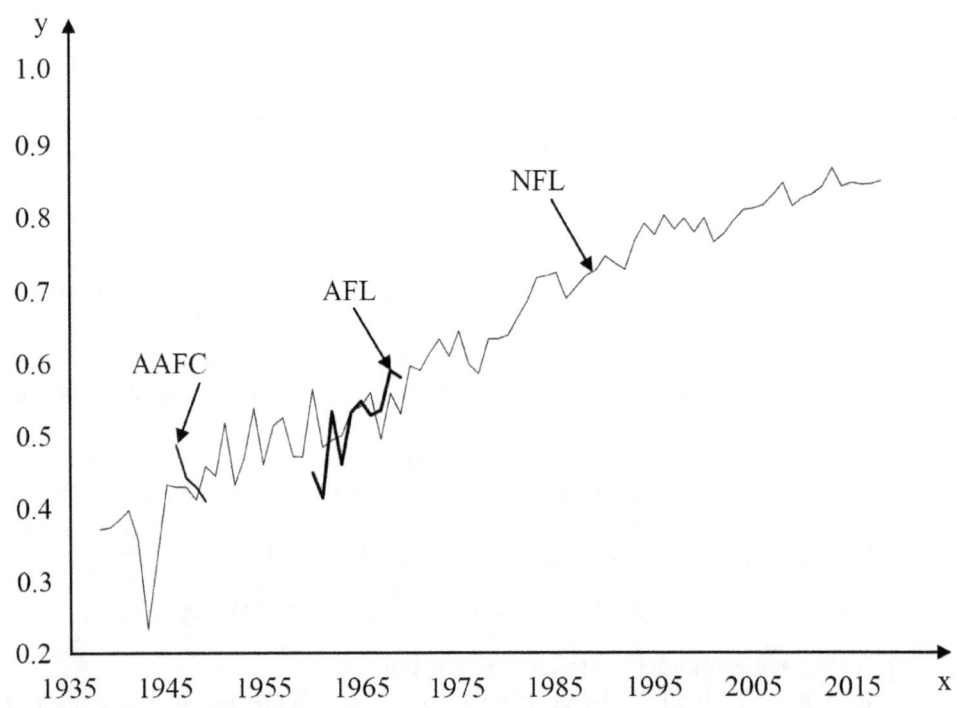

Figure 7.1. Field goal success rates by season, 1938–2018, NFL, AFL, AAFC.

field goal strategies to take into account the extra ten yards. In the early 1940s the field goal rates made a huge drop because of the lack of quality players due to World War II. The drop between 1975 and 1976 (which was caused by the expansion to 28 teams) was much greater than the drop between 1973 and 1974.

Next, we'll look at extra point rates throughout pro football history. Figure 7.2 is a graph of extra point percentage (y) by season (x). In 1974, the ten-yard extra point attempt suddenly became a twenty-yard extra point try, and the success rate dropped like a stone from 97 percent to less than 91 percent. It didn't improve quickly because there was an expansion in 1976, when Tampa Bay and Seattle joined the NFL; two kickers who weren't of NFL quality in 1975 were kicking in the league in 1976 and their less than stellar stats did not help the league kicking rates.

During the first couple years of the AFL, the AFL extra point percentage was below the NFL, but by 1963, the AFL had pulled ahead of the NFL and stayed ahead for the remainder of its history. In 1965, the AFL as a whole was a perfect 267 of 267 in extra point attempts.

At the right end of the graph you can see the drop between 2014 and 2015, where it dropped from 99.35 percent to 94.17 percent when the extra point went from a 20-yard kick to a 33-yard kick. It dropped a shade in 2017, but I expect it to start increasing again, slowly but steadily, over the years to come.

There are reasons for the general increase in kicking percentages over the years, including improved strength and conditioning, modern medicine, the fact that all kickers do now is kick and can practice relentlessly, and train to be kickers since before high school, the advent of the "kicking ball" (the NFL went to a certain type of football just for kicking as opposed to regular play in 1999), and soccer-style kicking replacing straight-on kicking just to name a few.

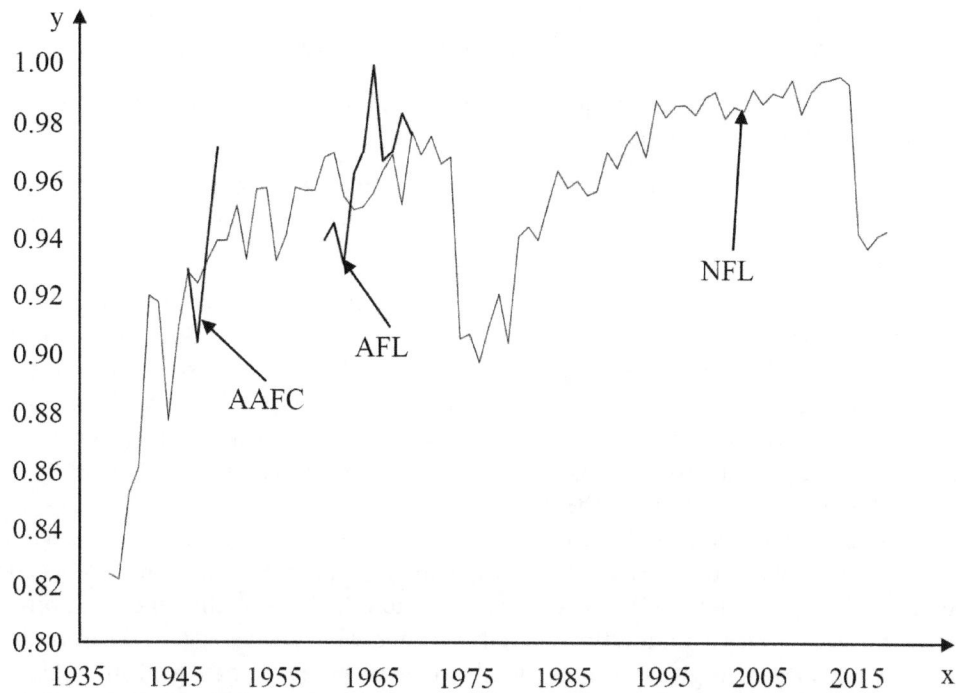

Figure 7.2. Extra point success rates by season, 1938–2018, NFL, AFL, AAFC.

For space reasons, I won't include a graph of K% by season, as it generally follows the field goal graph pretty closely.

In spite of K% steadily increasing over time, it is handy for comparing contemporary kickers from the same season, or kickers from the same era, but it does not work for comparing kickers from different eras. A good work-around would probably be to subtract the league K% from the player K% for evaluating players, and increase the number of decimal places from one to three.

We're not going to use K% very much from this point forward; it's just a simple evaluative tool for kickers. There is a table at the end of this chapter of all-time single season and career best in K%. I frankly don't use K% much because I came up with a much better way to rate kickers.

Points Above League

The second rating system I have developed is PAL, or Points Above League. The PAL formula is:

$$PAL = (KXPM + 3 \cdot KFGM) - (KXPA \cdot (LXPM - KXPM) / (LXPA - KXPA)) - 3 \cdot (KFGA \cdot (LFGM - KFGM) / (LFGA - KFGA))$$

KXPM, KXPA = Kicker Extra Points Made, Extra Points Attempted
KFGM, KFGA = Kicker Field Goals Made, Field Goals Attempted

LXPM, LXPA = League Extra Points Made, Extra Points Attempted
LFGM, LFGA = League Field Goals Made, Field Goals Attempted

The formula looks pretty complicated but is quite simple when you understand the three components of the PAL formula. Here's how it works:

PAL = (Kicker points) - (Kicker extra point attempts * League extra point success percentage) - (3*Kicker field goal attempts * League field goal success percentage)

Success percentage, of course, is defined as made over attempted.

The first part of the equation (from left to right) is kicker points, or how many points the kicker actually scores. The second (kicker extra point attempts times league extra point percentage) is how many extra points an average kicker from the season in question would have made given the same number of extra point attempts the kicker being rated had. The third part (three times kicker field goal attempts times league field goal percentage) is how many points from field goals an average league kicker would have made given the number of field goal attempts the kicker had.

The sum of the second and third parts of the equation is average kicker points, which is how many points an average kicker would actually score given the same number of extra point and field goal attempts as the kicker in question. PAL is the difference (in points) between what the kicker in question actually did, and what an average kicker from that season would have done given the same number of extra point and field goal attempts.

When I use the term "average kicker" in the context of rating a particular kicker against an "average kicker," what I really mean is the aggregate average of every other kicker in the league except for the one being rated. It is necessary to remove the statistics of the kicker being rated (in this case, Moseley), from the league totals for 1983 so that he is not being rated against his own performance. Moseley is competing against the aggregate performance of the rest of the NFL in 1983. This is similar to what we did with my other rating systems such as YRAA and NPR. With that in mind, here is the PAL calculation for Moseley in 1983 (using the stats from Moseley and the NFL from the K% calculations):

$$PAL = (62 + 3*33) - (63 * (1104 - 62) / (1160 - 63))$$
$$- 3 * (47 * (551 - 33) / (771 - 47)) = 0.28$$

PAL and PAL2 (which we will get to shortly) are rounded off to two decimal places.

In 1983, Mark Moseley is evaluated by the PAL formula as being a little over a quarter of a point above average. Over the course of a 16-game season, that works out to less than two-hundredths of a point per game above average, which is virtually meaningless. An average kicker in the NFL in 1983 (anybody besides Moseley), given 63 extra point attempts and 47 field goal attempts, would be expected to put up approximately 160.72 points. The fact that Moseley scored 161 points in that context is simply not impressive. It would have been impressive if Moseley had scored 170 or 175 points in the 1983 season if he had been given 63 extra point attempts and 47 field goal tries.

By comparison, the highest PAL score in 1983 belonged to Ali Haji-Sheikh of the New York Giants, who was successful in 22 of 23 extra points attempts and hit 35 of 42 field goals. His PAL score is:

$$PAL = (22 + 3*35) - (23 * (1104 - 22) / (1160 - 23))$$
$$- 3 * (42 * (551 - 35) / (771 - 42)) = 15.93$$

Haji-Sheikh scored nearly 16 points above what an average NFL kicker (anybody besides him) would have scored in 1983 given the same number of field goal and extra point attempts, which works out to about one point a game above average. An average NFL kicker in 1983 would have scored about 111 points given 23 extra point attempts and 42 field goal tries while Haji-Sheikh scored 127, which is why he scores a plus 16 in PAL.

PAL can also be used to evaluate team offenses (for teams with more than one kicker seeing time during the season) and defenses (to evaluate how many points above or below the league average a team allowed its opponents in the kicking game). One can even tie Offensive and Defensive Team PAL scores together into a single differential total in order to see how many points a good or bad kicking game on both sides of the ball can affect a team in terms of a swing of points. The formula for evaluating teams would be exactly the same as evaluating individuals, except for using the aggregate totals for every team except the team in question. In other words, subtract the particular team's kicking stats from the league stats for that season when using PAL or K%.

When one applies PAL on every kicker (or team) in the league, and then adds up the totals of all the teams or kickers, it never comes in exactly at zero, it's always either a little bit above zero or a little bit below zero. Intuitively, PAL must be a zero-sum game, meaning that the sum of the PAL scores for all the kickers or teams in the league should equal zero in any given season. However, sometimes the sum of all the scores for all the teams comes out nowhere near zero.

An extreme example occurred amongst the offenses in the 1960 AFL when rating them for Offensive PAL2. (We haven't gotten to PAL2 yet, but stick with me, the process for using this for PAL works just the same.) In this example we'll use four decimal places instead of two:

Table 7.1
Offensive PAL2 Values for 1960 AFL Teams

TM	PAL2
BOP	-3.2035
BUF	0.2743
DTX	-0.1341
DEN	18.0602
HOU	8.9702
LAC	4.5012
NYT	8.3966
OAK	-9.6007
SUM	27.2641

The sum of all the PAL2 scores for the entire league should be close to zero, but instead as you can see in Table 7.1 that the sum is 27.2641. The PAL2 scores for the teams need to be adjusted in a reasonable way so that the league sum comes out at zero. I came up with a creative way to do it.

The first thing I did in Table 7.2 (below) was to split the positive values from the negative values, creating two separate lists, a positive values list (P2+) and a negative values list (P2-) for the 1960 AFL teams. You will notice at the bottom a SUM row, which is the sum of the numbers in the column. Below that is absolute average, which is the average SUM P2+ and the absolute value of SUM P2- (which will turn the negative SUM P2- value positive); this is calculated as follows:

$$AAV = ((SUM\ P2+) + |(SUM\ P2-)|) / 2$$

In this case, it would be the average of 40.2025 and 12.9383, which is 26.5704.

The row below that is ARAT, short for Adjusted Ratio, where we will be creating a ratio of the absolute average and sum. ARAT will equal AAV/SUM, as shown:

Table 7.2
Splitting of Positive and Negative P2 Values for 1960 AFL Teams

TM	P2	P2+	P2-
BOP	-3.2035	0	-3.2035
BUF	0.2743	0.2743	0
DTX	-0.1341	0	-0.1341
DEN	18.0602	18.0602	0
HOU	8.9702	8.9702	0
LAC	4.5012	4.5012	0
NYT	8.3966	8.3966	0
OAK	-9.6007	0	-9.6007
SUM	27.2641	40.2025	-12.9383
AAV		26.5704	26.5704
ARAT		0.6609	-2.0536

The object is to adjust all of the values until the sum of the positive values reaches the adjusted average and the absolute sum of the negative values also reaches the adjusted average. Each of the P2+ values will be multiplied by the P2+ ARAT, and all of the P2- values will be multiplied by the P2- ARAT

For example, we'll look at the Boston Patriots (BOP); their P2+ is zero, so their P2A+ would also be zero, and their PP2- of 3.2035 is multiplied by -2.0536, with the resulting product of -6.5787 going in the P2A- column and also the P2A column.

Table 7.3 shows this process being performed to all the teams:

Table 7.3
PAL2 Adjustment (P2A) Values for All 1960 AFL Teams

TM	P2	P2+	P2-	PP2-	ADJ+	ADJ-	P2A+	P2A-	P2A
BOP	-3.2035	0	-3.2035	3.2035	0.6609	-2.0536	0	-6.5787	-6.5787
BUF	0.2743	0.2743	0	0	0.6609	-2.0536	0.1813	0	0.1813
DTX	-0.1341	0	-0.1341	0.1341	0.6609	-2.0536	0	-0.2755	-0.2755
DEN	18.0602	18.0602	0	0	0.6609	-2.0536	11.9362	0	11.9362
HOU	8.9702	8.9702	0	0	0.6609	-2.0536	5.9286	0	5.9286

TM	P2	P2+	P2-	PP2-	ADJ+	ADJ-	P2A+	P2A-	P2A
LAC	4.5012	4.5012	0	0	0.6609	-2.0536	2.9749	0	2.9749
NYT	8.3966	8.3966	0	0	0.6609	-2.0536	5.5494	0	5.5494
OAK	-9.6007	0	-9.6007	9.6007	0.6609	-2.0536	0	-19.7162	-19.7162
SUM	27.2641	40.2025	-12.9383	12.9383			26.5704	-26.5704	0
AVG		26.5704		26.5704					

The P2A+ and P2A- are the final positive and negative adjustments to PAL2, and P2A is the sum of the P2A+ and P2A- lists. As you can see, if you look at the sum of the P2A, it comes up at zero.

As I said before, this was a rare case, when you had one team that was very good in a small league. This adjustment is applied to all seasons all leagues, PAL and PAL2, kickers and teams. Since 1970, the adjustment is very small, less than four percent plus or minus for PAL and less than seven percent plus or minus for PAL2, but in most cases the adjustment is less than one percent either way after the merger. The adjustment is much larger pre–1970, particularly in leagues where we don't have all the missed field goal distances because this adjustment is forced to correct for the field goal distances that are currently unaccounted for.

The adjustment did not lower Moseley's 1983 PAL score, it remained at 0.28, but it did lower Haji-Sheikh slightly, from 15.93 to 15.82.

If you calculate PAL for every season of a kicker's career, you can tell how many points above or below average he was over the course of his career simply by adding together the PAL scores for each season. I will present career PAL totals later in this chapter, best and worst, single season and career for kickers and teams. The career leader in highest PAL and PAL2 score (and he leads both by a sizeable margin among those for whom we have complete or nearly complete field goal miss data) is a mild surprise, but I'll spring that on you later. This particular kicker has never been mentioned seriously as a Hall of Fame candidate, although he has made the preliminary list in every season that he has been eligible for enshrinement (I think), but this book and the results of my research could be used to help make a case on his behalf.

Missed Field Goal Distances

The major advantage to PAL is that it is easy to calculate for any kicker or team in NFL history. All you need is the statistics for the kicker or team and the league totals for that particular season and you can plug them into the formula quickly; these totals are available in any number of pro football encyclopedias or websites.

Another advantage to PAL is that a PAL score of +15 is just as impressive in 1983 as it is in 2013. I find a good rule of thumb is one point per game played is an excellent measure of a kicker's quality; if a kicker in a 16-game per season league has a +16 in PAL, it is an outstanding score, comparable to a +14 in a 14-game per season league.

When you try to compare kickers from the 16-game era against kickers from the 14 or 12-game era, you need to divide PAL by games played to compare from different eras, but it's a simple adjustment. I also have kickers rated on a per-game basis in order to remove this bias; these tables are located in the tables at the end of the chapter.

There is, however, a major drawback to PAL, and it is that PAL weighs all field goal attempts (and misses) equally as if they are all kicked from the same distance. It is obviously much more difficult to kick a 50-yard field goal as opposed to a 25-yard chip shot, but PAL just looks at the raw totals of success and failure and gives a result. In short, PAL tends to overrate kickers who attempt shorter field goals and underrate kickers who attempt longer field goals. There is a way to correct this problem, and that is to look at the distances of all field goal attempts, makes and misses, and evaluate the kicker compared to how successful the league was in kicking from each particular distance. This is the fundamental basis of PAL2; that we would need to examine the distance of every field goal the kicker attempted in order to accurately evaluate him.

The problem with this is that we would need all field goal attempt distances for each particular kicker, successes and misses. Successful field goal distances have been part of the scoring summary in box scores throughout NFL history, so we have those from 1933 to present and we have most from the 1920–1932 era also. However, field goal miss distances were not added to the standard box score until the early 1980s.

Before 1960 the only public source for finding such information seems to be found in newspaper stories about the games ("George Blanda missed a game-winning 43-yard field goal attempt as time expired") or NFL media guides for certain teams, or a few game books, or play-by-play documents, or grainy black and white game films of old games. Even with all those resources, and I've scoured all of them, not every field goal miss distance can be found. In fact, the earliest field goal miss data I've found in a media guide is in the Packers guide where they give miss distance data for 1959 to present, and there were more than 2000 missed field goals in the NFL and AAFC from 1933 to 1958.

There have been 36,632 successful field goals between 1938 and 2018, and 15,575 missed field goals in that time, regular season between NFL, AFL and AAFC. I started building my kicker database in 2002 in order to calculate PAL and PAL2 for all kickers and teams, and in order to do that, I started keeping track of the distances of all made and missed field goals. After a couple thousand hours of going through old newspapers and exhausting every possible resource, and along with the assistance of Ken Pullis and Pete Palmer and others, we've gotten the number of unknown missed field goal distances from 1938 to 2018 down 15,575 to 313. That is not a misprint; we've found the distances of about 98 percent of the missed field goals, and we are finding more as time goes on.

This database is not and should never be considered by any means official. We have all the missed field goal distances for the NFL for 1961 and 1963 and from 1968 to 2018 and for the AFL for their entire history (1960–69). By the time this book is published we'll also have other seasons from the 1950s and 1960s complete, and the number of unknown missed field goal distances should be under 250 as the PFRA game books collection effort is filling in the gaps.

Individual and team kicking statistics before 1938 are suspect and not 100 percent complete and accurate at this time and I've chosen to ignore the 1933 through 1937 seasons and instead use the 1938 through 2018 seasons, NFL, AFL and AAFC, when evaluating kickers and teams.

Points Above League 2

The format of PAL2 is very similar to PAL, it is:

PAL2 = Kicker Points—(Kicker XPA * League XPM/League XPA) - 3* (Kicker FGA at X yards * League FGM at X yards/League FGA at X yards for each attempt distance)

Note that the extra point portion of the PAL2 formula is the same as PAL, but instead of lumping all field goals together, I am instead lumping together field goal attempts at each particular distance, like 38-yard attempts, or 52-yard attempts, and comparing the kicker to the league average of field goal attempts that season at 38 and 52 yards.

In 1983, Moseley attempted field goals from the following distances, in yards:

Table 7.4
Distances, in Yards, of 1983 Mark Moseley Field Goal Attempts, Makes and Misses Separated, and Ranked from Highest to Lowest

MAKES					MISSES	
51	42	34	30	23	56	42
47	39	34	29	23	52	40
46	38	33	28	22	49	39
43	38	33	28	22	47	39
43	37	32	28	19	43	36
42	36	32	26		43	35
42	35	31	24		43	31

Combining all the attempts from Table 7.4 into a single list, with quantities from each distance:

Table 7.5
Distances of 1983 Mark Moseley Field Goal Attempts in Yards (YDS), Ranked Highest to Lowest with Quantity (QTY)

YDS	QTY	YDS	QTY	YDS	QTY
56	1	39	3	30	1
52	1	38	2	29	1
51	1	37	1	28	3
49	1	36	2	26	1
47	2	35	2	24	1
46	1	34	2	23	2
43	5	33	2	22	2
42	4	32	2	19	1
40	1	31	2		

Table 7.6 will compare Mark Moseley's (which we'll abbreviate MM) 1983 field goal performance in terms of how the rest of the league (which is the total league statistics with Moseley's stats removed) did from attempts at the same distances:

Table 7.6
Distances of 1983 Mark Moseley Field Goal Attempts, Attempt Values Multiplied by Number of Attempts at Distance

DIST OF 1983 MM ATTS	1983 NFL AT DIST (MK-MS)	1983 MM ATT AT DIST (MK-MS)	NFL MINUS MM (MK-MS)	VALUE OF ATT (MK-MS)	MM ATT * ATT VALUE
56	3 (2–1)	1 (0–1)	2 (2–0)	2/2 = 1.000	1.000
52	20 (8–12)	1 (0–1)	19 (8–11)	8/19 = 0.421	0.421
51	9 (4–5)	1 (1–0)	8 (3–5)	3/8 = 0.375	0.375
49	21 (11–10)	1 (0–1)	20 (11–9)	11/20 = 0.550	0.550
47	27 (13–14)	2 (1–1)	25 (12–13)	12/25 = 0.480	0.960
46	22 (7–15)	1 (1–0)	21 (6–15)	6/22 = 0.286	0.286
43	19 (13–6)	5 (2–3)	14 (11–3)	11/14 = 0.786	3.929
42	40 (31–9)	4 (3–1)	36 (28–8)	28/36 = 0.778	3.111
40	19 (14–5)	1 (0–1)	18 (14–4)	14/18 = 0.778	0.778
39	22 (15–7)	3 (1–2)	19 (14–5)	14/19 = 0.737	2.211
38	24 (18–6)	2 (2–0)	22 (16–6)	16/22 = 0.727	1.455
37	33 (24–9)	1 (1–0)	32 (23–9)	23/32 = 0.719	0.719
36	19 (13–6)	2 (1–1)	17 (12–5)	12/17 = 0.706	1.412
35	30 (19–11)	2 (1–1)	28 (18–10)	17/28 = 0.643	1.286
34	23 (16–7)	2 (2–0)	21 (14–7)	14/21 = 0.667	1.333
33	16 (12–4)	2 (2–0)	14 (10–4)	10/14 = 0.714	1.429
32	30 (28–2)	2 (2–0)	28 (26–2)	26/28 = 0.929	1.857
31	22 (18–4)	2 (1–1)	20 (17–3)	17/20 = 0.850	1.700
30	21 (18–3)	1 (1–0)	20 (17–3)	17/20 = 0.850	0.850
29	23 (21–2)	1 (1–0)	21 (20–2)	20/22 = 0.909	0.909
28	22 (20–2)	3 (3–0)	19 (17–2)	17/19 = 0.895	2.684
26	18 (14–4)	1 (1–0)	17 (13–4)	13/17 = 0.765	0.765
24	19 (16–3)	1 (1–0)	18 (15–3)	15/18 = 0.833	0.833
23	30 (28–2)	2 (2–0)	28 (26–2)	26/28 = 0.929	1.857
22	18 (18–0)	2 (2–0)	16 (16–0)	16/16 = 1.000	2.000
19	17 (16–1)	1 (1–0)	16 (15–1)	15/16 = 0.938	0.938
TOTALS		47 (33–14)			35.646

The leftmost column of Table 7.6 is of Moseley's attempt distances, misses and makes combined, from highest distance to lowest distance. After that is the total of league (NFL) kickers who had attempts at that distance, with the make-miss ratio in parentheses. The third column is the number of attempts Moseley had at that distance, with his make-miss ratio in parentheses. The following column covers the subtraction process, where Moseley's stats are removed from the NFL stats, and the totals in that column are the totals of the rest of the league except for Moseley from that distance, with the make-miss ratio in parentheses. The fifth column sets the value of field goal attempt at each distance for Moseley in 1983, by taking the make-miss ratio in the fourth column and converting it into a percentage by [make / (make plus miss)]. This is the success percentage from each distance by all kickers except for Moseley. The rightmost column is the product of the number of Moseley attempts (column three) multiplied by the field goal attempt value (column five).

Note that in the above table all field goal percentages have been rounded to three decimal places; in the spreadsheet they are about a dozen decimal places and when rounding the numbers off there can be slight differences between the figures in these PAL2 charts and the spreadsheets.

Here is how you read Table 7.6:

Moseley attempted a field goal from 56 yards, and he missed it. The NFL as a whole in 1983 attempted three field goals from 56 yards, going 2–3 in the attempts. The missed 56-yard attempt in the NFL in 1983 was, obviously, from Moseley. Subtracting the Moseley attempt from the league totals, the rest of the league was 2–2 in attempts, for a success rate of 1.000 (100 percent). And when multiplying column three by column five, one times one is one.

At 52 yards, Moseley attempted a field goal and missed it. The 1983 NFL as a whole was 8–20 in field goals from 52 yards away: Subtracting the Moseley miss, the remainder of the league was 8–19 in 52-yard field goal attempts, for a 0.421 percentage. One times 0.421 equals 0.421.

Just to show how to deal with multiple kicker attempts, at 43 yards, Moseley attempted five field goals, and was successful on two of them. The entire NFL in 1983 was 13–20 from 43 yards out. Everybody else in the league besides Moseley went 11–15 (0.733) from 43 yards away. Five times 0.733 equals 3.667, and so on.

The totals row at the bottom gives Moseley's actual totals (he hit on 33 of 47 field goal attempts) and the sum of column six, Moseley's attempts times the value of attempts, is 35.646. That total of 35.646 is the number of field goals an average kicker in the NFL in 1983 (other than Moseley) would have been successful on given attempts from the same distances that Moseley attempted them from.

Plugging this total into the PAL2 formula:

$$PAL2 = (62 + 3*33) - (63 * (1104 - 62)/ (1160 - 63)) - 3 * (35.646) = -5.78$$

The PAL2 system estimates that Moseley cost his team about five and three-quarter points over the course of the 1983 season. An average NFL kicker in 1983 not named Mark Moseley would have been expected to score approximately 166.78 points given the number of extra points Moseley attempted and field goals at the distances that Moseley kicked from. With the final averaging adjustment, Moseley's final PAL2 score stands at - 5.89

We'll do one more, Ali Haji-Sheikh (which we'll abbreviate AHS) of the New York Giants in 1983:

Table 7.7
Distances of 1983 Ali Haji-Sheikh Field Goal Attempts, Makes and Misses Separated, Ranked Highest to Lowest

MAKES									MISSES	
56	45	44	37	32	30	27	25	20	66	45

154 A Statistical History of Pro Football

MAKES									MISSES	
56	45	40	37	31	29	27	25	20	61	44
48	44	39	35	31	28	27	21	19	52	35
48	44	37	32	31	28	27	21		46	

Table 7.8
Distances of 1983 Ali Haji-Sheikh Field Goal Attempts,
Ranked Highest to Lowest with Quantity

YDS	QTY	YDS	QTY	YDS	QTY	YDS	QTY
66	1	45	3	32	2	27	4
61	1	44	4	31	3	25	2
56	2	40	1	30	1	21	2
52	1	39	1	29	1	20	2
48	2	37	3	28	2	19	1
46	1	35	2				

Table 7.9
Distances of 1983 Ali Haji-Sheikh Field Goal Attempts,
Attempt Values Multiplied by Number of Attempts at Distance

DIST OF 1983 AHS ATTS	1983 NFL AT DIST (MK-MS)	1983 AHS ATT AT DIST (MK-MS)	NFL MINUS AHS (MK-MS)	VALUE OF ATT (MK-MS)	AHS ATT * ATT VALUE
66	1 (0–1)	1 (0–1)	0 (0–0)	0/0 = 0.000	0.000
61	1 (0–1)	1 (0–1)	0 (0–0)	0/0 = 0.000	0.000
56	3 (2–1)	2 (2–0)	1 (0–1)	0/1 = 0.000	0.000
52	20 (8–12)	1 (0–1)	19 (8–11)	8/19 = 0.421	0.421
48	23 (14–9)	2 (2–0)	21 (12–9)	12/21 = 0.571	1.143
46	22 (7–15)	1 (0–1)	21 (7–14)	7/21 = 0.333	0.333
45	27 (16–11)	3 (2–1)	24 (14–10)	14/24 = 0.583	1.750
44	21 (11–10)	4 (3–1)	17 (8–9)	8/17 = 0.471	1.882
40	19 (14–5)	1 (1–0)	18 (13–5)	13/18 = 0.722	0.722
39	22 (15–7)	1 (1–0)	21 (14–7)	14/21 = 0.667	0.667
37	33 (24–9)	3 (3–0)	30 (21–9)	21/30 = 0.700	2.100
35	30 (19–11)	2 (1–1)	28 (18–10)	18/28 = 0.630	1.286
32	30 (28–2)	2 (2–0)	28 (26–2)	26/28 = 0.926	1.857
31	22 (18–4)	3 (3–0)	19 (15–4)	15/19 = 0.789	2.368
30	21 (18–3)	1 (1–0)	20 (17–3)	17/20 = 0.850	0.850
29	23 (21–2)	1 (1–0)	22 (20–2)	20/22 = 0.870	0.909
28	22 (20–2)	2 (2–0)	20 (18–2)	18/20 = 0.900	1.800

DIST OF 1983 AHS ATTS	1983 NFL AT DIST (MK-MS)	1983 AHS ATT AT DIST (MK-MS)	NFL MINUS AHS (MK-MS)	VALUE OF ATT (MK-MS)	AHS ATT * ATT VALUE
27	27 (24-3)	4 (4-0)	23 (20-3)	20/23 = 0.870	3.478
25	12 (12-0)	2 (2-0)	10 (10-0)	10/10 = 1.000	2.000
21	11 (10-1)	2 (2-0)	9 (8-1)	8/9 = 0.889	1.778
20	19 (19-0)	2 (2-0)	17 (17-0)	17/17= 1.000	2.000
19	17 (16-1)	1 (1-0)	16 (15-1)	15/16 = 0.938	0.938
TOTALS		42 (35-7)			28.282

PAL2 = (22 + 3*35) - (23 * (1104 - 22)/ (1160 - 23)) - 3 * (28.282) = 20.27

Haji-Sheikh actually scored 127 points, but an average NFL kicker in 1983 would have scored approximately 106.73 (or 127–20.27) points given the same number of field goal attempts from the same distances Haji-Sheikh attempted them from and the same number of extra point attempts. His Adjusted PAL2 (or APAL2) score of 19.89 is one of the 20 highest single-season PAL2 scores of all time and would in most seasons lead the NFL. However, Raul Allegre led the NFL in APAL2 in 1983 with a score of 24.90.

One thing you'll notice in the above table—at 66 and 61 yards, Haji-Sheikh was the only kicker in the NFL to attempt field goals from those distances. When you subtract his stats from the league stats, you get a 0/0 in the fifth column, but I put a 0.000 in there as the result because dividing by zero is still zero.

The fact that nobody in the league was successful with a field goal from that distance means an attempt from that distance should have zero value. The spreadsheet is set up so that in situations of that kind where you are dividing by zero, it just changes the value of the cell to zero. In other words, you don't get penalized by PAL2 if you are unsuccessful in attempting a field goal from a distance that nobody else in the league attempted.

Moseley's Career

During his NFL career, Mark Moseley had a career APAL score of 15.90, meaning he was nearly 60 points above average over the course of 213 career regular season NFL games, which puts him at number 63 on the all-time APAL list. The career APAL score is calculated by adding together the APAL scores for every season of the kicker's career. Moseley's career APAL score is not very good considering the length of his career; the leader in career APAL score is over 130.

However, Moseley's career APAL2 was 53.66, which was very good and put him at number 17 all-time. In some cases, career APAL and career APAL2 do differ greatly. If the APAL2 is much higher than the APAL when it comes to career scores, that means the kicker had a strong leg and was thus underrated. If the career APAL is much higher than the career APAL2, that tends to indicate a weaker leg and thus he is probably overrated.

If you get the feeling that I think that Mark Moseley was a lousy kicker because of his

1983 season, that is simply not the case. He was a very good kicker over the course of his career, and APAL2 was a much better indicator of his true value, I tend to follow that. His career APAL2 score put him sixteenth all time, which is in the neighborhood of where I would rate him among the all-time kickers; in fact, I would probably rate him a little higher.

For one thing, he was one of the only pure kickers in pro football history who was a team leader on a championship team. For the 1982 Super Bowl winning Redskins, the team leaders were Theismann, Riggins and Moseley. The only other kickers I would put in that company are Adam Vinatieri, Jan Stenerud, and Lou Groza, although Groza wasn't a pure kicker. That's a company of four kickers, three of which are either in the Hall of Fame or will be, along with Moseley.

There is also the 1982 NFL MVP award, the only time a pure kicker has won the award, and I'm sure it was due in part to the uniqueness of the 1982 season but I doubt it will ever happen again. For those reasons, I think Mark Moseley was probably one of the dozen greatest kickers ever; I'd probably put him near the bottom, number 11 or 12. I doubt the Redskins would have won Super Bowl XVII without him because he won a number of games with late field goals, thus giving the Redskins home field advantage throughout the NFC playoffs. And in the 1982 playoffs, John Riggins carried the Redskins to the NFL Championship.

Without Moseley, the Redskins might very well have been a 5–4 team instead of an 8–1 team, and a number five seed instead of a number one seed. Really? Here are the facts:

In Week 1, Moseley nailed a 48-yard field goal at the end of regulation to tie the game at 34–34 and defeated the Eagles with a 26-yard field goal five minutes into OT.

In Week 4, the Redskins beat the Eagles again, 13–7, as Moseley provided the difference with 45 and 43-yard field goals.

The Redskins offense couldn't punch it into the end zone in Week 6, and Moseley won the game with four short field goals (32, 30, 20 and 24 yards) as the Redskins defeated the Cardinals 12–7.

Moseley kicked three field goals, including a 42-yarder with under 10 seconds to play, as the Redskins defeated the Giants 15–14 in Week 7.

If you swap the two Eagles wins and Giants wins to losses, and adjust the points allowed for the Eagles and Giants to account for the now-missed field goals:

It makes the Cowboys the top NFC seed at 6–3, and the Packers would become the second seed at 5–3–1, and would put the Redskins at 5–4, and also put the Eagles and Giants at 5–4, setting up a mind-boggling seven-way third place tiebreaker between the Redskins, Eagles, Giants, Cardinals, Vikings, Bucs and Falcons for third place in the NFC. I am not making this up, check this out yourself if you don't believe me. A seven-way tie.

I'm pretty good with the NFL tiebreakers, but I took this to my friend and colleague Ivan Urena (who understands tiebreakers much better than I do), and we both worked through the seven-way tiebreaker and concluded that the Vikings and Falcons would have been the third and fourth seeds, respectively. The Redskins, Cardinals, Eagles and Giants would have been the fifth, sixth, seventh and eighth place seeds, respectively, with the Bucs being the ninth seed and thus, missing out on the postseason.

In this scenario, the Redskins would have probably been on the road the entire way for the 1982 NFC playoffs; they would most likely have had to win three road games, against Atlanta in the first round, and most likely at Dallas in the Divisional game and either at Green Bay or Minnesota in the NFC Championship. They could have run the table and won all three, with Riggins at full throttle, but I wouldn't have bet on it.

On the other hand, having home field advantage throughout the NFC playoffs made the Redskins the prohibitive favorite to go to the Super Bowl, and that is why Mark Moseley in my opinion deserved the 1982 MVP award.

Although he scored a lot of points in 1983, I just don't think he had a very good season. I needed to use a kicker as an example to show how the system works and I chose Moseley because I thought he was a good case of how points scored can be misleading.

Best and Worst Disclaimer

All seasonal kicker best and worst listings are based on a minimum of four Kicker Points per scheduled team game from 1938 to 2018. Career leaders are based on a minimum of 200 Kicker Points from 1938 to 2018. Team best and worst seasonals are from 1938 to 2018. Kicker Points are points scored just from field goals and extra points.

When evaluating Team Season Defensive APAL and APAL2 results, a team that gives up fewer points than expected is above average and a team that gives up more points than expected is below average, therefore a negative score is better than a positive score with respect to Defensive APAL or APAL2. Offensive statistics are always the opposite of defensive statistics. Teams who score the most points have the best offenses, and teams who give up the fewest have the best defenses. With that in mind, defensively it is better to have a negative PAL score, the lower the better.

Also, in the APAL2 lists, you will see a column called MISS (sometimes abbreviated MS or M), this is the number of misses we have not yet ascertained a distance for this particular kicker, and it will be expressed as a number such as 3. That is the number of unknown missed field goals we are seeking for a particular season for a particular kicker. In some occasions, the miss column will read 0 (zero), which means all of his miss distances have been ascertained, but there are other missed field goals in the league that season for which we are still seeking the distances, and as we find those misses, the kickers' PAL2 and APAL2 will fractionally change. If the MISS column reads N/A, it means all the miss distances have been found for all the kickers in that particular season, and those APAL2 totals won't change.

For career APAL2 lists, the MISS column list is total career unknown miss distances, and as before, if it is N/A for a particular kicker, it means his APAL2 numbers are complete and won't change unless we find a more reliable source with a different miss distance.

If a kicker played in the AAFC, or in the NFL between 1938 and 1967 (except for 1961 and 1963), his APAL2 scores are not 100 percent accurate, but the smaller the miss number, the more accurate his APAL2 score is. Every time we ascertain a hitherto unknown missed field goal distance, it fractionally changes the APAL2 score of every kicker in the league in that particular season. For kickers who played only in the AFL between 1960 and 1969 or who started in the NFL after 1967, they get a N/A in the MISS column.

Table 7.10
25 Highest Qualifying Career Average Field Goal Attempt Distance (AAT), Average Field Goal Made Distance (AMK) and Average Field Goal Miss Distance (AMS) Values

RK	KICKER	AAT	RK	KICKER	AMK	RK	KICKER	AMS
1	J Myers	39.80	1	J Myers	38.51	1	J Tucker	50.70
2	G Zuerlein	39.51	2	J Elliott	38.05	T2	G Zuerlein	49.01
3	J Tucker	39.28	3	J Tucker	38.03	T2	D Hopkins	49.01
4	S Janikowski	39.14	4	G Zuerlein	37.65	4	B McManus	48.46
5	J Elliott	38.95	5	P Edinger	37.33	5	S Janikowski	47.94
6	B Walsh	38.71	6	M Prater	37.24	T6	Wil Lutz	47.40
7	J Lambo	38.66	7	J Lambo	37.20	T6	J Lambo	47.40
8	M Prater	38.65	8	K Fairbairn	37.19	8	D Igwebuike	47.39
9	D Igwebuike	38.41	9	B Walsh	37.11	9	D Carpenter	47.13
10	P Edinger	38.39	10	S Janikowski	37.01	10	H Butker	47.00
11	K Fairbairn	38.36	11	D Bailey	36.98	11	J Myers	46.74
12	J Scobee	38.30	12	C Boswell	36.90	12	J Hanson	46.63
13	D Bailey	38.23	13	Wil Lutz	36.53	13	D Bailey	46.35
14	J Hanson	38.17	14	J Scobee	36.45	14	B Walsh	46.22
15	B McManus	38.09	15	G Gano	36.43	15	M Crosby	46.18
16	K Willis	38.08	T16	R Bironas	36.39	16	C Sturgis	46.14
17	D Carpenter	37.98	T16	C Barth	36.39	T17	M Prater	46.07
18	C Barth	37.97	18	J Hanson	36.36	T17	Nick Novak	46.07
19	Wil Lutz	37.91	19	M Luckhurst	36.30	19	C Santos	45.95
T20	M Luckhurst	37.83	T20	D Carpenter	36.22	20	R Succop	45.80
T20	G Gano	37.83	T20	S Hauschka	36.22	21	J Scobee	45.68
T22	D Biasucci	37.80	T22	R Succop	36.21	22	C Barth	45.66
T22	M Crosby	37.80	T22	Josh Brown	36.21	23	A Henery	45.58
T22	C Boswell	37.80	24	R Bullock	36.18	24	J Kasay	45.52
25	R Succop	37.77	25	K Forbath	36.14	T25	R Bullock	45.18
						T25	J Nedney	45.18

Table 7.11
25 Highest Qualifying Single-Season and Career Kicker Points per Game (PPG)

RK	KICKER	TM	YL	PTS	GP	PPG	RK	KICKER	PTS	GP	PPG
1	Greg Zuerlein	L A	17N	158	14	11.29	1	H Butker	279	29	9.62
2	H Butker	K C	17N	142	13	10.92	2	S Gostkowski	1743	200	8.72

7. Kicker Ratings

RK	KICKER	TM	YL	PTS	GP	PPG	RK	KICKER	PTS	GP	PPG
3	Greg Zuerlein	L A	18N	116	11	10.55	3	Wil Lutz	409	48	8.52
4	David Akers	S F	11N	166	16	10.38	4	Justin Tucker	952	112	8.50
5	Jim Turner	NYJ	68A	145	14	10.36	5	Nate Kaeding	895	114	7.85
6	G Anderson	MIN	98N	164	16	10.25	6	M Vanderjagt	1067	137	7.79
7	Jeff Wilkins	SLR	03N	163	16	10.19	7	D Hopkins	415	54	7.69
8	M Andersen	N O	87N	121	12	10.08	T8	Caleb Sturgis	398	52	7.65
9	Mark Moseley	WAS	83N	161	16	10.06	T8	Mason Crosby	1469	192	7.65
T10	S Gostkowski	N E	13N	158	16	9.88	10	Dan Bailey	927	122	7.60
T10	Matt Bryant	ATL	16N	158	16	9.88	11	David Akers	1721	227	7.58
12	M Vanderjagt	IND	03N	157	16	9.81	12	K Fairbairn	242	32	7.56
13	Mike Mercer	OKC	66A	98	10	9.80	13	Jason Elam	1983	263	7.54
T14	Bob Thomas	CDT	82N	39	4	9.75	14	Chris Boswell	436	58	7.52
T14	S Gostkowski	N E	14N	156	16	9.75	15	Cairo Santos	461	62	7.44
T14	S Gostkowski	N E	17N	156	16	9.75	16	Blair Walsh	655	89	7.36
17	S Gostkowski	N E	12N	153	16	9.56	T17	Jake Elliott	228	31	7.35
18	John Carney	NYG	08N	143	15	9.53	T17	Jason Myers	397	54	7.35
19	S Gostkowski	N E	15N	151	16	9.44	T17	S Hauschka	1051	143	7.35
20	Chris Boswell	PIT	15N	113	12	9.42	T17	Robbie Gould	1528	208	7.35
T21	S Graham	NEG	10N	75	8	9.38	21	Mike Prater	1240	169	7.34
T21	Mike Prater	DEN	13N	150	16	9.38	22	A Vinatieri	2598	355	7.32
T21	Cody Parkey	PHI	14N	150	16	9.38	T23	Matt Bryant	1710	234	7.31
T21	K Fairbairn	HOU	18N	150	16	9.38	T24	Jeff Wilkins	1416	194	7.30
25	Neil Rackers	ARZ	05N	140	15	9.33	T24	Graham Gano	978	134	7.30

After 13 seasons, Stephen Gostkowski is number 12 on the all-time career scoring list for Kicker Points with 1,743 points through field goals and extra points. Gostkowski has averaged 134 points per season during his career, which is excellent. Adam Vinatieri, by comparison, has averaged about 113 points per season throughout his career. At this rate, Gostkowski will break Vinatieri's current mark of 2,598 points in 6.4 seasons, but it may go much higher before he retires.

In pro football history, there have been 15 times where a kicker has scored more than 150 points in a season just through his kicking. Gostkowski has done it five times. Nobody else has done it more than once.

Table 7.12
25 Highest Qualifying Single-Season and Career Kicking Percentages (K%)

RK	KICKER	TM	YL	K%	RK	KICKER	K
T1	Gary Anderson	MIN	98N	100.0	1	Justin Tucker	92.3

RK	KICKER	TM	YL	K%
T1	M Vanderjagt	IND	03N	100.0
T1	Jeff Wilkins	SLR	00N	100.0
T1	Garrett Hartley	N O	08N	100.0
5	Tony Zendejas	L A	91N	98.7
6	Mike Prater	DEN	13N	98.0
T7	Justin Tucker	BAR	16N	97.9
T7	Adam Vinatieri	IND	14N	97.9
T9	Norm Johnson	ATL	93N	97.4
T9	Gary Anderson	MIN	00N	97.4
T9	Shayne Graham	NEG	10N	97.4
12	Eddie Murray	DET	89N	97.0
13	Aldrick Rosas	NYG	18N	96.9
14	Pete Stoyanovich	K C	97N	96.6
15	S Gostkowski	N E	14N	96.3
T16	Chris Boniol	DAL	95N	96.2
T16	Robbie Gould	S F	18N	96.2
18	Steven Hauschka	SEA	13N	96.0
T19	Adam Vinatieri	N E	04N	95.9
T19	Neil Rackers	ARZ	05N	95.9
21	Jason Hanson	DET	03N	95.8
22	Jason Hanson	DET	08N	95.7
T23	Dan Bailey	DAL	13N	95.6
T23	Jason Elam	ATL	08N	95.6
T23	Adam Vinatieri	IND	10N	95.6
T23	Shaun Suisham	PIT	13N	95.6

RK	KICKER	K
2	Harrison Butker	91.8
3	S Gostkowski	91.3
4	Nate Kaeding	91.0
5	M Vanderjagt	90.7
6	Robbie Gould	90.5
7	Dan Bailey	90.4
8	Wil Lutz	90.3
9	Matt Bryant	89.8
10	Shayne Graham	89.6
11	Kai Forbath	89.5
12	Rob Bironas	89.4
13	S Hauschka	89.1
14	Adam Vinatieri	88.4
T15	Garrett Hartley	88.2
T15	Josh Brown	88.2
T17	Chris Boswell	88.1
T17	Shaun Suisham	88.1
T17	Ryan Longwell	88.1
20	Dustin Hopkins	87.9
T21	Matt Stover	87.8
T21	Aldrick Rosas	87.8
23	Mike Prater	87.7
24	Alex Henery	87.6
25	Cody Parkey	87.5

There are no big surprises on the single-season list, other than Tony Zendejas finishing fifth; in 1991 he hit on all his field goal attempts but missed an extra point try. Of the top 26 single-season totals on the list (there was a four-way tie at number 23), they were all from 1989 forward, and 20 of the seasons have occurred since 2000. Adam Vinatieri appears on the list three times, while Gary Anderson and Jason Hanson each made the list twice. Morten Andersen, number two on the career-scoring list, did not make the single-season list in any particular season.

From the career list, all have been active since at least 2006 when Mike Vanderjagt retired.

Table 7.13
25 Highest and Lowest Single-Season Adjusted Points Above League (APAL)

RK	KICKER	TM	YL	APAL	RK	KICKER	TM	YL	APAL
1	Lou Groza	CLE	53N	36.88	1	John Aveni	WAS	61N	-28.96
2	Jim Bakken	STL	67N	26.37	2	Paul Hornung	G B	64N	-27.01
3	M Vanderjagt	IND	03N	24.64	3	Fred Steinfort	BNE	83N	-24.99
4	Jim Turner	NYJ	68A	24.34	4	Ali Haji-Sheikh	NYG	84N	-22.75
5	Jan Stenerud	K C	69A	23.71	5	B Timberlake	NYG	65N	-22.59
6	Gary Anderson	MIN	98N	23.18	6	P Martinovich	BKA	47F	-22.07
7	Pat Summerall	NYG	59N	22.74	7	Bill Capece	T B	83N	-21.83
8	Gene Mingo	DEN	62A	22.37	8	Dick Guesman	DEN	64A	-20.89
9	Fred Cox	MIN	69N	21.82	9	Ken Vinyard	ATL	70N	-20.52
10	Jan Stenerud	K C	68A	21.10	10	Mason Crosby	G B	12N	-20.45
11	Nick Lowery	K C	90N	20.68	11	Mike Cofer	S F	91N	-20.02
12	Ben Agajanian	LAA	47F	20.42	12	Art Michalik	PIT	55N	-19.61
13	Jan Stenerud	G B	81N	20.11	13	G Cappelletti	BOP	69A	-19.42
14	George Blair	S D	62A	19.54	14	Joe Geri	CHC	52N	-19.33
15	Lou Groza	CLE	52N	19.13	15	David Akers	S F	12N	-19.25
16	Neil Rackers	ARZ	05N	18.98	16	Shane Marler	JAX	03N	-18.69
17	Jeff Wilkins	SLR	03N	18.63	17	Chip Lohmiller	WAS	93N	-18.15
18	Fred Cone	G B	55N	18.57	18	Jerry DePoyster	DET	68N	-18.02
19	Scott Norwood	BUF	88N	18.55	19	Scott Sisson	N E	93N	-17.87
20	Tony Fritsch	HOU	79N	18.39	20	Jim O'Brien	BAL	72N	-17.80
21	Lou Michaels	PIT	62N	18.30	21	Greg Davis	PHX	92N	-17.65
22	Errol Mann	DET	69N	18.19	22	Happy Feller	PHI	71N	-17.56
23	Jim Bakken	STL	64N	18.07	23	Larry Barnes	OAK	60A	-17.33
24	M Andersen	N O	86N	18.04	24	Gene Mingo	PIT	70N	-17.05
25	Don Chandler	NYG	62N	17.95	25	Greg Zuerlein	SLR	15N	-17.01

I feel very confident that the highest single season APAL score will never be broken, or even seriously approached. In 1953 Lou Groza hit 23 of 26 field goal attempts (88.5 percent) when the rest of the NFL kickers hit barely over 40 percent. Gary Anderson in 1998 hit 59 of 59 extra points and 35 of 35 field goals during the regular season for number six on the list, and he didn't even come close to approaching Groza's mark. In order to break Groza's single season APAL mark without missing a field goal, Gary Anderson would have had to have perfect in 57 field goal attempts during his 1998 season.

The most amazing thing about Groza's record is that he did it in only 12 games. Even though it was more than 60 years ago, Lou Groza had, in my opinion, the greatest season of any kicker in pro football history, and he should have won the MVP award although in 1953 it went to his teammate Otto Graham. Groza did win the Sporting News MVP award the following season.

I think the Luckman Effect might be in play with respect to the PAL all-time best and worst seasons, to an extent; it does seem that there are an abnormal number of kickers from smaller (12 teams or less) leagues near the top of the lists. In spite of that, of the 25 lowest single season APAL scores, there is a pretty good mix of kickers from the 1950s through the modern era. No kicker appears on this list more than once.

One oddity was the aforementioned Ali Haji-Sheikh, who led the NFL in APAL in 1983 during Mark Moseley's prolific season. In 1984, Haji-Sheikh had one of the worst seasons in pro football history according to APAL, as he was more than 22 points below average. Haji-Sheikh, along with Mason Crosby and David Akers in 2012, were the only kickers on the worst APAL list whose teams made it to the playoffs during the season in question.

One kicker on the list whose performance probably cost his team a spot in the playoffs was Mike Cofer, whose 49ers finished 10–6 in 1991 and missed the playoffs due to being on the short end of a tie-breaker with Atlanta. Had the Niners had an average kicker in 1991, they would have easily made the postseason. I won't do an analysis on Cofer, but I'll do one on Paul Hornung.

Paul Hornung's dismal kicking performance in 1964 (12-38 in field goals), I am going to argue, kept Green Bay out of the postseason. The Packers finished 8–5–1 behind the 12–2 Colts, but if you review the missed field goals and reconstruct history, it is easy to see that the Packers perhaps should have finished 11–2–1 with the Colts at 10–4 if Green Bay had a decent kicker.

The Packers finished 8–5–1, but if you review their losses and the tie:

In Week 2 Green Bay lost to Baltimore 21–20, but Hornung missed field goals of 32 and 46 yards and an extra point. If he had made either of those field goals, the Packers would have won. The rest of the NFL except for Hornung was 1-6 from 46 yards out, and 9-1 from 32 yards away. The 46-yard try was a low-probability try, but the 32-yard field goal should have been makeable, and Green Bay should have won that game, or at least tied it, if he had hit the extra point. Add one win to Green Bay and subtract a win from Baltimore.

In Week 4 Green Bay lost to Minnesota 24–23, and Hornung was 1–1 on his field goal attempt from 20 yards out but missed an extra point. Green Bay should have had a tie here, add a tie to Green Bay, and subtract a loss.

In Week 6 Green Bay lost to Baltimore 24–21, and Hornung missed five field goals, from 17, 33 and 43 yards and two from 46. One of the misses from 46 was blocked, so I won't dock him for that one. As we mentioned before, the 46-yard field goal was low-probability, but from 43 yards the rest of the NFL was 7–13 from 43 yards away, so it was about 50–50 and Hornung could have been expected to hit it. That leaves 33 and 17 yards, and from 33 yards everybody in the NFL was 2–6 but in reality, there was probably a 60–70 percent probability of making it. Hornung missed two field goals from 17 yards away in 1964, while no other NFL kicker missed from that distance. Hornung should have hit the 17-yard field goal and hit from either 33 yards or one of the longer ones and the Packers win. Add another win to GB, subtract another loss from Baltimore.

In Week 7 Green Bay lost to Los Angeles 27–17, and Hornung missed two field goals. I can't blame Hornung for this one.

In Week 10 Green Bay lost to San Francisco 24–14, and Hornung missed four field goals including one that was blocked from 34 yards. Hornung would have had to hit all four field goals (the others were from 43, 38 and 17 yards), and I doubt most kickers in 1964 would have been able to do it.

In Week 14 Green Bay tied Los Angeles 24–24. Number 5 missed three field goals (one was blocked) and one of the misses was from 13 yards. The Pack should have won this game. Add a win to Green Bay, subtract a loss.

In the final analysis, add two wins, change a loss to a tie and a tie to a win to Green Bay and subtract two wins from Baltimore, which is a net plus three wins for Green Bay and a net two losses for Baltimore. You wind up with Green Bay at 11-2-1 and Baltimore at 10-4.

Don Chandler joined the Packers in 1965, took over the kicking job, and Paul Hornung's kicking career was over.

Table 7.14
25 Highest and Lowest Career Adjusted Points Above League (APAL)

RK	KICKER	APAL	RK	KICKER	APAL
1	Nick Lowery	132.32	1	Greg Davis	-66.27
2	Gary Anderson	116.00	2	Neil O'Donoghue	-50.49
3	Lou Groza	114.57	3	Michael Husted	-49.42
4	Jim Bakken	98.00	4	Mike Cofer	-45.33
5	M Andersen	97.72	5	Chris Bahr	-44.64
6	Jan Stenerud	97.36	6	S Mike-Mayer	-43.28
7	Matt Stover	88.03	7	Billy Cundiff	-41.81
8	Fred Cox	85.13	8	Wayne Walker	-40.74
9	Garo Yepremian	74.19	9	Mason Crosby	-39.82
10	John Carney	69.79	10	John Hall	-36.83
11	Jim Turner	67.15	11	Joe Danelo	-36.72
12	M Vanderjagt	64.48	12	Kris Brown	-32.15
13	Eddie Murray	61.28	13	Fred Steinfort	-31.64
14	Don Cockroft	58.51	14	Nick Folk	-30.08
15	Adam Vinatieri	56.91	15	N Mike-Mayer	-29.73
16	Bruce Gossett	56.59	16	Tommy Davis	-29.36
17	Stephen Gostkowski	54.82	17	Josh Scobee	-28.23
18	Robbie Gould	54.06	18	Chip Lohmiller	-25.34
19	Justin Tucker	52.46	19	Mike Nugent	-24.79
20	Sam Baker	51.40	20	Wade Richey	-24.59
21	Jason Hanson	50.59	21	S Janikowski	-24.35
22	Pat Leahy	50.43	22	Bob Thomas	-23.15
23	Matt Bryant	48.06	23	Graham Gano	-21.24
24	Norm Johnson	46.90	24	Dean Biasucci	-20.71
25	Tony Fritsch	44.82	25	Paul Edinger	-20.55

It was a bit of a surprise that the top career APAL score belonged to Nick Lowery. When I was compiling the data, I figured the career leader would either be Gary Anderson or Morten Andersen based on sheer longevity, and neither of them would have lasted very long if they weren't outstanding kickers. The reason Lowery finished first by a big margin is that he never really had a bad season until the final season of his career. The only seasons in which he had a negative APAL score were in his rookie season of 1978 (when he missed his only field goal try of the season despite hitting all seven extra point attempts), 1984 (APAL score of -0.8) and his final season in 1996 (PAL of -7.4). Six seasons he had an APAL above 10, and one year was above 20. And he accomplished his career APAL total in only 17 seasons, when Gary and Morten needed 23 and 25 seasons, respectively, to get where they are.

Adam Vinatieri is at number one on the career points list, but he's only had an APAL above 10 three times (in 23 seasons) and was below zero in APAL seven seasons, and in four other seasons, had an APAL between zero and one. His career APAL2 of 56.91 puts him at number 15 all time. In other words, despite the fact that he has spent most of his career playing for outstanding offenses led by Tom Brady and Peyton Manning and Andrew Luck giving him all the point opportunities, the APAL system sees him as an average to above average kicker, not one of the greatest kickers of all time.

For one thing, Vinatieri has only led the NFL in scoring one time in his career, and on two other occasions he was third in the league. A lot of his fame rides on three clutch playoff field goals, against the Raiders in the Tuck Rule game, and the other two to win Super Bowls XXXVI and XXXVIII in the final seconds. He is a future Hall of Famer for sure, probably first ballot, but I feel that Adam Vinatieri is overrated.

Greg Davis, who kicked for the Cardinals and other teams in the 1980s and 1990s, tops the list of career worst in APAL. In an era where the league field goal percentage was between 75 and 80 percent, Davis had a fairly long career where he kicked at a success rate of just under 69 percent. Over the course of more than 300 field goal attempts, that is going to make for a low career APAL total.

Chris Bahr is probably the single biggest surprise on the list, but he had one really good season and five really bad ones.

Table 7.15
25 Highest and Lowest Single-Season Adjusted Points Above League 2 (APAL2)

RK	KICKER	TM	YL	A2	M	RK	KICKER	TM	YL	A2	M
1	Jim Bakken	STL	67N	30.09	0	1	P Hornung	G B	64N	-31.55	0
2	Lou Groza	CLE	53N	27.51	1	2	F Steinfort	BNE	83N	-25.79	
3	M Moseley	WAS	79N	27.15		3	Martinovich	BKA	47F	-22.53	2
4	Jan Stenerud	K C	69A	26.56		4	Scott Sisson	N E	93N	-21.37	
5	Gene Mingo	DEN	62A	24.97		5	C Lohmiller	WAS	93N	-20.72	
6	Raul Allegre	BAL	83N	24.90		6	G Cappelletti	BOP	69A	-20.65	

7. Kicker Ratings

RK	KICKER	TM	YL	A2	M	RK	KICKER	TM	YL	A2	M
7	Neil Rackers	ARZ	05N	23.48		7	Haji-Sheikh	NYG	84N	-20.41	
8	Jan Stenerud	K C	68A	23.36		8	Bill Capece	T B	83N	-20.08	
9	Justin Tucker	BAR	16N	23.31		9	Gary Glick	PIT	57N	-19.70	0
10	Mike Mercer	OKC	66A	23.30		10	B Timberlake	NYG	65N	-19.28	
11	M Andersen	N O	85N	22.98		11	Joe Nedney	MIA	96N	-18.86	
12	F Steinfort	DEN	80N	22.84		12	Shane Marler	JAX	03N	-18.63	
13	Jim Bakken	STL	64N	21.78	1	13	David Akers	SF	12N	-17.48	
14	B Agajanian	LAA	47F	21.14	1	14	Jim O'Brien	BAL	72N	-17.42	
15	Jan Stenerud	K C	70N	20.74		15	R Aguayo	TB	16N	-17.30	
16	S Janikowski	OAK	09N	20.58		16	Happy Feller	PHI	71N	-17.14	
17	P Summerall	NYG	59N	20.51	1	17	C Gilchrist	BUF	62A	-17.04	
18	G Anderson	MIN	98N	20.13		18	Keith Lincoln	S D	64A	-16.90	
19	G Cappelletti	BOP	61A	20.03		19	Ken Vinyard	ATL	70N	-16.89	
20	Haji-Sheikh	NYG	83N	19.89		20	Art Michalik	PIT	55N	-16.70	0
21	Tony Fritsch	HOU	79N	19.85		21	Tim Mazzetti	ATL	79N	-16.35	
22	Tony Franklin	PHI	79N	19.69		22	M Crosby	GB	12N	-16.34	
T23	Lou Groza	CLE	52N	19.47	1	23	J DePoyster	DET	68N	-16.32	
T23	Sam Baker	PHI	66N	19.45	0	24	Kris Brown	HOT	09N	-16.26	
25	Gene Mingo	DEN	63A	19.15		25	Mike Mercer	G B	69N	-16.22	

It has to be kept in mind that APAL2 is only really accurate with the 1960 through 1969 AFL and the 1961 and 1963 and 1968 through 2018 NFL seasons. One day when the missed field goal distance data is complete, or nearly complete, this list should look much different. By contrast, in the 1953 NFL there are 24 missed field goals for which we do not know the difference, and only one of them belongs to Lou Groza.

Jan Stenerud appears three times in the top 25 highest APAL2 list, along with Bakken. Lou the Toe finished in the top 25 twice. Nobody else appeared more than once.

As I previously explained how to read the MISS (M) column, in 1967 Jim Bakken has all of his missed field goal distances accounted for, but there are still two field goals whose distances are not accounted for, and when they are found one day, they will fractionally change Bakken's APAL2, maybe by a few hundredths of a point, meaning his current APAL2 is not 100 percent accurate, but it is close.

Ali Haji-Sheikh, who if you will remember had the APAL2 of 19.51 in 1983, had a truly terrible season in 1984. Gary Anderson followed up his stellar 1998 season with a horrendous 1999 season. No kicker appears on this list more than once, but 15 of the 25 worst APAL seasons also appear on the bottom PAL2 list.

Paul Hornung's 1964 season tops the APAL2 list, and it is doubtful his -31.30 score will be topped anytime soon.

Table 7.16
25 Highest and Lowest Career Adjusted Points Above League 2 (APAL2)

RK	KICKER	APAL2	MISS	RK	KICKER	APAL2	MISS
1	Lou Groza	139.61	20	1	Billy Cundiff	-47.69	N/A
2	Nick Lowery	138.27	N/A	2	Neil O'Donoghue	-44.10	N/A
3	Morten Andersen	128.95	N/A	3	Steve Mike-Mayer	-40.23	N/A
4	Jan Stenerud	124.55	N/A	4	Greg Davis	-39.76	N/A
5	Jim Bakken	104.50	0	5	Mike Cofer	-37.98	N/A
6	Jason Hanson	99.86	N/A	6	Paul Hornung	-37.63	0
7	Gary Anderson	96.71	N/A	7	Roger LeClerc	-35.50	1
8	Sam Baker	86.57	0	8	Mike Nugent	-35.23	N/A
9	Garo Yepremian	77.80	0	9	John Hall	-34.19	N/A
10	George Blanda	77.79	15	10	Chip Lohmiller	-31.74	N/A
11	Fred Cox	67.48	0	11	Chris Bahr	-31.44	N/A
12	Eddie Murray	66.03	N/A	12	Mason Crosby	-31.39	N/A
13	Justin Tucker	64.06	N/A	13	Michael Husted	-29.67	N/A
14	John Kasay	60.47	N/A	14	Bobby Walston	-29.65	5
15	Matt Stover	55.73	N/A	15	Wade Richey	-27.80	N/A
16	Mike Vanderjagt	55.16	N/A	16	Nick Folk	-27.47	N/A
17	Mark Moseley	53.66	N/A	17	Matt Bahr	-27.07	N/A
18	Norm Johnson	50.23	N/A	18	Gerry Soltau	-27.01	5
19	Jason Elam	47.54	N/A	19	David Treadwell	-26.90	N/A
20	Robbie Gould	46.79	N/A	20	Fred Steinfort	-25.71	N/A
21	S Janikowski	46.35	N/A	21	Bob Thomas	-25.54	N/A
22	Don Cockroft	45.42	N/A	22	D Van Raaphorst	-24.58	N/A
23	D Igwebuike	44.80	N/A	23	Nick Novak	-24.11	N/A
24	Ben Agajanian	43.67	16	24	Mac Percival	-24.05	N/A
25	Rafael Septien	41.61	N/A	25	Kris Brown	-23.84	N/A

One could look at the list on the left as a ranking of sorts of the best kickers of the all-time, I'm not quite sure of the order, but I agree with the top four. There are a few surprises; one is Donald Igwebuike at number 21 on the APAL2 list. Another surprise is Mike Vanderjagt at number 15, ranking higher than guys like Norm Johnson and Elam and John Carney whose careers were almost twice as long.

Sebastian Janikowski is one of five active kickers in 2018 on the list, along with Justin Tucker and Robbie Gould. The other two are Adam Vinatieri, and the man who replaced Vinatieri in New England, Stephen Gostkowski. As I mentioned earlier, Gostkowski is scoring points at a record pace, but like Vinatieri he too seems to be maybe a little overrated. Gostkowski's career APAL2 is 27.88, good for 45th best all-time, while Vinatieri's APAL2 of 40.64 comes in at number 26.

The current kicker who is quickly shooting up the career APAL2 list is Justin Tucker of Baltimore. After seven seasons, his career APAL2 score is 64, and that includes a monster season with an APAL2 of 23, and other outstanding seasons of 11, 10 of 9. He is the best kicker of this era.

Although Lou Groza is the current career leader in APAL2, as each of those 20 missed field goal distances are located, they will most likely lower his score, which means in time, Nick Lowery should be the career APAL2 leader. My guess is that when we have all of the missed field goal distances for Groza's career, his career APAL2 score should be expected to drop 15 to 20 points from where it is now.

The big surprise on the worst career APAL2 list is that Billy Cundiff is at number one. Mason Crosby is within two very bad seasons of overtaking Cundiff, and his career high in APAL2 for a season was in 2013 when he scored a 2.94.

Chris and Matt Bahr both appear on the worst career APAL2 list.

Anderson Vs. Andersen

It is interesting to note that Morten Andersen finished significantly ahead of Gary Anderson in APAL2 where Gary had a big edge in APAL. With APAL2 being a more accurate system for rating kickers than APAL, I am forced to conclude that Morten is a little better than Gary. One way of comparing the two is by career average field goal make and miss distance. In career average successful field goal distance Morten leads Gary 34.8 to 34.1; in career average missed field goal distance Morten again has a big edge of 44.5 to 42.4.

One might think that having a higher average miss distance is a bad thing, but it is actually an indication of a kicker with a stronger leg.

If you compare the two at various distance ranges (40–44 yards, 45–49 yards and so on), the differences between the two become clear. I have data on every make and miss for both of them, as they both debuted in 1982. I'll throw in Nick Lowery, since I've been touting him quite a bit in this chapter. I also added the aggregate NFL totals for the entire 1981–2007 era, which completely covers all their careers except for the first full season of Lowery's career.

Table 7.17 should be pretty much self-explanatory:

Table 7.17
Field Goal Distance Data for Anderson, Andersen, Lowery, NFL 1981–2007

Kicker	Dist.	17–24	25–29	30–34	35–39	40–45	45–49	50–54	55+	SUM
Gary Anderson	Make	88	95	93	88	107	55	11	1	538
	Att	91	106	102	106	138	89	33	5	670
	%	96.7	89.6	91.2	83.0	77.5	61.8	33.3	20.0	80.3

Kicker	Dist.	17–24	25–29	30–34	35–39	40–45	45–49	50–54	55+	SUM
Morten Andersen	Make	78	95	93	77	79	58	33	7	520
	Att	80	98	102	92	113	89	70	13	657
	%	97.5	96.9	91.2	83.7	69.9	65.2	47.1	53.8	79.1
Nick Lowery	Make	63	49	64	72	60	37	16	2	363
	Att	64	51	74	85	76	59	33	9	451
	%	98.4	96.1	86.5	84.7	78.9	62.7	48.5	22.2	80.5
NFL 1981 to 2007	Make	4745	4249	4221	4075	3711	3053	1619	204	25877
	Att	4906	4608	4890	5083	5194	4842	2920	586	33029
	%	96.7	92.2	86.3	80.2	71.4	63.1	55.4	34.8	78.3

Morton Andersen beats Gary Anderson by a sizeable margin in APAL2 (over 30 points) on the basis of making more than three times as many field goals from over 50 yards (40 to 12). The fact that Morten hit on over half his kicks from 55 or more yards is mind-boggling; the rest of the league besides Andersen hit about a third of their attempts from 55 or more.

After reviewing this chart, I am convinced that Morton Andersen has had a slightly more impressive career than Gary Anderson simply on the basis of greater leg strength. As their careers have run exactly parallel to one another so one does not really have an edge based on longevity over the other and we would not have the arguments associated with comparing kickers from different eras. Morten leads Gary in every distance category except for 40 to 44 yards and Gary also has a slim lead in 35–39 of one percent.

I think Morten and Gary are both Hall of Fame caliber kickers, and I was surprised it took Morten Andersen five tries to get into Canton. Gary Anderson hasn't gone in yet but he will eventually. If Nick Lowery joined them in Canton I would not have a problem with his being there, either, but I think it is doubtful he will get in. Lowery is more of a HOVG (Hall of Very Good) type.

The Field Goal Success Curve

Of the seasons for which we have complete field goal make and miss distance data, 1960–69 AFL and 1961 and 1963 and 1968–2018 NFL, Table 7.18 displays the aggregate data by distance (YD) with makes (MK), attempts (ATT) and percentage (PCT):

Table 7.18
Field Goal by Distance Data, 1960–69 AFL,
1961, 1963, 1968–2018 NFL

YD	MK	ATT	PCT	YD	MK	ATT	PCT	YD	MK	ATT	PCT
76	0	1	0.000	52	365	832	0.439	28	1138	1311	0.868

YD	MK	ATT	PCT
75	0	0	0.000
74	0	1	0.000
73	0	1	0.000
72	0	0	0.000
71	0	2	0.000
70	0	1	0.000
69	0	1	0.000
68	0	3	0.000
67	0	2	0.000
66	0	7	0.000
65	0	7	0.000
64	1	8	0.125
63	4	24	0.167
62	2	20	0.100
61	5	24	0.208
60	6	34	0.176
59	11	42	0.262
58	17	71	0.239
57	28	98	0.286
56	46	135	0.341
55	97	241	0.402
54	178	386	0.461
53	318	636	0.500
51	414	834	0.496
50	496	990	0.501
49	583	1122	0.520
48	715	1380	0.518
47	793	1499	0.529
46	710	1238	0.574
45	801	1366	0.586
44	776	1314	0.591
43	882	1397	0.631
42	1026	1640	0.626
41	884	1291	0.685
40	983	1420	0.692
39	937	1311	0.715
38	1043	1410	0.740
37	1161	1603	0.724
36	897	1178	0.761
35	998	1293	0.772
34	970	1253	0.774
33	1158	1424	0.813
32	1203	1486	0.810
31	986	1171	0.842
30	1014	1229	0.825
29	1015	1196	0.849
27	1256	1442	0.871
26	959	1166	0.822
25	1055	1116	0.945
24	1019	1126	0.905
23	1181	1278	0.924
22	1171	1260	0.929
21	919	975	0.943
20	926	983	0.942
19	686	733	0.936
18	305	305	1.000
17	126	126	1.000
16	104	118	0.881
15	115	125	0.920
14	106	112	0.946
13	101	111	0.910
12	150	156	0.962
11	71	74	0.959
10	85	91	0.934
9	63	65	0.969
8	31	32	0.969
7	2	2	1.000
SUM	33092	45329	0.730

When we graph distance or YD from Table 7.18 (x) versus success percentage or PCT (y), we get Figure 7.3. The graph in Figure 7.3 is fairly smooth, and the thinner, curved line is the trendline. For a 50-yard field goal, the success rate is about 50 percent, and at 60 yards, a field goal is about 20 percent successful.

The lighter, smooth curve is the least squares curve (polynomial degree 6), that intersects at zero percent at approximately 66 or 67 yards, which would be the upper limit of kicking a field goal for an average kicker under normal conditions. But other factors have to be taken into account, including the stadium and kicking with the wind and a warm temperature, and a kicker with a strong leg which could increase the maximum distance.

It also must be taken into consideration that the curve displayed in Figure 7.3 includes all field goal attempts over the past 50 seasons, and if you're attempting to determine the maximum distance of a field goal in the modern era, the data should probably be limited to field goal attempts over the past 10 seasons, with a field goal curve being generated from that data.

Figure 7.3. Graph of field goal attempt distance (YD) versus success percentage (PCT) data from Table 7.18.

Table 7.19
Highest and Lowest Qualifying APAL Values for Every League 1938–1969 NFL, 1946–1949 AAFC, 1960–1969 AFL and for AFC and NFC 1970–2018

YL	BEST KICKER, TEAM, APAL			WORST KICKER, TEAM, APAL		
38N	Ward Cuff	NYG	7.14	Hank Reese	PHI	-4.64
39N	Chuck Hanneman	DET	6.42	Clarke Hinkle	G B	-10.59
40N	Clarke Hinkle	G B	12.74	George Somers	PHI	-4.64
41N	Andy Marefos	NYG	7.25	Mel Condit	BKN	-6.99
42N	Frank Maznicki	CHI	7.92	Armond Niccolai	PIT	-9.70
43N	Don Hutson	G B	8.59	Joe Aguirre	WAS	-3.90
44N	Ken Strong	NYG	9.26	Bernie Masterson	BKN	-5.52
45N	Ben Agajanian	PPG	6.18	Joe Kuharich	CHC	-3.95
46F	Steve Nemeth	CHA	12.27	Bob Nelson	LAA	-4.60
46N	Bob Waterfield	L A	9.74	Bill Dudley	PIT	-4.38
47F	Ben Agajanian	LAA	20.42	Phil Martinovich	BKA	-22.07
47N	Pat Harder	CHC	11.23	Cliff Patton	PHI	-11.13

7. Kicker Ratings

YL	BEST KICKER, TEAM, APAL			WORST KICKER, TEAM, APAL		
48F	Rex Grossman	BAA	11.52	Ben Agajanian	LAA	-4.21
48N	Cliff Patton	PHI	13.94	Joe Muha	PHI	-6.61
49F	Rex Grossman	BAA	5.60	Lou Groza	CLE	-6.00
49N	Ben Agajanian	NYG	8.25	Ted Fritsch	GB	-15.64
50N	Lou Groza	CLE	17.16	Ted Fritsch	G B	-16.15
51N	Ray Poole	NYG	12.90	Gordie Soltau	S F	-11.30
52N	Lou Groza	CLE	19.13	Joe Geri	CHC	-19.33
53N	Lou Groza	CLE	36.88	Fred Cone	G B	-9.06
54N	Lou Groza	CLE	11.06	Jim Martin	DET	-6.95
55N	Fred Cone	G B	18.57	Art Michalik	PIT	-19.61
56N	Bobby Layne	DET	15.84	Bert Rechichar	BAL	-13.27
57N	Lou Groza	CLE	12.87	Gary Glick	PIT	-16.03
58N	Paige Cothren	L A	9.57	Gordie Soltau	S F	-8.87
59N	Pat Summerall	NYG	22.74	Lou Groza	CLE	-10.86
60A	Gene Mingo	DEN	17.87	Larry Barnes	OAK	-17.33
60N	Bobby Walston	PHI	9.14	John Aveni	CHI	-7.66
61A	George Blanda	HOU	16.41	Jack Spikes	DTX	-7.07
61N	Lou Groza	CLE	15.88	John Aveni	WAS	-28.96
62A	Gene Mingo	DEN	22.37	Cookie Gilchrist	BUF	-9.94
62N	Lou Michaels	PIT	18.30	Bobby Walston	PHI	-11.06
63A	Gino Cappelletti	BOP	16.53	Jack Spikes	K C	-13.18
63N	Jim Martin	BAL	13.90	Tommy Davis	S F	-16.65
64A	Gino Cappelletti	BOP	16.68	Dick Guesman	DEN	-20.89
64N	Jim Bakken	STL	18.07	Paul Hornung	G B	-27.01
65A	Pete Gogolak	BUF	10.48	Tommy Brooker	K C	-11.65
65N	Fred Cox	MIN	15.61	Bob Timberlake	NYG	-22.59
66A	Mike Mercer	OKC	14.66	Mike Eischied	OAK	-7.41
66N	Sam Baker	PHI	13.21	Don Chandler	G B	-12.08
67A	George Blanda	OAK	14.05	Roger LeClerc	DEN	-6.90
67N	Jim Bakken	STL	26.37	Wayne Walker	DET	-7.18
68A	Jim Turner	NYJ	24.34	John Wittenborn	HOU	-11.77
68N	Mac Percival	CHI	17.21	Jerry DePoyster	DET	-18.02
69A	Jan Stenerud	K C	23.71	Gino Cappelletti	BOP	-19.42
69N	Fred Cox	MIN	21.82	Mike Mercer	G B	-12.03
70A	Jan Stenerud	K C	16.73	Gene Mingo	PIT	-17.05
70N	Curt Knight	WAS	12.29	Ken Vinyard	ATL	-20.52

YL	BEST KICKER, TEAM, APAL			WORST KICKER, TEAM, APAL		
71A	Garo Yepremian	MIA	14.99	Bobby Howfield	NYJ	-10.15
71N	Fred Cox	MIN	10.59	Happy Feller	PHI	-17.56
72A	Don Cockroft	CLE	16.95	Jim O'Brien	BAL	-17.80
72N	Chester Marcol	G B	12.67	Curt Knight	WAS	-13.14
73A	Don Cockroft	CLE	8.37	Ray Wersching	S D	-16.37
73N	Bruce Gossett	S F	16.95	Curt Knight	WAS	-12.98
74A	Don Cockroft	CLE	15.10	Dennis Partee	S D	-5.50
74N	Errol Mann	DET	10.87	Bruce Gossett	S F	-10.60
75A	Roy Gerela	PIT	13.32	David Green	CIN	-11.73
75N	Jim Bakken	STL	14.15	Steve Mike-Mayer	S F	-13.73
76A	Toni Linhart	BAL	16.61	Errol Mann	DTO	-12.09
76N	Efren Herrera	DAL	16.95	Joe Danelo	NYG	-12.80
77A	Don Cockroft	CLE	13.01	Garo Yepremian	MIA	-8.16
77N	Efren Herrera	DAL	5.26	Steve Mike-Mayer	DET	-9.67
78A	Garo Yepremian	MIA	13.45	Roy Gerela	PIT	-11.08
78N	Tim Mazzetti	ATL	10.34	Fred Steinfort	ATL	-10.41
79A	Tony Fritsch	HOU	18.39	Toni Linhart	BNJ	-11.03
79N	Mark Moseley	WAS	16.97	Steve Little	STL	-11.24
80A	John Smith	N E	16.91	Chris Bahr	OAK	-14.71
80N	Tim Mazzetti	ATL	5.61	Mark Moseley	WAS	-10.62
81A	U von Schamann	MIA	12.29	Dave Jacobs	CLE	-12.40
81N	Jan Stenerud	G B	20.11	Benny Ricardo	N O	-9.41
82A	Nick Lowery	K C	9.33	Matt Bahr	CLE	-9.02
82N	Mark Moseley	WAS	15.84	John Roveto	CHI	-14.51
83A	Gary Anderson	PIT	15.95	Fred Steinfort	BNE	-24.99
83N	Ali Haji-Sheikh	NYG	15.82	Bill Capece	T B	-21.83
84A	Norm Johnson	SEA	9.50	U von Schamann	MIA	-15.82
84N	Jan Stenerud	MIN	10.92	Ali Haji-Sheikh	NYG	-22.75
85A	Nick Lowery	K C	15.49	Rich Karlis	DEN	-15.13
85N	Morten Andersen	N O	17.14	Jan Stenerud	MIN	-11.87
86A	Tony Franklin	N E	13.03	Jim Breech	CIN	-14.42
86N	Morten Andersen	N O	18.04	Eric Schubert	STL	-14.50
87A	Dean Biasucci	IND	16.65	Tony Franklin	N E	-9.45
87N	Roger Ruzek	DAL	14.87	Jim Gallery	STL	-13.02
88A	Scott Norwood	BUF	18.55	Teddy Garcia	N E	-14.60
88N	Eddie Murray	DET	15.12	Roger Ruzek	DAL	-10.52

7. Kicker Ratings

YL	BEST KICKER, TEAM, APAL			WORST KICKER, TEAM, APAL		
89A	David Treadwell	DEN	9.78	Norm Johnson	SEA	-8.87
89N	Eddie Murray	DET	15.75	Luis Zendejas	PDA	-9.52
90A	Nick Lowery	K C	20.68	Tony Zendejas	HOU	-6.14
90N	Steve Christie	T B	10.01	Al Del Greco	PHX	-8.47
91A	Jeff Jaeger	LAR	12.37	Dean Biasucci	IND	-12.32
91N	Tony Zendejas	L A	13.49	Mike Cofer	S F	-20.02
92A	Nick Lowery	K C	15.04	Dean Biasucci	IND	-15.25
92N	Morten Andersen	N O	13.27	Greg Davis	PHX	-17.65
93A	Gary Anderson	PIT	16.60	Scott Sisson	N E	-17.87
93N	Norm Johnson	ATL	17.52	Chip Lohmiller	WAS	-18.15
94A	John Carney	S D	13.03	Dean Biasucci	IND	-8.63
94N	Fuad Reveiz	MIN	10.52	Michael Husted	T B	-14.26
95A	Matt Stover	CLE	11.22	Mike Cofer	IND	-8.85
95N	Chris Boniol	DAL	15.24	Steve McLaughlin	SLR	-13.11
96A	Cary Blanchard	IND	12.88	Joe Nedney	MIA	-16.70
96N	Chris Boniol	DAL	9.29	Greg Davis	ARZ	-6.56
97A	Pete Stoyanovich	K C	14.63	Cole Ford	OAK	-14.47
97N	R Cunningham	DAL	16.24	Jeff Wilkins	SLR	-11.79
98A	Al Del Greco	TEN	15.90	Greg Davis	OAK	-13.47
98N	Gary Anderson	MIN	23.18	Wade Richey	S F	-12.10
99A	Mike Vanderjagt	IND	14.41	Michael Husted	OAK	-12.38
99N	Wade Richey	S F	8.90	R Cunningham	DCA	-14.22
00A	Matt Stover	BAR	12.49	Neil Rackers	CIN	-14.41
00N	Joe Nedney	DNC	11.79	Wade Richey	S F	-9.48
01A	Jason Elam	DEN	11.56	Neil Rackers	CIN	-14.09
01N	John Carney	N O	10.95	Ryan Longwell	G B	-11.54
02A	Adam Vinatieri	N E	12.09	Todd Peterson	PIT	-13.82
02N	John Carney	N O	12.56	James Tuthill	WAS	-8.07
03A	Mike Vanderjagt	IND	24.64	Shane Marler	JAX	-18.69
03N	Jeff Wilkins	SLR	18.63	M Grammatica	T B	-14.73
04A	Adam Vinatieri	NE	13.86	Kris Brown	HOU	-7.13
04N	Josh Brown	SEA	8.94	M Grammatica	TB	-14.26
05A	Mike Vanderjagt	IND	9.19	S Janikowski	OAK	-12.93
05N	Neil Rackers	ARZ	18.98	Paul Edinger	MIN	-7.47
06A	Matt Stover	BAR	11.41	Olindo Mare	MIA	-10.14
06N	Robbie Gould	CHI	8.83	Michael Koenen	ATL	-13.11

YL	BEST KICKER, TEAM, APAL			WORST KICKER, TEAM, APAL		
07A	Shayne Graham	CIN	9.25	S Janikowski	OAK	-10.57
07N	Morten Andersen	ATL	5.86	Neil Rackers	ARZ	-12.42
08A	S Gostkowski	NE	7.08	Mike Prater	DEN	-12.43
08N	John Carney	NYG	9.20	Shaun Suisham	WAS	-13.65
09A	Nate Kaeding	SD	10.88	Kris Brown	HOT	-15.89
09N	Ryan Longwell	MIN	9.91	Nick Folk	DAL	-14.14
10A	Adam Vinatieri	IND	9.58	Dan Carpenter	MIA	-11.55
10N	Matt Bryant	ATL	8.08	Graham Gano	WAS	-14.74
11A	Rob Bironas	TEN	7.86	Shaun Suisham	PIT	-8.14
11N	Matt Bryant	ATL	9.41	Graham Gano	WAS	-10.21
12A	Phil Dawson	CLE	9.44	Adam Vinatieri	IND	-5.00
12N	Blair Walsh	MIN	9.94	Mason Crosby	GB	-20.45
13A	S Gostkowski	NE	8.13	S Janikowski	OAK	-15.16
13N	Steven Hauschka	SEA	8.67	Garrett Hartley	NO	-12.05
14A	Adam Vinatieri	IND	12.57	Billy Cundiff	CLE	-7.13
14N	Josh Brown	NYG	6.93	Blair Walsh	MIN	-10.41
15A	S Gostkowski	N E	11.15	Josh Scobee	PIT	-8.06
15N	Josh Brown	NYG	10.82	Greg Zuerlein	SLR	-17.01
16A	Justin Tucker	BAR	17.78	Mike Nugent	CIN	-8.69
16N	Matt Bryant	ATL	11.55	Roberto Aguayo	TB	-12.59
17A	Justin Tucker	BAR	11.02	Brandon McManus	DEN	-7.66
17N	Robbie Gould	S F	14.46	Nick Folk	T B	-11.50
18A	Justin Tucker	BAR	7.30	Chris Boswell	PIT	-14.47
18N	Aldrick Rosas	NYG	13.40	Zane Gonzalez	CLA	-11.14

Table 7.20
Highest and Lowest Qualifying APAL2 Values for Every League 1960–1969 AFL, 1961 and 1963 NFL and for AFC and NFC 1970–2018

YL	BEST KICKER, TEAM, APAL2			WORST KICKER, TEAM, APAL2		
60A	Gene Mingo	DEN	12.92	Larry Barnes	OAK	-15.93
61A	Gino Cappelletti	BOP	20.03	Dick Guesman	NYJ	-13.70
61N	Paul Hornung	G B	14.37	John Aveni	WAS	-12.83
62A	Gene Mingo	DEN	24.97	Cookie Gilchrist	BUF	-17.04
63A	Gene Mingo	DEN	19.15	Mack Yoho	BUF	-16.05
63N	Don Chandler	CLE	10.60	Bob Jencks	CHI	-11.40
64A	Gino Cappelletti	BOP	16.86	Keith Lincoln	S D	-16.90

7. Kicker Ratings

YL	BEST KICKER, TEAM, APAL2			WORST KICKER, TEAM, APAL2		
65A	Pete Gogolak	BUF	7.38	Greg Kroner	DEN	-8.29
66A	Mike Mercer	OKC	23.30	Jim Turner	NYJ	-10.09
67A	Jan Stenerud	K C	17.57	Jim Turner	NYJ	-12.88
68A	Jan Stenerud	K C	23.36	Dale Livingston	CIN	-13.26
68N	Fred Cox	MIN	15.11	Jerry DePoyster	DET	-16.32
69A	Jan Stenerud	K C	26.56	Gino Cappelletti	BOP	-20.65
69N	Fred Cox	MIN	15.73	Mike Mercer	G B	-16.22
70A	Jan Stenerud	K C	20.74	Gene Mingo	PIT	-13.64
70N	Curt Knight	WAS	10.85	Ken Vinyard	ATL	-16.89
71A	Garo Yepremian	MIA	12.39	Bobby Howfield	NYJ	-6.64
71N	Tom Dempsey	PHI	10.62	Happy Feller	PHI	-17.14
72A	Don Cockroft	CLE	13.01	Jim O'Brien	BAL	-17.42
72N	Chester Marcol	G B	12.98	Curt Knight	WAS	-13.69
73A	Jim Turner	DEN	11.63	Ray Wersching	S D	-13.03
73N	Nick Mike-Mayer	ATL	13.72	Happy Feller	N O	-12.98
74A	Don Cockroft	CLE	10.71	Dennis Partee	S D	-7.49
74N	Chester Marcol	G B	14.71	David Ray	L A	-11.41
75A	Jim Turner	DEN	7.67	David Green	CIN	-15.38
75N	Tom Dempsey	L A	13.86	Steve Mike-Mayer	S F	-10.05
76A	Toni Linhart	BAL	13.96	Don Cockroft	CLE	-5.35
76N	Rich Szaro	N O	11.32	Joe Danelo	NYG	-14.33
77A	Errol Mann	OAK	12.19	Jan Stenerud	K C	-7.12
77N	Mark Moseley	WAS	10.52	Fred Cox	MIN	-9.89
78A	Pat Leahy	NYJ	16.84	Toni Linhart	BAL	-9.80
78N	Mark Moseley	WAS	15.17	Jim Bakken	STL	-9.28
79A	Tony Fritsch	HOU	19.85	Toni Linhart	BNJ	-15.45
79N	Mark Moseley	WAS	27.15	Tim Mazzetti	ATL	-16.35
80A	Fred Steinfort	DEN	22.84	Steve Mike-Mayer	BAL	-8.55
80N	Neil O'Donoghue	STL	7.29	Tom Birney	G B	-9.15
81A	Nick Lowery	K C	13.36	Dave Jacobs	CLE	-13.21
81N	Jan Stenerud	G B	16.86	Benny Ricardo	N O	-9.02
82A	Nick Lowery	K C	15.45	Matt Bahr	CLE	-11.69
82N	Mark Moseley	WAS	12.18	John Roveto	CHI	-9.33
83A	Raul Allegre	BAL	24.90	Fred Steinfort	BNE	-25.79
83N	Ali Haji-Sheikh	NYG	19.89	Bill Capece	T B	-20.08
84A	Gary Anderson	PIT	6.72	U von Schamann	MIA	-14.42

YL	BEST KICKER, TEAM, APAL2			WORST KICKER, TEAM, APAL2		
84N	Jan Stenerud	MIN	11.99	Ali Haji-Sheikh	NYG	-20.41
85A	Nick Lowery	K C	18.27	Chris Bahr	LAR	-12.88
85N	Morten Andersen	N O	22.98	Jan Stenerud	MIN	-15.75
86A	Tony Franklin	N E	10.26	Rolf Benirschke	S D	-10.77
86N	Morten Andersen	N O	15.59	Eric Schubert	STL	-14.87
87A	Dean Biasucci	IND	17.40	Tony Franklin	N E	-7.62
87N	Roger Ruzek	DAL	13.78	Jim Gallery	STL	-14.53
88A	Dean Biasucci	IND	14.81	Tony Zendejas	HOU	-6.11
88N	Eddie Murray	DET	11.48	Al Del Greco	PHX	-8.02
89A	Scott Norwood	BUF	6.47	Teddy Garcia	N E	-12.41
89N	Eddie Murray	DET	18.00	Roger Ruzek	DAP	-12.59
90A	Nick Lowery	K C	18.15	Scott Norwood	BUF	-9.90
90N	Morten Andersen	N O	10.54	Mike Lansford	L A	-9.29
91A	Jeff Jaeger	LAR	12.61	Pat Leahy	NYJ	-11.55
91N	Tony Zendejas	L A	11.17	Mike Cofer	S F	-16.01
92A	Nick Lowery	K C	9.00	John Kasay	SEA	-7.61
92N	Morten Andersen	N O	12.99	Greg Davis	PHX	-15.23
93A	Gary Anderson	PIT	12.55	Scott Sisson	N E	-21.37
93N	Norm Johnson	ATL	18.05	Chip Lohmiller	WAS	-20.72
94A	Doug Pelfrey	CIN	10.24	Dean Biasucci	IND	-9.07
94N	Fuad Reveiz	MIN	11.26	David Treadwell	NYG	-11.78
95A	Al Del Greco	HOU	14.22	Matt Bahr	N E	-12.36
95N	Morten Andersen	ATL	12.61	Steve McLaughlin	SLR	-13.21
96A	Cary Blanchard	IND	14.51	Joe Nedney	MIA	-18.86
96N	Chris Boniol	DAL	9.03	Greg Davis	ARZ	-8.35
97A	Pete Stoyanovich	K C	18.49	Cole Ford	OAK	-14.24
97N	R Cunningham	DAL	11.72	Jeff Wilkins	SLR	-12.00
98A	Al Del Greco	TEN	14.69	Greg Davis	OAK	-15.29
98N	Gary Anderson	MIN	20.13	Wade Richey	S F	-14.30
99A	Olindo Mare	MIA	16.45	Doug Pelfrey	CIN	-13.60
99N	Jason Hanson	DET	14.38	Gary Anderson	MIN	-15.36
00A	Matt Stover	BAR	11.49	Neil Rackers	CIN	-15.26
00N	Ryan Longwell	G B	13.54	Michael Husted	WAS	-9.92
01A	Jason Elam	DEN	13.23	Neil Rackers	CIN	-14.80
01N	Paul Edinger	CHI	9.40	Ryan Longwell	G B	-7.74
02A	Adam Vinatieri	N E	14.12	Todd Peterson	PIT	-15.56

7. Kicker Ratings

YL	BEST KICKER, TEAM, APAL2			WORST KICKER, TEAM, APAL2		
02N	John Carney	N O	13.17	James Tuthill	WAS	-10.65
03A	Mike Vanderjagt	IND	18.39	Shane Marler	JAX	-18.63
03N	Jeff Wilkins	SLR	14.36	Owen Pochman	S F	-12.58
04A	Matt Stover	BAR	10.01	Kris Brown	HOU	-5.41
04N	David Akers	PHI	8.18	M Grammatica	TB	-15.89
05A	Matt Stover	BAR	8.54	S Janikowski	OAK	-8.22
05N	Neil Rackers	ARZ	23.48	Robbie Gould	CHI	-8.05
06A	Rian Lindell	BUF	8.49	Olindo Mare	MIA	-9.05
06N	John Kasay	CAR	11.34	Michael Koenen	ATL	-10.74
07A	Rob Bironas	TEN	10.42	Adam Vinatieri	IND	-12.83
07N	Ryan Longwell	MIN	8.44	Olindo Mare	N O	-7.77
08A	Rob Bironas	TEN	8.41	Mike Prater	DEN	-11.30
08N	Jason Hanson	DET	11.09	Shaun Suisham	WAS	-11.29
09A	S Janikowski	OAK	20.58	Kris Brown	HOT	-16.26
09N	Neil Rackers	ARZ	6.08	Jason Elam	ATL	-12.50
10A	Neil Rackers	HOT	9.48	Jeff Reed	PSF	-8.62
10N	John Kasay	CAR	7.51	Graham Gano	WAS	-11.01
11A	S Janikowski	OAK	13.11	Billy Cundiff	BAR	-9.92
11N	Connor Barth	TB	11.82	Graham Gano	WAS	-9.49
12A	S Janikowski	OAK	10.73	S Gostkowski	NE	-6.35
12N	Blair Walsh	MIN	12.43	David Akers	SF	-17.48
13A	Justin Tucker	BAR	10.81	S Janikowski	OAK	-13.92
13N	Phil Dawson	SF	7.64	Garrett Hartley	NO	-15.66
14A	S Gostkowski	NE	12.01	Billy Cundiff	CLE	-8.15
14N	Matt Bryant	ATL	10.54	Nate Freese	DET	-9.65
15A	S Gostkowski	N E	12.46	Josh Scobee	PIT	-8.78
15N	Dan Bailey	DAL	10.87	Kyle Brindza	T B	-14.04
16A	Justin Tucker	BAR	23.31	Mike Nugent	CIN	-13.27
16N	Matt Bryant	ATL	13.69	Roberto Aguayo	TB	-17.30
17A	Justin Tucker	BAR	11.43	Brandon McManus	DEN	-10.47
17N	Robbie Gould	S F	17.44	Aldrick Rosas	NYG	-12.80
18A	Jason Myers	NYJ	10.81	Chris Boswell	PIT	-13.05
18N	Aldrick Rosas	NYG	10.87	Cody Parkey	CHI	-10.89

Table 7.21
Career Kicking Points Leaders, Through 2018,
Minimum 200 Career Kicker Points Scored

KICKER	PTS	K%	APAL	P%	AP2	P2%	TG	PPG	P16	P216	MS
Adam Vinatieri	2598	88.4	56.91	2.19	40.64	1.56	355	7.32	2.56	1.83	0
M Andersen	2544	85.2	97.72	3.84	128.95	5.07	375	6.78	4.17	5.50	0
Gary Anderson	2434	85.6	116.00	4.77	96.71	3.97	353	6.90	5.26	4.38	0
Jason Hanson	2150	86.8	50.59	2.35	99.86	4.64	328	6.55	2.47	4.87	0
John Carney	2062	86.7	69.79	3.38	40.47	1.96	302	6.83	3.70	2.14	0
Matt Stover	2004	87.8	88.03	4.39	55.73	2.78	297	6.75	4.74	3.00	0
Jason Elam	1983	86.3	28.18	1.42	47.54	2.40	263	7.54	1.71	2.89	0
John Kasay	1970	86.1	40.07	2.03	60.47	3.07	301	6.54	2.13	3.21	0
George Blanda	1948	67.6	16.22	0.83	77.79	3.99	342	5.70	0.76	3.64	15
S Janikowski	1913	85.4	-24.35	-1.27	46.35	2.42	285	6.71	-1.37	2.60	0
Phil Dawson	1841	87.3	22.17	1.20	0.88	0.05	306	6.02	1.16	0.05	0
S Gostkowski	1743	91.3	54.82	3.15	27.88	1.60	200	8.72	4.39	2.23	0
Norm Johnson	1736	83.7	46.90	2.70	50.23	2.89	275	6.31	2.73	2.92	0
David Akers	1721	86.0	-9.37	-0.54	-8.30	-0.48	227	7.58	-0.66	-0.59	0
Nick Lowery	1711	85.3	132.32	7.73	138.27	8.08	262	6.53	8.08	8.44	0
Matt Bryant	1710	89.8	48.06	2.81	35.24	2.06	234	7.31	3.29	2.41	0
Jan Stenerud	1699	74.7	97.36	5.73	124.55	7.33	263	6.46	5.92	7.58	0
Ryan Longwell	1687	88.1	38.06	2.26	38.38	2.27	240	7.03	2.54	2.56	0
Lou Groza	1602	70.4	114.57	7.15	139.61	8.71	272	5.89	6.74	8.21	20
Eddie Murray	1594	82.0	61.28	3.84	66.03	4.14	250	6.38	3.92	4.23	0
Al Del Greco	1584	83.5	28.77	1.82	36.39	2.30	248	6.39	1.86	2.35	0
Olindo Mare	1555	85.9	11.39	0.73	-7.37	-0.47	233	6.67	0.78	-0.51	0
Robbie Gould	1528	90.5	54.06	3.54	46.79	3.06	208	7.35	4.16	3.60	0
Steve Christie	1476	83.6	7.34	0.50	-8.22	-0.56	229	6.45	0.51	-0.57	0
Pat Leahy	1470	78.9	50.43	3.43	21.37	1.45	250	5.88	3.23	1.37	0
Mason Crosby	1469	86.2	-39.82	-2.71	-31.39	-2.14	192	7.65	-3.32	-2.62	0
Jay Feely	1445	87.2	16.38	1.13	16.41	1.14	211	6.85	1.24	1.24	0
Jim Turner	1433	71.4	67.15	4.69	32.37	2.26	228	6.29	4.71	2.27	0
Matt Bahr	1422	79.9	22.24	1.56	-27.07	-1.90	237	6.00	1.50	-1.83	0
Jeff Wilkins	1416	87.2	31.22	2.21	39.28	2.77	194	7.30	2.58	3.24	0
Josh Brown	1395	88.2	18.15	1.30	35.37	2.54	202	6.91	1.44	2.80	0
Mark Moseley	1382	73.4	15.90	1.15	53.66	3.88	213	6.49	1.19	4.03	0
Jim Bakken	1380	72.7	98.00	7.10	104.50	7.57	227	6.08	6.91	7.37	0

7. Kicker Ratings

KICKER	PTS	K%	APAL	P%	AP2	P2%	TG	PPG	P16	P216	MS
Fred Cox	1365	71.7	85.13	6.24	67.48	4.94	210	6.50	6.49	5.14	0
Rian Lindell	1350	86.3	0.08	0.01	-3.60	-0.27	212	6.37	0.01	-0.27	0
Shayne Graham	1260	89.6	35.10	2.79	22.33	1.77	181	6.96	3.10	1.97	0
Jim Breech	1246	79.9	16.82	1.35	-8.38	-0.67	198	6.29	1.36	-0.68	0
Mike Prater	1240	87.7	-8.50	-0.69	-2.17	-0.17	169	7.34	-0.80	-0.21	0
P Stoyanovich	1236	85.2	36.78	2.98	33.35	2.70	180	6.87	3.27	2.96	0
Chris Bahr	1213	73.0	-44.64	-3.68	-31.44	-2.59	210	5.78	-3.40	-2.40	0
Kevin Butler	1208	80.1	-5.99	-0.50	-22.12	-1.83	185	6.53	-0.52	-1.91	0
Neil Rackers	1164	85.1	-13.38	-1.15	5.39	0.46	180	6.47	-1.19	0.48	0
Kris Brown	1123	82.9	-32.15	-2.86	-23.84	-2.12	179	6.27	-2.87	-2.13	0
Ray Wersching	1122	76.6	17.02	1.52	33.19	2.96	203	5.53	1.34	2.62	0
Mike Nugent	1122	85.6	-24.79	-2.21	-35.23	-3.14	164	6.84	-2.42	-3.44	0
Joe Nedney	1113	85.3	1.21	0.11	5.94	0.53	175	6.36	0.11	0.54	0
Don Cockroft	1080	74.9	58.51	5.42	45.42	4.21	188	5.74	4.98	3.87	0
Nick Folk	1077	85.4	-30.08	-2.79	-27.47	-2.55	154	6.99	-3.13	-2.85	0
Garo Yepremian	1074	76.6	74.19	6.91	77.80	7.24	181	5.93	6.56	6.88	0
M Vanderjagt	1067	90.7	64.48	6.04	55.16	5.17	137	7.79	7.53	6.44	0
S Hauschka	1051	89.1	14.59	1.39	4.46	0.42	143	7.35	1.63	0.50	0
Josh Scobee	1046	84.9	-28.23	-2.70	-6.28	-0.60	171	6.12	-2.64	-0.59	0
Todd Peterson	1043	84.9	8.47	0.81	3.40	0.33	159	6.56	0.85	0.34	0
Rob Bironas	1032	89.4	24.07	2.33	36.33	3.52	144	7.17	2.67	4.04	0
Bruce Gossett	1031	70.5	56.59	5.49	19.63	1.90	154	6.69	5.88	2.04	0
Ryan Succop	1019	87.4	-1.40	-0.14	-5.87	-0.58	160	6.37	-0.14	-0.59	0
Jeff Jaeger	1008	80.4	-13.42	-1.33	-3.24	-0.32	165	6.11	-1.30	-0.31	0
Dan Carpenter	999	87.1	-4.56	-0.46	3.70	0.37	140	7.14	-0.52	0.42	0
Graham Gano	978	85.8	-21.24	-2.17	-11.83	-1.21	134	7.30	-2.54	-1.41	0
Sam Baker	965	69.3	51.40	5.33	86.57	8.97	171	5.64	4.81	8.10	0
Greg Davis	962	75.7	-66.27	-6.89	-39.76	-4.13	168	5.73	-6.31	-3.79	0
Rafael Septien	960	79.9	44.10	4.59	41.61	4.33	151	6.36	4.67	4.41	0
Jeff Reed	959	87.2	7.71	0.80	-15.21	-1.59	132	7.27	0.93	-1.84	0
Justin Tucker	952	92.3	52.46	5.51	64.06	6.73	112	8.50	7.49	9.15	0
Lou Michaels	947	66.5	32.69	3.45	38.25	4.04	141	6.72	3.71	4.34	3
Chris Jacke	944	83.0	3.61	0.38	5.87	0.62	146	6.47	0.40	0.64	0
Fuad Reveiz	931	82.5	6.68	0.72	9.55	1.03	147	6.33	0.73	1.04	0
Lawrence Tynes	927	87.3	-6.63	-0.71	-17.73	-1.91	129	7.19	-0.82	-2.20	0
Dan Bailey	927	90.4	22.82	2.46	26.65	2.88	122	7.60	2.99	3.50	0

KICKER	PTS	K%	APAL	P%	AP2	P2%	TG	PPG	P16	P216	MS
Doug Brien	915	85.2	7.86	0.86	18.94	2.07	149	6.14	0.84	2.03	0
Chip Lohmiller	913	78.6	-25.34	-2.78	-31.74	-3.48	136	6.71	-2.98	-3.73	0
Shaun Suisham	907	88.1	3.96	0.44	-8.44	-0.93	125	7.26	0.51	-1.08	0
Roy Gerela	903	70.4	4.40	0.49	-19.37	-2.14	145	6.23	0.49	-2.14	0
Nate Kaeding	895	91.0	27.90	3.12	11.18	1.25	114	7.85	3.92	1.57	0
John Hall	889	80.7	-36.83	-4.14	-34.19	-3.85	134	6.63	-4.40	-4.08	0
Mike Hollis	879	85.2	14.42	1.64	11.54	1.31	124	7.09	1.86	1.49	0
Tony Zendejas	874	80.7	6.46	0.74	3.98	0.45	152	5.75	0.68	0.42	0
Tony Franklin	872	76.0	-5.27	-0.60	12.61	1.45	140	6.23	-0.60	1.44	0
Gino Cappelletti	870	64.1	12.25	1.41	18.70	2.15	149	5.84	1.32	2.01	0
Pete Gogolak	863	69.8	20.58	2.38	4.47	0.52	150	5.75	2.19	0.48	0
Errol Mann	846	72.9	43.41	5.13	35.57	4.20	136	6.22	5.11	4.18	0
Dean Biasucci	823	77.6	-20.71	-2.52	11.11	1.35	154	5.34	-2.15	1.15	0
Billy Cundiff	823	82.7	-41.81	-5.08	-47.69	-5.80	131	6.28	-5.11	-5.83	0
Nick Novak	802	86.3	-15.67	-1.95	-24.11	-3.01	115	6.97	-2.18	-3.35	0
Rich Karlis	799	79.0	6.23	0.78	-2.29	-0.29	119	6.71	0.84	-0.31	0
Mike Lansford	789	80.8	12.51	1.59	1.58	0.20	124	6.36	1.61	0.20	0
Rolf Benirschke	766	78.5	21.74	2.84	19.02	2.48	122	6.28	2.85	2.49	0
Tony Fritsch	758	76.3	44.82	5.91	37.21	4.91	125	6.06	5.74	4.76	0
Bob Thomas	756	72.2	-23.15	-3.06	-25.54	-3.38	144	5.25	-2.57	-2.84	0
Greg Zuerlein	753	87.2	-4.73	-0.63	21.49	2.85	104	7.24	-0.73	3.31	0
Tommy Davis	738	62.6	-29.36	-3.98	-7.81	-1.06	141	5.23	-3.33	-0.89	2
Tom Dempsey	729	69.0	2.51	0.34	39.12	5.37	127	5.74	0.32	4.93	0
Connor Barth	726	87.2	-0.90	-0.12	5.65	0.78	121	6.00	-0.12	0.75	0
Mike Clark	724	70.0	19.40	2.68	0.18	0.03	125	5.79	2.48	0.02	2
Horst Muhlman	707	72.6	31.35	4.43	22.63	3.20	122	5.80	4.11	2.97	0
Mike Cofer	702	76.7	-45.33	-6.46	-37.98	-5.41	102	6.88	-7.11	-5.96	0
M Grammatica	693	82.6	-7.79	-1.12	-2.49	-0.36	105	6.60	-1.19	-0.38	0
John Smith	692	77.2	37.25	5.38	23.39	3.38	116	5.97	5.14	3.23	0
Cary Blanchard	683	82.1	-3.66	-0.54	1.91	0.28	111	6.15	-0.53	0.28	0
Scott Norwood	670	80.7	4.71	0.70	-1.72	-0.26	108	6.20	0.70	-0.26	0
Doug Pelfrey	660	82.4	-9.02	-1.37	-1.56	-0.24	112	5.89	-1.29	-0.22	0
Ben Agajanian	655	68.0	38.08	5.81	43.67	6.67	132	4.96	4.62	5.29	16
Blair Walsh	655	85.7	-16.58	-2.53	-6.96	-1.06	89	7.36	-2.98	-1.25	0
Joe Danelo	639	68.4	-36.72	-5.75	-22.37	-3.50	137	4.66	-4.29	-2.61	0
Michael Husted	618	77.4	-49.42	-8.00	-29.67	-4.80	115	5.37	-6.88	-4.13	0

7. Kicker Ratings

KICKER	PTS	K%	APAL	P%	AP2	P2%	TG	PPG	P16	P216	MS
Bobby Walston	605	70.8	5.08	0.84	-29.65	-4.90	138	4.38	0.59	-3.44	5
Efren Herrera	604	77.3	39.56	6.55	33.49	5.55	108	5.59	5.86	4.96	0
Raul Allegre	594	79.4	14.54	2.45	33.18	5.59	91	6.53	2.56	5.83	0
Mike Mercer	594	67.2	-1.61	-0.27	3.12	0.53	118	5.03	-0.22	0.42	0
David Treadwell	587	82.3	14.01	2.39	-26.90	-4.58	91	6.45	2.46	-4.73	0
N O'Donoghue	576	69.9	-50.49	-8.76	-44.10	-7.66	112	5.14	-7.21	-6.30	0
N Mike-Mayer	571	67.5	-29.73	-5.21	-20.55	-3.60	129	4.43	-3.69	-2.55	0
Paul Edinger	569	80.8	-20.55	-3.61	0.30	0.05	96	5.93	-3.43	0.05	0
Chris Boniol	567	83.6	-4.21	-0.74	-16.83	-2.97	90	6.30	-0.75	-2.99	0
Roger Ruzek	566	78.9	-8.92	-1.58	-15.89	-2.81	93	6.09	-1.53	-2.73	0
Mick Luckhurst	558	78.8	9.58	1.72	12.47	2.24	95	5.87	1.61	2.10	0
Pat Summerall	557	61.8	-12.73	-2.29	13.41	2.41	109	5.11	-1.87	1.97	12
Gene Mingo	551	62.8	8.88	1.61	26.81	4.87	117	4.71	1.21	3.67	0
Brad Daluiso	544	81.6	-13.30	-2.44	-22.37	-4.11	94	5.79	-2.26	-3.81	0
Uwe von Schamann	540	77.5	4.61	0.85	-5.47	-1.01	89	6.07	0.83	-0.98	0
Kai Forbath	539	89.5	8.15	1.51	5.09	0.94	77	7.00	1.69	1.06	0
C Catanzaro	539	86.7	-6.17	-1.15	-11.04	-2.05	77	7.00	-1.28	-2.29	0
Don Chandler	530	71.5	35.54	6.71	28.67	5.41	86	6.16	6.61	5.33	1
Randy Bullock	527	86.4	-10.78	-2.05	-16.50	-3.13	78	6.76	-2.21	-3.38	0
Paul McFadden	520	79.6	15.64	3.01	23.13	4.45	79	6.58	3.17	4.68	0
Chester Marcol	519	68.7	4.62	0.89	5.32	1.02	102	5.09	0.72	0.83	0
B McManus	506	85.9	-10.10	-2.00	-10.69	-2.11	80	6.33	-2.02	-2.14	0
David Ray	497	70.1	5.14	1.03	-16.86	-3.39	69	7.20	1.19	-3.91	0
Bob Waterfield	495	74.3	35.86	7.25	32.08	6.48	93	5.32	6.17	5.52	12
Gordie Soltau	494	68.7	3.33	0.67	-27.01	-5.47	108	4.57	0.49	-4.00	5
D Villanueva	491	68.1	10.45	2.13	-12.12	-2.47	93	5.28	1.80	-2.08	0
Bobby Howfield	487	69.7	-7.48	-1.54	-1.77	-0.36	88	5.53	-1.36	-0.32	0
John Leypoldt	482	70.5	-5.67	-1.18	10.09	2.09	92	5.24	-0.99	1.75	0
D Igwebuike	477	81.0	16.56	3.47	44.80	9.39	80	5.96	3.31	8.96	0
Curt Knight	475	67.9	-7.08	-1.49	-0.19	-0.04	70	6.79	-1.62	-0.04	0
Mac Percival	466	63.2	-20.03	-4.30	-24.05	-5.16	101	4.61	-3.17	-3.81	0
Cairo Santos	461	87.0	-3.05	-0.66	-5.72	-1.24	62	7.44	-0.79	-1.48	0
Benny Ricardo	447	73.8	1.52	0.34	2.57	0.57	92	4.86	0.26	0.45	0
Cody Parkey	446	87.5	-2.17	-0.49	-11.16	-2.50	65	6.86	-0.53	-2.75	0
Chris Boswell	436	88.1	3.80	0.87	2.08	0.48	58	7.52	1.05	0.57	0
Jim Martin	434	58.3	-19.75	-4.55	20.79	4.79	97	4.47	-3.26	3.43	6

KICKER	PTS	K%	APAL	P%	AP2	P2%	TG	PPG	P16	P216	MS
Garrett Hartley	433	88.2	-7.51	-1.73	-17.14	-3.96	60	7.22	-2.00	-4.57	0
Toni Linhart	425	71.5	-0.46	-0.11	-10.97	-2.58	82	5.18	-0.09	-2.14	0
Dustin Hopkins	415	87.9	4.66	1.12	-1.34	-0.32	54	7.69	1.38	-0.40	0
Wil Lutz	409	90.3	12.35	3.02	12.50	3.06	48	8.52	4.12	4.17	0
Caleb Sturgis	398	84.0	-16.28	-4.09	-16.51	-4.15	52	7.65	-5.01	-5.08	0
Fred Cone	398	73.3	20.19	5.07	21.23	5.33	96	4.15	3.36	3.54	0
Jason Myers	397	85.2	-8.39	-2.11	5.44	1.37	54	7.35	-2.48	1.61	0
Paul Hornung	388	63.2	-14.11	-3.64	-37.63	-9.70	69	5.62	-3.27	-8.73	0
Roger LeClerc	382	62.0	-8.62	-2.26	-35.50	-9.29	81	4.72	-1.70	-7.01	1
Josh Lambo	381	87.2	0.23	0.06	2.06	0.54	55	6.93	0.07	0.60	0
Dennis Partee	380	70.6	-3.37	-0.89	-3.45	-0.91	73	5.21	-0.74	-0.76	0
Frank Corral	379	71.2	-6.94	-1.83	-5.05	-1.33	64	5.92	-1.73	-1.26	0
Wade Richey	376	79.8	-24.59	-6.54	-27.80	-7.39	61	6.16	-6.45	-7.29	0
R Cunningham	371	85.3	5.25	1.42	-3.95	-1.07	52	7.13	1.62	-1.22	0
Chuck Nelson	364	78.6	-8.60	-2.36	-16.65	-4.57	63	5.78	-2.18	-4.23	0
Rick Danmeier	364	75.4	5.44	1.50	-2.77	-0.76	73	4.99	1.19	-0.61	0
S Mike-Mayer	362	63.7	-43.28	-11.96	-40.23	-11.11	80	4.53	-8.66	-8.05	0
Alex Henery	346	87.6	-5.74	-1.66	-10.96	-3.17	50	6.92	-1.84	-3.51	0
Skip Butler	340	66.1	-18.25	-5.37	-6.01	-1.77	71	4.79	-4.11	-1.35	0
Lin Elliot	338	81.4	-3.91	-1.16	-12.92	-3.82	50	6.76	-1.25	-4.13	0
Wayne Walker	331	58.6	-40.74	-12.31	-15.95	-4.82	86	3.85	-7.58	-2.97	1
Doak Walker	330	73.0	25.83	7.83	15.52	4.70	71	4.65	5.82	3.50	9
Ali Haji-Sheikh	323	74.1	-12.63	-3.91	-7.21	-2.23	50	6.46	-4.04	-2.31	0
Steve Myhra	312	67.5	-5.61	-1.80	0.63	0.20	55	5.67	-1.63	0.18	3
Fred Steinfort	311	66.0	-31.64	-10.17	-25.71	-8.27	63	4.94	-8.04	-6.53	0
Pat Harder	303	73.7	25.04	8.26	22.78	7.52	83	3.65	4.83	4.39	13
Brett Conway	299	81.7	-5.09	-1.70	0.00	0.00	45	6.64	-1.81	0.00	0
Jim O'Brien	289	66.3	-15.43	-5.34	-17.78	-6.15	47	6.15	-5.25	-6.05	0
Harrison Butker	279	91.8	13.16	4.72	7.60	2.72	29	9.62	7.26	4.19	0
Ward Cuff	279	61.2	25.75	9.23	21.56	7.73	98	2.85	4.20	3.52	13
Cliff Patton	278	70.9	13.82	4.97	-5.94	-2.14	60	4.63	3.69	-1.59	13
George Blair	272	72.5	34.61	12.72	14.97	5.50	45	6.04	12.31	5.32	1
Tommy Brooker	272	66.3	-10.25	-3.77	-0.96	-0.35	49	5.55	-3.35	-0.31	0
Charlie Gogolak	270	68.2	-1.19	-0.44	10.67	3.95	57	4.74	-0.33	2.99	0
Harvey Johnson	262	78.0	25.37	9.68	26.08	9.96	66	3.97	6.15	6.32	7
Jose Cortez	258	80.1	-13.70	-5.31	-21.55	-8.35	39	6.62	-5.62	-8.84	0

7. Kicker Ratings

KICKER	PTS	K%	APAL	P%	AP2	P2%	TG	PPG	P16	P216	MS
Ken Willis	255	77.3	-9.37	-3.68	-1.57	-0.62	45	5.67	-3.33	-0.56	0
Dick Van Raaphorst	247	64.3	-6.50	-2.63	-24.58	-9.95	42	5.88	-2.48	-9.36	0
Chester Durkee	243	62.1	-8.81	-3.63	-0.20	-0.08	46	5.28	-3.06	-0.07	0
Ka'imi Fairbairn	242	87.4	0.52	0.22	0.51	0.21	32	7.56	0.26	0.26	0
Joe Vetrano	235	77.0	-0.65	-0.28	3.55	1.51	54	4.35	-0.19	1.05	3
J Staurovsky	231	74.3	-13.13	-5.68	-10.99	-4.76	46	5.02	-4.57	-3.82	0
Tim Mazzetti	230	74.7	4.78	2.08	-11.37	-4.95	42	5.48	1.82	-4.33	0
Jake Elliott	228	86.7	-1.75	-0.77	-1.12	-0.49	31	7.35	-0.91	-0.58	0
Bobby Layne	222	81.0	29.70	13.38	0.80	0.36	84	2.64	5.66	0.15	1
Cole Ford	221	80.4	-13.99	-6.33	-15.43	-6.98	37	5.97	-6.05	-6.67	0
Bill Dudley	220	67.7	8.37	3.81	-3.40	-1.55	69	3.19	1.94	-0.79	3
Shane Blanton	210	81.4	-9.71	-4.62	-6.53	-3.11	33	6.36	-4.71	-3.17	0
Bob Khayat	204	65.0	1.69	0.83	2.53	1.24	40	5.10	0.68	1.01	0
Booth Lusteg	202	62.0	-17.02	-8.43	-18.17	-9.00	36	5.61	-7.57	-8.08	0
Aldrick Rosas	201	87.8	2.17	1.08	-1.94	-0.96	32	6.28	1.08	-0.97	0

Note: P% or P2% and P16 or P216 are two different ways to put APAL and APAL2 into a context. P%, which is APAL Percentage, or P2%, APAL2 Percentage, is merely career APAL or APAL2 per career points scored, multiplied by 100. This measure puts kickers on a similar context for the amount of APAL or APAL2 they would gain in a very good (100-point) season. P16 is APAL divided by games played, multiplied by 16, and P216 is APAL2 divided by games played, multiplied by 16, which puts all kickers on a similar context of a 16-game season.

Table 7.22
25 Highest and Lowest Single-Season Offensive Team APAL Values

RK	TM	YL	APAL	RK	TM	YL	APAL
1	CLE	53N	37.03	1	BAL	72N	-33.13
2	STL	67N	26.72	2	NYG	65N	-32.18
3	NYJ	68A	24.87	3	WAS	61N	-28.80
4	IND	03N	24.69	4	G B	64N	-28.73
5	K C	69A	23.78	5	T B	83N	-26.87
6	MIN	98N	23.25	6	N E	83N	-24.22
7	DEN	62A	23.03	7	BUF	83N	-23.90
8	MIN	69N	21.97	T8	CHI	99N	-23.81
9	NYG	59N	21.75	T8	DET	68N	-23.81
10	K C	66A	21.72	10	NYG	84N	-23.67
11	K C	68A	21.56	11	PIT	57N	-23.06

RK	TM	YL	APAL	RK	TM	YL	APAL
12	ARZ	05N	20.88	12	WAS	67N	-22.41
13	K C	90N	20.74	13	PIT	70N	-21.93
14	LAA	47F	20.64	14	STL	85N	-21.92
15	G B	81N	20.26	15	BKA	47F	-21.84
16	CLE	52N	19.34	16	BOP	69A	-21.52
17	S D	62A	18.94	17	DET	14N	-21.35
18	G B	55N	18.81	18	ATL	70N	-20.45
19	SLR	03N	18.67	19	G B	12N	-20.43
20	BUF	88N	18.63	20	G B	88N	-20.18
21	HOU	79N	18.48	21	BAL	56N	-20.00
22	CLE	50N	18.42	22	S F	91N	-19.99
23	DET	69N	18.31	23	STL	86N	-19.88
T24	N O	86N	18.12	24	CHC	52N	-19.36
T24	PIT	62N	18.12	25	S F	12N	-19.23

Table 7.23
25 Highest and Lowest Single-Season Offensive Team APAL Values

RK	TM	YL	APAL	RK	TM	YL	APAL
1	PHI	85N	-23.99	1	DEN	64A	32.17
2	OAK	64A	-22.70	2	STL	64N	29.03
3	S F	76N	-22.66	3	BUF	76N	27.85
4	S F	98N	-22.59	4	HOU	72N	27.34
5	CHI	57N	-22.34	5	NYG	91N	22.53
6	DTX	60A	-21.41	6	ATL	96N	22.06
7	CHI	68N	-21.22	7	ATL	71N	20.80
8	MIN	76N	-21.12	8	LAR	88N	20.12
9	NYG	00N	-20.73	9	G B	80N	19.78
10	N E	02N	-20.18	10	NYJ	76N	19.69
11	G B	85N	-20.02	11	L A	69N	19.60
12	PIT	01N	-19.80	12	WAS	68N	18.93
13	ATL	91N	-19.71	13	SEA	77N	18.64
14	DET	69N	-19.57	14	N E	71N	18.22
15	CHI	56N	-19.26	15	CLE	84N	17.84
16	BOP	63A	-19.13	16	MSA	46F	17.73
17	BUF	96N	-18.77	17	N E	73N	17.12
18	BAR	01N	-18.72	18	PHI	82N	16.91

RK	TM	YL	APAL	RK	TM	YL	APAL
19	L A	17N	-18.57	19	BUF	81N	16.87
20	DAL	72N	-18.14	20	CIN	87N	16.68
21	BAL	71N	-17.72	21	HOU	94N	16.64
22	HOU	61A	-17.53	22	N O	72N	16.32
23	K C	98N	-17.51	23	ATL	89N	15.85
24	ATL	84N	-17.44	24	PHI	68N	15.75
25	DEN	76N	-17.13	25	MIA	86N	15.66

Table 7.24
25 Highest and Lowest Single-Season Offensive Team APAL2 Values

RK	TM	YL	APAL2	MS	RK	TM	YL	APAL2	MS
1	STL	67N	30.37	0/2	1	G B	64N	-34.64	0/6
2	CLE	53N	27.52	1/17	2	S D	64A	-33.12	N/A
3	WAS	79N	27.28	N/A	3	NYG	65N	-32.12	0/2
T4	K C	69A	26.64	N/A	4	PIT	57N	-27.15	0/3
T4	K C	66A	26.64	N/A	5	T B	83N	-25.93	N/A
6	DEN	62A	25.13	N/A	6	CLE	49F	-25.75	0/3
7	BAL	83N	24.99	N/A	7	N E	83N	-25.13	N/A
8	ARZ	05N	23.79	N/A	8	BAL	72N	-25.03	N/A
9	K C	68A	23.59	N/A	9	CHI	99N	-24.95	N/A
10	BAR	16N	23.28	N/A	10	BUF	62A	-23.81	N/A
11	N O	85N	23.07	N/A	11	WAS	67N	-23.65	0/2
12	DEN	80N	22.95	N/A	12	BKA	47F	-22.91	0/9
13	STL	64N	21.89	0/6	13	BOP	69A	-22.84	N/A
14	LAA	47F	20.97	0/9	14	LAC	17N	-22.57	N/A
15	K C	70N	20.80	N/A	15	BUF	83N	-22.01	N/A
16	OAK	09N	20.64	N/A	16	NYG	84N	-21.39	N/A
17	MIN	98N	20.17	N/A	17	NYJ	79N	-21.12	N/A
18	NYG	83N	19.96	N/A	18	MIN	87N	-20.94	N/A
19	HOU	79N	19.95	N/A	19	STL	86N	-20.70	N/A
20	PHI	79N	19.79	N/A	20	WAS	93N	-20.67	N/A
21	CLE	52N	19.75	1/21	21	WAS	39N	-20.46	1/9
22	PHI	66N	19.53	0/1	22	STL	87N	-19.96	N/A
23	DEN	63A	19.41	N/A	23	OAK	60A	-19.72	N/A
24	NYG	59N	19.38	1/3	24	DET	14N	-19.71	N/A
25	MIN	65N	19.20	0/2	25	N E	93N	-19.64	N/A

Table 7.25
25 Highest and Lowest Single-Season Defensive Team APAL2 Values

RK	TM	YL	APAL2	MS	RK	TM	YL	APAL2	MS
1	BFA	49F	-27.82	0/3	1	BUF	76N	24.78	N/A
2	G B	85N	-23.53	N/A	2	DEN	64A	22.05	N/A
3	DEN	66A	-23.29	N/A	3	SEA	91N	21.85	N/A
4	CHC	48N	-23.22	5/14	4	HOU	72N	20.66	N/A
5	CPT	44N	-23.04	0/14	5	STL	64N	19.53	0/6
6	BUF	96N	-22.69	N/A	6	L A	69N	19.04	N/A
7	K C	98N	-22.19	N/A	7	SEA	77N	18.38	N/A
8	L A	64N	-21.82	0/6	8	NYG	91N	18.31	N/A
9	CHI	57N	-21.81	0/3	9	N E	71N	18.08	N/A
10	HOU	61A	-21.79	N/A	10	MIA	02N	17.60	N/A
11	OAK	64A	-21.70	N/A	11	LAR	88N	17.56	N/A
12	S F	76N	-21.60	N/A	12	G B	65N	17.34	0/2
13	PIT	86N	-20.99	N/A	13	NYJ	76N	17.19	N/A
14	MIN	76N	-20.35	N/A	14	NYT	62A	17.10	N/A
15	BAR	01N	-20.15	N/A	15	WAS	68N	16.91	N/A
16	TEN	08N	-19.94	N/A	16	ATL	71N	16.88	N/A
17	S F	98N	-19.83	N/A	17	ATL	96N	16.86	N/A
18	CLR	41N	-19.48	3/8	18	CHI	77N	16.43	N/A
19	NYG	74N	-19.22	N/A	19	DET	87N	16.32	N/A
20	G B	78N	-19.13	N/A	20	S F	73N	15.84	N/A
21	PHI	85N	-18.99	N/A	21	OAK	70N	15.76	N/A
T22	BOP	63A	-18.58	0/1	22	DEN	93N	15.60	N/A
T22	PIT	01N	-18.58	N/A	23	PHI	82N	15.42	N/A
24	NYG	00N	-18.50	N/A	24	HOU	94N	15.17	N/A
25	DET	18N	-18.44	N/A	25	DTX	52N	15.11	9/21

8

Punter Ratings: 1961 and 2018

You could say I've never been enamored with the way the NFL rates punters, by gross punting average. The major reason I've always disliked it is because it seems to favor punters on lesser teams who tend to punt from worse field position and thus are not sacrificing distance on said punts due to proximity to the end zone per my 60-yard theory, which we'll get to. Also, there are a number of important things that punters do that do not necessarily show up in the punting average, such as being able to punt out of bounds inside the 20-yard line, avoiding touchbacks, and being able to maximize distance on longer punts over 60 yards from the end zone he is punting toward. Many of the important things that punters do, in fact, reduce their gross punting average.

While I like net punting average, to me it is very dependent on the special teams and the guy returning the kick, and I am strictly trying to evaluate the punter, not the special teams.

Before I get into my system for rating punters, I wanted to take a quick look at how punting averages have changed over the years. Table 8.1 lists punting data per season from 1940 to present (N is NFL, A is AFL and F is AAFC):

Table 8.1
League Punting Data, 1940–2018 NFL, 1960–69 AFL, 1946–49 AAFC, Summary

YR	LG	PUNTS	YDS	AVG	YR	LG	PUNTS	YDS	AVG
1940	N	716	28335	39.57	1990	N	1917	77404	40.38
1941	N	657	26674	40.60	1991	N	1987	82237	41.39
1942	N	676	26948	39.86	1992	N	2057	86544	42.07
1943	N	506	19391	38.32	1993	N	2118	89380	42.20
1944	N	596	22353	37.51	1994	N	2189	91191	41.66
1945	N	513	19679	38.36	1995	N	2193	91668	41.80
1946	N	579	23746	41.01	1996	N	2325	99731	42.90
1947	N	649	26960	41.54	1997	N	2473	105640	42.72
1948	N	690	28081	40.70	1998	N	2441	105547	43.24
1949	N	666	26998	40.54	1999	N	2578	107495	41.70
1950	N	890	35944	40.39	2000	N	2471	102924	41.65
1951	N	814	32900	40.42	2001	N	2479	103967	41.94

YR	LG	PUNTS	YDS	AVG	YR	LG	PUNTS	YDS	AVG
1952	N	859	35468	41.29	2002	N	2447	100179	40.94
1953	N	825	33907	41.10	2003	N	2550	104470	40.97
1954	N	748	30322	40.54	2004	N	2524	105435	41.77
1955	N	760	31187	41.04	2005	N	2511	106427	42.38
1956	N	696	28232	40.56	2006	N	2489	107560	43.21
1957	N	716	29507	41.21	2007	N	2353	101669	43.21
1958	N	668	27238	40.78	2008	N	2307	100766	43.68
1959	N	691	29722	43.01	2009	N	2451	107733	43.95
1960	N	750	31617	42.16	2010	N	2466	107002	43.39
1961	N	860	36642	42.61	2011	N	2488	112047	45.03
1962	N	833	34969	41.98	2012	N	2469	112340	45.50
1963	N	895	38406	42.91	2013	N	2527	113614	44.96
1964	N	970	41863	43.16	2014	N	2387	106899	44.78
1965	N	911	38686	42.47	2015	N	2440	110322	45.21
1966	N	1004	40873	40.71	2016	N	2334	105854	45.35
1967	N	1110	44704	40.27	2017	N	2444	110878	45.37
1968	N	1053	42098	39.98	2018	N	2214	99544	44.96
1969	N	1092	43729	40.04					
1970	N	1900	77928	41.01	1960	A	566	21403	37.81
1971	N	1743	71044	40.76	1961	A	557	22642	40.65
1972	N	1610	65843	40.90	1962	A	555	22004	39.65
1973	N	1767	72463	41.01	1963	A	553	22789	41.21
1974	N	1991	77686	39.02	1964	A	561	23152	41.27
1975	N	1966	77854	39.60	1965	A	604	25667	42.50
1976	N	2266	87477	38.60	1966	A	637	26098	40.97
1977	N	2267	87090	38.42	1967	A	653	27576	42.23
1978	N	2458	94866	38.59	1968	A	777	32577	41.93
1979	N	2323	91419	39.35	1969	A	724	30348	41.92
1980	N	2174	87507	40.25					
1981	N	2240	91754	40.96	1946	F	610	24745	40.57
1982	N	1250	50755	40.60	1947	F	501	20393	40.70
1983	N	2249	91697	40.77	1948	F	505	20890	41.37
1984	N	2260	92721	41.03	1949	F	432	17391	40.26
1985	N	2279	94272	41.37					
1986	N	2311	93474	40.45	NFL	SUM	131264	5475116	41.71
1987	N	2140	83950	39.23	AFL	SUM	6187	254256	41.10

YR	LG	PUNTS	YDS	AVG	YR	LG	PUNTS	YDS	AVG
1988	N	2179	87519	40.16	AAFC	SUM	2048	83419	40.73
1989	N	2083	83695	40.18	ALL	SUM	139499	5812791	41.67

I guess you can see a graph of the Table 8.1 data coming next, and of course you would be correct. We'll graph the league punting average or AVG (y) per season or YR (x):

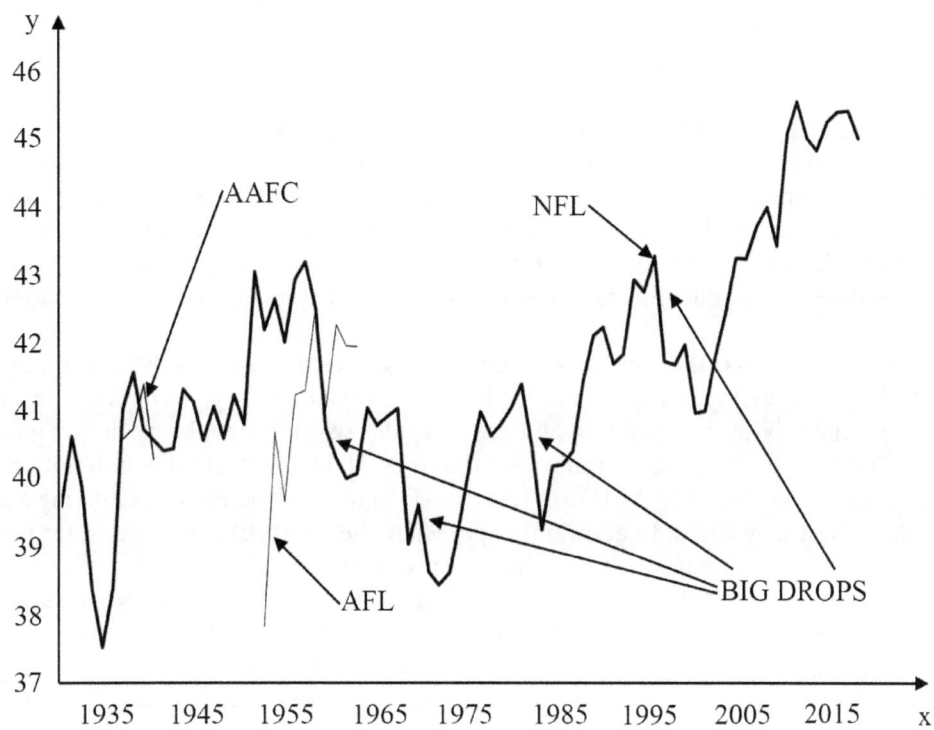

Figure 8.1. Graph of league punting average (AVG) by season (YR), 1933–2018 for NFL, AAFC and AFL from Table 8.1 data.

The major thing to take away from Figure 8.1 is that, with the exception of two sharp drops (1985–86 and 1998–2002), the annual punting average in the NFL has been increasing pretty steadily since the 1976 expansion, from 38.4 yards per punt in 1976 to 45.4 yards per punt in 2018. There was also a huge drop of six yards per punt between 1964 and 1968, and another four yards between 1973 and 1974. The 1985–86 drop was also about four yards, and between 1998 and 2002 was another four yards. I would be open to any theories as to why these drops occurred.

Another interesting thing to consider is that the average of 4.32 punts per team per game in 2018 was the third-lowest annual total since 1940, only behind 1990's 4.28 and 1962's 4.25. It makes sense that points scored and punts per game are inversely related, when scoring goes up, the number of punts per game goes down, and vice versa. As scoring was up 7.4 percent in 2018 from 2017, punts were down about 10 percent.

Punts and Play-by-Play

I've always felt if I had data on every single punt for every single punter for a single season, I would learn a lot about punting and could probably develop a pretty good system for evaluating punters. Having an entire season's worth of punting data would also allow us to look at different things, such as home-away data, punting average by week, and whether this 60-yard theory really holds up.

With that in mind, I decided to go through the game books for every regular season game in the 2018 season and for every punt, I would record three things—the line of scrimmage (distance from the point the ball was snapped to the goal line the punter was punting the ball toward), the distance of the kick and if the punt went out of bounds or not.

The game book is the statistical form that is compiled by the official statisticians at every pro football game, and it contains play-by-play accounts and statistics for each game, along with the rosters, and starters, and halftime stats, and other things. It is the complete and official statistical record of each game. From these game books, the NFL compiles game and seasonal statistics. Game books are, in a sense, the DNA of pro football; sacred documents, if you consider football a religion. I do, as a matter of fact.

I have collected the game books for all the games of the entire 1961 AFL season (which was the earliest season for which I have a complete set of game books) and went through the play-by-play for each and every regular season game. Many thanks go out to various PR and media personnel with the Bills, Titans (formerly the Oilers), Chargers, and Chiefs (formerly the Dallas Texans [AFL]) who helped fill in the missing game books as best they could. In addition, I appreciate the efforts of the Broncos, for being the first NFL team to make all their historical game books available for download on their team website about 15 years ago. I already had the Patriots and Raiders game books through the Pro Football Researchers Association (PFRA), where we are in the process of collecting game books for every pro football game for which they are available. Thanks also to the Raiders and Patriots for making them available to us for this at some point in the past.

First things first, the play-by-play accounts for the 1961 AFL season is not 100 percent complete. We are missing the play-by-play for one entire game, the 12/17/61 contest with the New York Titans, now known as the New York Jets, at the Dallas Texans (AFL), now known as the Kansas City Chiefs. The 12/3/61 Texans at Titans game, we are missing the play-by-play for the entire fourth quarter, and the 9/24/61 Oilers at Chargers game, we are missing a page of the gamebook that has the final seven minutes of play-by-play for the second period. I contacted all the teams involved and they don't have it. I figure I have about 54.625 of 56 games, which is about 97.5 percent of the 1961 AFL season. It will have to suffice.

Needless to say, because the old game books were hand-compiled and typed instead of entered into a computer like they are today, there was not much of a double-checking process used, which means there are occasionally mathematical errors in the figures. For this reason, the final totals I present for players may not exactly equal their final official statistics; they may be a few yards off here and there.

In most cases the single game errors were one or two yards, which is acceptable, but in a couple cases it was ten yards or more. There was one game (Buffalo at Dallas Texans

(AFL), 11/12/61 where the Bills punting totals were off by a whopping 37 yards because there were three occasions where the official scorer apparently carried a two instead of carrying a one when computing the distance of the punt because he was ten yards too high on the actual distance of the punt.

In addition, I've also gone through the play-by-play for the 2018 NFL punt situations. We'll compare and contrast the two seasons, and evaluate the punters from both seasons.

League Data

Here are the 1961 AFL and 2018 NFL regular season punting data:

Table 8.2
Comparison of 1961 AFL and 2018 NFL League Punting Data

1961A	TOTAL	HOME	AWAY	2018N	TOTAL	HOME	AWAY
PUNTS	538	266	272	PUNTS	2198	1083	1115
YARDS	22048	11073	10975	YARDS	99534	48841	50693
ADST	40.98	41.63	40.35	ADST	45.28	45.10	45.46
ALOS	68.86	69.03	67.46	ALOS	65.57	65.19	65.94

The total number of punts in Table 8.2 does not include 8 blocked punts for the 1961 AFL and 16 for the 2018 NFL; they have been omitted from the study.

ADST is short for Average or Gross Punt Distance, and ALOS is Average Line of Scrimmage, which was the average line of scrimmage (distance from the goal line the punter is punting toward) of the snap of the punt.

Initial observations: the ADST for the modern punters is up about five yards across the board, and the ALOS (average line of scrimmage) is down a yard and a half. I'm not quite sure what to make of the difference in ALOS between 1961 and 2018, but I guess I need data from more seasons in between to conclude if one of those two sets of totals is not a fluke.

I did not break down the data by week or by stadium, or by domes, because for one or two seasons, there is just not enough data to form any kind of conclusion. After 20 or 30 seasons worth of data, we would have enough data to know if stadiums other than Heinz Field or Denver would affect punting. My guess is that the effects would be negligible, a fraction of a yard at best. The long-term data on punting in domed stadiums versus open air stadiums is likely interesting.

60-Yard Theory

Having an entire modern season's worth of data should validate my 60-yard theory on punting. The 60-yard theory states that once the line of scrimmage (where the ball is snapped to the punter) gets within 60 yards of the end zone the punter is punting in the direction of, the punting average begins to drop off precipitously. This occurs because the punter begins to sacrifice average by aiming for the sidelines or trying to avoid a touchback. If the line of scrimmage (LOS) is more than 60 yards away, the punter is generally trying to kick the ball as hard and far as he possibly can.

Table 8.3 lists the punting average by LOS for the 2018 NFL (L is short for LOS; P is short for Punts):

Table 8.3
2018 NFL League Punting Data Broken Down by Line of Scrimmage

L	P	YDS	AVG	L	P	YDS	AVG	L	P	YDS	AVG
99	3	163	54.33	76	60	2918	48.63	53	33	1477	44.76
98	7	343	49.00	75	66	3215	48.71	52	41	1726	42.10
97	5	242	48.40	74	53	2564	48.38	51	32	1344	42.00
96	4	221	55.25	73	61	3008	49.31	50	43	1666	38.74
95	6	296	49.33	72	59	2801	47.47	49	32	1329	41.53
94	18	835	46.39	71	68	3270	48.09	48	37	1456	39.35
93	7	341	48.71	70	68	3312	48.71	47	42	1566	37.29
92	5	267	53.40	69	60	2757	45.95	46	26	979	37.65
91	15	701	46.73	68	53	2525	47.64	45	39	1426	36.56
90	17	855	50.29	67	60	2906	48.43	44	31	1126	36.32
89	16	759	47.44	66	78	3807	48.81	43	23	814	35.39
88	26	1247	47.96	65	44	2023	45.98	42	21	710	33.81
87	23	1046	45.48	64	35	1570	44.86	41	23	799	34.74
86	23	1107	48.13	63	46	2161	46.98	40	24	780	32.50
85	27	1314	48.67	62	38	1791	47.13	39	20	652	32.60
84	29	1418	48.90	61	44	2151	48.89	38	14	446	31.86
83	19	874	46.00	60	50	2356	47.12	37	12	326	27.17
82	42	2074	49.38	59	42	1849	44.02	36	3	88	29.33
81	33	1658	50.24	58	35	1571	44.89	35	3	93	31.00
80	55	2730	49.64	57	39	1769	45.36	34	1	22	22.00
79	37	1747	47.22	56	43	1965	45.70	33	1	33	33.00
78	44	2175	49.43	55	57	2579	45.25	32	1	17	17.00
77	42	1894	45.10	54	33	1457	44.15	31	1	27	27.00
								SUM	2198	99534	45.28

Graphing the data from Table 8.3, line of scrimmage or L (x) vs. Punting Average or AVG (y), with a polynomial trendline degree six running through the data. The data on the right end of Figure 8.2, for the LOS between 90 and 99 yards, fluctuates quite a bit because of a lack of data. As a comparison, there is more than three times as much data in the 80–89 area than the 90–99 area. You can see the same thing happening on the left side of the curve because of the lack of data. The more data you have, the less fluctuation you have and the less jagged the graph is.

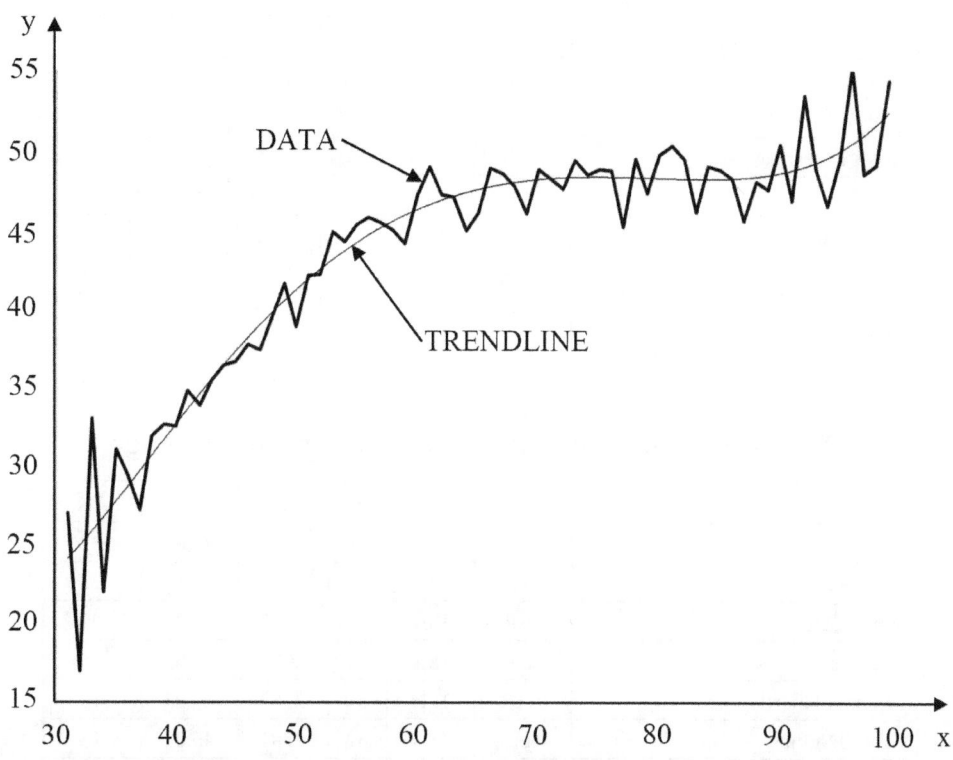

Figure 8.2. Graph of line of scrimmage (L) versus average punt distance (AVG) from Table 8.3 data.

In case you're wondering why I didn't include the corresponding data and graph for the 1961 AFL, the reason is because the graph didn't work; there just isn't enough data for the graph to work right. It is an example of a sample size that is too small. You have to remember the 1961 AFL consisted of eight teams playing a 14-game schedule (559 punts) as opposed to 32 teams in the 2018 NFL playing a 16-game schedule (2198 punts), four times as much data. For the AFL data to have much significance, you would probably need four complete seasons worth of punting data (say, 1960–63) to generate a significant graph.

Punter Rating System

Here are the individual yards per average punting stats for the 1961 AFL (Table 8.4) and 2018 NFL (Table 8.5) punters who qualified for the league punting title (P is Punts, Y is Yards, A is Average, and RK is Rank, with one being lowest):

Table 8.4
1961 AFL Punters with Rank of Gross Punting Average

PUNTER	TM	YL	P	Y	A	RK
Tom Yewcic	BOP	61A	62	2384	38.45	1

PUNTER	TM	YL	P	Y	A	RK
Billy Atkins	BUF	61A	84	3718	44.26	8
Cotton Davidson	DAT	61A	57	2288	40.14	3
George Herring	DEN	61A	80	3170	39.63	2
Jim Norton	HOU	61A	48	1949	40.60	4
Curley Johnson	NYT	61A	60	2583	43.05	7
Wayne Crow	OAK	61A	61	2618	42.92	6
Paul Maguire	S D	61A	61	2534	41.54	5

Table 8.5
2018 NFL Punters with Rank of Gross Punting Average

PUNTER	TM	YL	P	Y	A	RK
Andy Lee	ARZ	18N	94	4568	48.60	32
Matthew Bosher	ATL	18N	60	2729	45.48	23
Sam Koch	BAR	18N	60	2842	47.37	29
Corey Bojorquez	BUF	18N	45	2028	45.07	16
Michael Palardy	CAR	18N	61	2759	45.23	19
Pat O'Donnell	CHI	18N	62	2791	45.02	13
Kevin Huber	CIN	18N	71	3119	43.93	6
Britton Colquitt	CLE	18N	83	3767	45.39	21
Chris Jones	DAL	18N	60	2670	44.50	7
Colby Wadman	DEN	18N	65	2905	44.69	9
Sam Martin	DET	18N	74	3310	44.73	10
JK Scott	GB	18N	71	3176	44.73	11
Trevor Daniel	HOT	18N	74	3237	43.74	5
Rigoberto Sanchez	IND	18N	57	2629	46.12	25
Logan Cooke	JAX	18N	86	3872	45.02	14
Dustin Colquitt	KC	18N	45	2021	44.91	12
Johnny Hekker	L A	18N	43	1992	46.33	26
Donnie Jones	LAC	18N	47	1990	42.34	1
Matt Haack	MIA	18N	87	3884	44.64	8
Matt Wile	MIN	18N	72	3254	45.19	18
Ryan Allen	N E	18N	64	2885	45.08	17
Thomas Morstead	N O	18N	43	1996	46.42	27
Riley Dixon	NYG	18N	71	3226	45.44	22
Lac Edwards	NYJ	18N	82	3763	45.89	24
Johnny Townsend	OAK	18N	70	3022	43.17	2
Cameron Johnston	PHI	18N	61	2937	48.15	30
Jordan Berry	PIT	18N	63	2753	43.70	3

PUNTER	TM	YL	P	Y	A	RK
Bradley Pinion	S F	18N	68	2973	43.72	4
Michael Dickson	SEA	18N	78	3759	48.19	31
Bryan Anger	T B	18N	57	2567	45.04	15
Brett Kern	TEN	18N	74	3483	47.07	28
Tress Way	WAS	18N	79	3581	45.33	20

While punting average is an important statistic, I think we need to look at segregating punting statistics between long punts (LOS 99 to 61 yards) and shorter punts (LOS 60 or fewer yards). This is the segregated data for the two leagues (L/S is Long/Short) in Table 8.6:

Table 8.6
Comparison of 1961 AFL and 2018 NFL Punts, Segregated Between LOS of 60 Yards

1961 AFL							2018 NFL					
L/S	L	P	YDS	AVG	PCT		L/S	L	P	YDS	AVG	PCT
LG	61–99	384	16069	41.85	0.714		LG	61–99	1396	67086	48.06	0.635
SH	31–60	154	5979	38.82	0.286		SH	31–60	802	32448	40.46	0.365
	SUM	538	22048	40.98				SUM	2198	99534	45.28	

The comparison in Table 8.6 is quite different, and indicative of how punting has changed over the years. In the early years, and even into the 1960s, punters (and kickers) played a secondary position, as rosters were smaller and teams could not tie up an entire roster spot on a pure punter or placekicker. Also, with the substitution rules, of the 1930s and into the 1940s, when a player came into a game, he had to stay on the field, barring injury, for the remainder of the quarter. (This form of limited substitution was done away with altogether in 1950 which ended the era of the two-way player.) The earliest pure punter I could find was Dick Deschaines of Green Bay and Cleveland from 1955 to 1958. The earliest pure kicker I know of was the "Toeless Wonder," Ben Agajanian, who began his two-decade career with the Eagles and Steelers in 1945.

For the record, there were no pure punters in the AFL in 1961 (Bobby Joe Green of Chicago was the only one in the NFL), and for that reason, it was enough just to have somebody who could punt the ball satisfactorily. There was no such thing as measuring "hang time" or a "coffin corner" punt in 1961, and those who weren't pure punters didn't get much time to practice punting as they spent most of their time working on their offensive or defensive positions.

For this reason, the punting average was not as high as it is now. Now, kids start punting in high school, probably earlier, and most never play another position; all they ever do is punt. All college and pro teams have kicking coaches, which they didn't have in the 1960s. Like kicking, punting has become highly specialized in the modern era. There hasn't been a punter who played a secondary position in the NFL since Danny White, who was the full-time punter and quarterback for the Cowboys through the 1982 season.

This overall difference between the punters of then and now can be seen in the LONG (61 to 99-yard LOS) punt averages, which have increased over seven yards from 1961 to 2018. The SHORT (31 to 60-yard LOS) punts increased by less than two yards over that span. Another interesting factoid is that the percentage (PCT) of short punts has increased from 28.6 percent in 1961 to 36.5 in 2018. I would have expected the percentage of short punts to be lower in 2018, not higher, due to the longer number of field goal attempts these days as opposed to 1961.

When the player punt attempts are split between short and long punts, this is what we have for the two league-seasons, 1961 AFL (Table 8.7) followed by 2018 NFL (Table 8.8). P is for Punts, Y for Yards, A for Average, RK for Rank of Average, highest average ranked at the total number of teams in the league, 8 or 32, down to lowest ranked at number one, and DIFF for Differential of long average minus short average:

Table 8.7
1961 AFL Punters, Data Segregated Between LOS of 60 Yards, Ranked by Average

			LOS 61–99 YARDS				LOS 31–60 YARDS				
PUNTER	TM	YL	P	Y	A	RK	P	Y	A	RK	DIFF
Tom Yewcic	BOP	61A	38	1501	39.50	1	24	883	36.79	1	2.71
Billy Atkins	BUF	61A	62	2771	44.69	8	22	947	43.05	8	1.65
Cotton Davidson	DTX	61A	39	1589	40.74	3	18	699	38.83	3	1.91
George Herring	DEN	61A	61	2493	40.87	2	19	677	35.63	2	5.24
Jim Norton	HOU	61A	39	1575	40.38	4	9	374	41.56	4	-1.17
Curley Johnson	NYT	61A	40	1770	44.25	7	20	813	40.65	7	3.60
Wayne Crow	OAK	61A	45	1943	43.18	6	16	675	42.19	6	0.99
Paul Maguire	S D	61A	42	1811	43.12	5	19	723	38.05	5	5.07

Table 8.8
2018 NFL Punters, Data Segregated Between LOS of 60 Yards

			LOS 61–99 YARDS				LOS 31–60 YARDS				
PUNTER	TM	YL	P	Y	A	RK	P	Y	A	RK	DIFF
Andy Lee	ARZ	18N	53	2775	52.36	32	41	1793	43.73	28	8.63
Matthew Bosher	ATL	18N	32	1521	47.53	11	28	1208	43.14	24	4.39
Sam Koch	BAR	18N	23	1202	52.26	30	37	1640	44.32	30	7.94
Corey Bojorquez	BUF	18N	21	1004	47.81	14	24	1024	42.67	20	5.14
Michael Palardy	CAR	18N	29	1396	48.14	16	32	1363	42.59	19	5.54
Pat O'Donnell	CHI	18N	23	1119	48.65	20	39	1672	42.87	23	5.78
Kevin Huber	CIN	18N	41	1916	46.73	6	30	1203	40.10	2	6.63
Britton Colquitt	CLE	18N	44	2138	48.59	19	39	1629	41.77	15	6.82
Chris Jones	DAL	18N	35	1589	45.40	3	25	1081	43.24	25	2.16
Colby Wadman	DEN	18N	32	1529	47.78	13	33	1376	41.70	14	6.08
Sam Martin	DET	18N	32	1565	48.91	21	42	1745	41.55	10	7.36

			LOS 61-99 YARDS				LOS 31-60 YARDS				
PUNTER	TM	YL	P	Y	A	RK	P	Y	A	RK	DIFF
JK Scott	GB	18N	37	1751	47.32	8	34	1425	41.91	17	5.41
Trevor Daniel	HOT	18N	27	1279	47.37	9	47	1958	41.66	13	5.71
Rigoberto Sanchez	IND	18N	29	1379	47.55	12	28	1250	44.64	31	2.91
Logan Cooke	JAX	18N	41	1948	47.51	10	45	1924	42.76	21	4.76
Dustin Colquitt	KC	18N	21	1033	49.19	23	24	988	41.17	5	8.02
Johnny Hekker	L A	18N	16	837	52.31	31	27	1155	42.78	22	9.53
Donnie Jones	LAC	18N	26	1110	42.69	1	21	880	41.90	16	0.79
Matt Haack	MIA	18N	40	1936	48.40	18	47	1948	41.45	8	6.95
Matt Wile	MIN	18N	42	2012	47.90	15	30	1242	41.40	7	6.50
Ryan Allen	N E	18N	34	1675	49.26	24	30	1210	40.33	3	8.93
Thomas Morstead	N O	18N	22	1129	51.32	29	21	867	41.29	6	10.03
Riley Dixon	NYG	18N	41	1978	48.24	17	30	1248	41.60	12	6.64
Lac Edwards	NYJ	18N	52	2460	47.31	7	30	1303	43.43	26	3.87
Johnny Townsend	OAK	18N	37	1699	45.92	5	33	1323	40.09	1	5.83
Cameron Johnston	PHI	18N	33	1686	51.09	26	28	1251	44.68	32	6.41
Jordan Berry	PIT	18N	30	1358	45.27	2	33	1395	42.27	18	2.99
Bradley Pinion	S F	18N	40	1835	45.88	4	28	1138	40.64	4	5.23
Michael Dickson	SEA	18N	46	2358	51.26	28	32	1401	43.78	29	7.48
Bryan Anger	T B	18N	26	1282	49.31	25	31	1285	41.45	9	7.86
Brett Kern	TEN	18N	34	1738	51.12	27	40	1745	43.63	27	7.49
Tress Way	WAS	18N	40	1960	49.00	22	39	1621	41.56	11	7.44

I removed from Tables 6.7 and 6.8 the non-qualifiers for the punting title, those who did not have enough punts during the season; there were a total of three from 1961 and six from 2018.

Here is the 1961 AFL (Table 8.9) and 2018 NFL (Table 8.10) data for touchbacks (TB) with percentage of attempts and rank, with lowest percentage getting a rank score of the number of teams in the league, 8 or 32, going down to the highest percentage getting a rank score of one.

Table 8.9
1961 AFL Punters Ranked by Touchback Percentage

PUNTER	TM	YL	P	TB	TB%	RK
Tom Yewcic	BOP	61A	62	4	6.45	5
Billy Atkins	BUF	61A	84	9	10.71	2
Cotton Davidson	DTX	61A	57	5	8.77	3
George Herring	DEN	61A	80	4	5.00	6
Jim Norton	HOU	61A	48	0	0.00	8
Curley Johnson	NYT	61A	60	10	16.67	1

PUNTER	TM	YL	P	TB	TB%	RK
Wayne Crow	OAK	61A	61	5	8.20	4
Paul Maguire	S D	61A	61	3	4.92	7

Table 8.10
2018 NFL Punters Ranked by Touchback Percentages

PUNTER	TM	YL	P	TB	TB%	RK
Andy Lee	ARZ	18N	94	7	7.45	12
Matthew Bosher	ATL	18N	60	3	5.00	26
Sam Koch	BAR	18N	60	5	8.33	9
Corey Bojorquez	BUF	18N	45	4	8.89	7
Michael Palardy	CAR	18N	61	4	6.56	18
Pat O'Donnell	CHI	18N	62	7	11.29	3
Kevin Huber	CIN	18N	71	3	4.23	28
Britton Colquitt	CLE	18N	83	6	7.23	13
Chris Jones	DAL	18N	60	2	3.33	30
Colby Wadman	DEN	18N	65	7	10.77	5
Sam Martin	DET	18N	74	4	5.41	25
JK Scott	GB	18N	71	9	12.68	1
Trevor Daniel	HOT	18N	74	5	6.76	17
Rigoberto Sanchez	IND	18N	57	5	8.77	8
Logan Cooke	JAX	18N	86	7	8.14	10
Dustin Colquitt	KC	18N	45	5	11.11	4
Johnny Hekker	L A	18N	43	2	4.65	27
Donnie Jones	LAC	18N	47	3	6.38	20
Matt Haack	MIA	18N	87	6	6.90	16
Matt Wile	MIN	18N	72	2	2.78	31
Ryan Allen	N E	18N	64	5	7.81	11
Thomas Morstead	N O	18N	43	4	9.30	6
Riley Dixon	NYG	18N	71	4	5.63	24
Lac Edwards	NYJ	18N	82	5	6.10	22
Johnny Townsend	OAK	18N	70	5	7.14	14
Cameron Johnston	PHI	18N	61	7	11.48	2
Jordan Berry	PIT	18N	63	4	6.35	21
Bradley Pinion	S F	18N	68	4	5.88	23
Michael Dickson	SEA	18N	78	5	6.41	19
Bryan Anger	T B	18N	57	4	7.02	15
Brett Kern	TEN	18N	74	3	4.05	29
Tress Way	WAS	18N	79	0	0.00	32

The touchback percentages haven't changed much between 1961 (7.4 percent) and 2018 (6.9 percent) and this fluctuation is well within the range of random chance.

Finally, we'll look at percentage of punts that go out of bounds inside the opponents' 20-yard line (I20) and the percentage of punts for the 1961 AFL (Table 8.11) and 2018 NFL (Table 8.12). These used to be called coffin corner punts in the 1970s and 1980s, but the term is no longer used. The highest percentage gets a rank equal to the number of teams in the league, 32 or 8, going down to the team with the lowest percentage getting a rank of one.

Table 8.11
1961 AFL Punters Ranked by Punts Out of Bounds Inside the 20

PUNTER	TM	YL	P	I20	I20%	RK
Tom Yewcic	BOP	61A	62	0	0.00	2.5
Billy Atkins	BUF	61A	84	0	0.00	2.5
Cotton Davidson	DTX	61A	57	1	1.75	6
George Herring	DEN	61A	80	1	1.25	5
Jim Norton	HOU	61A	48	2	4.17	8
Curley Johnson	NYT	61A	60	0	0.00	2.5
Wayne Crow	OAK	61A	61	2	3.28	7
Paul Maguire	S D	61A	61	0	0.00	2.5

Table 8.12
2018 NFL Punters Ranked by Punts Out of Bounds Inside the 20

PUNTER	TM	YL	P	I20	I20%	RK
Andy Lee	ARZ	18N	94	2	2.13	13
Matthew Bosher	ATL	18N	60	1	1.67	10
Sam Koch	BAR	18N	60	2	3.33	20
Corey Bojorquez	BUF	18N	45	3	6.67	28
Michael Palardy	CAR	18N	61	2	3.28	19
Pat O'Donnell	CHI	18N	62	0	0.00	3
Kevin Huber	CIN	18N	71	0	0.00	3
Britton Colquitt	CLE	18N	83	3	3.61	21
Chris Jones	DAL	18N	60	0	0.00	3
Colby Wadman	DEN	18N	65	3	4.62	24
Sam Martin	DET	18N	74	1	1.35	6
JK Scott	GB	18N	71	1	1.41	8
Trevor Daniel	HOT	18N	74	2	2.70	17
Rigoberto Sanchez	IND	18N	57	1	1.75	12
Logan Cooke	JAX	18N	86	4	4.65	25
Dustin Colquitt	KC	18N	45	1	2.22	14
Johnny Hekker	L A	18N	43	5	11.63	31

PUNTER	TM	YL	P	I20	I20%	RK
Donnie Jones	LAC	18N	47	2	4.26	22
Matt Haack	MIA	18N	87	2	2.30	15
Matt Wile	MIN	18N	72	1	1.39	7
Ryan Allen	N E	18N	64	3	4.69	26
Thomas Morstead	N O	18N	43	5	11.63	30
Riley Dixon	NYG	18N	71	2	2.82	18
Lac Edwards	NYJ	18N	82	2	2.44	16
Johnny Townsend	OAK	18N	70	0	0.00	3
Cameron Johnston	PHI	18N	61	1	1.64	9
Jordan Berry	PIT	18N	63	3	4.76	27
Bradley Pinion	S F	18N	68	3	4.41	23
Michael Dickson	SEA	18N	78	6	7.69	29
Bryan Anger	T B	18N	57	1	1.75	11
Brett Kern	TEN	18N	74	9	12.16	32
Tress Way	WAS	18N	79	0	0.00	3

The percentage of coffin corner punts in 1961 (1.1 percent) is a mere third of the 2018 figure of 3.3 percent. However, I have to wonder how many of the 1961 punts in the play-by-play were not described correctly as having gone out of bounds. However, in this day and age, punting has become more of a science, and punting has clearly been going through a renaissance over the past 20 years.

Now we'll put the rankings together, and since Michael Dickson of Seattle was the consensus All-Pro punter in the NFL in 2018, we'll use him as the example. Here are his rankings for the five categories—GPA is Gross Punting Average, LPA is Long Punt Average, SPA is Short Punt Average, TB% is Touchback percentage and I20% is Inside the 20 and Out of Bounds (Coffin Corner) percentage:

Table 8.13
2018 Punting Category Ranks of Michael Dickson

PUNTER	TM	YL	GPA	LPA	SPA	TB%	I20%
Michael Dickson	SEA	18N	31	28	29	19	29

As you can see, Dickson had an outstanding year, as he finished in the top five (from 28 to 32 in rank) in four of the five categories. To tie the five numbers together into a final ranking, I decided to use a harmonic mean. The formula for PUR (Punt Rating) is:

$$PUR = \text{(The five rankings multiplied together)} \wedge (1/5)$$

Applying the ranking to Dickson:

$$PUR = ((31 * 28 * 29 * 19 * 29)) \wedge 0.2 = 26.817$$

Due to the differing number of teams in leagues, I chose to divide the final ranking by the number of punters in the ranking process, so that the maximum value in PUR a punter could possibly achieve is 1.000 and the minimum value is 0.000. There were 32 punters being rated in 2018, which means the harmonic average will be divided by 32. Therefore:

PUR = 26.817 / 32 = 0.838

Because I wanted to get a PUR score with a maximum high of one for the best punter, it made more sense to reverse the values of the rankings for the five categories, giving the highest numeric rank to the best rating and going down to the worst rating in the category getting a score of one.

Here are the final PUR scores for the eligible punters in the two leagues, 1961 AFL (Table 8.14) and 2018 NFL (Table 8.15):

Table 8.14
1961 AFL Punters Ranked by Punter Rating

PUNTER	TM	YL	GPA	LPA	SPA	TB%	I20%	PUR
Wayne Crow	OAK	61A	6	6	6	4	7	0.713
Jim Norton	HOU	61A	4	4	4	8	8	0.660
Billy Atkins	BUF	61A	8	8	8	2	2.5	0.601
Paul Maguire	S D	61A	5	5	5	7	2.5	0.582
Curley Johnson	NYT	61A	7	7	7	1	2.5	0.483
Cotton Davidson	DAT	61A	3	3	3	3	6	0.431
George Herring	DEN	61A	2	2	2	6	5	0.374
Tom Yewcic	BOP	61A	1	1	1	5	2.5	0.207

Table 8.15
2018 NFL Punters Ranked by Punter Rating

PUNTER	TM	YL	GPA	LPA	SPA	TB%	I20%	PUR
Brett Kern	TEN	18N	28	27	27	29	32	0.892
Johnny Hekker	L A	18N	26	31	22	27	31	0.849
Michael Dickson	SEA	18N	31	28	29	19	29	0.838
Sam Koch	BAR	18N	29	30	30	9	20	0.675
Andy Lee	ARZ	18N	32	32	28	12	13	0.668
Michael Palardy	CAR	18N	19	16	19	18	19	0.568
Riley Dixon	NYG	18N	22	17	12	24	18	0.565
Britton Colquitt	CLE	18N	21	19	15	13	21	0.546
Matthew Bosher	ATL	18N	23	11	24	26	10	0.543
Lac Edwards	NYJ	18N	24	7	26	22	16	0.540
Rigoberto Sanchez	IND	18N	25	12	31	8	12	0.484
Corey Bojorquez	BUF	18N	16	14	20	7	28	0.483
Thomas Morstead	N O	18N	27	29	6	6	30	0.479
Logan Cooke	JAX	18N	14	10	21	10	25	0.466
Bryan Anger	T B	18N	15	25	9	15	11	0.441

PUNTER	TM	YL	GPA	LPA	SPA	TB%	I20%	PUR
Tress Way	WAS	18N	20	22	11	32	3	0.425
Cameron Johnston	PHI	18N	30	26	32	2	9	0.422
Matt Wile	MIN	18N	18	15	7	31	7	0.414
Ryan Allen	N E	18N	17	24	3	11	26	0.401
Sam Martin	DET	18N	10	21	10	25	6	0.393
Matt Haack	MIA	18N	8	18	8	16	15	0.383
Colby Wadman	DEN	18N	9	13	14	5	24	0.358
Trevor Daniel	HOT	18N	5	9	13	17	17	0.347
Dustin Colquitt	KC	18N	12	23	5	4	14	0.297
Jordan Berry	PIT	18N	3	2	18	21	27	0.283
Pat O'Donnell	CHI	18N	13	20	23	3	3	0.276
Chris Jones	DAL	18N	7	3	25	30	3	0.269
Bradley Pinion	S F	18N	4	4	4	23	23	0.252
JK Scott	GB	18N	11	8	17	1	8	0.204
Donnie Jones	LAC	18N	1	1	16	20	22	0.184
Kevin Huber	CIN	18N	6	6	2	28	3	0.178
Johnny Townsend	OAK	18N	2	5	1	14	3	0.105

Most of the AFL punters you've probably never heard of, except for Paul Maguire, who punted for the Chargers and Bills during the entire history of the AFL, and whose 712 regular season punts between 1960 and 1969 will forever be the most in American Football League history. Maguire, of course, had a long career as a sports broadcaster. Curley Johnson, who was the punter for the 1968 Jets in Super Bowl III, was second in career AFL punts with 537, and Jim Norton was right behind Johnson with 522 career punts, and as a defensive back, his 45 career interceptions are the second-most in AFL history.

The Sporting News, *New York Daily News*, and the AFL selected their own all-AFL teams for 1961, but none of those teams included a punter.

Among the 2018 NFL punters, Michael Dickson wound up finishing third in the league in PUR, behind Brett Kern of Tennessee, the AFC Pro Bowl kicker, and Johnny Hekker of the LA Rams, who was second team AP All-Pro.

All in all, I think we did fine with this first attempt at a punter rating system. I think some will disagree about not using net punting average as a category, but I was trying to focus solely on the performance of the punter, and in time, I may come around on this. I'm sure with the release of this book that others will come forward with suggestions that will improve this system (and I welcome their suggestions), but I have reached the conclusion that reviewing each punt on an individual basis instead of a collective basis is the correct way to look at the issue.

9

Coding

In doing research, I have always felt the need to develop a shorthand, if you will, that could be used to take a team's statistics and boil them down from a stream of hundreds or thousands of digits into a simplified code that can be used to quickly compare and contrast teams. Such a technique could be applied to a myriad of different studies, and also to express the degree of similarity (or the lack thereof) between two teams. I finally gave it a shot and developed such a process; I call it coding.

Coding is a system that assigns for each team in each season a series of letter grades, or codes if you will, for different aspects of a team's performance based on statistical tables. The codes cover offense and defense and special teams, and the code letters will fall into one of five categories:

A = Superior = 80–100 percent
B = Above Average = 60–79 percent
C = Average = 40–59 percent
D = Below Average = 20–39 percent
E = Very Bad = 0–19 percent

In rare situations, there will be a code X assigned when there is no data for the category for that particular season, but we'll cross that bridge when we get to it.

Each team has a total of 36 codes, 18 for offense and 18 for defense, and the code categories are the same for both offense and defense:

Points Scored (or allowed)
First Downs
Penalties
Fumbles per Rushing Attempt
Yards Rushing per Game
Yards per Rushing Attempt
YRAA/G (Yards Rushing Above Average per Game—See Chapter 5)
Rushing Touchdowns per Attempt
Rushing Grade (based on an overall ranking of the above five rushing categories)
Pass Completion Percentage
Passing Yards per Attempt
Pass Touchdown Percentage
Interception Percentage
Sack Percentage (Sacks divided by Pass Attempts)
Passing Grade (based on an overall ranking of above five passing categories)

Yards per Play
Yards per Point
Kicking (PAL or PAL2—See Chapter 7)

I wanted to keep the number of codes as small as possible, which is why there are not separate codes for punting and kickoff returns and things like that. On the other hand, I wanted there to be just enough codes to ensure the most similar teams are identified.

The 1955 NFL Season

A sample league will be needed to demonstrate the process, and I have chosen the 1955 NFL. For all categories we will be using regular season statistics only. We'll begin with the offensive categories. The first category is Points Scored or PS. Table 9.1 lists the points scored for each of the ten teams (TM is short for team) in the 1955 NFL, and PS, ranked in order from highest to lowest:

Table 9.1
Points Scored (PS) for All 1955 NFL Teams

TM	PS
CLE	349
CHI	294
NYG	267
L A	260
G B	258
PHI	248
WAS	246
DET	230
CHC	224
S F	216
BAL	214
PIT	195

In order to assign a letter grade (or code) for Points Scored, you must consider the number of teams in the league that season, and that the code letters should roughly cover five equal regions. I put together Table 9.2, which lists the number of teams that will be assigned each particular code for each of the categories based on the total number of teams in that league.

Table 9.2
Dispersion of Codes Per Number of Teams in League

CODE	NUMBER OF TEAMS IN LEAGUE												
	7	8	9	10	12	13	14	15	16	26	28	30	31	32
A	1	1	2	2	2	2	3	3	3	5	6	6	6	6

	NUMBER OF TEAMS IN LEAGUE												
B	2	2	2	2	3	3	3	3	3	5	5	6	6	7
C	1	2	1	2	2	3	2	3	4	6	6	6	7	6
D	2	2	2	2	3	3	3	3	3	5	5	6	6	7
E	1	1	2	2	2	2	3	3	3	5	6	6	6	6

The idea is to try to make Table 9.2 so that an equal number of teams each season will get the same code, as each of the five grades gets 20 percent. This is impossible, of course, in most leagues, but over time it will generally even out.

From Table 9.2, for a 12-team league, there will be two As, three Bs, two Cs, three Ds and two Es. Applying that to a 12 to 1 list, with 12 being highest, it would correspond like this:

Table 9.3
Dispersion of Codes for a 12-Team League

RANK	CODE
12	A
11	A
10	B
9	B
8	B
7	C
6	C
5	D
4	D
3	D
2	E
1	E

Putting Table 9.3 together with Table 9.1, this should immediately make sense, as the highest scores get the highest codes (RK is short for Rank, CD is short for Code in Table 9.4):

Table 9.4
Points Scored Codes for 1955 NFL Teams

TM	PS	RK	CD
CLE	349	12	A
CHI	294	11	A
NYG	267	10	B
L A	260	9	B
G B	258	8	B

TM	PS	RK	CD
PHI	248	7	C
WAS	246	6	C
DET	230	5	D
CHC	224	4	D
S F	216	3	D
BAL	214	2	E
PIT	195	1	E

Note, if two teams tie in a category, they get the same code. Sometimes that violates Table 9.2 for how many of each code to disperse per number of teams in the league. In those tie situations, the rule is to always grade upward. There was a tie in the Offensive First Downs (FD) category for the 1955 NFL, as shown in Table 9.5:

Table 9.5
First Down Codes for 1955 NFL Teams

TM	FD	RK	CD
CHI	235	12	A
L A	233	11	A
CLE	**224**	**9.5**	**B**
DET	**224**	**9.5**	**B**
PHI	219	8	B
G B	213	7	C
PIT	211	6	C
BAL	206	5	D
S F	204	4	D
WAS	193	3	D
NYG	189	2	E
CHC	150	1	E

In Table 9.5, the Browns and Lions were tied with 224 First Downs (in bold and italic) and both wound up with the same code of B, but if after applying the code letters, one had been on the B side and the other on the C side, I would grade up, and make both of them Bs. It is important to notice that their rank, also in bold, is the total number of points (19, or nine plus ten) is split by both teams. And, of course, 9 plus 10 equals 19, which divided by two equals 9.5, and that is why they get a rank of 9.5.

Penalties are the next category, and this is contrary to most statistical categories in that a low number of penalties on offense (which are actually team penalties) and a higher number of penalties on defense (which are opposition penalties) gets the higher codes, which makes logical sense. Here are the codes for Offensive or Team Penalties:

Table 9.6
Penalty Codes for 1955 NFL Teams

TM	PEN	RANK	CODE
G B	41	12	A
NYG	50	11	A
DET	51	10	B
CHI	57	9	B
BAL	59	8	B
WAS	60	7	C
PHI	61	6	C
CLE	64	4	D
L A	64	4	D
S F	64	4	D
PIT	67	2	E
CHC	82	1	E

Note that the Browns, Rams and 49ers all tied with 64 penalties, and all of them got the same code. The 12 total rank points (five, four and three) were split equally three ways, which equals four.

For Rushing, the five categories used to determine the Rushing Grade are Rushing Attempts per Fumble, Rushing Yards per Game, Rushing Yards per Attempts, Yards Rushing Above Average per Game or YRAA/G and Rushing Touchdowns per 100 Attempts.

Although it's not really the best way to do it, for Fumbles per Rushing Attempt, what I used for fumbles in this category is Fumbles Lost, which is not necessarily due to fumbles from rushing but also from passing and kick returns and bad quarterback snaps and the like. I had to get Fumbles Lost in here somehow so this is where they will go, like it or not.

Table 9.7 lists the Teams, Games Played (G), Rushing Attempts (ATT), Rushing Yards (YDS), Fumbles Lost (FL), and Rushing Touchdowns (TD), Attempts per Fumble (ATT/F), Rushing Yards per Game (RY/G), Rushing Yards per Attempt (Y/A), Yards Rushing Above Average per Game (YRAA/G) and Rushing Touchdowns per 100 Attempts (TD%):

Table 9.7
Offensive Rushing Grade Statistics for 1955 NFL Teams

TM	G	ATT	YDS	FL	TD	ATT/F	RY/G	Y/A	YRAA/G	TD%
BAL	12	456	1833	8	15	57.000	152.750	4.020	1.158	3.289
CHI	12	487	2388	18	19	27.056	199.000	4.903	40.735	3.901
CHC	12	438	1626	20	10	21.900	135.500	3.712	-11.122	2.283
CLE	12	536	2020	18	20	29.778	168.333	3.769	-11.092	3.731
DET	12	392	1477	19	11	20.632	123.083	3.768	-7.902	2.806
G B	12	433	1883	25	11	17.320	156.917	4.349	14.020	2.540

TM	G	ATT	YDS	FL	TD	ATT/F	RY/G	Y/A	YRAA/G	TD%
L A	12	451	1943	10	17	45.100	161.917	4.308	12.993	3.769
NYG	12	414	1693	16	12	25.875	141.083	4.089	3.648	2.899
PHI	12	392	1317	21	9	18.667	109.750	3.360	-22.300	2.296
PIT	12	420	1284	17	13	24.706	107.000	3.057	-35.529	3.095
S F	12	408	1713	18	12	22.667	142.750	4.199	7.611	2.941
WAS	12	478	2000	21	17	22.762	166.667	4.184	8.414	3.556

Table 9.8 displays the ranks and codes for each of the five categories. In all five categories, the higher statistical value gets the higher rank number.

Table 9.8
Rushing Grade Ranks for 1955 NFL Teams Based on Data from Table 9.7

	ATT/F		RY/G		Y/A		YRAA/G		TD%	
TM	RK	CD	RK	CD	RK	CD	RK	CD	RK	CD
BAL	12	A	7	C	6	C	6	C	8	B
CHI	9	B	12	A	12	A	12	A	12	A
CHC	4	D	4	D	3	D	3	D	1	E
CLE	10	B	11	A	5	D	4	D	10	B
DET	3	D	3	D	4	D	5	D	4	D
G B	1	E	8	B	11	A	11	A	3	D
L A	11	A	9	B	10	B	10	B	11	A
NYG	8	B	5	D	7	C	7	C	5	D
PHI	2	E	2	E	2	E	2	E	2	E
PIT	7	C	1	E	1	E	1	E	7	C
S F	5	D	6	C	9	B	8	B	6	C
WAS	6	C	10	B	8	B	9	B	9	B

I developed an averaging technique for combining the five ranks into one. It involves first taking an arithmetic mean, and then a harmonic mean, of the five ranks for each team, and then, taking a harmonic mean of the arithmetic and harmonic means. An arithmetic mean, of course, is a simple average of the five ranks. A harmonic mean of the five ranks would be the product of the five ranks multiplied together, raised to the 0.2 or 1/5th power, or:

$$HAR = (RY/G * RY/A * RA/F * YRAA/G * TD\%) \wedge (1/5)$$

The final score, a harmonic mean of the average and the above harmonic mean, would be derived as follows:

$$FIN = (AVG * HAR) \wedge (1/2)$$

The reason for using harmonic means in addition to averages as opposed to just using a simple average to determine a final score was to cut down on the number of final ranks that wind up tied. This is more of an issue with larger leagues than smaller leagues.

9. Coding

For the Browns, the numerical average of 10, 11, 5, 4 and 10 is simply 40 divided by five, or 8.0. The harmonic mean is calculated as:

$$HAR = (10 * 11 * 5 * 4 * 10) \wedge (1/5) = (22{,}000) \wedge (0.2) = 7.387$$

The final score for Offensive Rushing Grade (ORG) would be:

$$OR = (8.0 * 7.387) \wedge (1/2) = (59.082) \wedge (0.5) = 7.688$$

This process is applied to the other teams in the 1955 NFL in Table 9.9, with the five ranks, the arithmetic mean or average (AVG), the harmonic mean (HAR), the harmonic mean between the two means or Final Mean (FM), the rank of FM from highest to lowest (RK) and the code for Offensive Rushing:

Table 9.9
Offensive Rushing Grade (ORG) Calculation Table for 1955 NFL Teams

TM	ATT/F	RY/G	Y/A	YRAA/G	TD%	AVG	HAR	ORG	RK	CD
BAL	12	7	6	6	8	7.8	7.529	7.663	8	B
CHI	9	12	12	12	12	11.4	11.329	11.364	12	A
CHC	4	4	3	3	1	3.0	2.702	2.847	3	D
CLE	10	11	5	4	10	8.0	7.387	7.688	9	B
DET	3	3	4	5	4	3.8	3.728	3.764	4	D
G B	1	8	11	11	3	6.8	4.927	5.788	5	D
L A	11	9	10	10	11	10.2	10.172	10.186	11	A
NYG	8	5	7	7	5	6.4	6.284	6.342	6	C
PHI	2	2	2	2	2	2.0	2.000	2.000	1	E
PIT	7	1	1	1	7	3.4	2.178	2.721	2	E
S F	5	6	9	8	6	6.8	6.645	6.722	7	C
WAS	6	10	8	9	9	8.4	8.278	8.339	10	B

In 1933 and 1934, we have no information on defensive fumbles, so we have to put Xs in there. In some of the early seasons, there is no statistical information available to fill the category. We will discuss how to deal with the X more as we get into similarity.

However, if you really, really must work out the codes for the 1933 and 1934 NFL right now, we will remove RA/F from both the mean and harmonic averages for defenses, which will make the harmonic formula (using rank numbers):

$$HAR = (RY/G * RY/A * YRAA/G * TD\%) \wedge (1/4)$$

Passing is next, and we will use five different categories—Completion Percentage (C/A), Yards per Attempt (Y/A), Pass Touchdown Percentage (TD/A), Interception Percentage (I/A) and Sack Percentage (S/A), ranking each team in each of the categories and then using the same technique to determine a final score for each team. In Table 9.10, the relevant passing stats for the 1955 NFL teams are listed:

Table 9.10
Offensive Passing Grade Statistics for 1955 NFL Teams

TM	ATT	COMP	YARDS	TD	INT	SK	C/A	Y/A	T/A	I/A	S/A
BAL	266	134	1795	11	22	21	0.504	6.748	0.041	0.083	0.079
CHI	306	145	2108	17	23	23	0.474	6.889	0.056	0.075	0.075
CHC	280	106	1520	14	25	22	0.379	5.429	0.050	0.089	0.079
CLE	234	130	2225	21	11	34	0.556	9.509	0.090	0.047	0.145
DET	400	204	2542	15	22	17	0.510	6.355	0.038	0.055	0.043
G B	348	159	2004	17	19	28	0.457	5.759	0.049	0.055	0.080
L A	344	175	2206	9	18	18	0.509	6.413	0.026	0.052	0.052
NYG	292	137	1865	17	15	13	0.469	6.387	0.058	0.051	0.045
PHI	400	198	2696	19	24	28	0.495	6.740	0.048	0.060	0.070
PIT	390	189	2550	12	30	20	0.485	6.538	0.031	0.077	0.051
S F	303	151	2225	17	28	36	0.498	7.343	0.056	0.092	0.119
WAS	257	101	1549	11	21	25	0.393	6.027	0.043	0.082	0.097

Table 9.11 displays the ranks and codes for the five passing categories. Note that for interceptions and sacks, having a lower number or percentage on offense and a higher number or percentage on defense is preferable, so in those two categories, the lower numbers on offense get the higher ranking:

Table 9.11
Offensive Passing Grade Ranks for 1955 NFL Teams, Based on Data from Table 9.10

	C/A		Y/A		T/A		I/A		SK	
TM	RK	CD	RK	CD	RK	CD	RK	CD	RK	CD
BAL	9	B	9	B	4	D	3	D	5	D
CHI	5	D	10	B	9	B	6	C	7	C
CHC	1	E	1	E	8	B	2	E	6	C
CLE	12	A	12	A	12	A	12	A	1	E
DET	11	A	4	D	3	D	8	B	12	A
G B	3	D	2	E	7	C	9	B	4	D
L A	10	B	6	C	1	E	10	B	9	B
NYG	4	D	5	D	11	A	11	A	11	A
PHI	7	C	8	B	6	C	7	C	8	B
PIT	6	C	7	C	2	E	5	D	10	B
S F	8	B	11	A	10	B	1	E	2	E
WAS	2	E	3	D	5	D	4	D	3	D

Finally, Table 9.12 displays the various ranks: average, harmonic, Offensive Passing Grade (OPG), final rank, and Offensive Passing Code for the teams in the 1955 NFL:

Table 9.12
Offensive Passing Grade Calculation Table for 1955 NFL Teams

TM	C/A	Y/A	T/A	I/A	S/A	AVG	HAR	OPG	RK	CD
BAL	9	9	4	3	5	6.0	5.462	5.725	6	C
CHI	5	10	9	6	7	7.4	7.166	7.282	10	B
CHC	1	1	8	2	6	3.6	2.491	2.995	1	E
CLE	12	12	12	12	1	9.8	7.300	8.458	12	A
DET	11	4	3	8	12	7.6	6.616	7.091	8	B
G B	3	2	7	9	4	5.0	4.324	4.650	3	D
L A	10	6	1	10	9	7.2	5.578	6.337	7	C
NYG	4	5	11	11	11	8.4	7.674	8.029	11	A
PHI	7	8	6	7	8	7.2	7.160	7.180	9	B
PIT	6	7	2	5	10	6.0	5.305	5.642	5	D
S F	8	11	10	1	2	6.4	4.458	5.341	4	D
WAS	2	3	5	4	3	3.4	3.245	3.322	2	E

The harmonic mean (HAR) would be calculated as (using rank numbers):

$$HAR = (C/A * Y/A * T/A * I/A * S/A)^{(1/5)}$$

Sack information for offense and defense is currently not available from 1933 to 1949, which means teams will have an X in these categories. For these seasons, the mean will have to have the sack numeric rankings removed because there are none, and the harmonic mean formula will need to be adjusted to be:

$$HAR = (C/A * Y/A * T/A * I/A)^{(1/4)}$$

The next category is Offensive Yards per Play (Y/PL), which of course is total yards (rushing and passing divided by total attempts (rushing plus passing):

Table 9.13
Offensive Yards Per Play Codes for 1955 NFL Teams

	RUSHING		PASSING		TOTAL				
TM	ATT	YDS	ATT	YDS	ATT	YDS	Y/PL	RK	CD
BAL	456	1833	266	1795	722	3628	5.025	5	D
CHI	487	2388	306	2108	793	4496	5.670	12	A
CHC	438	1626	280	1520	718	3146	4.382	1	E
CLE	536	2020	234	2225	770	4245	5.513	10	B
DET	392	1477	400	2542	792	4019	5.074	8	B
G B	433	1883	348	2004	781	3887	4.977	4	D
L A	451	1943	344	2206	795	4149	5.219	9	B
NYG	414	1693	292	1865	706	3558	5.040	6	C
PHI	392	1317	400	2696	792	4013	5.067	7	C
PIT	420	1284	390	2550	810	3834	4.733	2	E

TM	RUSHING		PASSING		TOTAL		Y/PL	RK	CD
	ATT	YDS	ATT	YDS	ATT	YDS			
S F	408	1713	303	2225	711	3938	5.539	11	A
WAS	478	2000	257	1549	735	3549	4.829	3	D

After that is Offensive Yards per Point (Y/PT), or Total Yards (YARDS) divided by Points Scored (PTS), and in this category, a lower score on offense and a higher score on defense are ranked higher:

Table 9.14
Offensive Yards Per Point Codes for 1955 NFL Teams

TM	YARDS	PTS	YD/PT	RK	CD
BAL	3628	214	16.953	4	D
CHI	4496	294	15.293	7	C
CHC	3146	224	14.045	10	B
CLE	4245	349	12.163	12	A
DET	4019	230	17.474	3	D
G B	3887	258	15.066	8	B
L A	4149	260	15.958	6	C
NYG	3558	267	13.326	11	A
PHI	4013	248	16.181	5	D
PIT	3834	195	19.662	1	E
S F	3938	216	18.231	2	E
WAS	3549	246	14.427	9	B

The final offensive category is PAL or Points Above League. (For seasons in which all missed field goal distances are available, PAL2, is used, but in the 1955 NFL, PAL was used because I'm still missing the distances of about 15 missed field goals for the 1955 season.)

Here are the PAL scores, rank and grades for the 1955 NFL:

Table 9.15
Offensive PAL Codes for 1955 NFL Teams

TM	PAL	RK	CD
BAL	-2.23	6	C
CHI	14.53	11	A
CHC	-6.39	4	D
CLE	5.36	9	B
DET	3.87	8	B
G B	18.8	12	A
L A	-1.07	7	C
NYG	11.41	10	B

TM	PAL	RK	CD
PHI	-4.49	5	D
PIT	-18.2	1	E
S F	-8.91	3	D
WAS	-12.68	2	E

As a recap, here are all the offensive codes for the 1955 NFL teams:

Table 9.16
Offensive Codes for 1955 NFL Teams

TM	POINTS	FD	PENS	RUSH FUM/ATT	RUSH YDS/GM	RUSH YDS/ATT	RUSH YRAA/G	RUSH TD/ATT	RUSH	PASS COMP %	PASS YDS/ATT	PASS TD %	PASS INT %	PASS SK %	PASS	YDS/PL	YDS/PT	PAL
BAL	E	D	B	A	C	C	C	B	B	B	B	D	D	D	C	D	D	C
CHI	A	A	B	B	A	A	A	A	A	D	B	B	C	C	B	A	C	A
CHC	D	E	E	D	D	D	D	E	D	E	E	B	E	C	E	E	B	D
CLE	A	B	D	B	A	D	D	B	B	A	A	A	A	E	A	B	A	B
DET	D	B	B	D	D	D	D	D	D	A	D	D	B	A	B	B	D	B
G B	B	C	A	E	B	A	A	D	D	D	E	C	B	D	D	D	B	A
L A	B	A	D	A	B	B	B	A	A	B	C	E	B	B	C	B	C	C
NYG	B	E	A	B	D	C	C	D	C	D	D	A	A	A	A	C	A	B
PHI	C	B	C	E	E	E	E	E	E	C	B	C	C	B	B	C	D	D
PIT	E	C	E	C	E	E	E	C	E	C	C	E	D	B	D	E	E	E
S F	D	D	D	D	C	B	B	C	C	B	A	B	E	E	D	A	E	D
WAS	C	D	C	C	B	B	B	B	B	E	D	D	D	D	E	D	B	E

Below are the defensive codes, and the process is exactly the same except the ranking rationale is all opposite. In other words, in all categories, the lowest totals are ranked highest with the exception of penalties, interceptions, sacks, and yards per point.

Table 9.17
Defensive Codes for 1955 NFL Teams

TM	POINTS	FD	PENS	RUSH FUM/ATT	RUSH YDS/GM	RUSH YDS/ATT	RUSH YRAA/G	RUSH TD/ATT	RUSH	PASS COMP %	PASS YDS/ATT	PASS TD %	PASS INT %	PASS SK %	PASS	YDS/PL	YDS/PT	PAL
BAL	C	D	A	E	D	D	D	D	D	D	D	A	C	B	C	E	A	E

TM	POINTS	FD	PENS	RUSH FUM/ATT	RUSH YDS/GM	RUSH YDS/ATT	RUSH YRAA/G	RUSH TD/ATT	RUSH	PASS COMP %	PASS YDS/ATT	PASS TD %	PASS INT %	PASS SK %	PASS	YDS/PL	YDS/PT	PAL
CHI	C	C	D	D	D	E	E	C	E	D	C	B	D	A	C	E	B	B
CHC	D	D	B	B	D	D	D	D	C	A	A	B	B	E	B	B	B	B
CLE	A	A	C	B	A	A	B	A	A	A	A	C	B	D	A	A	E	B
DET	D	D	B	A	C	D	D	D	D	E	E	E	E	D	E	D	C	A
G B	D	B	D	D	E	E	E	B	E	B	D	D	A	E	D	D	D	D
L A	B	E	E	D	B	C	C	E	C	E	E	D	A	C	E	D	A	E
NYG	B	C	E	C	B	B	A	C	B	C	D	B	C	D	D	C	B	A
PHI	B	A	D	B	B	B	B	A	B	B	C	C	D	B	B	B	D	D
PIT	E	B	B	C	C	B	B	B	B	D	B	E	E	A	D	A	E	C
S F	E	E	C	E	E	C	C	E	D	B	B	A	B	C	A	C	D	D
WAS	A	B	A	A	A	A	B	A	C	B	D	D	B	B	B	C	C	C

There are two major applications for coding: similarity (offensive, defensive, and overall) and it can be used to study various types of football related questions.

Similarity Overview

Which team is the most statistically similar to the 1975 Baltimore Colts? How about the 2012 Baltimore Ravens? Which offense is most similar to the 1999 St. Louis Rams? Which defense is most similar to the 1985 Chicago Bears? We can now answer questions of this nature with coding.

When we are talking about "most similar," we are talking about it in a relative way, that a team that gets an A for an offensive Passing Grade in 2018 is in the top 20 percent of the league for the 2018 season. A team that received an A for passing in 1958 was also, more or less, in the top 20 percent for that season. Does this make them statistically similar? No, but I think it makes them relatively similar when compared between eras. For years I've been wanting to create a system for making it possible to quantify similarity between teams of different eras, and didn't want to get bogged down in trying to compare ten billion numbers to one another. The answer was to simplify each team into a string of 36 letters to make things easier to work with.

In order to compare two teams to one another using codes, you need to know the weights of each of the 18 codes (How much is each category such as Penalties or Passing Grade worth?) and how to compare the codes of two teams in each category.

Table 9.18 lists the weights I have assigned to each of the 18 categories (offense and defense are the same):

Table 9.18
Weights of Categories for Similarity in Coding

Category	Weight	Category	Weight
Points Scored	25	Pass Comp %	1
First Downs	5	Yards / Pass Att	3
Penalties	3	Pass TD %	2
Fumbles / Rush Att	1	Pass Int %	3
Rush Yards / Game	2	Sack %	1
Yards / Rush Att	3	Passing Grade	15
YRAA / Game	3	Yards / Play	5
TD / Rush Att	1	Yards / Point	5
Rushing Grade	15	PAL/PAL2	7

The total number of weights is 200, 100 for offense and 100 for defense. Rushing and passing each make up 25 percent of offense and defense, points make up another 25 percent, and the other 25 percent is split between the intangibles and miscellaneous—first downs, penalties, yards per play, yards per point and PAL or PAL2.

Looking at Table 9.18, it seems that a category such as rushing yards per game is a little underrepresented because it is only worth two points, but in reality, it is worth much more as it drives a good portion of the Rushing Grade, and that first downs, not to mention yards per play and yards per point and points scored, are directly related to rushing yards per game. Many of the secondary categories that are worth only a few points are interrelated to categories that are worth a lot more points.

The next step is to determine the numerical differences between letter grades, between comparing one team who has an A in a particular category and the other team who has a B in that category, or an A and a C. I came up with the following rules for the difference between letters when comparing a category between two teams:

- A difference of one letter grade (A to B, B to C, C to D, D to E) = 1 point
- A difference of two letter grades (A to C, B to D, C to E) = 8 points
- A difference of three letter grades (A to D, B to E) = 16 points
- A difference of four letter grades (A to E) = 32 points

Similarity Between Two Teams

I will compare the winner of the first Super Bowl, the 1966 Packers, and the winner of the 2018 Super Bowl, the New England Patriots? Table 9.19 lists the codes for each category, offensive and defensive, for the Packers and Patriots, with columns below showing the absolute letter grade difference (D) between the two teams, the score awarded for said letter grade difference according to the above list (S), the aforementioned weights for each category (W), and the product of the grade difference score and the category weight (PRD, which is S multiplied by W). On the bottom row, there is a SUM row for the sum of the PRDs. I added rows at the bottom for Similarity (SIM) and Team Similarity (TSIM) and I'll get to those in just a moment.

Table 9.19
Similarity Table for Comparing 1966 Packers to 2018 Patriots

	OFFENSE						DEFENSE					
	TM1	TM2	D	S	W	PRD	TM1	TM2	D	S	W	PRD
TEAM	G B	N E					G B	N E				
YL	66N	18N					66N	18N				
POINTS	B	A	1	1	25	25	A	B	1	1	25	25
FD	C	B	1	1	5	5	A	C	2	8	5	40
PENS	A	A	0	0	3	0	C	E	2	8	3	24
FUM/ATT	D	A	3	16	1	16	C	B	1	1	1	1
YDS/GM	C	A	2	8	2	16	B	B	0	0	2	0
YDS/ATT	E	D	1	1	3	3	B	E	3	16	3	48
YRAA/G	E	D	1	1	3	3	B	D	2	8	3	24
TD/ATT	B	B	0	0	1	0	A	C	2	8	1	8
RUSH	C	D	1	1	15	15	B	D	2	8	15	120
COMP %	A	C	2	8	1	8	C	A	2	8	1	8
YDS/ATT	A	B	1	1	3	3	A	B	1	1	3	3
TD %	B	B	0	0	2	0	A	C	2	8	2	16
INT %	A	B	1	1	3	3	A	E	4	32	3	96
SK %	C	A	2	8	1	8	A	E	4	32	1	32
PASS	A	A	0	0	15	0	A	D	3	16	15	240
YDS/PL	B	B	0	0	5	0	C	C	0	0	5	0
YDS/PT	B	B	0	0	5	0	B	A	1	1	5	5
PAL	E	C	2	8	7	56	E	D	1	1	7	7
SUM						161						697
SIM						474.8						391.1
TSIM												865.9

As you can see from Table 9.19, the two teams are much more similar offensively than defensively, because the sum of their various differences is much larger on defense (697), than it is on offense (161).

The maximum differential in any category or maximum S score (an A being compared to an E) is 32 points, and the sum of all of the weights in offense (and defense) is 100, which makes the maximum possible deviation (meaning an offense of As in every category being compared to an offense of Es in every category) would be 3,200. The deviation for both offense and defense will need to be subtracted from the maximum value, which would give us 3039 (or 3200 - 161) for offense and 2503 (or 3200 - 697) for defense.

To put those numbers into a more comfortable context, I chose the base number

9. Coding

500, for offense and defense, with Total Similarity, the sum of offense and defense, being 1000. Since those numbers are currently in a context of 3200, they need to be multiplied by a factor of 500/3200 or 5/32, as follows:

Offensive Similarity (or OSIM): 5/32* (3200–161) = 474.8
Defensive Similarity (or DSIM): 5/32 * (3200–697) = 391.1
Total Similarity (or TSIM): 474.8 + 391.1 = 865.9

The Similarity formula would be:

Similarity = 5/32 * (3200—Sum of Weights * Grade Difference Score)

The maximum similarity, offensive or defensive, is 500, which would occur if all the codes were exactly the same for both teams. The minimum, of course, would be zero, and that could only be achieved if you were comparing a team whose codes were all As against a team whose codes were nothing but Es.

What Do the Results Really Mean?

The Packers and Patriots were very similar offensively; of the 1,995 team-seasons from 1933 to 2018 ranked most similar to the 1966 Green Bay Packers, the Patriots finished number 59, tied with the 2009 Colts, which puts them in the top three percent, or 59/1995. The Patriots defensive similarity of 391.1 was about average, as the Patriots were tied at 971 (out of 1,995) with the 1956 Bears and 2008 Bengals in teams of similarity to the 1966 Packers. Average similarity is another way of saying they were neither similar nor dissimilar.

Which teams, then, are most similar to the 1966 Packers? Table 9.20 is a top ten list, in order, offensive, defensive, and total:

Table 9.20
10 Most-Similar Teams to 1966 Packers; Offense, Defense and Total

	OFFENSIVE			DEFENSIVE			TOTAL		
RK	OSIM	TM	YL	DSIM	TM	YL	TSIM	TM	YL
1	493.8	G B	10N	497.1	NYG	39N	967.8	K C	71N
2	493.0	PHI	80N	495.0	CLE	84N	967.3	S F	95N
3	491.3	NYJ	02N	494.1	NYG	85N	965.9	CLE	87N
4	490.0	CIN	15N	494.1	S D	92N	964.8	S D	10N
5	487.0	MIA	96N	493.0	NYG	37N	963.4	MIN	17N
6	486.1	NYG	72N	492.8	N O	91N	960.8	L A	74N
7	486.1	N O	94N	492.8	JAX	99N	960.2	DAL	94N
8	485.9	CHI	95N	491.3	DET	61N	958.4	MIN	74N
9	485.7	G B	33N	491.3	BUF	14N	958.1	PHI	80N
10	485.5	CLE	87N	490.6	OAK	67A	958.0	SEA	07N

It is interesting to note that of the Packers 10 most similar teams listed in Table 9.20, only two of them (1974 Vikings, 1980 Eagles) made the Super Bowl and both went home empty.

What about the most similar teams to the 2018 Patriots?

Table 9.21
10 Most-Similar Teams to 2018 Patriots; Offense, Defense and Total

	OFFENSIVE			DEFENSIVE			TOTAL		
RK	OSIM	TM	YL	DSIM	TM	YL	TSIM	TM	YL
1	495.6	S D	04N	491.1	K C	06N	973.1	G B	38N
2	495.5	N E	09N	488.8	G B	38N	967.8	G B	95N
3	493.1	N E	16N	486.3	OAK	65A	962.8	DEN	87N
4	492.2	DEN	87N	486.1	G B	95N	958.0	N E	09N
5	492.2	N E	07N	485.9	G B	54N	955.8	CLE	86N
6	489.5	N O	06N	485.3	NYJ	99N	953.6	NYG	72N
7	489.4	MIN	17N	484.8	DAL	93N	952.7	N O	06N
8	488.8	N E	11N	484.7	BOR	34N	952.3	N O	11N
9	488.3	NYG	72N	484.4	TEN	11N	950.2	S D	08N
10	487.8	ATL	11N	484.1	JAX	98N	948.8	PHI	61N

Of the ten most similar offenses to the Patriots in Table 9.21, four are from the Brady-Belichick era, and of the ten most similar teams, the 2009 Patriots made the top ten, and there were no Super Bowl winners or league champions.

I have found from experience that the average similarity from one offense or defense to another is about 400 and from one team to another is about 800. True similarity, which is being similar within one percent of all other team-seasons, is about 475 to 480, and for teams is about 940 or so.

Dealing with the Xs

We will check the similarity of the 1978 Pittsburgh Steelers to the 1941 Chicago Bears:

Table 9.22
Similarity Table for Comparing 1941 Bears to 1978 Steelers

	OFFENSE						DEFENSE					
	TM1	TM2	D	S	W	WX	PRD	TM1	TM2	D	S	W	WX	PRD
TM	CHI	PIT	0	0	0	0	0	CHI	PIT	0	0	0	0	0
YL	41N	78N	0	0	0	0	0	41N	78N	0	0	0	0	0
PTS	A	A	0	0	25	25	0	B	A	1	1	25	25	25
FD	A	A	0	0	5	5	0	B	B	0	0	5	5	0
PENS	E	C	2	8	3	3	24	A	C	2	8	3	3	24
FUM/A	D	B	2	8	1	1	8	B	A	1	1	1	1	1
YDS/G	A	C	2	8	2	2	16	A	A	0	0	2	2	0
YDS/A	A	E	4	32	3	3	96	B	A	1	1	3	3	3
YRAA	A	E	4	32	3	3	96	B	A	1	1	3	3	3
TD/A	A	D	3	16	1	1	16	E	B	3	16	1	1	16

9. Coding 219

	OFFENSE							DEFENSE						
	TM1	TM2	D	S	W	WX	PRD	TM1	TM2	D	S	W	WX	PRD
RUSH	A	D	3	16	15	15	240	A	A	0	0	15	15	0
C %	B	B	0	0	1	1	0	A	B	1	1	1	1	1
YDS/A	A	A	0	0	3	3	0	A	A	0	0	3	3	0
TD %	A	A	0	0	2	2	0	B	A	1	1	2	2	2
INT %	A	D	3	16	3	3	48	A	B	1	1	3	3	3
SK %	X	A	0	0	1	0	0	X	B	0	0	1	0	0
PASS	A	A	0	0	15	15	0	A	A	0	0	15	15	0
YDS/PL	A	C	2	8	5	5	40	B	A	1	1	5	5	5
YDS/PT	A	A	0	0	5	5	0	B	A	1	1	5	5	5
PAL	D	D	0	0	7	7	0	D	C	1	1	7	7	7
SUM							584							95
SIM							407.8							485
TSIM														892.8

I added a column WX in Table 9.22 for category weight provided neither of the teams had a code of X in that category; if either team had an X in that category, it came back as a zero, but if neither team had an X, it came back with the regular category weight. The only time it came into play was for the Sack categories, which each had a weight of one. For this reason, the Category Weight row total is 100 for offense and defense, but for the Category Weight No X row, the sum is 99.

To compensate for this, the Similarity formula will need to be tweaked a little:

$$\text{Similarity} = 5/32 * (3200 - * (100 / \text{Sum Category Weight No X}) * \text{Sum of Weights Grade Difference Scores})$$

For the comparison of the 1941 Bears to the 1978 Steelers:

Offensive Similarity = 5/32 * (3200 - (100/99) * 584) = 407.8
Defensive Similarity = 5/32 * (3200 - (100/99) * 95) = 485.0
Similarity = 407.8 + 485.0 = 892.8

The 1941 Bears and 1978 Steelers were not very similar offensively, but were pretty similar defensively, 141st most similar of 1,995 team-seasons, which puts them in the top ten percent. Both were probably the greatest team-seasons for each franchise in team history, although many will argue for the 1985 Bears.

Here are their ten most similar, Bears first, then Steelers:

Table 9.23
10 Most-Similar Teams to 1941 Bears; Offense, Defense and Total

	OFFENSIVE			DEFENSIVE			TOTAL		
RK	OSIM	TM	YL	DSIM	TM	YL	TSIM	TM	YL
1	498.1	DEN	97N	494.9	PIT	73N	987.5	SLR	01N
2	497.6	SLR	99N	492.7	G B	44N	983.1	SLR	99N

	OFFENSIVE			DEFENSIVE			TOTAL		
RK	OSIM	TM	YL	DSIM	TM	YL	TSIM	TM	YL
3	497.3	S F	98N	492.1	NYG	37N	982.2	DEN	96N
4	497.2	NYJ	82N	491.8	SLR	01N	973.8	CHI	35N
5	497.0	DAL	68N	490.9	G B	36N	972.9	CHI	38N
6	495.9	CHI	65N	490.1	BUF	04N	971.4	CHI	39N
7	495.9	DAL	71N	489.7	L A	69N	969.9	G B	36N
8	495.7	SLR	01N	489.7	ARZ	15N	969.4	CHI	65N
9	495.1	S F	91N	489.4	PIT	72N	969.1	DAL	71N
10	495.1	OAK	00N	489.0	MIA	02N	968.8	OAK	67A

Table 9.24
10 Most-Similar Teams to 1978 Steelers; Offense, Defense and Total

	OFFENSIVE			DEFENSIVE			TOTAL		
RK	OSIM	TM	YL	DSIM	TM	YL	TSIM	TM	YL
1	492.7	DEN	14N	499.0	WAS	39N	973.3	PHI	80N
2	490.9	BUF	93N	498.3	CLE	48F	973.1	CLE	87N
3	489.1	OAK	69A	497.8	G B	63N	972.8	S D	79N
4	488.9	S F	72N	497.6	DET	34N	971.4	IND	07N
5	488.0	CLE	87N	497.4	NYG	38N	970.2	PIT	04N
6	487.8	BAL	59N	497.3	PIT	72N	968.4	WAS	74N
7	487.0	BAL	70N	497.2	PIT	10N	966.4	N E	16N
8	487.0	N E	09N	497.2	PHI	48N	964.5	S F	95N
9	486.9	IND	07N	497.0	TEN	00N	963.4	MIN	17N
10	486.4	S D	11N	497.0	CAR	05N	962.8	WAS	73N

Perhaps when others start to use this, they will find that using a percentile rank or numerical rank sort of approach might work better than the similarity scores.

10

Dynasties

How do you compare the 1970s Steelers to the 1980s 49ers?

There are a number of ways to do it—position-by-position comparisons, postseason records, records against teams who made the postseason in regular season games, All-Pro seasons, I could rattle off a dozen or so of them, so could you.

I came up with a different way of looking at the issue, which involves defining a dynasty and rewarding teams based on how successful they are in each season within the dynasty, and when evaluating the dynasty, doing it in such a way as to accentuate peak value while also rewarding the size and length of the dynasty.

This is a two-stage system, where in stage one, teams are awarded Postseason Points, or PPT, for each individual season based on how deep they get into the postseason. In stage two, groups of consecutive seasons for teams are evaluated in chains to determine magnitude or greatness, which is measured in DPT or Dynasty Points.

We'll begin with Stage One:

Stage One: Post-Season Points (PPT)

In a nutshell, here is how PPT works—a team who wins the Super Bowl or league (in pre–Super Bowl seasons) championship is awarded 256 PPT for the season, a team that finishes at 0.5000 and does not make the playoffs receives 1 PPT for the season, and everybody that finishes above 0.5000 or makes the playoffs falls somewhere in between. Teams who finish below 0.5000 and do not make the playoffs get zero PPT. The further a team advances in the postseason, the more PPT they get. The number of PPT a team receives will always be a whole number, and a series of tiebreakers are used to break any ties between teams.

Format A—1990–2018 NFL Seasons

Here is how it works for a season in the modern era of 12 teams in the postseason and six teams per conference:

- The team that wins the Super Bowl is awarded 256 PPT for the season.
- The team that loses the Super Bowl is awarded 128 PPT for the season.
- The teams that lose the AFC or NFC Championship games each receive 64 PPT for the season.
- The teams that lose the AFC or NFC Divisional Playoff games get either 32 or 16

PPT, with the Divisional loser in each conference with the higher regular season winning percentage getting 32 PPT and the Divisional loser with the lesser regular season winning percentage getting 16 PPT. If the two teams in question have the same regular season record (splitting all ties as a half-win, half-loss), we apply a head-to-head tiebreaker between the two teams. More on the tiebreakers shortly.
- The AFC and NFC Wild Card Playoff game losers will receive 8 or 4 PPT, with the loser in each conference with the higher regular season winning percentage getting 8 PPT and the loser with the lesser regular season winning percentage getting 4 PPT. If both Wild Card losers from the same conference have the same record, tiebreakers are applied.
- If there are any teams remaining that finish above 0.5000 and don't make the postseason, they each get 2 PPT.
- Teams with a 0.500 record are awarded 1 PPT if they don't make the playoffs.
- Everybody else gets nothing.

Here are the tiebreakers (which we will refer to as the AA tiebreakers) that we will use to settle ties for the losers of Divisional and Wild Card games during 1967–2018 NFL and 1969 AFL seasons:

AA Tiebreakers
1. Best Winning Percentage (WPCT) in all regular season games.
2. Head-to-head sweep (applicable only if one club has defeated or lost to each of others)
3. Best WPCT (won-lost-tied percentage) in regular season games against other playoff teams in the season in question. (A tie is considered a half-win, half-loss.)
4. Best average net points in regular season games against other playoff teams in the season in question.
5. Team with the higher seeding as determined by the NFL playoff tiebreakers used during the season in question (1975 to present—we never got to this stage before 1975 so it was not necessary to create an additional pre–1975 tiebreaker.)

Does this system sound confusing? We'll use the 2017 season as an example for assigning PPT.

- Philadelphia won Super Bowl LII, so they get 256 PPT for the 2017 season.
- New England lost the Super Bowl, so they get 128 PPT for the 2017 season.
- The teams who lost the AFC and NFC Championship games, Jacksonville and Minnesota, will each receive 64 PPT.
- In the AFC, Pittsburgh and Tennessee lost the Divisional games, but since Pittsburgh has a better WPCT than Tennessee, they receive 32 PPT while the Titans receive 16 PPT.
- In the NFC, Atlanta and New Orleans lost the Divisional games, and New Orleans had a better record, so they get 32 PPT while the Falcons get 16 PPT.
- Among the AFC Wild Card losers, Kansas City had a better record than Buffalo, which means the Chiefs get 8 PPT and the Bills get 4 PPT.
- The two NFC Wild Card losers, the Rams and Panthers, both had the same record, and did not meet one another during the regular season. In regular

season games against the other teams who would appear in the 2017 postseason, the Rams had a 3–2 (0.6000) record while Carolina had a 5–4 (0.5556) record, which gives the tiebreaker to Los Angeles. The Rams will receive 8 PPT while Carolina receives 4 PPT.
- Baltimore, the LA Chargers, Dallas, Detroit and Seattle all had a better than 0.5000 (9–7) record and failed to make the playoffs, so they each receive 2 PPT.
- Arizona finished 8–8 (0.5000), and they receive 1 PPT.
- Everybody else receives zero PPT.

To summarize:

256 PPT—Philadelphia
128 PPT—New England
64 PPT—Jacksonville, Minnesota
32 PPT—Pittsburgh, New Orleans
16 PPT—Tennessee, Atlanta
8 PPT—Kansas City, LA Rams
4 PPT—Buffalo, Carolina
2 PPT—Baltimore, LA Chargers, Dallas, Detroit, Seattle
1 PPT—Arizona
0 PPT—Everybody else

Seems simple enough. Let's run it on 2012:

- Baltimore gets 256 PPT for winning the Super Bowl XLVII for the 2012 season.
- San Francisco gets 128 PPT for losing the Super Bowl.
- New England and Atlanta lost the Conference Championship games. They each receive 64 PPT.
- In the AFC Divisional playoffs, Denver and Houston lost. Denver had a 13–3 record, and Houston had a 12–4 record, which gives the Broncos 32 PPT and the Texans 16 PPT.
- In the NFC Divisional playoffs, Seattle and Green Bay lost. Both finished with an 11–5 record. The first tiebreaker is head-to-head play, and on 9/24/2012, Seattle defeated Green Bay 14–12, which means the Seahawks win the tiebreaker and thus they get the 32 PPT, and the Packers get 16 PPT.
- In the AFC Wild Card playoffs, Cincinnati and Indianapolis lost, but the Colts had a better record (11–5 vs.10–6 for the Bengals) so the Colts will get 8 PPT and the Bengals will get 4 PPT.
- In the NFC Wild Card playoffs, Washington and Minnesota lost, and both had a 10–6 record. On 10/14/2012, Washington defeated Minnesota 38–26, which means the Redskins win the tiebreaker and get the 8 PPT while the Vikings get 4 PPT.
- Chicago finished 10–6 but did not make the playoffs, nor did the 9–7 New York Giants make the postseason. Both will receive 2 PPT.
- The only 0.500 teams who did not make the playoffs were Pittsburgh and Dallas, and both will get 1 PPT each.

To summarize:

256 PPT—Baltimore
128 PPT—San Francisco

64 PPT—New England, Atlanta
32 PPT—Denver, Seattle
16 PPT—Houston, Green Bay
8 PPT—Indianapolis, Washington
4 PPT—Cincinnati, Minnesota
2 PPT—Chicago, New York Giants
1 PPT—Pittsburgh, Dallas
0 PPT—Everybody else

Now, a couple particular situations to demonstrate how the tiebreakers work:

In 2009, Cincinnati and New England lost the AFC Wild Card games, and both finished 10-6. The two teams did not meet one another during the regular season, so the next tiebreaker is best record against other postseason teams. In 2009, the Bengals played six regular season games against teams who would make the playoffs—two against Baltimore, and one each against Green Bay, Minnesota, San Diego and the Jets. In those six games, the Bengals went 3-3. The Patriots had a total of five games against teams who would make the postseason—two against the Jets, and one each against Baltimore, Indianapolis and New Orleans. In those five games, the Pats went 2-3. The Bengals win the tiebreaker because their 3-3 record (0.5000) is better than the Patriots 2-3 (0.4000) record. Therefore, the Bengals get 8 PPT and the Patriots get 4 PPT.

In the 2007 AFC Wild Card games, Pittsburgh and Tennessee lost. Both were 10-6, and the two teams did not meet in 2007. Pittsburgh played three games against playoff teams—Seattle, New England and Jacksonville, and went 1-2 in those three games. Tennessee played six games against playoff teams (two against Jacksonville, two against Indianapolis, and one each against San Diego and Tampa Bay). The Titans went 2-4 in these games. Both teams had an identical WPCT of 0.3333. Looking at average net points in games against playoff teams, Pittsburgh scored 56 points and gave up 63 points, for a net of minus seven, which divided by three is -2.3333. Tennessee scored 89 and gave up 106 in their six games against playoff teams for a net of -17, which divided by six is -2.8333. Pittsburgh won the tiebreaker for the higher net points in games against playoff teams.

Needless to say, if a team should happen to finish below 0.5000 and make the playoffs, which happened to Seattle in 2010 and to Carolina in 2014, they would receive PPT based on how far they advance in the postseason. Both teams won in the Wild Card round but lost in the Divisional round, so they would each receive 16 PPT for having the worst record of the team who lost the divisional playoff game. If a 7-9 team were to get into the playoffs and somehow win the Super Bowl, they would get 256 PPT for the season.

The above format is used from 1990 to 2018; we'll call it Format A. Even with the 2002 realignment in the NFL, Format A would still work because the playoff structure has not changed. There are still six teams from each conference in the playoffs, and the teams are still seeded in the same way. If the playoff system is modified to include seven or eight teams per conference, a new format will have to be created from Format A for assigning PPT to teams.

Format B—1978-81, 1983-89 NFL Seasons

At this point we will make our first adjustment to the system (which we will call Format B) to compensate for the fact that from 1978 to 1989 there were five teams per conference in the postseason (except for 1982, which we'll deal with later) instead of the current six. Format B works almost the same as Format A, except that the AFC and NFC Wild Card game losers receive an automatic 8 PPT and the team in each conference with the best 0.5000 or better record not already in the postseason (in other words, the sixth place team) gets 4 PPT. If there is no team that finishes at or above 0.5000 and does not make the playoffs, the 4 PPT are not awarded. The AA tiebreakers we established in Format A for awarding PPT to Divisional playoff game losers will still be in effect.

In cases such as this where we are essentially awarding additional wild cards in a particular season and there is an NFL tiebreaker system available for that season, we will use the NFL tiebreaker system that was in place for that season and apply it to determine the next wild card team.

Another rule I put in place with awarding fifth place teams is that if there is no fifth place team but there is a 0.5000 team, that 0.5000 team gets 4 PPT instead of 1 PPT, and if there are multiple teams with 0.5000 (which didn't happen) they would have gone to the NFL tiebreaker to decide the wild card team..

I won't run down the particular NFL tiebreakers for each season; there are sources out that have that information, but I will list the sixth-place teams for each season from 1978 to 1989 (except for 1982). In other words, if the NFL had a second wild card in each conference during this era, these are the teams who would have also been in the playoffs (along with a below 0.500 NFC team in 1987). As the sixth-place team according to the NFL tiebreakers used for each particular season, these teams will each receive 4 PPT:

1978—San Diego, Green Bay
1979—New England, Washington
1980—New England, Detroit
1981—Denver, Washington
1983—Cleveland, St. Louis
1984—New England, St. Louis
1985—Denver, Washington
1986—Cincinnati, Minnesota
1987—New England, (Dallas)
1988—New England, New York Giants
1989—Kansas City, Green Bay

Note: In 1987, there was no sixth place NFC team with a WPCT above 0.5000. But the Cowboys were the sixth-place team in the NFC in 1987 although they were below 0.5000 and thus, they receive no PPT. The parentheses are just in case you're curious who the sixth-place team actually was, even though they don't get rewarded.

We will do a full season example. I chose the 1983 season:

256 PPT—LA Raiders, for winning the Super Bowl.
128 PPT—Washington, for losing the Super Bowl.
64 PPT—Seattle and San Francisco, for losing the AFC and NFC Championship games.
32 PPT—Miami (for having a better record than Pittsburgh) and LA Rams (for

beating Detroit 21–10 on 10/2/1983 to win a head-to-head tiebreaker), who lost the Divisional games.

16 PPT—Pittsburgh and Detroit, who lost the Divisional games.

8 PPT—Denver and Dallas, for losing the AFC and NFC Wild Card games.

4 PPT—Cleveland and St. Louis, for being the sixth place teams in the AFC and NFC, respectively.

2 PPT—There were no seventh place teams, or other teams above 0.5000 that were not already in the postseason.

1 PPT—New England, Buffalo, Green Bay, Chicago, Minnesota and New Orleans, for finishing 0.5000.

Format C—1982 NFL Season

Due to the truncated nine-game regular season, the league decided to hold an eight team per conference format to determine a champion. We will refer to this adjustment as Format C, and it works pretty much the same as Format B at first:

256 PPT—Washington, for winning the Super Bowl.
128 PPT—Miami, for losing the Super Bowl.
64 PPT—NY Jets and Dallas, for losing the Conference Championship games.
32 PPT—LA Raiders and Green Bay
16 PPT—San Diego and Minnesota

Each conference had four wild card teams. Of the AFC wild card losers, Cincinnati (7–2) had the best record of the four, so they get 8 PPT. Pittsburgh (6–3) had the next best record, so they get 4 PPT. New England and Cleveland each get 2 PPT. I felt in this circumstance it was fair for a number eight seed to have played and lost a postseason game to have received two PPT, so in this instance we give the number seven and eight teams two PPT each.

In the NFC, it gets hairy. Of the four remaining NFC playoff teams, Atlanta, the Cardinals and Tampa Bay finished 5–4, while Detroit was 4–5. In the three-way AA tiebreaker between the Cards, Lions and Bucs, head-to-head did not apply because only St. Louis and Atlanta met, and it came down to WPCT in games against other playoff teams. In these games, Tampa Bay was 2–4, St. Louis was 1–3 and Atlanta is 0–3. Atlanta is eliminated, and it came down to Tampa Bay and St. Louis, where again it came down to WPCT against other playoff teams, where Tampa Bay won 2–4 to 1–3. Tampa Bay is awarded 8 PPT, while St. Louis gets 4 PPT, and Atlanta and Detroit will each get 2 PPT. Even though the Lions (like the Browns) had a losing record, they made the postseason and played in a playoff game and thus will receive 2 PPT.

There were no other teams who were above 0.5000 and did not make the playoffs.

Format D—1967–77 NFL, 1969 AFL Seasons

In the 1970–77 seasons, only four teams from each conference made the postseason, so another adjustment must be made. This will be Format D, and is similar to Format B, except that the wild card game loser from Format B is now the fifth place team (the team in each conference with the best record and not already in the playoffs) and gets 8

10. Dynasties

PPT provided they have a record above 0.5000. If there is a sixth place team that finishes above 0.5000, they get 4 PPT, and if there is a seventh place team above 0.5000, they get 2 PPT. Teams who finish 0.5000 and do not make the playoffs get 1 PPT. We will continue to use the prevailing NFL tiebreakers in each season to determine the fifth and sixth place teams, along with the AA tiebreakers I established in Format A for awarding PPT to Divisional playoff game losers.

Here are the fifth and sixth place teams (respectively) for each season from 1967 to 1977 under Format D, with the AFL team listed on the left and the NFL on the right. Below that are 1970–77 with AFC teams on the left and NFC teams on the right. Again, if the NFL had a six-team per conference playoff format in this era, these teams would have also been in the postseason (along with an average of about one below 0.500 team per season). The fifth place teams will receive 8 PPT, while the sixth place teams will receive 4 PPT. Parentheses denote teams who were sixth place teams but were below 0.5000 and do not receive PPT.

As we did previously, if there was no fifth or sixth place team that was over 0.5000, but there were 0.5000 teams, a 0.5000 team could be awarded the 4 PPT for sixth place. This occurred in the AFC and NFC in 1974 and went to tiebreakers in both conferences, with Houston and Philadelphia winning the tiebreakers:

1967—	Baltimore, Chicago
1968—	Los Angeles, St. Louis
1969—San Diego, (Denver)	Detroit, Baltimore
1970—Kansas City, Cleveland	Los Angeles, New York Giants
1971—Oakland, (New England)	Los Angeles, Detroit
1972—Cincinnati, Kansas City	Detroit, New York Giants
1973—Buffalo, Denver	Atlanta, (Detroit)
1974—Denver, Houston	Dallas, Philadelphia
1975—Houston, Miami	Washington, Detroit
1976—Cincinnati, Denver	St. Louis, San Francisco
1977—Miami, New England	Washington, Atlanta

Format D will also work with 1967–1969 NFL, along with the 1969 AFL as they also used a four-team postseason format. The only difference is that these leagues had no tiebreaker system as we know them today for breaking fifth and sixth place ties, but as it turned out, there were no situations that required such a tiebreaker.

We'll use the 1976 season as an example:

256 PPT—Oakland, for winning Super Bowl XI.
128 PPT—Minnesota, for losing the Super Bowl.
64 PPT—Pittsburgh and Los Angeles, for losing the AFC and NFC Championship games, respectively.
32 PPT—New England (for winning the "better record in regular season games against postseason teams" AA tiebreaker over Baltimore), and Dallas (for having a better record than Washington), who lost the Divisional games.
16 PPT—Baltimore and Washington, who lost the Divisional games.

8 PPT—Cincinnati and St. Louis, for being the fifth place teams in the AFC and NFC, respectively.

4 PPT—Denver (who beat Cleveland 44–13 on 9/26/1976 to win a head-to-head tiebreaker) and San Francisco, for being the sixth place teams in the AFC and NFC, respectively.

2 PPT—Cleveland, for being the seventh place team in the AFC. There was no seventh place team in the NFC.

1 PPT—There were no 0.5000 teams in 1976.

Format E—1966 NFL, 1966–68 AFL Seasons

The 1966 NFL, along with the 1966–68 AFL, utilized a two-division format (from this point back, the divisions were often referred to as conferences), in which only the division/conference leaders met for the championship. If the division leaders were tied at the end of the regular season, a tiebreaker game was held to decide who would appear in the title game as there was no system of tiebreakers.

It will be necessary to create a new set of tiebreakers (which I will refer to as the BB Tiebreakers) in order to split hairs between teams with similar records, and the goal should always be to select categories that would favor the better team. (There was no such thing as tiebreakers as we know them today until the NFL first developed them in 1967 to do away with the Divisional Tiebreaker game.) With that in mind, here are the tiebreakers for Formats E and F:

BB Tiebreakers

Division Ties:
1. Best WPCT in all regular season games.
2. Best WPCT in regular season head-to-head competition.
3. Best WPCT in regular season common games.
4. Best WPCT in regular season games against 0.500 or better teams.
5. Best WPCT in regular season games within the division/conference.

Different Divisions Ties
1. Best WPCT in all regular season games.
2. Head-to-head regular season sweep (applicable only if one club has defeated each of the others or lost to each of the others).
3. Best WPCT in regular season games against 0.500 or better teams.
4. Best net points in regular season games against 0.500 or better teams.

Notes
1. If any of the teams are from the same division/conference, apply Division tiebreaker first.
2. There should only be two teams remaining, one from each division/conference, at the point when you apply Different Divisions tiebreakers.
3. If more than one club remains tied after one or more teams are eliminated in any step in Division Ties, the Division Ties tiebreaker restarts at step one.
4. A team who loses a divisional tiebreaker game after the season and before

the championship game will automatically be awarded third place for the league, even if there is another team or teams in the other division/conference with a better record(s). (There are two exceptions to this rule. The first is in the 1950 NFL when both conferences were tied at the end of the season and there were two tiebreaker games. In that case, the above tiebreakers were used to award third and fourth place in the league. The other is the 1949 AAFC, which used a four-team playoff system. Again, the above tiebreakers will be used to award third and fourth place in the league, but in both occasions, it was simply best won-loss record.)

As we work our way back in time to 1933, the leagues will continue to get smaller, and divisions/conferences will shrink from eight to four teams. For this reason, it became necessary to put standards in place to prevent teams with not-so-good records from racking up a lot of PPT for finishing in third or fourth place in a league in a given season. I put it together in a table that combines finish in the league (based on highest WPCT) with the team's WPCT.

The division/conference champions are automatically first and second place in the league depending on who wins and loses the league championship game. Unless there is a divisional tiebreaker game, the third-place team is the team in the league with the next best WPCT (regardless of division/conference), provided their WPCT is over 0.5000. Same with fourth place, fifth place and sixth place, if applicable. After that, if there are still any teams remaining with a WPCT above 0.5000, they are automatically seventh place. Teams who finish 0.5000 receive one PPT unless they reach the playoffs, then they receive as many points as a team normally accumulates based on how far they advance.

Table 10.1 should make sense:

Table 10.1
PPT Dispersal Based on Finish and WPCT for Format E

	Format E–1966–68 AFL, 1966 NFL					
	Finish	3	4	5	6	7
WPCT	0.7001 and up	32	16	8	4	2
	0.6501–0.7000	24	12	8	4	2
	0.6001–0.6500	16	8	6	4	2
	0.5001–0.6000	8	6	4	3	2

With that in mind, here is how the 1966 NFL looks:

256 PPT: Green Bay, for winning the NFL title game and Super Bowl.
64 PPT: Dallas, for losing the NFL title game.

Cleveland, Philadelphia and Baltimore were all tied with a 9–5 (0.6429 WPCT) record for third place. Because there were three teams, and two of them (Cleveland and Philadelphia) are in the same conference, that tie needs to be broken first. The Browns and Eagles split their two games, and in common games, Cleveland had an 8–3 to 7–4 edge over Philadelphia, so Philadelphia is eliminated from third place and it's between Cleveland and Baltimore.

Since the Browns and Colts teams are in different conferences, it is a Different Divisions Tie, and in head-to-head, they did not meet. The second tiebreaker is best record against 0.5000-or-better teams, which essentially means all teams that will receive PPT. In this category, the Colts faced the Packers, 49ers and Rams, and Baltimore was swept by Green Bay and they swept the San Francisco and split against Los Angeles for a 3–3 record. However, Cleveland played nine games against 0.5000-or-above teams, splitting series against Dallas, St. Louis and Philadelphia, along with sweeping Washington and losing to Green Bay. The Browns managed a 5–4 record against PPT teams, and thus they win the third-place tiebreaker.

The battle for fourth place goes back to Baltimore and Philadelphia, and they did not meet, which means they also go to the best record against 0.5000-or-better competition tiebreaker. In this tiebreaker, the Eagles had a 3–5 record (splitting their series against Cleveland, Washington and Dallas and getting swept by the Cardinals) while the Colts were 3–3 as we had already done the calculation above. Baltimore gets fourth place, and the Eagles get fifth place.

The St. Louis football Cardinals will get sixth place with an 8–5–1 record, while the Los Angeles football Rams finished 8–6 (0.5714), good for seventh place. San Francisco and Washington both finished 0.5000 and will receive 1 PPT.

We will now need to consult Table 10.1 to award PPT for third through sixth place based on WPCT:

16 PPT: Cleveland, for third place with an WPCT between 0.6001 and 0.6501.
8 PPT: Baltimore, for fourth place with an WPCT between 0.6001 and 0.6501.
6 PPT: Philadelphia, for fifth place with an WPCT between 0.6001 and 0.6501.
4 PPT: St. Louis, for sixth place with an WPCT (0.6154) between 0.6001 and 0.6501.
2 PPT: Los Angeles, for seventh place.
1 PPT: Washington and San Francisco, for finishing 0.5000.

We will also do the 1966 AFL:

128 PPT: Kansas City, for winning the AFL title, although they lost the Super Bowl.
64 PPT: Buffalo, for losing the AFL Championship game.
24 PPT: Boston, for third place with an 8–4–2 record (0.6667 WPCT).
8 PPT: Oakland, for fourth place with an 8–5–1 record (0.6154 WPCT).
4 PPT: San Diego, for fifth place with a 7–6–1 record (0.5385 WPCT).
1 PPT: New York Jets, for finishing with a 6–6–2 record (0.5000 WPCT).

When we use Table 10.1 as we did above, the rule of thumb is to first determine the place for all the teams in the league, and then consult the chart to award the points.

Format F—1933–65 NFL, 1960–65 AFL, 1946–49 AAFC

For the 1933–65 NFL seasons, there was no Super Bowl game, which resets all the values we've established to this point. Without a Super Bowl, the value of a league championship becomes 256 PPT, and the loser of the league championship game gets 128 PPT. If there is a divisional/conference tiebreaker game, the team who loses that game automatically gets 64 PPT, and in those cases the fourth-place team can earn as many as 32 PPT. The tiebreakers we established in Format E will remain in place for our final iteration, Format F. The table we introduced in Format E will need to be modified for Format F, as the third-place team will now be eligible to receive as many as 64 PPT. We will use Table 10.2 for Format F:

Table 10.2
PPT Dispersal Based on Finish and WPCT for Format F

	Format F Table—1960–65 AFL, 1946–48 AAFC, 1933–65 NFL					
	Finish	3	4	5	6	7
WPCT	0.7001 and up	64	32	16	8	4
	0.6501–0.7000	32	24	16	8	4
	0.6001–0.6500	16	12	8	4	2
	0.5001–0.6000	8	6	4	3	2

Here are the results for the 1960 NFL.

256 PPT: Philadelphia, for winning the NFL Championship game
128 PPT: Green Bay, for losing the NFL Championship game
64 PPT: Cleveland, for finishing 8–3–1 (0.7273 WPCT) for third place
6 PPT: New York Giants, for finishing 6–4–2 (0.6000 WPCT) for fourth place)

Detroit and San Francisco tied for fifth place with a 7–5 (0.5833 WPCT) record, and they split their head-to-head games. The second tiebreaker for teams from the same division is common games, and here both teams finished 6–3. The third tiebreaker is games against 0.5000 or better teams, Detroit went 4–3 while San Francisco went 3–4, which gives fifth place to Detroit and sixth place to San Francisco.

According to Table 10.2, the Lions will receive 4 PPT and the 49ers will get 3 PPT.

2 PPT: St. Louis, for seventh place.
1 PPT: Baltimore, for finishing 6–6.

My logic for implementing Tables 10.1 and 10.2 is that if you look at teams from the Super Bowl era who have been awarded 32 PPT, those teams would have at least appeared in one or two playoff games to rise to a level to be awarded that many PPT for the season, and in most cases, would have won at least two thirds of their contests. To award 32 PPT to an 8–6 team who finishes in third place and didn't even appear in a postseason game seems too generous.

I created a study to look at PPT awarded between 1933 and 1969 as well as between 1970 and 2018, by PPT award number (256, 128, 64, etc.), along with quantity (NUM), and the average WPCT of those teams, to see how they differ between pre-merger and post-merger. Table 10.3 displays the results of the study:

Table 10.3
Comparison of PPT and Aggregate WPCT
for Pre- and Post-Merger Teams

	1933–69		1970–2018			1933–69		1970–2018	
PPT	NUM	AVG	NUM	AVG	PPT	NUM	AVG	NUM	AVG
256	47	0.8040	49	0.7909	6	17	0.5787	0	0.0000
128	47	0.7898	49	0.7690	4	25	0.5799	90	0.5966
64	36	0.7498	98	0.7195	3	11	0.5672	0	0.0000

	1933–69		1970–2018	
PPT	NUM	AVG	NUM	AVG
32	23	0.7266	98	0.7298
16	10	0.6377	98	0.6299
12	10	0.6335	0	0.0000
8	19	0.6500	98	0.6537

	1933–69		1970–2018	
PPT	NUM	AVG	NUM	AVG
2	11	0.5605	93	0.5696
1	42	0.5000	135	0.5000
SUM	298		808	
AVG		0.6759		0.6416

As you can see from Table 10.3, they're pretty even: the winning percentages awarded for the number of PPT awarded between 1933 and 1969 and between 1970–2018.

There is an interesting phenomenon with the post-merger data. If you look at 1970–2018 divisional playoff game losers who receive 32 or 16 PPT, the average WPCT of the team who gets 32 PPT (0.7298) is actually higher than the team who gets 64 PPT (0.7195) for losing the AFC or NFC Championship game. Now, look at the team who receives 8 PPT in 1970–2018 for fifth place. Their average WPCT is 0.6537, but the fourth-place team who loses the divisional game and receives 16 PPT has a worse average WPCT at 0.6299. I'm not sure what it means.

We'll use the 1950 season as an example of how to apply PPT, because this season is tricky:

In the 1950 NFL, both conferences were tied at the end of the season, and two divisional tiebreaker games were held to decide the teams who would meet in the NFL Championship game. The 32 PPT cannot be awarded to both teams who lost the tiebreaker games, which in this case were the New York Giants and Chicago Bears. Format F will work, but we'll just have to apply the Format F tiebreaker for third place Different Divisions which the Giants would win on best won-loss record.

Here is how it will shake out for 1950:

128 PPT: Cleveland, for winning the NFL Championship game.
64 PPT: LA Rams, for losing the NFL Championship game.
The NY Giants and Chicago Bears lost the tiebreaker games, the Giants (at 10–2) had a better WPCT than the Bears (at 9–3), so the Giants get the 32 PPT for third place while the Bears get 16 PPT for fourth place.
4 PPT: NY Yanks, for finishing 7–5 (0.5833) for fifth place
1 PPT: Pittsburgh, Philadelphia and Detroit, for finishing 0.5000.

In 1949, the AAFC had a similar four-team playoff format, and I decided to handle it as I did the 1950 NFL with two Divisional tiebreaker games, and apply the tiebreaker for third place, and it worked just the same.

In 1943, because of the war, the Rams suspended operations for the season and the Eagles and Steelers didn't have enough players to field teams on their own and were forced to merge to keep the league afloat. The Steagles, as they were known, finished 5–4–1, good for fifth place, and according to the above table, they were awarded 4 PPT. After the 1943 season the Steagles were disbanded and went back to being the Steelers and Eagles, and in this case, I awarded the 4 PPT to both the Eagles and Steelers for the 1943 season.

And that's how stage one of the dynasty evaluation system works. I refer to this as the Equal Championships (or EC) methodology, based on the logic that a Super Bowl Championship is equal to a pre–Super Bowl league championship. Table 10.4 is self-explanatory, and lists the six formats, the years and leagues to which they are applied, and how many PPT are applied. Below that is Table 10.5, which is the legend for deciphering the letter abbreviations in Table 10.4:

Table 10.4
Equal Championship Summary

	Equal Championships					
	Method					
PPT	A	B	C	D	E	F
256	G	G	G	G	G	G
128	H	H	H	H	H	H
64	J	J	J	J, K	K	See Format F Table
32	L	L	L	L	See Format E Table	
16	M	M	M	M		
8	N	T	N	W		
4	P	U	P	U		
2	R	R	V	X		
1	S	S	S	S	S	S
Tiebreakers	AA	AA	AA	AA	BB	BB
Years	1990–2018 NFL	1978–81, 1983–89 NFL	1982 NFL	1967–77 NFL, 1969 AFL	1966 NFL, 1966–68 AFL	1933–65 NFL, 1960–65 AFL, 1946–49 AAFC

Table 10.5
Equal Championships Legend

	Legend
G	Super Bowl/Pre-Super Bowl League Championship Game Winner
H	Super Bowl/Pre-Super Bowl League Championship Game Loser
J	AFC/NFC Championship Game Losers,
K	AFL/NFL Championship Game Losers (1966–1969)
L	Divisional Losers in Each Conference with Best Record
M	Divisional Losers in Each Conference with Second Best Record
N	Wild Card Loser with Better Record
P	Wild Card Loser with Second Best Record
V	Two Remaining Wild Card Losers in Each Conference
T	Wild Card Game Loser
W	Fifth Place Team Over 0.5000
U	Sixth Place Team Over 0.5000
X	Seventh Place Team Over 0.5000
R	Remaining Teams Over 0.5000 and not in Postseason
S	.5000 Teams not in Postseason

The Super Bowl and Unequal Championships

When I first developed this system in the mid-1980s and was evaluating dynasties from different eras, I did not figure into the basic system the concept of the Super Bowl. I had two pretty similar systems, one where I rated just teams from the Super Bowl era using Super Bowl results, and another where I rated teams from 1933 to present but I acted as though there was no such thing as a Super Bowl and I rated an AFL or NFL Championship from the pre–Super Bowl era equivalent to an AFC or NFC Championship from the modern era.

When I showed this system to my colleagues in the pro football historian community a decade back, there was some considerable debate about the system which forces you to ask one simple question, and how you answer this question says exactly where you come down on the issue. The question is "Do you believe the 1966 NFL and AFL Championship games to be of equal importance to the 1965 NFL and AFL Championship games?"

If you answer "Yes," then you believe the Super Bowl is on a higher level than the championship games from the years before the Super Bowl existed. If you answer "No," then you believe the Super Bowl winners are on an equal level as the championship game winners from the years before the Super Bowl existed.

Here's a way of laying out the argument with a table:

Table 10.6
Equal/Unequal Championship Argument Table

Are the 1965 and 1966 Championship games of equal importance?		
Answer	Yes	No
Conclusion	1966 Championship Games = 1965 Championship Games	1965 Championship Games > 1966 Championship Games
Hierarchy of Postseason Games—most important to least important	Super Bowl	Super Bowl and pre-1966 Championship Games
	All Championship Games	SB era Championship Games
	Divisional Games/Tiebreakers	Divisional Games/Tiebreakers
	Wild Card Games	Wild Card Games
Equal or Unequal Championships	Unequal Championships	Equal Championship

Some believe a pre-1966 league title as being roughly equal to a modern conference title, while others think a Super Bowl title should be equal to a pre–Super Bowl NFL, AFL or AAFC championship, in that the last game of the season should be weighed equally whether it be a league championship game from before 1965 or a Super Bowl. This is a matter we will have to discuss in order to lay out the remainder of this dynasty evaluation system.

Where do I come down on this issue? I think both schools of thought are correct, and neither is quite 100 percent correct. But forced to choose, I lean toward the notion that winning a conference title in the post-1966 era is roughly equivalent to winning an NFL, AFL or AAFC title through 1965. How do I arrive at this? In 1965, there were 14 teams in the NFL; today the AFC and NFC have 16 teams each. Doesn't it make sense to a degree that an NFL title in 1965 like the Packers won should be roughly equivalent to an NFC or AFC Championship in 2018? If we set the value of an NFL Championship pre-merger to being equal with a Super Bowl title, I worry it would overrate the teams from before the Super Bowl existed.

Here's another way of looking at it: in winning Super Bowl XXXIX, the 2004 New England Patriots were the best team from a 32-team league, but in winning the 1955 NFL Title, the Browns were the best team from a 12-team league. I don't know if I feel the two championships to be of a similar value as the Browns only had to play a 12-game regular season schedule and win one postseason game to claim their title while the Patriots had to play 16 regular season games and then win three playoff games to win the Super Bowl. It makes more sense to me to compare the Browns' 1955 NFL title as being closer to the Packers winning the 1997 NFC title or the Giants winning the 1990 NFC title or the Dolphins' 1984 AFC Championship.

Of course, it is easier to win a championship in a league with only ten teams as opposed to 16 due to the law of averages, but the system I have created does not tend to overrate teams from leagues with fewer teams as the teams who appear in the championship games get most of the points regardless of the year.

With that in mind, I have developed a similar, parallel methodology to the PPT system where we operate on the presumption that winning an NFL title in 1933 or an AFL title in 1960 is equivalent to winning an AFC or NFC title in 1998 or 1973, and the number of PPT for a pre-merger league championship or a post-merger conference championship will be the same. In this system, we ignore the Super Bowl results, and finish each season of the Super Bowl era with two conference champions instead of one league champion. For the era before the Super Bowl, we finish the season with one league champion.

When ignoring the Super Bowl results and comparing the Steelers dynasty of the 1970s to a pre–Super Bowl dynasty like the Bears of the 1940s, the Steelers' four Super Bowl wins are ignored, and instead their four AFC Championships in 1974, 1975, 1978 and 1979 are used as the basis for comparison against the Chicago Bears' NFL Championship wins from 1940, 1941, 1943 and 1946. Also, it looks at the Minnesota Vikings' four NFL/NFC Championships in 1969, 1973, 1974 and 1976 as a positive instead of looking at their four Super Bowl losses as a negative.

As far as the debate about a Super Bowl being equal to an NFL Championship, I respect the converse argument that many of my friends and colleagues in the field hold in that an NFL Championship from 1965 is equal to the Super Bowl I Championship from 1966. I like an open debate, I think both schools of thought have valid arguments here, and I will present both systems and both sets of final results. I'm sure this concept will be a major point of debate, probably the most intense point of debate, concerning this book.

The Equal Championship system I've already laid out for you so far is Plan A. Unequal Championships is Plan B and that is what follows.

I have developed an alternate methodology known as Unequal Championships (or UC) in which the pre–Super Bowl league championship winner will get 128 PPT and the loser of that game gets 64 PPT. For seasons in the Super Bowl era, the Super Bowl results are ignored, and the league (pre-1970) or conference championship winner will receive 128 PPT and the loser of the game will get 64 PPT. The rest of the PPT values will shift accordingly, and there have been a couple changes to which seasons are covered by which formats. The below Tables 10.7 and 10.8 should help make things clear:

Table 10.7
Unequal Championships Summary

	Unequal Championships					
	Method					
PPT	A	B	C	D	E	F
128	Y	Y	Y	Y	Y	Y
64	Z	Z	Z	Z	Z	Z
32	L	L	L	L	See Format E Table	See Format F Table
16	M	M	M	M		
8	N	T	N	W		
4	P	U	P	U		
2	R	R	V	X		
1	S	S	S	S	S	S
Tiebreakers	AA	AA	AA	AA	BB	BB
Years	1990–2018 NFL	1978–81, 1983–89 NFL	1982 NFL	1967–77 NFL, 1969 AFL	1966 NFL, 1966–68 AFL	1933–65 NFL, 1960–65 AFL, 1946–49 AAFC

Table 10.8
Unequal Championships Legend

	Legend
Y	Conference/Pre-Super Bowl Championship Game Winner
Z	Conference/Pre-Super Bowl Championship Game Loser
L	Divisional Losers in Each Conference with Best Record
M	Divisional Losers in Each Conference with Second Best Record
N	Wild Card Loser with Better Record
P	Wild Card Loser with Second Best Record
V	Two Remaining Wild Card Losers in Each Conference
T	Wild Card Game Loser
W	Fifth Place Team Over 0.5000
U	Sixth Place Team Over 0.5000
X	Seventh Place Team Over 0.5000
R	Remaining Teams Over 0.5000 and not in Postseason
S	.5000 Teams not in Postseason

All the procedures previously established with the Equal Championships methodology apply, and the AA and BB tiebreakers for UC will be the same ones used for EC.

For the post-merger era (1970 and later), the only difference between PPT values for EC and UC is that the Super Bowl winner's total is 256 in EC and 128 in UC. What this means is that, for example, in 1980, both the Oakland Raiders and Philadelphia Eagles each receive 128 UC, and the results of Super Bowl XV are ignored altogether. For pre–Super Bowl seasons, the UC values are often half of the EC values. Here are a few sample seasons from the pre-merger era:

Table 10.9
Comparison of EC and UC PPT Dispersals for 1940 NFL, 1952 NFL, 1962 NFL and 1962 AFL

1940 NFL	EC	UC
Chicago Bears	256	128
Washington	128	64
Brooklyn	64	32
NY Giants	6	6
Green Bay	4	4
Detroit	1	1
SUM	459	235

1962 NFL	EC	UC
Green Bay	256	128
NY Giants	128	64
Detroit	64	32
Chicago	12	8
Pittsburgh	8	6
Cleveland	3	3
Baltimore	1	1
SUM	472	242

1952 NFL	EC	UC
Detroit	256	128
Cleveland	128	64
Los Angeles	64	32
Philadelphia	6	6
NY Giants	4	4
San Francisco	3	3
Green Bay	1	1
SUM	462	238

1962 AFL	EC	UC
San Diego	256	128
Boston	128	64
Buffalo	64	32
Oakland	32	16
SUM	480	240

Next, we need to define the term "dynasty" for the purposes of this chapter.

What Is a Dynasty?

Once PPT are calculated for every team-season in AFL-NFL-AAFC history from 1933 to 2018, the team-seasons need to be grouped into dynasties. From my research, I have determined that there are 188 groups of team-eras that meet my definition of a dynasty throughout pro football history from 1933 to 2018. There are great dynasties, good dynasties, and lesser dynasties.

I define a dynasty within the scope of this methodology as a period of consecutive years in which the team in question collects PPT in at least every other season. If a team has two consecutive years in which they collect no PPT (that is, two straight seasons with losing records and no playoff appearances), then the dynasty is over. Also, in the first and final season of any dynasty (or sub-dynasty, which I'll get to later) they have to collect PPT. A dynasty can also last one season if there are at least two seasons in which they collect no PPT before and after the season in question. This probably sounds confusing until you see it in action.

I set the end of a dynasty as two straight losing seasons, because if a team finishes below 0.5000 twice in a row, they generally start making changes—the GM gets dumped and the new one starts cleaning house, usually starting with the head coach, or they change the dynamics of the team, bring in a new quarterback, new coordinators, things like that. One of the things I am trying to do here is to isolate a particular era for a team, a particular set of players, and I found if I set it to three consecutive losing seasons to break dynasties, the dynasties would get too large in some cases. The Minnesota Vikings, as an example, have not had three consecutive losing seasons in more than 50 years. Making it one losing season to end a dynasty was too harsh, as many great teams have had an off season here and there, but two off seasons in a row generally seemed about right to signal the end of an era.

Buffalo Bills Dynasty History

To demonstrate how to evaluate a dynasty we will examine the history of the Buffalo Bills AFL/AFC franchise in terms of PPT awarded per season, shown in Table 10.10. Here we are using Equal Championships but the stage two methodology would be the same for UC:

Table 10.10 Buffalo Bills PPT Awarded Per Season

Year	PPT	Year	PPT	Year	PPT	Year	PPT	Year	PPT
1960	0	1972	0	1984	0	1996	8	2008	0
1961	0	1973	8	1985	0	1997	0	2009	0
1962	6	1974	16	1986	0	1998	8	2010	0
1963	64	1975	2	1987	0	1999	8	2011	0
1964	256	1976	0	1988	64	2000	1	2012	0
1965	256	1977	0	1989	32	2001	0	2013	0
1966	64	1978	0	1990	128	2002	1	2014	2
1967	0	1979	0	1991	128	2003	0	2015	1
1968	0	1980	32	1992	128	2004	2	2016	0
1969	0	1981	16	1993	128	2005	0	2017	4
1970	0	1982	0	1994	0	2006	0	2018	0
1971	0	1983	1	1995	16	2007	0		

The dynasties are easy to spot in Table 10.10 when you remember the rules: in the first and last seasons of the dynasty, they have to receive PPT and there cannot be two straight goose eggs within a dynasty. I'll run the same list again, but this time, I'll remove all the occurrences of zero PPTs in consecutive seasons:

Table 10.11
Buffalo Bills PPT Awarded Per Season, with Zero PPT Seasons Left Blank

Year	PPT	Year	PPT	Year	PPT	Year	PPT	Year	PPT
1960		1972		1984		1996	8	2008	

10. Dynasties

Year	PPT	Year	PPT	Year	PPT	Year	PPT	Year	PPT
1961		1973	8	1985		1997	0	2009	
1962	6	1974	16	1986		1998	8	2010	
1963	64	1975	2	1987		1999	8	2011	
1964	256	1976		1988	64	2000	1	2012	
1965	256	1977		1989	32	2001	0	2013	
1966	64	1978		1990	128	2002	1	2014	2
1967		1979		1991	128	2003	0	2015	1
1968		1980	32	1992	128	2004	2	2016	0
1969		1981	16	1993	128	2005		2017	4
1970		1982	0	1994	0	2006		2018	
1971		1983	1	1995	16	2007			

They become much easier to identify now. In the history of the Buffalo Bills, there have been five dynasties according to my definition, and they show up clearly in Table 10.11. The first such dynasty occurs from 1962 to 1966; there is another from 1973 to 1975, and another from 1980 to 1983. There is a larger dynasty from 1988 to 2004, and a final one from 2014 to 2017 that is currently in progress. If the Bills have a below 0.5000 season or do not make the postseason in 2019, the dynasty is over, and another dynasty will not begin until the next season when they accumulate PPT. However, if the Bills either finish at or above 0.5000 or make the postseason in 2019, the dynasty is still active and will go on indefinitely.

There is no set length to a dynasty; theoretically, a dynasty can continue forever. Most dynasties last five seasons or less, some last much longer. The longest sustained dynasty in the history of pro football since 1933 is the 1973-to-2016 Denver Broncos at 44 seasons; they had not had back to back losing seasons since 1971–72 until they finished below 0.5000 in 2017 and 2018, which ended their dynasty. The Broncos next dynasty will begin the next time they make the postseason, or they have a 0.500 or better record.

Among other long-term dynasties, the Dolphins had a 34-year dynasty from 1970 to 2003. The Browns had a 28-year dynasty from 1946 to 1973, the Packers had one of 25 seasons from 1992 to 2016, the Raiders had one of 24 years from 1963 to 1986, as have the Giants from 1949 to 1972, and Washington from 1969 to 1992. Among current teams, the Patriots dynasty is at 25 years (1994–2018), the Ravens and Colts are 20 years (1999–2018) and the Steelers are at 19 years (2000–2018) and counting.

What I am attempting to do here is to identify and rank team-eras of determinate length despite the fact that a dynasty is of indeterminate length. I've decided to use the "chain" analogy to explain how to evaluate a dynasty. If you liken each season to a single link of a chain, these links are joined together in chronological order to form longer chains or dynasties. Figure 10.1 displays several examples of dynasty chains, with each season in a block being a link in a chain. As you can see in Figure 10.1, some chains are short and some are quite long, and some are only one link long. Some links are heavier than other links, as a team winning a league or conference championship is much more impressive than a team that loses in the first round of the playoffs. Some

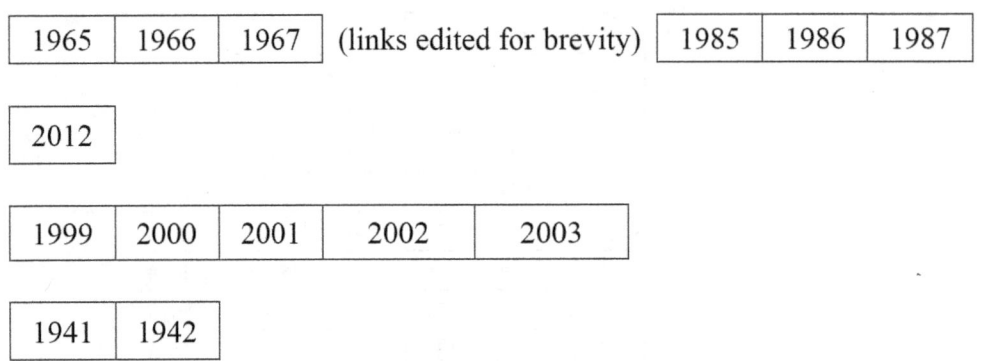

Figure 10.1. Several graphical depictions of dynasty chains.

chains have heavy links and lighter links joined together. We will examine certain parts of these chains to see if a particular number of links are collectively heavier than the same number of links on another chain. We will also examine the chains internally by cutting them apart (in a symbolic sense) and weighing certain portions of the chains separately. A season with a less than 0.500 record is considered a null link, a link with no weight; it exists merely to hold the two links on either side together, but it has no weight.

In terms of trying to isolate a set of key players and coaching as a dynasty (such as the 1972–84 Steelers or the 1959–69 Packers or the 2001 to present Patriots), we have to settle on a fixed number of consecutive seasons to compare. When I first came up with this, I set the standard at 10 consecutive seasons. But I've realized over the years that 10 is not necessarily the only correct number, as all but a few dynasties last 15 years or less I set the maximum limit at 15 consecutive seasons. Some teams for short periods, such as the 1971–74 Dolphins and the Buffalo and Dallas teams of the early 1990s, and I was curious how teams compared at lower levels so I set the lower limit at five consecutive seasons. So whichever length of time you want to compare (I'm going with 5, 10 and 15 years) we can answer that question. Which team had the best 5-year era? Which had the heaviest 15-link piece of chain?

Stage Two—Dynasty Points (DPT)

How do we compare the weights of chains? I have developed an analytical technique for evaluating the greatness of a dynasty. This is how it works, using the 1962–66 Bills dynasty as an example, the AFL Championship era. Here are the PPT awarded by season using the EC methodology:

    1962: 6 PPT
    1963: 64 PPT
    1964: 256 PPT
    1965: 256 PPT
    1966: 64 PPT

10. Dynasties

This is how the chronological and PPT chains look, respectively:

1962	1963	1964	1965	1966

6	64	256	256	64

Figure 10.2. Chronological and PPT chains for the 1962–66 Buffalo Bills dynasty.

To begin with, we're going to drop the first two digits off the season numbers to make them a little less cumbersome:

62	63	64	65	66

Figure 10.2. Chronological and PPT chains for the 1962–66 Buffalo Bills dynasty.

Next, we're going to merge the chronological and PPT links for each season into a single link, with the year on top in two-digit form and the PPT underneath, known as a YR/PPT link:

62	63	64	65	66
6	64	256	256	64

Figure 10.4. Merged chronological/PPT chain for the 1962–66 Buffalo Bills dynasty.

The PPT, the lower number, represents the weight of each link, if you will. What I am creating here is a schematic diagram of sorts to make this dynasty process easier to visualize and understand.

In order to evaluate the chain, you first identify the best individual season in the dynasty, PPT-wise, which would be the highest one-year peak. That was in 1964 and 1965 where they scored a 256 in each season.

Next, you group the dynasty into consecutive two-year blocks (62–63, 63–64, 64–65 and 65–66) and look at total PPT accumulated in the two-year sets:

1962–63: 6 + 64 = 70
1963–64: 64 + 256 = 320
1964–65: 256 + 256 = 512
1965–66: 256 + 64 = 320

Using the chain analogy, we are now looking for the two heaviest consecutive links in the sequence. The two-year peak would be 512, is located at 64–65.

Next, the three-year peaks. We'll look at three-year eras (1962–64, 1963–65 and 1964–66), and see which is the heaviest three consecutive links:

62–64: 6 + 64 + 256 = 326
63–65: 64 + 256 + 256 = 576
64–66: 256 + 256 + 64 = 576

The three-year peak is 576, which was compiled over the 63–65 and 64–66 seasons.

Four-year peaks, which are 1962–65 and 1963–66:

62–65: 6 + 64 + 256 + 256 = 582
63–66: 64 + 256 + 256 + 64 = 640

The four-year peak is 640.

Finally, we look at the five-year peak, and since there is only one five-year peak possible, it is the sum of the PPT accumulated during the five seasons in question:

62–66: 6 + 64 + 256 + 256 + 64 = 646

If we were evaluating a 10-year dynasty, we would have continued with six-, seven- eight-, nine-, and ten-year peaks. As far as Buffalo 62–66 is concerned, their 8, 10, 12 or 15-year peaks are the same as their final five-year peak, which was 646. They had already reached their peak.

Putting the peaks in order, we get:

1-year peak: 256
2-year peak: 512
3-year peak: 576
4-year peak: 640
5-year peak: 646

Next, we plug these numbers into the formula:

Dynasty Points or DPT = (1*1-year peak) + (2*2-year peak) + (3*3-year peak) + … + (X*X-year peak), where X is the final number of years in question.

At five years, the DPT would be:

DPT = (1*256) + (2*512) + (3*576) + (4*640) + (5*646) = 8798 DPT

The 1962–66 Bills' 8798 DPT is 14th best of 381 five-year EC dynasties, through 2018.

Next, we'll evaluate the Bills 1962–66 dynasty at 10-year levels:

We would continue as we did above, determining the peaks at six, seven, eight, nine and ten years. Since this particular dynasty only lasted five seasons, the peak would remain the same for six, seven, eight, etc., seasons. In addition, the DPT formula would also remain the same. Since the dynasty has already ended and we already know the peak (646) and we have the total through five years (8798), we can just plug them into the formula through five years, and condense the formula somewhat. Instead of:

DPT = (1*256) + (2*512) + (3*576) + (4*640) + (5*646) +
(6*646) + (7*646) + (8*646) + (9*646) + (10*646)

We can make it:

DPT = 8798 + (6*646) + (7*646) + (8*646) + (9*646) + (10*646) = 34638 DPT

The 1962–66 Bills 34638 DPT is 23th best (of 265) of all time. And finally, at 15 years:

$$DPT = 34368 + (11*646) + (12*646) + (13*646) + (14*646) + (15*646) = 76628$$

Their 76628 DPT is 26th best (of 221) of all time.

To summarize the dynasty at the differing year levels (using the form X Year: (last two years of the first and last years of the dynasty or partial dynasty in question)/ (PPT Peak over the years in question in PPT)/ (DPT over the years in question)):

5 Year: 6266/646 PPT/8798 DPT
10 Year: 6266/646 PPT/34638 DPT
15 Year: 6266/646 PPT/76628 DPT

And that is how one evaluates a smaller dynasty.

The Electric Company Era

Next, we will examine Buffalo from 1973 to 1975, and we'll use the YR/PPT links to save space:

73	74	75
8	16	2

Figure 10.5. Chronological/PPT chain for the 1973–75 Buffalo Bills dynasty.

1-year peak: 16
2-year peak: 24
3-year and above peak: 26

Again, it follows the form:

$$DPT = (1*16) + (2*24) + (3*26) + \ldots + (X*26)$$

Evaluating at the different levels:

5 Year: 7375/26 PPT/376 DPT
10 Year: 7375/26 PPT/1416 DPT
15 Year: 7375/26 PPT/3106 DPT

The Ground Chuck Era

For the 1980–83 dynasty, the Chuck Knox years:

80	81	82	83
32	16	0	1

Figure 10.6. Chronological/PPT chain for the 1980–83 Buffalo Bills dynasty.

1-year peak: 32
2-year peak: 48
3-year peak: 48
4 and higher peak: 49

5 Years: 8083/49 PPT/713 DPT
10 Years: 8083/49 PPT/2673 DPT
15 Years: 8083/49 PPT/5858 DPT

I think you get the hang of this when it deals with dynasties that are five years or less in length. When we deal with dynasties that are longer than five years it gets a little more complicated.

The Bills of the 1990s: Five Years

Evaluating the 1988–2004 Bills dynasty in PPT per season, we have:

88	89	90	91	92	93	94	95	96	97	98	99	00	01	02	03	04
64	32	128	128	128	128	0	16	8	0	8	8	1	0	1	0	2

Figure 10.7. Chronological/PPT chain for the 1988–2004 Buffalo Bills dynasty.

We'll start by evaluating the dynasty over a five-year interval. In terms of the chain analogy, we are going to cut the chain (represented in Figure 10.7) apart into pieces of five links or less in such a way as to maximize the five-year peaks. This is easier to demonstrate than to explain.

For the Bills, here is a complete YR/PPT link chain and a horizontal list of every five-year era within the dynasty, with the peaks generated, and the DPT formula run on each era (first and year abbreviation on top, DPT on the bottom):

YRS	8892	8993	9094	9195	9296	9397	9498	9599	9600	9701	9802	9903	0004
DPT	5856	6560	6400	5328	3896	2184	424	464	312	244	249	143	47

Figure 10.8. Horizontal list of all five-year eras and corresponding DPT values for the 1988–2004 Buffalo Bills dynasty.

Reviewing Figure 10.8, we see the highest five-year DPT peak for the Bills dynasty to be 6560 DPT from 1989 to 1993. In our chain analogy we will remove the 1989–93 YR/PPT link segment out of the chain, as shown:

88
64

94	95	96	97	98	99	00	01	02	03	04
0	16	8	0	8	8	1	0	1	0	2

89	90	91	92	93
32	128	128	128	128

10. Dynasties

After evaluating the 1989–93 sub-dynasty, we will add a line to the bottom of the era block listing the DPT for the era (in Figure 10.9, the piece that was cut out of the chain), but all of the sub-dynasties will be reassembled at the end:

89	90	91	92	93
32	128	128	128	128

6560 DPT

Figure 10.10. Chronological/PPT chain for the 1989-1993 Buffalo Bills sub-dynasty with DPT block underneath.

This piece can be set aside.

Next, we'll examine the two pieces that remain:

88
64

94	95	96	97	98	99	00	01	02	03	04
0	16	8	0	8	8	1	0	1	0	2

Figure 10.11. Remaining 1988 and 1994-2004 segments of the 1988-2004 Buffalo Bills dynasty that have yet to be analyzed for DPT.

We'll start with the single link since that will be easy to do. The 1988 season will be evaluated as though it were a dynasty that is one season in length.

88: 64
One-year peak: 64
PPT = (1*64) + (2*64) + (3*64) + (4*64) + (5*64) = 960 DPT

8864

| 960 |
| DPT |

Figure 10.12. Chronological/PPT chain for the 1988 Buffalo Bills sub-dynasty with DPT block underneath.

This piece can be set aside. We will get back to the piece that remains. The 1994 link is what I referred to earlier as a null link in which the Bills received zero PPT. We will remove the null link from the chain and consider the chain to run from 1995 to 2004 because for the first and last year of any dynasty, the team must receive PPT. Removing the zero PPT from the equation does not affect the final totals.

Opposite, bottom: **Figure 10.9. Chronological/PPT chain for the 1988-2004 Buffalo Bills dynasty with 1989-1993 seasons removed.**

94	95	96	97	98	99	00	01	02	03	04
0	16	8	0	8	8	1	0	1	0	2

Figure 10.13. Remaining 1994–2004 segment of the 1988–2004 Buffalo Bills dynasty that has yet to be analyzed for DPT.

We are left with:

95	96	97	98	99	00	01	02	03	04
16	8	0	8	8	1	0	1	0	2

Figure 10.14. Remaining 1995–2004 segment of the 1988–2004 Buffalo Bills dynasty that has yet to be analyzed for DPT.

At this point we will evaluate the chain to find the five-year peak. I think you can look at the chain and quickly deduce that the peak is from 1995 to 1999, so I will spare you the mathematics with the peaks, and we will cut the chain between 99 and 00 so that we will be left with two pieces of chain:

95	96	97	98	99
16	8	0	8	8

00	01	02	03	04
1	0	1	0	2

Figure 10.15. 1995–2004 segment of the 1988–2004 Buffalo Bills dynasty broken into separate sub-dynasties of 1995–99 and 2000–04.

After evaluating the peaks and running the DPT formula, you will find the DPT for the 9599 era is 464 and the DPT for 0004 is 47.

95	96	97	98	99
16	8	0	8	8
464 DPT				

00	01	02	03	04
1	0	1	0	2
47 DPT				

Figure 10.16. Chronological/PPT chain for the 1995–1999 and 2000–2004 Buffalo Bills sub-dynasties with DPT blocks underneath.

Finally, we can reassemble the various segments we have analyzed, pulling all the links back into chronological order and summarize the dynasty at the five-years level:

88	89	90	91	92	93	94	95	96	97	98	99	00	01	02	03	04
64	32	128	128	128	128	0	16	8	0	8	8	1	0	1	0	2
960 DPT	6560 DPT						464 DPT					47 DPT				

10. Dynasties

Using the shorthand form we've already established:

5 Years: 88/64 PPT/960 DPT
8993/544 PPT/6560 DPT
9599/40 PPT/464 DPT
0004/4 PPT/47 DPT

Note that the PPT for each of the sub-dynasties is equal to the sum of the PPTs of all the links in the sub-dynasty. The PPT or peak is nothing more than PPT, the total number of PPT is going to stay the same whether you evaluate it at 5 or 15 years.

You can see how all the sub-dynasties fit back together, except for the null links, to form the entire dynasty.

The Bills of the 1990s: 10 Years

88	89	90	91	92	93	94	95	96	97	98	99	00	01	02	03	04
64	32	128	128	128	128	0	16	8	0	8	8	1	0	1	0	2

Figure 10.18. Chronological/PPT chain for the 1988–2004 Buffalo Bills dynasty.

Since we're looking at 10-year eras, we'll begin by laying out all of the possible 10-year eras within the dynasty (1988–97, 1989–98, etc.) in a horizontal list, with the DPT amounts for the ten-year eras above it, similar to what we did in Table 10.8 for the five-year eras:

YRS	8897	8998	9099	9100	9201	9302	9403	9504
DPT	31464	29160	28024	22026	15603	8893	2131	2151

Figure 19.19. Horizontal list of all 10-year eras and corresponding DPT values for the 1988–2004 Buffalo Bills dynasty.

The peak was 31464 from 1988 to 1997 according to Figure 10.19. Because the first and last year of any sub-dynasty cannot be a zero, the sub-dynasty was evaluated from 1988 to 1996. The 8896 part of the chain is removed (and the DPT block added underneath), and the null link at 1997 is also removed from the chain:

Opposite, bottom: Figure 10.17. Reassembled and fully analyzed 1988–2004 Buffalo Bills dynasty at five-year levels with DPT blocks underneath.

98	99	00	01	02	03	04
8	8	1	0	1	0	2

97
0

88	89	90	91	92	93	94	95	96
64	32	128	128	128	128	0	16	8
31464 DPT								

Figure 10.20. Chronological/PPT chain for 1988–2004 Buffalo Bills dynasty with 1988–1996 seasons removed (DPT block added) along with null 1997 season.

We are left with the 9804 part, which is shown in Figure 10.21, and this piece will be evaluated:

98	99	00	01	02	03	04
8	8	1	0	1	0	2

Figure 10.21. Remaining 1998–2004 segment of the 1988–2004 Buffalo Bills dynasty that has yet to be analyzed for DPT.

I think you get the hang of how the peaks work at this point, so I won't list them. This one is pretty simple to figure out if you look at it.

$$DPT = (1*8) + (2*16) + (3*17) + (4*17) + (5*18) + (6*18) + (7*20) + (8*20) + (9*20) + (10*20) = 1037\ DPT$$

98	99	00	01	02	03	04
8	8	1	0	1	0	2
1037 DPT						

Figure 10.22. Chronological/PPT chain for the 1998–2004 Buffalo Bills sub-dynasty with DPT block underneath.

Reassembling the pieces:

88	89	90	91	92	93	94	95	96	97	98	99	00	01	02	03	04
64	32	128	128	128	128	0	16	8	0	8	8	1	0	1	0	2
31464 DPT									1037 DPT							

At 10 years, the final result is:

10 Years: 8896/632 PPT/31464 DPT
9804/20 PPT/1037 DPT

The Bills of the 1990s: 15 Years

Last, but not least, at 15-year intervals:

88	89	90	91	92	93	94	95	96	97	98	99	00	01	02	03	04
64	32	128	128	128	128	0	16	8	0	8	8	1	0	1	0	2

Figure 10.24. Chronological/PPT chain for the 1988–2004 Buffalo Bills dynasty.

There are three possible 15-year intervals within the 1988–2004 dynasty:

YRS	8802	8903	9004
DPT	73553	67203	64041

Figure 10.25. Horizontal list of all 15-year eras and corresponding DPT values for the 1988–2004 Buffalo Bills dynasty.

The peak is at 8802; cutting the chain between 2002 and 2003 and removing the null link at 2003:

04
2

03
0

88	89	90	91	92	93	94	95	96	97	98	99	00	01	02
64	32	128	128	128	128	0	16	8	0	8	8	1	0	1
73553 DPT															

Figure 10.26. Chronological/PPT chain for the 1988–2004 Buffalo Bills dynasty with 1988–2002 seasons removed (DPT block added) along with null 2003 season.

Opposite, bottom: Figure 10.23 Reassembled and fully analyzed 1988–2004 Buffalo Bills dynasty at 10-year levels with DPT blocks underneath

We are left with the single link at 04 with a PPT of 2:

$$DPT = (1*2) + (2*2) + (3*2) + (4*2) + (5*2) + (6*2) +$$
$$(7*2) + (8*2) + (9*2) + (10*2) + (11*2) + (12*2) +$$
$$(13*2) + (14*2) + (15*2) = 240 \text{ DPT}$$

04
2
240 DPT

Figure 10.27. Chronological/PPT chain for the 2004 Buffalo Bills sub-dynasty with DPT block underneath.

When the sub-dynasties are reassembled:

88	89	90	91	92	93	94	95	96	97	98	99	00	01	02	03	04
64	32	128	128	128	128	0	16	8	0	8	8	1	0	1	0	2
73553 DPT																240 DPT

Figure 10.28. Reassembled and fully analyzed 1988–2004 Buffalo Bills dynasty at 15-year levels with DPT blocks underneath.

15 Years: 8802/650 PPT/73553 DPT
04/2 PPT/240 DPT

The final summary of the 1988–2004 Bills Dynasty:

5 Years: 88/64 PPT/960 DPT
8993/544 PPT/6560 DPT
9599/40 PPT/464 DPT
0004/4 PPT/47 DPT
10 Years: 8896/632 PPT/31464 DPT
9804/20 PPT/1037 DPT
15 Years: 8802/650 PPT/73553 DPT
04/2 PPT/240 DPT

Contemporary Bills Dynasty

The Bills have another dynasty that is currently in progress:

Figure 10.29. Chronological/PPT chain for the 2014–17 Buffalo Bills dynasty.

14	15	16	17
2	1	0	4

1-year peak: 4 (2017)
2-year peak: 4 (16–17)
3-year peak: 5 (15–17)
4-year peak: 7 (14–17)

5 Years: 1417/5 PPT/90 DPT
10 Years: 1417/5 PPT/164 DPT
15 Years: 1417/5 PPT/825 DPT

Keep in mind this dynasty is in progress, and if the Bills are awarded PPT in 2019, then this dynasty will need to be reevaluated, as will every team that is awarded PPT in 2019 that has an active dynasty. If the Bills do not receive any PPT in 2019, then this dynasty has ended as they did not receive any PPT in 2018 and will require no further evaluation.

Evaluating dynasties using this method focuses on the peak seasons, and can be used to compare the 89–93 Bills against the 2001–05 Patriots or any other five-year era for any other dynasty. If you believe that a dynasty should be rated over 10 seasons, or 15 seasons, that can also be done. If you want to see what it would look like at 6 or 9 or 12 seasons, that can also be done, using this methodology.

I believe that the evaluation method I've developed is a great way to compare dynasties and can be used in other ways to compare team-eras of quality. And, with a few modifications, a similar system would work for all team sports, especially baseball, for rating teams over periods of years.

Another thing I like about using this type of evaluation is that it rewards teams who "bunch" their best years together. We'll take two hypothetical teams over a 5-year period, team A and team B, with the number of PPT they accumulate per season:

Team A	Team B
Year 1: 4	Year 1: 0
Year 2: 0	Year 2: 4
Year 3: 16	Year 3: 16
Year 4: 0	Year 4: 8
Year 5: 8	Year 5: 0

In each case the team accumulated 28 PPT. Which dynasty is more impressive?

Team A	Team B
1-year peak: 16	1-year peak: 16
2-year peak: 16	2-year peak: 24
3-year peak: 24	3-year peak: 28
4-year peak: 24	
5-year peak: 28	
5-year DPT = 356	5-year DPT = 400
10-year DPT = 1476	10-year DPT = 1520
15-year DPT = 3296	15-year DPT = 3340

As you can tell, in every case, the team with the seasons that were better grouped together scored higher in the DPT system.

Browns/49ers

One franchise evaluation needs to be discussed, and that is the Cleveland Browns, and to a lesser extent, the San Francisco 49ers. In 1946 the Browns and 49ers began to play in the AAFC (All-America Football Conference) and played in the AAFC until 1949 when they were admitted to the NFL in 1950 and the rest of the league folded. The original Baltimore Colts team also came over from the AAFC to the NFL but folded after one season in the NFL. (In 1953, another team also named the Baltimore Colts joined the NFL, but this time it was successful and eventually became the Indianapolis Colts.)

The Browns ran roughshod over the AAFC, winning all four AAFC Championship games. It could be argued that the Browns of 1948 and 1949 were stronger than the World Champion Eagles of 1948 and 1949. The problem was that the rest of the AAFC (except for San Francisco) was relatively much weaker than the NFL, and for that reason it is like trying to compare apples to oranges measuring Cleveland's dominance in the AAFC against their dominance of the NFL. However, the Browns dispelled this question of their dominance when they won the NFL Championship in 1950, their initial season in the NFL, and went to the NFL Championship game in each of the first six seasons in the NFL, winning three of them.

Cleveland had a dynasty that ran from 1946 to 1973, including the AAFC years. To rate them strictly against NFL teams, I created a second, separate but parallel Cleveland Browns dynasty that omitted the AAFC years and ran from 1950 to 1973, and evaluated this alternate dynasty only based on the NFL seasons. I left both dynasties in the listings, and I abbreviated the 1950–73 Cleveland dynasty as CLN while the 1946–73 dynasty is abbreviated CLE. In cases where both dynasties overlapped, say, each had a similar five-year sub-dynasty of the same PPT and DPT from 1951 to 1955, I omitted the CLN entry from the lists. But if they differed in the years involved in the various sub-dynasties, I included CLE and CLN.

As San Francisco also accumulated PPT in the AAFC and NFL, to be consistent I created a separate but parallel SFN evaluation to separate their NFL only accomplishments from their AAFC accomplishments. The SFN dynasty runs from 1951 to 1954.

Concerns About Rating Dynasties

There is the inevitable concern that some leagues are weaker than others. The AFL through most of the '60s was a relatively weaker league than the NFL, although by the end of the decade the best AFL teams were as good as the best NFL teams. This gap continued into the '70s as the three teams who moved from the NFL to AFC during the 1970 realignment (Colts, Steelers and Browns) snagged 15 of 42 available AFC playoff spots and five Super Bowl wins between them during the 1970s. The addition of the Browns and Colts, and the Steelers and Dolphins developing into powerhouse teams, quickly narrowed the gap between the leagues and, by the mid–1970s, the AFC and

NFC were both relatively equal in talent top to bottom. The AAFC of the late 1940s (Cleveland excepted) was relatively much weaker than the NFL of the same era. Since we are trying to measure dominance over a period of consecutive years, I think the relative strength of the league in question is a moot point.

If I have the Packers of the '60s rated higher than the modern-day Patriots does that mean I think Starr and company would have beaten Brady and company if Lombardi's team could step into a time machine and beat Belichick's teams of today? I would have to say they would not, as players of the modern era are generally bigger and faster than players of the 1960s. It only stands to reason that an average modern team, say, the 2013 8–8 Pittsburgh Steelers, would surely win a best-of-seven series against the 1950 Cleveland Browns, and in fact, would probably sweep the series. It would be like an average modern NFL team playing an average modern college team.

Rating the '60s Packers ahead of the Patriots in this methodology means that I believe the Packers were more dominant in the era they played in than the Patriots were in theirs. Had there been a Super Bowl from 1960 to 1966, the NFL probably would have won all six of the games against the AFL with the possible exception of the 1963 or 1964 game (neither of which would have involved the Packers), and that would have given the Packers five Super Bowl wins in five tries.

Lists

Here is the payoff; the top 50 lists in DPT for EC or Equal Championships (where the Super Bowl champion is equivalent to a pre–Super Bowl Championship), and Unequal Championships or UC (where a modern Conference Champion is equal to pre–Super Bowl Championships), each for 5, 10 and 15-year eras.

Let the arguments begin:

Table 10.12
50 Highest Five-Year Sub-Dynasties, EC and UC

RK	TM ERA	PK	DPT	RK	TM ERA	PK	DPT
1	CLE 4650	1280	14080	1	CLE 4650	640	7040
2	CHI 3943	928	11424	2	BUF 8993	544	6560
3	G B 6367	844	10924	3	N E 1418	576	6464
4	CLE 5155	896	10752	4	DAL 9195	480	5792
5	DAL 9195	864	10656	5	CHI 3943	464	5712
6	N E 0418	960	10560	6	MIA 7074	448	5696
7	N E 0105	786	9874	7	MIN 7377	480	5568
8	PGH 7478	848	9616	8	G B 6367	424	5480
9	MIA 7074	704	9408	9	CLE 5155	448	5376
10	DET 5256	704	9280	10	DAL 7579	432	5328
11	PHI 4549	670	9134	11	PGH 7478	464	5264

RK	TM ERA	PK	DPT	RK	TM ERA	PK	DPT
12	G B 5962	646	9014	12	DAL 6973	416	5216
13	HOU 6062	640	8960	13	N E 0307	464	5120
14	BUF 6266	646	8798	14	DEN 8589	389	4905
15	S F 8690	624	8560	T15	G B 9397	368	4848
16	G B 3539	684	8240	T15	S F 8690	368	4848
17	L A 4953	608	7904	17	BUF 6266	358	4798
18	DEN 9598	545	7817	18	MIA 8185	384	4704
19	BAL 5761	521	7515	19	DET 5256	352	4640
20	S D 6064	640	7424	20	PHI 4549	338	4594
21	NYG 3337	544	7328	21	G B 5962	326	4534
22	DAL 7579	560	7248	T22	HOU 6062	320	4480
23	WAS 3640	608	7232	T22	OAK 7377	384	4480
24	DAL 6973	544	7136	24	WAS 8286	356	4452
25	S F 8185	584	7104	T25	PHI 0004	352	4320
26	CHI 3337	582	6920	T25	SEA 1216	320	4320
27	WAS 4145	524	6900	27	DEN 1115	336	4272
28	PGH 0408	585	6868	28	BAL 6771	332	4248
29	NYG 3842	519	6861	29	G B 3539	352	4184
30	G B 9397	496	6768	30	DEN 9600	296	4136
31	OAK 8084	552	6656	31	L A 7579	352	4096
32	NYG 5660	520	6604	T32	S F 8185	328	4032
33	BUF 8993	544	6560	T32	S F 9296	320	4032
34	OAK 7377	512	6400	34	L A 4953	304	3952
35	WAS 8286	484	6372	35	N E 0913	292	3892
36	CLE 6468	480	6288	36	BAL 5771	265	3803
37	SEA 1216	448	6240	37	PGH 0408	329	3796
38	DEN 1115	464	6192	T38	K C 6670	312	3752
39	BAL 6771	460	6168	T38	S D 6064	320	3712
40	S F 9296	448	5952	T40	WAS 3640	312	3712
41	CHC 4649	394	5740	T40	NYG 3438	344	3672
42	CHI 4650	440	5680	42	SLR 9903	292	3672
43	K C 6670	440	5672	43	CHI 8488	304	3664
44	G B 4044	420	5652	44	IND 0610	304	3656
45	NYG 8690	548	5616	45	PGH 9397	276	3604
46	NYG 0711	547	5598	46	S F 1114	257	3593
47	SLR 9903	420	5592	47	OAK 8084	296	3584

RK	TM ERA	PK	DPT	RK	TM ERA	PK	DPT
48	CHI 8488	432	5584	T48	CHI 3337	294	3496
49	IND 0610	432	5576	T48	BAR 0812	288	3472
50	MIN 7377	480	5568	50	CLE 6468	288	3472

Table 10.13
50 Highest 10-Year Sub-Dynasties, EC and UC

RK	TM ERA	PK	DPT	RK	TM ERA	PK	DPT
1	CLE 4655	2176	85632	1	CLE 4655	1088	42816
2	G B 5967	1490	67198	2	N E 0918	868	38344
3	CLN 5059	1347	61534	3	G B 5967	750	33754
4	CHI 3948	1288	59048	4	DAL 6978	840	33480
5	N E 0918	1252	57800	5	PGH 7281	691	31872
6	PGH 7281	1203	56704	6	BUF 8897	632	31464
7	S F 8190	1208	49712	7	CLN 5059	675	30782
8	N E 9908	981	48290	8	MIN 6978	689	29954
9	DET 5057	969	48011	9	CHI 3746	668	29548
10	NYG 3342	1063	46948	10	S F 8897	706	29282
11	WAS 3645	1132	46232	11	N E 9908	597	28376
12	DAL 9199	888	46040	12	DAL 9199	504	25816
13	G B 3544	1104	45404	13	WAS 8291	630	25450
14	DAL 6978	1096	44872	14	OAK 6776	680	25120
15	OAK 7483	996	41236	15	MIA 7079	484	24304
16	L A 4554	879	40486	16	DET 5057	487	24095
17	NYG 5463	911	40438	17	DEN 8392	494	24027
18	WAS 8291	1014	39120	18	NYG 3342	543	23932
19	S D 6069	790	39034	19	WAS 3645	576	23580
20	PHI 4352	745	38735	20	PGH 0110	555	23219
21	MIA 7079	740	38256	21	G B 3544	564	23056
22	PGH 0110	811	36527	22	L A 7180	464	22120
23	BUF 6266	646	34638	23	PHI 0009	453	21027
24	HOU 6062	640	34560	24	IND 0210	440	20792
25	BAL 5766	724	34551	25	BAL 6271	439	20712
26	DEN 8998	746	32979	26	K C 6271	479	20591
27	BUF 8897	632	31464	27	MIA 8190	420	20511
28	K C 6271	735	31087	28	L A 4554	447	20486
29	CHI 3338	586	30360	29	NYG 5463	463	20470

RK	TM ERA	PK	DPT	RK	TM ERA	PK	DPT
30	CLE 5766	702	30328	30	G B 9302	403	20360
31	CLN 6069	651	30121	31	S D 6069	406	19770
32	MIN 6978	689	29954	32	PHI 4352	381	19635
33	NYG 8493	613	29215	33	BUF 6266	358	19118
34	NYG 0512	561	28009	34	S F 8187	376	18880
35	IND 0210	568	27832	T35	CLE 6069	409	18611
36	S F 9198	546	27574	T35	OAK 7786	397	18490
37	G B 9302	531	27400	37	DEN 0816	340	17838
38	DEN 0716	468	24878	38	SEA 1018	342	17806
39	SEA 1018	470	24846	39	HOU 6062	320	17280
40	BAL 6771	460	24568	40	CHI 8391	345	17153
41	CHI 8391	473	24193	41	G B 0716	412	17068
42	G B 0716	540	24108	42	SLR 9906	325	16659
43	SLR 9906	453	23699	43	NYG 8493	357	16415
44	BAR 0614	449	22920	44	DEN 9302	308	16289
45	L A 7180	464	22120	45	PGH 8997	326	16282
46	CHC 4649	394	21500	46	BAR 0614	321	15880
47	CHI 5463	511	21348	47	NYG 0512	305	15209
48	OAK 6573	448	21296	48	BAL 5761	262	14264
49	PHI 0009	453	21027	49	S F 0914	258	13913
50	MIA 8190	420	20511	50	TEN 9603	243	12728

Table 10.14
50 Highest 15-Year Sub-Dynasties, EC and UC

RK	TM ERA	PK	DPT	RK	TM ERA	PK	DPT
1	CLE 4660	2435	237719	1	CLE 4660	1219	118903
2	CHI 3347	1810	166258	2	N E 0418	1206	106878
3	G B 5969	1492	164178	3	DAL 6983	1056	98488
4	CLN 5064	1710	158575	4	S F 8195	986	86896
5	N E 0418	1718	153214	5	CHI 3347	910	83474
6	S F 8195	1626	145242	6	G B 5969	751	82569
7	PGH 7284	1287	138711	7	PGH 7284	775	80599
8	NYG 3346	1383	130827	8	CLN 5064	860	79571
9	DAL 6680	1336	125976	9	OAK 6680	884	78570
10	WAS 3448	1140	120144	10	MIN 6882	737	76691
11	G B 3447	1121	118012	11	BUF 8802	650	73553

RK	TM ERA	PK	DPT
12	OAK 6983	1228	115016
13	DET 5057	969	110996
14	L A 4558	1032	106679
15	WAS 7791	1031	105651
16	NYG 4963	1044	104428
17	DAL 9199	888	103760
18	BAL 5771	1184	103019
19	MIA 7084	1061	98869
20	DEN 8498	1039	94418
21	PGH 0115	845	90394
22	S D 6069	790	90384
23	PHI 4354	765	88456
24	K C 6073	749	79564
25	MIN 6882	737	76691
26	BUF 6266	646	76628
27	HOU 6062	640	76160
28	N E 9403	671	75400
29	BUF 8802	650	73553
30	IND 0014	676	70684
31	CLE 6173	622	70051
32	NYG 8494	615	69190
33	G B 9307	620	65269
34	BAR 0014	747	64498
35	NYG 0512	561	64474
36	DEN 0216	544	59930
37	SEA 1018	470	55396
38	L A 6680	530	55358
39	CHI 5468	527	55349
40	CHI 8391	473	54938
41	G B 0916	476	54344
42	SLR 9906	453	53144
43	PHI 0014	468	51048
44	CHC 4649	394	47110
45	DET 3340	375	44494
46	N O 0013	381	42962
47	T B 9702	365	42898

RK	TM ERA	PK	DPT
12	DEN 8498	783	68880
13	MIA 7084	805	68277
14	WAS 7892	655	67831
15	NYG 3346	703	66619
16	WAS 3448	584	61352
17	BAL 5771	704	61038
18	G B 3447	581	60564
19	PGH 0115	589	60446
20	DAL 9199	504	58576
21	DET 5057	487	55750
22	L A 6680	529	55343
23	IND 0014	548	55324
24	L A 4558	524	54091
25	NYG 4963	532	53068
26	K C 6073	493	52428
27	PHI 0014	468	51048
28	G B 9307	492	49909
29	S D 6069	406	46160
30	PHI 4354	395	45286
31	CLE 6173	412	45271
32	N E 9404	415	45176
33	DEN 0216	416	44570
34	BAR 0014	491	43762
35	BUF 6266	358	42388
36	SEA 1018	342	40036
37	NYG 8494	359	39750
38	CHI 8391	345	39578
39	G B 0916	348	38984
40	HOU 6062	320	38080
41	SLR 9906	325	37784
42	PGH 8797	328	37602
43	NYG 0512	305	35034
44	S F 0914	258	30683
45	CHI 5468	295	30401
46	CIN 8190	286	30136
47	CLN 6573	259	29361

RK	TM ERA	PK	DPT	RK	TM ERA	PK	DPT
48	PHI 5961	322	38570	48	TEN 9603	243	28523
49	NYA 4649	320	37888	49	N O 0013	253	27602
50	S F 4669	367	37650	50	T B 9702	237	27538

Glossary

The chapter where the term primarily appears is given, if applicable

A16G, Y16G—Attempts per 16 Games, Yards per 16 Games—Putting a rusher's career totals into a 16-game context, in which his career totals are divided by the number of games played and then multiplied by 16. (Chapter 5)

AAFC or F—All-America Football League (1946–1949). The AAFC disbanded after the 1949 season but the Cleveland Browns, San Francisco 49ers and Baltimore Colts (AAFC) joined the NFL for the 1950 season. (The Colts disbanded after the 1950 season, and are not to be confused with the Baltimore Colts franchise who began play in 1953; they are two separate franchises.) AAFC statistics are not recognized by the NFL but they are recognized in this book. In some cases, I segregated the NFL and AAFC statistics of some teams and players.

Absolute Value—Absolute Value signifies the magnitude of the number and ignores whether the value of the number inside the vertical lines is positive or negative. It is mathematically expressed with vertical lines around both sides of the area that is under absolute value. The result is always positive. For example, |23| is referred to as "the absolute value of 23" and is equal to 23, and |-23| is referred to as "the absolute value of negative 23," and is also equal to 23.

AEWP—Adjusted Estimated Winning Percentage—NPCT in which the schedule adjustment (OPCT) has been removed using a reverse-engineered form of Bayes Theorem. In other words, the team's Estimated Winning Percentage has been adjusted for how it would play against an average or 0.5000 schedule. (Chapter 2)

AFC or A—American Football Conference (1970–2018)—After the AFL-NFL merger took effect in 1970, the AFL teams, along with Baltimore, Cleveland and Pittsburgh, were renamed the American Football Conference. The three NFL teams moved to the AFC in order to give each conference 13 teams.

AFL or A—American Football League (1960–1969), merged with NFL starting in the 1970 season. All AFL statistics are officially recognized by NFL.

Aggregate—A statistical term for sum or total or collective.

Average Home Point Differential—Total points scored in home games minus total points allowed in home games divided by the number of home games played. (Chapter 1)

Average Point Differential—Total points scored minus total points against divided by games played. (Chapter 1)

Average Road Point Differential—Same as Home Point but road instead of home. (Chapter 1)

Bayes Theorem—A standard statistical formula for measuring the effect of two objects competing against one another. (Chapter 2)

Bell Curve or Normal Curve—A statistical curve depicting how data is normally distributed. The distance from the top of the curve is marked off in Standard Deviations or SD. (Chapter 2)

Cinderella Team—A team who played below 0.5000 in each of the previous two seasons, failed to make the postseason in the third-most recent season, and in the season in question (target season) made the postseason and appeared in a league (pre–Super Bowl era) or conference championship game or better. An example would be the 1981 San Francisco 49ers. (Chapter 4)

Coding–A methodology for assigning a particular letter grade (either A, B, C, D, E or X) to 36 different statistical categories for each team. These grades, or codes, can be used to determine the degree of similarity between two particular offenses or defenses or teams in general, and the research possibilities for doing various studies using coding are endless. (Chapter 9)

Coefficient—The number that the variable (or variable being raised to the power) is being multiplied by. In the $12 = 3 \times X^2$ equation, the coefficient is 3.

Defensive Similarity—DSIM—The degree to which two teams are statistically similar defensively. (Chapter 9)

DP—Data Point—A point on a graph that represents one or more pieces of data.

Dynasty—For the purposes of this book, an era of consecutive seasons in which a team accumulates at least one PPT in every other season. If a team goes two straight seasons and fails to make the playoffs or finish at or above 0.5000 in either season, the dynasty is over, and a new dynasty begins the next season in which the team makes the postseason or finishes at or above 0.5000. A dynasty can last one season or go on forever; there is no set length to a dynasty. (Chapter 10)

Dynasty Points or DPT—A methodology in which groups of PPT are evaluated in year-eras to determine the peak number of PPT, and these various peaks are plugged into a formula to compare dynasties. (Chapter 10)

EPCT—Estimated Winning Percentage—A mathematical equation that predicts the winning percentage of a particular team-season based upon their points scored and points allowed. (Chapter 2)

Equal Championships or EC—The rationale that a Super Bowl Championship is relatively equivalent to a pre–Super Bowl NFL, AFL or AAFC Championship. When thinking in terms of EC, the 1956 NFL title or the 1963 AFL title are roughly equal to the Super Bowl XVIII Championship. (Chapter 10)

Factorial or !—Used in probability, the easiest way to explain factorial is by giving an example. Eight factorial (or 8!) is $8 \times 7 \times 6 \times 5 \times 4 \times 3 \times 2 \times 1$ or 40,320. 2! = 2×1 or 2.

G, GP—Game(s), Games Played.

Harmonic Mean—A different method for averaging numbers; instead of adding the numbers, one multiplies the numbers together, then raises the product to the (1/x) root, where X is the number of items in the set being averaged. For example, the harmonic mean of the numbers 1, 3, 6, 9, and 10 are $(1 \times 3 \times 6 \times 9 \times 10)$ ^ (1/5) or (1620) ^ (0.2) or 4.3843.

HFA—Home Field Advantage—A combination of both the advantage a team has by playing in their home stadium and in front of a home crowd and the disadvantage the opposing team has of having to travel to a foreign stadium and play in front of a hostile crowd. There are probably many things that contribute to HFA, including the intensity of the crowd, which seems to be more of a factor in football than baseball. The type of HFA that is more of an advantage in baseball than football is related to the unique design and architecture of the stadium, and the manner in which teams tailor their rosters to take advantage of that. (Chapter 1)

HPA—Home Field Point Advantage—Home field advantage with respect to point differential. It is the difference between a team's home and road average point differential, divided by two. (Chapter 1)

HPCT—Home Winning Percentage—Winning percentage in home games only. (Chapter 1)

HWA—Home Field Winning Advantage—Home Field Advantage with respect to winning percentage. For a team, it is half of the difference between a team's home and road winning percentage (HPCT, RPCT). (Chapter 1)

Kicker Points—The number of points a kicker scores from field goals and extra points only. For virtually all modern kickers, Kicker Points and Points Scored by kickers are synonymous, but there were kickers in the past who played offensive positions (such as George Blanda and Paul Hornung) and they scored points both from offensive touchdowns and from kicking field goals and extra points. Kicker Points separates the points they scored as an offensive player from those they scored as a kicker. As an example, many football fans know that George Blanda scored 2,002 points during his career, however, Blanda actually scored 1,948 Kicker Points during his career along with nine rushing touchdowns (54 points) which added up to his 2,002 career points scored. (Chapter 7)

Kicking Percentage or K%–A ratio, multiplied by 100, of the number of points a kicker scored on field goals and extra points in a season, divided by the number of points he would have scored had he been successful on all of his field goal and extra point attempts in the same season. (Chapter 7)

Least Squares Curve—Also known as a trendline, a mathematical curve derived from the data which bests explains the data. The degree of the curve refers to the highest power any of the elements of the curve equation are raised to. For example, a sixth-degree curve will have a "^6" in it and will be the highest number raised to a power. In many cases, a least square curve is a straight line (degree one), because the data tends to follow a straight line.

Luckman Effect—Named for Sid Luckman, Hall of Fame quarterback for the Chicago Bears in the 1930s and 1940s who had great statistical seasons in leagues where the rest of the passers he was being compared to were rather mediocre. When rated against his peers (and his stats were removed from the league totals), it often overrated his performance to an extreme degree as he is being compared against a small league of players, none of whom were remotely as good as he was and the aggregate performance of the rest of the league is slightly below average or well below average. This can happen in small leagues with a good or very good performance by a single player or in seasons with a lower average quality of play (such as the World War II era NFL). It is a mathematical anomaly that I have been unable to work around; perhaps somebody smarter than me can find a way to compensate for the Luckman Effect. (Chapter 6)

Mean—A statistical term for average, or the sum of a list of items divided by the numbers of items in the list. Mean and average are the same thing, but statisticians use the term mean instead of average.

MOM—Momentum—Momentum Winning Percentage (MWP) minus Winning Percentage (WPCT). (Chapter 3)

Momentum—In mathematical or scientific terms, mass multiplied by acceleration. In sports terms, I define it as a positive or negative carryover from one play to the next, one possession to the next, one game to the next, and perhaps, one season to the next. What I have defined as momentum in this book is actually a weighted formula for calculating acceleration and deceleration, the degree to which a team's winning percentage is increasing or decreasing. (Chapter 3)

MW—Momentum Wins—The result of the Momentum Weight (MW) for the week in question multiplied by 1 if the team wins that week, 0.5 if the team ties that week, and zero if the team loses that week. (Chapter 3)

MWP—Momentum Winning Percentage—The sum of all MWs accumulated to a particular point in the season divided by the sum of all MWTs to the same point in the season. (Chapter 3)

MWT—Momentum Weight—A weight assigned to each particular week of the season, with the first week weighted at 1.0, and the weight of each successive week raised by a level of 0.2, (Week 2 MWT = 1.2, Week 3 MWT = 1.4, Week 4 MWT = 1.6 and so on.) (Chapter 3)

NFC or N—National Football Conference (1970–2018)—After the AFL-NFL merger took effect in 1970, the remaining 13 NFL teams were renamed the National Football Conference. The NFL remains today as the parent league, with the AFC and NFC underneath it as children conferences.

NFL or N—National Football League—(1920–2018) In 1920–21, the league was known as the APFA, the American Professional Football Association. In this book we are just examining the teams and players from 1933 to 2018.

NPR—Normalized Passer Rating—An attempt to fix the errors in the PRS; instead of using fixed standards, the PRS rates passers against the league averages for the season in question in the four categories. (Chapter 6)

Offensive Similarity—OSIM—The degree to which two teams are statistically similar offensively, according to their codes and the weights accorded to each code category. The maximum possible similarity between any two offenses, or defenses, is 500.00, and can only occur if each of the 18 code letters are exactly the same for both teams. The minimum possible similarity is 0.00, which can only occur if one team's codes consist of all As and the other team's codes consist of all Es. The average similarity between any two offensive or defensive teams is about 400 to 425. (Chapter 9)

One-Year Wonder—OYW—A team who in the middle season (target season) of a five, seven, nine, or eleven-year span, has a year whose WPCT exceeds the weighted average WPCT of the other seasons of the span except for the target season by an amount greater than 0.3000. There are rules in place to curtail the number of OYW teams, such as OYW teams cannot make the postseason in the year before or the year after the target season, and a team must have an above 0.5000 record during an OYW season. An OYW can also be either a Cinderella team or a surprise team. An example of a one-year wonder team is the 2008 Miami Dolphins. (Chapter 4)

OSCH—Schedule—An adjustment to EPCT to adjust for the schedule the particular team plays. (Chapter 2)

PCT—Percentage—A ratio of one number to another, measured in decimal terms relative to 100, such as a 45 percent chance of it raining today implies 45 percent of 100. This always involves division.

Point Differential—Points for minus points against. (Chapter 1)

Points Above League or PAL—A formula for evaluating a kicker based on how many points an average kicker in the league in the same season would have scored given the same number of field goal or extra point attempts. Can also be used to evaluate teams, offensively or defensively. (Chapter 7)

Points Above League 2 or PAL2—A more complex and accurate version of PAL that requires data on missed field goal attempt distances. As this data is not complete for many kickers before the late 1960s, the PAL2 data for these kickers is not accurate. I have been spearheading an effort to ascertain the distances of all missed field goal attempts, and at this point that number of unknown miss distances from 1938 to 2018 has been reduced to about 375. (Chapter 7)

Postseason Points or PPT—Points that are awarded to teams each season based on their accomplishments during the season. The maximum number of points that can be awarded in a season is 256 PPT when applying Equal Championships or 128 PPT when applying Unequal Championships for the season, and the minimum number is zero for teams who finish below 0.5000 or do not make the postseason. Teams who finish 0.5000 and do not make the postseason receive one PPT for the season, and all other teams who finish above 0.5000 earn additional PPT based on either their final WPCT and or how far they advance in the postseason. PPT are always expressed in whole numbers greater than or equal to zero. (Chapter 10)

PRS—Passer Rating System—Used by the NFL since 1972 to rate passers against fixed mathematical standards in four different categories—completion percentage, yards per attempt, touchdown percentage and interception percentage. This final result is known as a Passer Rating or PR. (Chapter 6)

PS, PA—Points Scored, Points Allowed.

PUR—Punter Rating—A rating calculated from a punter's ranking among his peers in five different categories—gross punting average, punting average in punts with an LOS (Line of Scrimmage of 60 yards or less), punting average in punts with an LOS of more than 60 yards, percentage of punts out of bounds inside the 20-yard line and percentage of punts that are touchbacks. (Chapter 8)

Pythagorean Formula—Created by Bill James and first appeared (as far as I know) in his *1980 Baseball Abstract*. It is for predicting a team's winning percentage based on the number of runs they score and give up. (Chapter 2)

^—Raised to a power of—A^B means "A raised to the power of B." 2^2 = 2 × 2 = 4, 3^3 = 3 × 3 × 3 = 27

RPCT—Road Winning Percentage—Winning percentage in road games only. (Chapter 1)

Sample Size—The number of items being examined from a much larger group for various statistical standards. The smaller the sample size, the less confident we are about the data as representative of the whole. The larger the sample size, the more confident we are about the data being representative of the entire group.

60 yards theory on punts—A punting theory I developed. When the LOS is more than 60 yards away from the end zone, the punter will generally kick it as hard and straight as he can and will not think about kicking toward the sidelines or sacrificing distance to pin the ball deep inside the opponents' territory. Once the LOS is 60 yards from the end zone, the punt average begins to drop off and it is clear that the punter is sacrificing distance and or angling toward the sidelines. This theory needs data from more stadiums (not to mention input from professional punters on the subject) in order to see if this is a generalized rule of thumb. (Chapter 8)

Standard Deviation or SD—A basic statistical tool used to measure how spread out a series of numbers (or data) are from the center. (Chapter 2)

Straw—Coined by Baseball Hall of Famer Reggie Jackson, the Straw is the X factor, the missing player/players, event or catalyst for the occurrence of a Surprise Team, Cinderella Team, or One-Year Wonder. If you examine these types of teams carefully enough between the season in question, and the previous season, you will almost always find a straw. (Chapter 4)

Surprise Team—A team who played below 0.5000 in each of the previous two seasons, failed to make the postseason in the third-most recent season, and in the season in question (target season) made the postseason but came up short of a league (pre-Super Bowl era) or conference championship game. An example would be the 2016 Oakland Raiders. (Chapter 4)

Team Similarity—TSIM—The degree to which two teams are statistically similar. It is the sum of OSIM and DSIM. (Chapter 9)

TM—Team—Franchise name in two or three-letter abbreviation such as GB for Green Bay or NYG for New York Giants. (See Team Abbreviations section.)

Total Adjustment—An adjustment made to each of the point totals obtained from the four factors of the PRS (C%P, Y/A P, TD% P, I% P) that adjusts each passer's NPR so that the league NPR for each season comes out very close to 66.6667. The total adjustments are different for each of the four factors and are different for each season. Total adjustments are also applied to offensive and defensive team passing statistics in order to adjust team NPR ratings. (Chapter 6)

TS—Team-Season—A particular season for a particular team, such as the 1948 New York Giants, or the 1971 Kansas City Chiefs or the 2015 Kansas City Chiefs.

Unequal Championships or UC—The rationale that an AFC or NFC Championship from the Super Bowl era is relatively equivalent to a pre–Super Bowl NFL, AFL or AAFC Championship. In other words, the 1962 NFL title is of equal importance to either the 2015 AFC or NFC conference titles. When thinking in terms of UC, Super Bowl results are ignored because there was no equivalent game to the Super Bowl before the 1965 season. (Chapter 10)

Variable—Any letter (or abbreviated phrase in the context of this book) that is being used in an equation in place of a number in order to solve the equation. For example, in the equation $12 = 3 \times X^2$, X is the variable, which you are generally solving for.

WPCT—Winning Percentage—Defined as wins plus half of losses divided by wins plus losses plus ties. Until 1971, WPCT was defined as wins divided by wins plus losses, meaning ties were ignored in computing winning percentage. From 1972–2016, a tie is considered a half-win and a half-loss.

X-Axis, Y-Axis—Both the X- and Y-axis define a system of numerical coordinates in a positive and negative direction. The X-axis runs horizontally, and the Y-axis runs vertically. The X and Y axis meet at the origin, which is (0,0).

YL—Year League—A three-character abbreviation used to denote the year and league associated with a particular team or player. It is always in NNL form, where the first two characters are numbers, and the third character is a letter. The first two numbers are the last two numbers of the year in question, and the letter is either N for NFL, F for AAFC, or A for AFL. A YL of 34N is an abbreviation for 1934 NFL, and a YL of 62A is an abbreviation for 62 AFL.

YR—Year or season, often abbreviated in two-digit form with the first two digits of the year number removed, such as 64 instead of 1964 or 00 for 2000.

YRAA—Yards Rushing Above Average—The number of yards a rusher gains in a season minus the rusher attempts times the league rushing average, with the rusher's statistics removed from the league statistics. For teams, it is the number of yards a team gains (or allows) in a season minus the team rushing attempts times the league rushing average with the team's rushing statistics removed from the league statistics. (Chapter 5)

YRAA/G—Yards Rushing Above Average per Game. (Chapter 5)

YRS—A four-digit shorthand for denoting the beginning and end of an era, in which the first two digits of the year numbers are removed, and the dash (-) sign between them is also removed. An example would be the era 1945–1951, which would be abbreviated 4551. 1996–2003 would be abbreviated 9603. 2006–2015 would be abbreviated 0615.

Z-Score—The number of SDs an item is from the group's mean. The higher the Z-score, the more unique (for better or worse) the item is. (Chapter 2)

Bibliography

1945 Record and Rules Manual (Chicago, IL: National Football League, 1945).
1963 NFL Record Manual (New York, NY: National Football League, 1963).
1964 NFL Record Manual (New York, NY: National Football League, 1964).
1965 NFL Record Manual (New York, NY: National Football League, 1965).
1967 NFL Record Manual (New York, NY: National Football League, 1967)
1968 NFL Record Manual (New York, NY: National Football League, 1968).
1969 NFL Record Manual (New York, NY: National Football League, 1969).
1970 National Football League Record Book (New York, NY: National Football League, 1970).
1971 National Football League Record Book (New York, NY: National Football League, 1971).
1976 National Football League Record Manual (New York, NY: National Football League, 1976).
1982 National Football League Record Manual (New York, NY: National Football League, 1982).
1983 National Football League Record Manual (New York, NY: National Football League, 1983).
1984 NFL Record and Fact Book (New York, NY: National Football League, 1984).
1985 NFL Record and Fact Book (New York, NY: National Football League, 1985).
1986 NFL Record and Fact Book (New York, NY: National Football League, 1986).
1987 NFL Record and Fact Book (New York, NY: National Football League, 1987).
1988 NFL Record and Fact Book (New York, NY: National Football League, 1988).
1989 NFL Record and Fact Book (New York, NY: National Football League, 1989).
1990 NFL Record and Fact Book (New York, NY: National Football League, 1990).
1991 NFL Record and Fact Book (New York, NY: National Football League, 1991).
1992 NFL Record and Fact Book (New York, NY: National Football League, 1992).
1993 NFL Record and Fact Book (New York, NY: National Football League, 1993).
1994 NFL Record and Fact Book (New York, NY: National Football League, 1994).
1995 NFL Record and Fact Book (New York, NY: National Football League, 1995).
1996 NFL Record and Fact Book (New York, NY: National Football League, 1996).
1997 NFL Record and Fact Book (New York, NY: National Football League, 1997).
1998 NFL Record and Fact Book (New York, NY: National Football League, 1998).
1999 NFL Record and Fact Book (New York, NY: National Football League, 1999).
2000 NFL Record and Fact Book (New York, NY: National Football League, 2000).
2001 NFL Record and Fact Book (New York, NY: National Football League, 2001).
2002 NFL Record and Fact Book (New York, NY: National Football League, 2002).
2003 NFL Record and Fact Book (New York, NY: National Football League, 2003).
2004 NFL Record and Fact Book (New York, NY: National Football League, 2004).
2005 NFL Record and Fact Book (New York, NY: National Football League, 2005).
2006 NFL Record and Fact Book (New York, NY: National Football League, 2006).
2007 NFL Record and Fact Book (New York, NY: National Football League, 2007).
2008 NFL Record and Fact Book (New York, NY: National Football League, 2008).
2009 NFL Record and Fact Book (New York, NY: National Football League, 2009).
2010 NFL Record and Fact Book (New York, NY: National Football League, 2010).
2011 NFL Record and Fact Book (New York, NY: National Football League, 2011).
2012 NFL Record and Fact Book (New York, NY: National Football League, 2012).

2013 NFL Record and Fact Book (New York, NY: National Football League, 2013).
2014 NFL Record and Fact Book (New York, NY: National Football League, 2014).
2015 NFL Record and Fact Book (New York, NY: National Football League, 2015).
2016 NFL Record and Fact Book (New York, NY: National Football League, 2016).
2017 NFL Record and Fact Book (New York, NY: National Football League, 2017).
2018 NFL Record and Fact Book (New York, NY: National Football League, 2018).
2019 NFL Record and Fact Book (New York, NY: National Football League, 2019).
All-America Football Conference 1947 Record Manual (New York, NY: All-America Football Conference, 1947).
All-America Football Conference 1948 Record Manual (New York, NY: All-America Football Conference, 1948).
All-America Football Conference 1949 Record Manual (New York, NY: All-America Football Conference, 1949).
All-America Football Conference Supplement to 1949 Record Manual (Bogota, NJ: Dancey Printing Company, 1949).
American Football Guide Official Guide 1962 (St. Louis, MO: *The Sporting News*, 1962).
American Football Guide Official Guide 1963 (St. Louis, MO: *The Sporting News*, 1963).
American Football Guide Official Guide 1964 (St. Louis, MO: *The Sporting News*, 1964).
American Football Guide Official Guide 1965 (St. Louis, MO: *The Sporting News*, 1965).
American Football Guide Official Guide 1966 (St. Louis, MO: *The Sporting News*, 1966).
American Football Guide Official Guide 1967 (St. Louis, MO: *The Sporting News*, 1967).
American Football Guide Official Guide 1968 (St. Louis, MO: *The Sporting News*, 1968).
American Football Guide Official Guide 1969 (St. Louis, MO: *The Sporting News*, 1969).
The American Football Guide Record and Press Manual (St. Louis, MO: *The Sporting News*, 1961).
Carroll, Bob; Gershman, Michael; Neft, David; Thorn, John, *Total Football* (New York, NY: Harper/Collins, 1997).
James, Bill, *1979 Baseball Abstract* (Lawrence, KS, Bill James, 1979), 29.
James, Bill, *1980 Baseball Abstract* (Lawrence, KS, Bill James, 1980), 104.
National Football Guide 1970 Edition (St. Louis, MO: *The Sporting News*, 1970).
National Football Guide 1971 Edition (St. Louis, MO: *The Sporting News*, 1971).
National Football Guide 1972 Edition (St. Louis, MO: *The Sporting News*, 1972).
National Football Guide 1973 Edition (St. Louis, MO: *The Sporting News*, 1973).
National Football Guide 1974 Edition (St. Louis, MO: *The Sporting News*, 1974).
National Football Guide 1975 Edition (St. Louis, MO: *The Sporting News*, 1975).
National Football Guide 1976 Edition (St. Louis, MO: *The Sporting News*, 1976).
National Football Guide 1977 Edition (St. Louis, MO: *The Sporting News*, 1977).
National Football Guide 1978 Edition (St. Louis, MO: *The Sporting News*, 1978).
National Football Guide 1979 Edition (St. Louis, MO: *The Sporting News*, 1979).
National Football Guide 1980 Edition (St. Louis, MO: *The Sporting News*, 1980).
National Football Guide 1981 Edition (St. Louis, MO: *The Sporting News*, 1981).
National Football League 1946 Record and Rules Manual (New York, NY: National Football League, 1946).
National Football League 1947 Record and Rules Manual (Philadelphia, PA: National Football League, 1947).
National Football League 1948 Record and Rules Manual (Philadelphia, PA: National Football League, 1948).
National Football League 1949 Record and Rules Manual (Philadelphia, PA: National Football League, 1949).
National Football League 1950 Record and Rules Manual (Philadelphia, PA: National Football League, 1950).
National Football League 1951 Record and Rules Manual (Philadelphia, PA: National Football League, 1951).
National Football League 1952 Record and Rules Manual (Philadelphia, PA: National Football League, 1952).

National Football League 1953 Record and Rules Manual (Philadelphia, PA: National Football League, 1953).
National Football League 1954 Record and Rules Manual (Philadelphia, PA: National Football League, 1954).
National Football League 1955 Record and Rules Manual (Philadelphia, PA: National Football League, 1955).
National Football League 1956 Record and Rules Manual (Philadelphia, PA: National Football League, 1956).
National Football League 1957 Record and Rules Manual (Bala Cynwyd, PA: National Football League, 1957).
National Football League 1958 Record and Rules Manual (Bala Cynwyd, PA: National Football League, 1958).
National Football League 1959 Record and Rules Manual (Bala Cynwyd, PA: National Football League, 1959).
National Football League 1960 Record and Rules Manual (New York, NY: National Football League, 1960).
National Football League 1961 Record and Rules Manual (New York, NY: National Football League, 1961).
National Football League 1962 Record Manual (New York, NY: National Football League, 1962).
Official 1970 National Football League Record Manual (New York, NY: National Football League, 1970).
Official 1971 National Football League Record Manual (New York, NY: National Football League, 1971).
Official 1972 National Football League Record Manual (New York, NY: National Football League, 1972).
Official 1973 National Football League Record Manual (New York, NY: National Football League, 1973).
Official 1974 National Football League Record Manual (New York, NY: National Football League, 1974).
Official 1975 National Football League Record Manual (New York, NY: National Football League, 1975).
Official 1976 National Football League Record Manual (New York, NY: National Football League, 1976).
Official 1977 National Football League Record Manual (New York, NY: National Football League, 1977).
Official 1978 National Football League Record Manual (New York, NY: National Football League, 1978).
Official 1979 National Football League Record Manual (New York, NY: National Football League, 1979).
Official 1980 National Football League Record Manual (New York, NY: National Football League, 1980).
Official 1981 National Football League Record Manual (New York, NY: National Football League, 1981).
Official Guide of the National Football League 1935 (New York, NY: American Sports Publishing, 1935).
Official Guide of the National Football League 1936 (New York, NY: American Sports Publishing, 1936).
Official Guide of the National Football League 1937 (New York, NY: American Sports Publishing, 1937).
Official Guide of the National Football League 1938 (New York, NY: American Sports Publishing, 1938).
Official Guide of the National Football League 1939 (New York, NY: American Sports Publishing, 1939).
Official Guide of the National Football League 1940 (New York, NY: American Sports Publishing, 1940).
Palmer, Pete; Pullis, Ken; Lahman, Sean; Maher, Tod; Silverman, Matthew; Gillette, Gary, *The ESPN Pro Football Encyclopedia, Second Edition* (New York, NY, Sterling Publishing, 2007).
Pro Football Guide 1982 Edition (St. Louis, MO: *The Sporting News*, 1982).
Pro Football Guide 1983 Edition (St. Louis, MO: *The Sporting News*, 1983).
Pro Football Guide 1984 Edition (St. Louis, MO: *The Sporting News*, 1984).
Pro Football Guide 1985 Edition (St. Louis, MO: *The Sporting News*, 1985).
Pro Football Guide 1986 Edition (St. Louis, MO: *The Sporting News*, 1986).
Pro Football Guide 1987 Edition (St. Louis, MO: *The Sporting News*, 1987).
Pro Football Guide 1988 Edition (St. Louis, MO: *The Sporting News*, 1988).
Pro Football Guide 1989 Edition (St. Louis, MO: *The Sporting News*, 1989).
Pro Football Guide 1990 Edition (St. Louis, MO: *The Sporting News*, 1990).
Pro Football Guide 1991 Edition (St. Louis, MO: *The Sporting News*, 1991).
Pro Football Guide 1992 Edition (St. Louis, MO: *The Sporting News*, 1992).
Pro Football Guide 1993 Edition (St. Louis, MO: *The Sporting News*, 1993).
Pro Football Guide 1994 Edition (St. Louis, MO: *The Sporting News*, 1994).
Pro Football Guide 1995 Edition (St. Louis, MO: *The Sporting News*, 1995).
Pro Football Guide 1996 Edition (St. Louis, MO: *The Sporting News*, 1996).

Pro Football Guide 1997 Edition (St. Louis, MO: *The Sporting News*, 1997).
Pro Football Guide 1998 Edition (St. Louis, MO: *The Sporting News*, 1998).
Pro Football Guide 1999 Edition (St. Louis, MO: *The Sporting News*, 1999).
Pro Football Guide 2000 Edition (St. Louis, MO: *The Sporting News*, 2000).
Pro Football Guide 2001 Edition (St. Louis, MO: *The Sporting News*, 2001).
Pro Football Guide 2002 Edition (St. Louis, MO: *The Sporting News*, 2002).
Pro Football Guide 2003 Edition (St. Louis, MO: *The Sporting News*, 2003).
Pro Football Guide 2004 Edition (St. Louis, MO: *The Sporting News*, 2004).
Pro Football Guide 2005 Edition (St. Louis, MO: *The Sporting News*, 2005).
Pro Football Guide 2006 Edition (St. Louis, MO: *The Sporting News*, 2006).

Player Index

Addai, Joseph 105
Agajanian, Ben 161, 165, 166, 170, 171, 180, 195
Aguayo, Roberto 165, 174, 177
Aguirre, Joe 170
Aikman, Troy 136
Ajayi, Jay 65
Akers, David 142, 159, 161, 162, 165, 177, 178
Albert, Frankie 121, 122, 126, 128, 140
Alexander, Shaun 85, 101
Allegre, Raul 155, 164, 175, 181
Allen, Eric 69
Allen, Josh 128
Allen, Marcus 82, 87, 100
Allen, Ryan 194, 197, 198, 200, 202
Allen, Terry 101
Alstott, Mike 104
Ameche, Alan 106
Andersen, Morten 70, 159, 161, 163–168, 172–174, 176, 178
Anderson, Derek 77, 123, 140
Anderson, Donny 104
Anderson, Gary 142, 143, 159–168, 172, 173, 175, 176, 178
Anderson, Jamal 82, 103
Anderson, Ken 65, 122, 128, 137
Anderson, Mike 106
Anderson, Morten 142, 160
Anderson, Neal 102
Anderson, Ottis 82, 101
Andrews, William 83, 103
Anger, Bryan 195, 197, 198, 200, 201
Armstrong, Otis 81, 105
Arnett, Jon 106
Atkins, Billy 194, 196, 197, 199, 201
Avellini, Bob 127
Aveni, John 161, 171, 174

Bahr, Chris 163, 164, 166, 172, 176, 179
Bahr, Matt 143, 166, 167, 172, 175, 176, 178
Bailey, Dan 158–160, 177, 179
Baker, Sam 163, 165, 166, 171, 179
Bakken, Jim 161, 163–166, 171, 172, 175, 178
Banaszak, Pete 106
Banks, Tony 139
Barber, Marion 104
Barber, Tiki 81, 83, 101

Barlow, Kevan 106
Barnes, Larry 161, 171, 174
Barth, Connor 158, 177, 180
Bartkowski, Steve 76, 137
Bass, Dick 103
Batch, Charlie 140
Baugh, Sammy 121, 124–128, 138
Belichick, Bill 69, 159, 253
Bell, Greg 104
Bell, Le'Veon 85, 86, 103
Benirschke, Rolf 176, 180
Bennett, Edgar 82, 84, 106
Bennett, Michael 107
Benson, Cedric 70, 82, 84, 102
Berry, Jordan 194, 197, 198, 200, 202
Bettis, Jerome 82, 87, 88, 100
Beuerlein, Steve 138
Biasucci, Dean 158, 163, 172, 173, 176, 180
Birney, Tom 175
Bironas, Rob 158, 160, 174, 177, 179
Blair, George 161, 182
Blake, Jeff 138
Blanchard, Cary 173, 176, 180
Blanda, George 123, 124, 128, 137, 150, 166, 171, 178
Blanton, Shane 183
Bledsoe, Drew 69, 136
Bleier, Rocky 106
Blount, LeGarrette 65, 77, 103
Bojorquez, Corey 194, 196, 198, 199, 201
Boller, Kyle 123, 141
Boniol, Chris 160, 173, 176, 181
Bono, Steve 140
Boozer, Emerson 104
Bortles, Blake 123, 139
Bosher, Matthew 194, 196, 198, 199, 201
Boswell, Chris 158–160, 174, 177, 181
Bowles, Todd 77
Bradford, Sam 138
Bradshaw, Ahmad 104
Bradshaw, Terry 109, 116, 121, 126, 128, 137
Brady, Tom 2, 108, 117–122, 125–128, 135, 159, 164, 253
Bratkowski, Zeke 129
Brazile, Robert 76
Breech, Jim 172, 179
Brees, Drew 121, 122, 126, 135

Brett, George 124
Brien, Doug 180
Brindza, Kyle 177
Brister, Bubby 139
Brockington, John 103
Brodie, John 126, 136
Brooker, Tommy 171, 182
Brooks, Aaron 138
Brooks, James 102
Brown, Bill 84, 103
Brown, Dave 123, 140
Brown, Ed 123, 140
Brown, Gary 105
Brown, Jim 80, 81, 83, 85–87, 100
Brown, Josh 158, 160, 173, 174, 178
Brown, Kris 163, 165, 166, 173, 174, 177, 179
Brown, Larry 103
Brown, Mike 70, 77
Brown, Ronnie 103
Brown, Ted 105
Brown, Timmy 106
Brunell, Mark 65, 70, 136
Bryant, Matt 159, 160, 163, 174, 177, 178
Buchanon, Willie 68, 76
Bukich, Rudy 126
Bulger, Mark 138
Bullock, Randy 158, 181
Bush, Reggie 103
Bussey, Dexter 104
Butker, Harrison 158, 160, 182
Butler, Kevin 179
Butler, Skip 182
Butts, Marion 104
Byner, Earnest 101

Cahill, Ronnie 128
Campbell, Calais 65
Campbell, Earl 81, 85, 101
Campbell, Jason 139
Canadeo, Tony 105
Capece, Bill 161, 165, 172, 175
Cappelletti, Gino 161, 164, 165, 171, 174, 175, 180
Carlson, Cody 60
Carney, Elam 166
Carney, John 159, 163, 166, 173, 174, 177, 178
Carpenter, Dan 158, 174, 179
Carpenter, Rob 105
Carr, David 123, 139
Carr, Derek 122, 123, 139

Player Index

Carroll, Bob 86
Casares, Rick 103
Cassel, Matt 123, 129, 139
Catanzaro, Chandler 181
Chandler, Chris 137
Chandler, Don 161, 163, 171, 174, 181
Charles, Jamaal 81, 83, 102
Christie, Steve 173, 178
Clark, Mike 180
Cobb, Reggie 84, 106
Cockroft, Don 163, 166, 172, 175, 179
Cofer, Mike 161, 162, 163, 166, 173, 176, 180
Collins, Kerry 65, 117–120, 128, 136
Collins, Tony 104
Colquitt, Britton 194, 196, 198, 199, 201
Colquitt, Dustin 194, 197, 198, 199, 202
Condit, Mel 170
Cone, Fred 161, 171, 182
Conerly, Charlie 126, 128, 138
Conway, Brett 182
Cooke, Logan 194, 197, 198, 199, 201
Corral, Frank 182
Cortez, Jose 182
Cothren, Paige 171
Couch, Tim 140
Cousins, Kirk 121, 139
Cowher, Bill 88
Cox, Fred 161, 163, 166, 171, 172, 175, 179
Craig, Roger 101
Crennel, Romeo 71, 77
Cribbs, Joe 69, 103
Crosby, Mason 158–163, 165–167, 174, 178
Crow, John David 81, 104
Crow, Wayne 194, 196, 198, 199, 201
Csonka, Larry 101
Cuff, Ward 170, 182
Culpepper, Daunte 122, 126, 128, 138
Cundiff, Billy 163, 166, 167, 174, 177, 180
Cunningham, Randall 83, 104, 128, 137, 173, 176, 182
Cunningham, Sam 103
Cutler, Jay 136

Dalton, Andy 122, 137
Daluiso, Brad 181
Danelo, Joe 163, 172, 175, 180
Daniel, Trevor 194, 197–199, 202
Daniels, Clem 104
Danielson, Gary 140
Danmeier, Rick 182
Darragh, Dan 128
Davidson, Cotton 122, 123, 140, 194, 196, 197, 199, 201
Davis, Al 76
Davis, Clarence 107
Davis, Greg 161, 163, 164, 166, 173, 176, 179

Davis, Stephen 65, 101
Davis, Terrell 78–81, 83, 85, 86, 102
Davis, Tommy 163, 171, 180
Dawson, Len 76, 121, 124–128, 137
Dawson, Phil 174, 177, 178
Dayne, Ron 84, 107
DeBerg, Steve 127, 136
Del Greco, Al 173, 176, 178
Delhomme, Jake 65, 77, 128, 138
Dempsey, Tom 175, 180
DePoyster, Jerry 161, 165, 171, 175
Deschaines, Dick 195
Dickerson, Eric 69, 78, 79, 80, 83, 85, 87, 100
Dickey, Curtis 106
Dickey, Lynn 138
Dickson, Michael 195, 197, 198, 200, 201
Dilfer, Trent 123, 138
Dillon, Corey 85, 87, 101
Dixon, Riley 194, 197, 198, 200, 201
Doleman, Chris 70
Dorsett, Tony 87, 100
Douglass, Bobby 126, 127, 129
Droughns, Reuben 107
Dudley, Bill 170, 183
Dunn, Warrick 70, 87, 101
Durkee, Chester 183

Eason, Tony 141
Edinger, Paul 158, 163, 173, 176, 181
Edwards, Lac 194, 197, 198, 200, 201
Eischied, Mike 171
Elam, Jason 159, 160, 166, 173, 176–178
Elliot, Lin 182
Elliott, Ezekiel 77
Elliott, Jake 158, 159, 183
Ellis, Gerry 106
Elway, John 108, 136
Esiason, Boomer 76, 136
Everett, Jim 136

Fairbairn, Ka'imi 158–159, 183
Farr, Miller 65, 76
Faulk, Kevin 107
Faulk, Marshall 65, 87, 100
Favre, Brett 77, 117–120, 126, 135
Feathers, Beattie 80, 81
Feely, Jay 178
Feller, Happy 161, 165, 172, 175
Ferguson, Joe 136
Ferragamo, Vince 129, 140
Fiedler, Jay 140
Filchock, Frank 124, 127
Fisher, Jeff 60
Fisher, Tony 117–120
Fitzpatrick, Ryan 77, 123, 129, 137
Flacco, Joe 136
Flores, Tom 76, 140
Flutie, Doug 140
Foles, Nick 65, 122, 125–127, 140
Folk, Nick 163, 166, 174, 179
Forbath, Kai 158, 160, 181
Ford, Cole 173, 176, 183
Foreman, Chuck 103
Forsett, Justin 106

Forte, Matt 101
Foster, Arian 85, 102
Foster, Barry 106
Foster, DeShaun 117–120
Fournette, Leonard 65
Fouts, Dan 136
Fox, John 70
Franklin, Tony 165, 172, 176, 180
Freeman, Josh 77, 123, 140
Freese, Nate 177
Frerotte, Gus 138
Fritsch, Ted 171
Fritsch, Tony 161, 163, 165, 172, 175, 180

Gabriel, Roman 76, 136
Gado, Samkon 117–120
Galbreath, Tony 106
Gallery, Jim 172, 176
Galloway, Joey 77
Gannon, Rich 137
Gano, Graham 158, 159, 163, 174, 177, 179
Garcia, Jeff 122, 137
Garcia, Teddy 172, 176
Garner, Charlie 102
Garrard, David 139
Garrett, Carl 105
Garrett, Mike 103
Garrison, Walt 106
George, Eddie 82, 84, 85, 101
George, Jeff 137
Gerela, Roy 172, 180
Geri, Joe 161, 171
Gifford, Frank 107
Gilchrist, Cookie 89, 105, 165, 171, 174
Gilmer, Harry 127, 129
Girard, Jug 127
Glick, Gary 165, 171
Goff, Jared 71
Gogolak, Charlie 182
Gogolak, Pete 171, 175, 180
Gonzalez, Zane 174
Goode, Rob 88
Gordon, Melvin 80
Gore, Frank 87, 100
Gossett, Bruce 163, 172, 179
Gostkowski, Stephen 158–160, 163, 166, 174, 177, 178
Gould, Robbie 159, 160, 163, 166, 173, 174, 177, 178
Graham, Otto 108, 121, 124–128, 139, 162
Graham, Shayne 2, 159, 160, 174, 179
Grammatica, Martin 173, 177, 180
Granger, Hoyle 107
Grant, Ryan 105
Grbac, Elvis 139
Green, Ahman 101
Green, Bobby Joe 195
Green, David 172, 175
Green, Harold 105
Green, Trent 137
Green-Ellis, BenJarvus 84, 106
Greene, Shonn 106
Griese, Bob 122, 138
Griese, Brian 128, 139

Player Index

Griffin, Robert, III 71, 77
Grigas, John 127
Grogan, Steve 137
Grossman, Rex 122, 141, 171
Groza, Lou 2, 124, 156, 161–167, 171, 178
Guesman, Dick 161, 171, 174
Gurley, Todd 71

Haack, Matt 194, 197, 198, 200, 202
Hadl, John 123, 124, 136
Haji-Sheikh, Ali 146, 147, 153–155, 161, 162, 165, 172, 175, 176, 182
Hall, Dante 77
Hall, John 163, 166, 180
Hall, Parker 127
Hammer, MC 69, 76
Hampton, Dave 105
Hampton, Rodney 82, 102
Hanneman, Chuck 170
Hanson, Jason 158, 160, 163, 166, 176–178
Harbaugh, Jim 137
Hardeman, Don 76
Harder, Pat 170, 182
Harrington, Joey 123, 139
Harris, Franco 65, 80, 82, 87, 88, 100
Hart, Jim 123, 136
Hartley, Garrett 143, 160, 174, 177, 182
Hasselbeck, Matt 136
Hauschka, Steven 158–160, 174, 179
Hayes, Wendell 106
Haynes, Abner 105
Haynes, Mike 76
Hearst, Garrison 102
Hebert, Bobby 69, 76, 138
Hector, Johnny 105
Hekker, Johnny 194, 197–199, 201, 202
Henery, Alex 158, 160, 182
Henne, Chad 123, 140
Henry, Travis 102
Herber, Arnie 124, 125, 127–128
Herrera, Efren 172, 181
Herring, George 127–128, 194, 196, 197, 199, 201
Heyward, Craig 105
Hilger, Rusty 127
Hill, Calvin 102
Hilliard, Dalton 84, 105
Hinkle, Clarke 106, 170
Hipple, Eric 141
Hoak, Dick 84, 106
Hoard, Leroy 106
Hoernschemeyer, Bob 105
Hollis, Mike 180
Holmes, Priest 83, 101
Hopkins, Dustin 158–160, 182
Hornung, Paul 107, 161–166, 171, 174, 182
Hostetler, Jeff 139
Houston, Ken 65, 76
Howfield, Bobby 172, 175, 181
Hoying, Bobby 127, 128
Hubbard, Marv 105
Huber, Kevin 194, 196, 198, 199, 202

Humphries, Stan 139
Husted, Michael 163, 166, 173, 176, 180
Hutson, Don 170

Igwebuike, Donald 158, 166, 181
Ingram, Mark 103
Isbell, Cecil 124–125, 127–128
Ivory, Chris 104

Jacke, Chris 179
Jackson, Earnest 79, 105
Jackson, Fred 103
Jackson, Keith 69
Jackson, Steven 82, 87, 101
Jackson, Wilbur 106
Jacobs, Brandon 104
Jacobs, Dave 172, 175
Jacobs, Jack 127–128
Jaeger, Jeff 173, 176, 179
James, Edgerrin 82, 85, 87, 88, 100
Janikowski, Sebastian 158, 163, 165, 166, 173, 174, 177, 178
Jaworski, Ron 137
Jencks, Bob 174
Jennings, Rashad 106
Johnson, Brad 137
Johnson, Charley 138
Johnson, Chris 78–81, 85, 101
Johnson, Curley 194, 196, 197, 199, 201, 202
Johnson, Harvey 182
Johnson, John Henry 102
Johnson, Johnny 106
Johnson, Keyshawn 117–120
Johnson, Larry 102
Johnson, Norm 160, 163, 166, 172, 173, 176, 178
Johnson, Pete 103
Johnson, Randy 129
Johnson, Ron A. 84, 105
Johnson, Rudi 84, 103
Johnston, Cameron 194, 197, 198, 200, 202
Jones, Bert 122, 125, 127, 139
Jones, Chris 194, 196, 198, 199, 202
Jones, Donnie 194, 197, 198, 200, 202
Jones, James R. 84, 107
Jones, Julius 104
Jones, Thomas 82, 84, 87, 101
Jones-Drew, Maurice 101
Jordan, LeMont 106
Jurgensen, Sonny 121, 137

Kaeding, Nate 159, 160, 174, 180
Kaepernick, Colin 122, 140
Kamara, Alvin 71
Kapp, Joe 126, 128
Karlis, Rich 172, 180
Kasay, John 158, 166, 176–178
Kaufman, Napoleon 83, 104
Keenum, Case 140
Kelly, Jim 136
Kelly, Leroy 102
Kemp, Jeff 122, 138
Kenney, Bill 139
Kern, Brett 195, 197, 198, 200–202
Khayat, Bob 183

Kiick, Jim 84, 106
Kilmer, Bill 138
Kitna, Jon 137
Kizer, DeShone 128
Knight, Curt 171, 172, 175, 181
Koch, Sam 194, 196, 198, 199, 201
Koenen, Michael 173, 177
Kosar, Bernie 138
Kramer, Erik 139
Kramer, Tommy 137
Krieg, Dave 65, 136
Kroner, Greg 175
Kuharich, Joe 170

Lacy, Eddie 107
Lambo, Josh 158, 182
Lamonica, Daryle 122, 139
Landry, Greg 139
Lane, MacArthur 104
Lansford, Mike 176, 180
Layne, Bobby 123, 137, 171, 183
Leaf, Ryan 123, 127–129
Leahy, Pat 163, 175, 176, 178
LeBaron, Eddie 123, 126–128, 140
LeClerc, Roger 166, 171, 182
Lee, Andy 194, 196, 198, 199, 201
Leftwich, Byron 140
Levens, Dorsey 104
Lewis, Jamal 77–82, 85, 87, 101
Lewis, Ray 77
Leypoldt, John 181
Lincoln, Keith 165, 174
Lindell, Rian 177, 179
Linhart, Toni 172, 175, 182
Little, Floyd 89, 102
Little, Steve 172
Livingston, Dale 175
Livingston, Mike 123, 140
Lohmiller, Chip 161, 163, 164, 166, 173, 176, 180
Lomax, Neil 138
Longwell, Ryan 160, 173, 174, 176–178
Lott, Ronnie 65, 76
Lowe, Paul 83, 104
Lowery, Nick 161, 163, 164, 166–168, 172, 173, 175, 176, 178
Luck, Andrew 121, 138, 164
Luckhurst, Mick 158, 181
Luckman, Sid 121, 124, 126, 127, 140
Lusteg, Booth 183
Lutz, Wil 158, 159, 160, 182
Lynch, Marshawn 101

Mack, Kevin 104
Maguire, Paul 194, 196, 198, 199, 201, 202
Mahomes, Patrick 126
Majkowski, Don 76, 140
Malone, Mark 122, 123, 127–128, 140
Mann, Errol 161, 172, 175, 180
Manning, Archie 123, 127, 137
Manning, Eli 117–120, 136
Manning, Peyton 108, 109, 116, 120–129, 135, 164
Marangi, Gary 126, 128
Marchibroda, Ted 69, 76
Marcol, Chester 68, 76, 172, 175, 181

Player Index

Mare, Olindo 173, 176–178
Marefos, Andy 170
Marino, Dan 122, 126, 128, 136
Mariota, Marcus 122, 140
Marler, Shane 161, 165, 173, 177
Marshall, Brandon 77
Martin, Curtis 76, 82, 85, 87, 88, 100
Martin, Doug 105
Martin, Jim 171, 181
Martin, Sam 194, 196, 198, 199, 202
Martinovich, Phil 161, 164, 170
Mason, Tommy 105
Masterson, Bernie 170
Mathews, Ryan 103
Mathis, Bill 84, 107
Matson, Ollie 104
Matte, Tom 104
Maznicki, Frank 170
Mazzetti, Tim 165, 172, 175, 183
McAllister, Deuce 102
McCarthy, Mike 70
McCormick, John 127, 128
McCown, Josh 126, 128, 129, 139
McCoy, LeSean 85, 101
McCullough, Hugh 126, 128
McCutcheon, Lawrence 102
McElhenny, Hugh 103
McFadden, Darren 103
McFadden, Paul 181
McGahee, Willis 101
McHan, Lamar 129
McLaughlin, Steve 173, 176
McMahon, Jim 139
McManus, Brandon 158, 174, 177, 181
McMillan, Randy 106
McNabb, Donovan 70, 136
McNair, Steve 77, 107, 136
McNeil, Freeman 101
McVay, Sean 71
Means, Natrone 84, 103
Mendenhall, Rashard 84, 105
Mercer, Mike 159, 165, 171, 175, 181
Meredith, Don 139
Metcalf, Eric 70
Metcalf, Terry 69
Michaels, Lou 161, 171, 179
Michalik, Art 161, 165, 171
Mike-Mayer, Nick 163, 175, 181
Mike-Mayer, Steve 163, 166, 172, 175, 182
Miller, Chris 138
Miller, Lamar 104
Miller, Red 67
Mingo, Gene 161, 164, 165, 171, 174, 175, 181
Mirer, Rick 122, 123, 140
Mitchell, Lydell 102
Mitchell, Scott 139
Mitchell, Stump 104
Montana, Joe 108, 121, 122, 125–127, 136
Montgomery, Wilbert 69, 102
Moon, Warren 60, 69, 136
Moore, Lenny 104
Moreno, Knowshon 107
Morrall, Earl 139
Morris, Alfred 71, 77, 103

Morris, Bam 106
Morris, Joe 82, 103
Morris, Maurice 107
Morris, Mercury 83, 105
Morstead, Thomas 194, 197, 198, 200, 201
Morton, Craig 67, 137
Moseley, Mark 142, 143, 146, 149, 151–153, 155–157, 159, 164, 166, 172, 175, 178
Moss, Santana 70
Motley, Marion 83, 104
Muha, Joe 171
Muhlman, Horst 180
Muncie, Chuck 102
Munoz, Anthony 2
Munson, Bill 140
Murray, DeMarco 102
Murray, Eddie 160, 163, 166, 172, 173, 176, 178
Murrell, Adrian 82, 103
Myers, Jason 158, 159, 177, 182
Myhra, Steve 182

Namath, Joe 123–124, 127–128, 137
Nance, Jim 103
Nedney, Joe 158, 165, 173, 176, 179
Nelsen, Bill 140
Nelson, Bob 170
Nelson, Chuck 182
Nelson, Darrin 105
Nemeth, Steve 170
Newhouse, Robert 104
Newton, Cam 83, 105, 137
Niccolai, Armond 170
Nofsinger, Terry 129
Norton, Jim 194, 196, 197, 199, 201, 202
Norton, Rick 127, 128
Norwood, Scott 161, 172, 176, 180
Novak, Nick 158, 166, 180
Nugent, Mike 163, 166, 174, 177, 179

O'Brien, Jim 161, 165, 172, 175, 182
O'Brien, Ken 137
O'Donnell, Neil 138
O'Donnell, Pat 194, 196, 198, 199, 202
O'Donoghue, Neil 163, 166, 175, 181
Okoye, Christian 89, 104
Ortmann, Chuck 126, 128
Orton, Kyle 139
Osborn, Dave 105
Otis, Jim 105

Pagel, Mike 123, 141
Palardy, Michael 194, 196, 198, 199, 201
Palmer, Carson 70, 117–120, 122, 136
Palmer, Pete 86, 150
Panciera, Don 126, 128
Parcells, Bill 70, 77
Pardee, Jack 60
Parilli, Babe 123, 127, 128, 138
Parker, Ace 128
Parker, Willie 103
Parkey, Cody 159, 160, 177, 181
Partee, Dennis 172, 175, 182

Pastorini, Dan 123, 127, 138
Patterson, Billy 126, 128
Patton, Cliff 170, 171, 182
Payton, Walter 79, 80, 82, 85–87, 100
Peaks, Clarence 107
Pearson, Preston 107
Peete, Rodney 123, 139
Pelfrey, Doug 176, 180
Pennington, Chad 70, 77, 121, 139
Percival, Mac 166, 171, 181
Perkins, Don 102
Perry, Joe 81, 83, 101
Peterson, Adrian L. 77–80, 83, 85, 87, 100
Peterson, Todd 173, 176, 179
Phillips, Bum 76
Phillips, Wade 70
Phipps, Mike 122, 127, 140
Pietrosante, Nick 106
Pinion, Bradley 195, 197, 198, 200, 202
Pisarcik, Joe 127
Pittman, Michael 103
Plum, Milt 125, 126, 127, 139
Plummer, Jake 128, 137
Plunkett, Jim 123, 127, 137
Pochman, Owen 177
Podolak, Ed 105
Pollard, Frank 106
Poole, Ray 171
Portis, Clinton 81, 85, 101
Powell, Art 76
Prater, Mike 158–160, 174, 177, 179
Prescott, Dak 77
Price, Eddie 88, 89
Pruitt, Greg 103
Pruitt, Mike 102
Pullis, Ken 150

Rackers, Neil 159–161, 165, 173, 174, 176, 177, 179
Ralston, John 67
Ramsey, Steve 67
Ray, David 175, 181
Rechichar, Bert 171
Reed, Jeff 177, 179
Reese, Hank 170
Reid, Andy 70
Reveiz, Fuad 173, 176, 179
Reynolds, Jack 65, 76
Rhett, Errict 84, 105
Ricardo, Benny 172, 175, 181
Rice, Jerry 2
Rice, Ray 102
Richardon, Bucky 60
Richey, Wade 163, 166, 173, 176, 182
Riggins, John 80, 82, 87, 88, 101, 156, 157
Riggs, Gerald 101
Rivera, Ron 70
Rivers, Phillip 121, 136
Robinson, Paul 89
Rodgers, Aaron 121, 122, 124–128, 136
Roethlisberger, Ben 121, 136
Rogers, George 85, 102
Roland, Johnny 106
Romanik, Steve 127

Player Index

Romo, Tony 121, 122, 126, 137
Rosas, Aldrick 160, 174, 177, 183
Rosen, Josh 128
Ross, Bobby 69
Rote, Tobin 123, 127, 128, 138
Roveto, John 172, 175
Rozier, Mike 69, 105
Russell, JaMarcus 128
Russell, Leonard 84, 106
Ruzek, Roger 172, 176, 181
Ryan, Frank 140
Ryan, Matt 121, 122, 126, 128, 136
Rypien, Mark 139

Saban, Nick 69
Sanchez, Mark 122, 139
Sanchez, Rigoberto 194, 197–199, 201
Sanders, Barry 78–80, 83, 85–87, 100
Sanders, Spec 81
Sandler, B.J. 117–120
Santos, Cairo 158, 163, 159, 181
Sayers, Gale 83, 89, 104
Schaub, Matt 60, 122, 138
Schroeder, Jay 138
Schubert, Eric 172, 176
Schwenk, Bud 127
Scobee, Josh 158, 163, 174, 177, 179
Scott, J.K. 194, 197–199, 202
Septien, Rafael 166, 179
Shaw, Dennis 127
Shofner, Del 76
Simms, Phil 136
Simpson, OJ. 76–80, 83, 85, 87, 89, 101
Sims, Billy 83, 85, 86, 104
Sinkwich, Frank 129
Sipe, Brian 137
Sisson, Scott 161, 164, 173, 176
Smith, Alex 136
Smith, Antowain 84, 102
Smith, Daryl 60
Smith, Emmitt 81, 85, 86, 100
Smith, Geno. 129
Smith, J.D. 104
Smith, John 172, 180
Smith, Lamar 82, 84, 104
Smith, Robert 83, 102
Smukler, David 127
Snead, Norm 123, 127, 137
Snell, Matt 105
Soltau, Gerry 166
Soltau, Gordie 171, 181
Somers, George 170
Spikes, Jack 171
Stabler, Ken 125, 127, 128, 137
Stafford, Matthew 71, 77, 122, 128, 136
Staley, Duce 103
Starr, Bart 122, 126, 128, 138, 253
Staubach, Roger 109, 121, 125, 127–128, 138
Staurovsky, Jason 183
Steinfort, Fred 161, 163–166, 172, 175, 182
Stenerud, Jan 156, 161, 163–166, 171, 172, 175, 176, 178
Stewart, James 82, 103

Stewart, Jonathan 102
Stewart, Kordell 123, 139
Stover, Matt 160, 163, 166, 173, 176–178
Stoyanovich, Pete 2, 160, 173, 176, 179
Strong, Ken 170
Sturgis, Caleb 158, 159, 182
Succop, Ryan 158, 179
Suisham, Shaun 160, 174, 177, 180
Summerall, Pat 161, 165, 171, 181
Szaro, Rich 175

Taliaferro, George 127, 128
Taliaferro, Mike 127, 128
Tannehill, Ryan 138
Tarkenton, Fran 107, 122, 136
Taylor, Altie 84, 105
Taylor, Chester 104
Taylor, Fred 83, 85, 87, 101
Taylor, Jim 101
Taylor, Lawrence 60, 69
Testaverde, Vinny 76, 127, 136
Theismann, Joe 87, 137, 156
Thomas, Anthony 70, 77, 84, 106
Thomas, Bob 159, 163, 166, 180
Thomas, Mike 105
Thomas, Pierre 106
Thomas, Thurman 65, 87, 101
Thomason, Bobby 129
Thompson, Tommy 126, 128
Thorn, John 86
Timberlake, Bob 161, 165, 171
Tittle, Y.A. 122, 126, 137
Todd, Richard 138
Tolliver, Billy Joe 60, 123, 140
Tomczak, Mike 123, 139
Tomlinson, LaDainian 82, 85, 87, 100
Townsend, Johnny 194, 197, 198, 200, 202
Treadwell, David 166, 173, 176, 181
Tripucka, Frank 122, 127, 129, 140
Trubinsky, Mitchell 71
Trudeau, Jack 123, 140
Tucker, Justin 158–160, 163, 165–167, 174, 177, 179
Turner, Jim 159, 161, 163, 171, 175, 178
Turner, Michael 70, 102
Turner, Norv 69
Tuthill, James 173, 177
Tyler, Wendell 83, 102
Tynes, Lawrence 179

Unitas, John 126, 136
Urena, Ivan 156
Urlacher, Brian 70
Utley, Mike 65, 76

Van Brocklin, Norm 121, 138
Van Buren, Steve 83, 103
Vanderjagt, Mike 143, 159–161, 163, 166, 173, 177
van Eeghen, Mark 102
Van Raaphorst, Dick 166, 183
Vetrano, Joe 183
Vick, Michael 70, 80, 81, 83, 102, 138
Villanueva, Danny 181

Vinatieri, Adam 156, 159–160, 163–164, 166, 173, 174, 176–178
Vinyard, Ken 161, 165, 171, 175
von Schamann, Uwe 172, 175, 181

Wade, Bill 76, 126, 139
Wadman, Colby 194, 196, 198, 199, 202
Walker, Doak 182
Walker, Herschel 101
Walker, Wayne 163, 171, 182
Walls, Wesley 65
Walsh, Blair 158, 159, 174, 177, 180
Walston, Bobby 166, 171, 181
Walter, Andrew 128
Warner, Kurt 65, 102, 121, 122, 126, 127, 137
Warren, Chris 102
Washington, Joe 104
Waterfield, Bob 64, 123, 140, 170, 181
Watters, Ricky 85, 87, 101
Way, Tress 195, 197, 198, 200, 202
Webster, Alex 105
Weis, Charlie 71, 77
Wersching, Ray 172, 175, 179
Westbrook, Brian 102
Wheatley, Tyrone 104
Whelihan, Craig 127, 128
White, Byron "Whizzer" 89
White, Charles 89
White, Danny 138, 195
White, Lorenzo 105
White, Whizzer 89
Wilder, James 79, 82, 103
Wile, Matt 194, 197, 198, 200, 202
Wilkins, Jeff 143, 159–161, 173, 176–178
Willard, Ken 102
Williams, Cadillac 77, 84, 106
Williams, DeAngelo 77, 101
Williams, Delvin 103
Williams, Doug 139
Williams, Harvey 106
Williams, John L. 104
Williams, Ricky 82, 101
Willis, Ken 158, 183
Wilson, Marc 122, 123, 140
Wilson, Russell 71, 121, 122, 126, 138
Wilson, Wade 139
Winder, Sammy 84, 103
Winston, Jameis 140
Wittenborn, John 171
Wood, Dick 127, 128
Woods, Ickey 76

Yepremian, Garo 163, 166, 172, 175, 179
Yewcic, Tom 193, 196, 197, 199, 201
Yoho, Mack 174
Young, Rickey 107
Young, Steve 83, 105, 121–122, 125–128, 137
Younger, Tank 107

Zendejas, Luis 173
Zendejas, Tony 160, 173, 176, 180
Zorn, Jim 123, 127, 138
Zuerlein, Greg 158, 159, 161, 174, 180

www.ingramcontent.com/pod-product-compliance
Lightning Source LLC
Chambersburg PA
CBHW060337010526
44117CB00017B/2868